1 & 2
THESSALONIANS

Brazos Theological Commentary on the Bible

1 & 2
THESSALONIANS

D O U G L A S   F A R R O W

BrazosPress
a division of Baker Publishing Group
Grand Rapids, Michigan

© 2020 by Douglas Farrow

Published by Brazos Press
a division of Baker Publishing Group
PO Box 6287, Grand Rapids, MI 49516-6287
www.brazospress.com

Paperback edition published 2021
ISBN 978-1-58743-548-5

Printed and bound by CPI Group (UK) Ltd, Croydon, CR0 4YY

The Library of Congress has cataloged the hardcover edition as follows:
Names: Farrow, Douglas, 1953– author.
Title: 1 & 2 Thessalonians / Douglas Farrow.
Other titles: First and Second Thessalonians
Description: Grand Rapids, Michigan : Brazos Press, a division of Baker Publishing Group, 2020. | Series: Brazos theological commentary on the Bible | Includes bibliographical references and index.
Identifiers: LCCN 2019052621 | ISBN 9781587431685 (cloth)
Subjects: LCSH: Bible. Thessalonians—Commentaries.
Classification: LCC BS2725.53 .F374 2020 | DDC 227/.8107—dc23
LC record available at https://lccn.loc.gov/2019052621

The translation of 1 and 2 Thessalonians and Scripture quotations labeled AT are the author's own.

All other Scripture quotations, unless otherwise indicated, are taken from the Revised Standard Version of the Bible—Second Catholic Edition (Ignatius Edition) Copyright © 2006 National Council of the Churches of Christ in the United States of America. Used by permission. All rights reserved worldwide.

Scripture quotations labeled KJV are from the King James Version of the Bible.

Scripture quotations labeled NIV are from THE HOLY BIBLE, NEW INTERNATIONAL VERSION®, NIV® Copyright © 1973, 1978, 1984, 2011 by Biblica, Inc.® Used by permission. All rights reserved worldwide.

for

Josiah, Celia, Nicholas, William, and Benedict

with prayers that you and yours
will be ready to greet the Lord when he comes

CONTENTS

SERIES PREFACE

Near the beginning of his treatise against gnostic interpretations of the Bible, *Against Heresies*, Irenaeus observes that scripture is like a great mosaic depicting a handsome king. It is as if we were owners of a villa in Gaul who had ordered a mosaic from Rome. It arrives, and the beautifully colored tiles need to be taken out of their packaging and put into proper order according to the plan of the artist. The difficulty, of course, is that scripture provides us with the individual pieces, but the order and sequence of various elements are not obvious. The Bible does not come with instructions that would allow interpreters to simply place verses, episodes, images, and parables in order as a worker might follow a schematic drawing in assembling the pieces to depict the handsome king. The mosaic must be puzzled out. This is precisely the work of scriptural interpretation.

Origen has his own image to express the difficulty of working out the proper approach to reading the Bible. When preparing to offer a commentary on the Psalms he tells of a tradition handed down to him by his Hebrew teacher:

> The Hebrew said that the whole divinely inspired scripture may be likened, because of its obscurity, to many locked rooms in our house. By each room is placed a key, but not the one that corresponds to it, so that the keys are scattered about beside the rooms, none of them matching the room by which it is placed. It is a difficult task to find the keys and match them to the rooms that they can open. We therefore know the scriptures that are obscure only by taking the points of departure for understanding them from another place because they have their interpretive principle scattered among them.[1]

---

1. Fragment from the preface to *Commentary on Psalms 1–25*, preserved in the *Philokalia*, in *Origen*, trans. Joseph W. Trigg (London: Routledge, 1998), 70–71.

As is the case for Irenaeus, scriptural interpretation is not purely local. The key in Genesis may best fit the door of Isaiah, which in turn opens up the meaning of Matthew. The mosaic must be put together with an eye toward the overall plan.

Irenaeus, Origen, and the great cloud of premodern biblical interpreters assumed that puzzling out the mosaic of scripture must be a communal project. The Bible is vast, heterogeneous, full of confusing passages and obscure words, and difficult to understand. Only a fool would imagine that he or she could work out solutions alone. The way forward must rely upon a tradition of reading that Irenaeus reports has been passed on as the rule or canon of truth that functions as a confession of faith. "Anyone," he says, "who keeps unchangeable in himself the rule of truth received through baptism will recognize the names and sayings and parables of the scriptures."[2] Modern scholars debate the content of the rule on which Irenaeus relies and commends, not the least because the terms and formulations Irenaeus himself uses shift and slide. Nonetheless, Irenaeus assumes that there is a body of apostolic doctrine sustained by a tradition of teaching in the church. This doctrine provides the clarifying principles that guide exegetical judgment toward a coherent overall reading of scripture as a unified witness. Doctrine, then, is the schematic drawing that will allow the reader to organize the vast heterogeneity of the words, images, and stories of the Bible into a readable, coherent whole. It is the rule that guides us toward the proper matching of keys to doors.

If self-consciousness about the role of history in shaping human consciousness makes modern historical-critical study actually critical, then what makes modern study of the Bible actually modern is the consensus that classical Christian doctrine distorts interpretive understanding. Benjamin Jowett, the influential nineteenth-century English classical scholar, is representative. In his programmatic essay "On the Interpretation of Scripture," he exhorts the biblical reader to disengage from doctrine and break its hold over the interpretive imagination. "The simple words of that book," writes Jowett of the modern reader, "he tries to preserve absolutely pure from the refinements or distinctions of later times." The modern interpreter wishes to "clear away the remains of dogmas, systems, controversies, which are encrusted upon" the words of scripture. The disciplines of close philological analysis "would enable us to separate the elements of doctrine and tradition with which the meaning of scripture is encumbered in our own

2. *Against Heresies* 9.4.

day."[3] The lens of understanding must be wiped clear of the hazy and distorting film of doctrine.

Postmodernity, in turn, has encouraged us to criticize the critics. Jowett imagined that when he wiped away doctrine he would encounter the biblical text in its purity and uncover what he called "the original spirit and intention of the authors."[4] We are not now so sanguine, and the postmodern mind thinks interpretive frameworks inevitable. Nonetheless, we tend to remain modern in at least one sense. We read Athanasius and think of him stage-managing the diversity of scripture to support his positions against the Arians. We read Bernard of Clairvaux and assume that his monastic ideals structure his reading of the Song of Songs. In the wake of the Reformation, we can see how the doctrinal divisions of the time shaped biblical interpretation. Luther famously described the Epistle of James as an "epistle of straw," for, as he said, "it has nothing of the nature of the gospel about it."[5] In these and many other instances, often written in the heat of ecclesiastical controversy or out of the passion of ascetic commitment, we tend to think Jowett correct: doctrine is a distorting film on the lens of understanding.

However, is what we commonly think actually the case? Are readers naturally perceptive? Do we have an unblemished, reliable aptitude for the divine? Have we no need for disciplines of vision? Do our attention and judgment need to be trained, especially as we seek to read scripture as the living word of God? According to Augustine, we all struggle to journey toward God, who is our rest and peace. Yet our vision is darkened and the fetters of worldly habit corrupt our judgment. We need training and instruction in order to cleanse our minds so that we might find our way toward God.[6] To this end, "the whole temporal dispensation was made by divine Providence for our salvation."[7] The covenant with Israel, the coming of Christ, the gathering of the nations into the church—all these things are gathered up into the rule of faith, and they guide the vision and form of the soul toward the end of fellowship with God. In Augustine's view, the reading of scripture both contributes to and benefits from this divine pedagogy. With countless variations in both exegetical conclusions and theological frameworks, the same pedagogy of a doctrinally ruled reading of scripture characterizes the broad sweep of the

---

3. Benjamin Jowett, "On the Interpretation of Scripture," in *Essays and Reviews* (London: Parker, 1860), 338–39.

4. Jowett, "On the Interpretation of Scripture," 340.

5. *Luther's Works*, vol. 35, ed. E. Theodore Bachmann (Philadelphia: Fortress, 1959), 362.

6. *On Christian Doctrine* 1.10.

7. *On Christian Doctrine* 1.35.

Christian tradition from Gregory the Great through Bernard and Bonaventure, continuing across Reformation differences in both John Calvin and Cornelius à Lapide, Patrick Henry and Bishop Bossuet, and on to more recent figures such as Karl Barth and Hans Urs von Balthasar.

Is doctrine, then, not a moldering scrim of antique prejudice obscuring the Bible, but instead a clarifying agent, an enduring tradition of theological judgments that amplifies the living voice of scripture? And what of the scholarly dispassion advocated by Jowett? Is a noncommitted reading—an interpretation unprejudiced—the way toward objectivity, or does it simply invite the languid intellectual apathy that stands aside to make room for the false truism and easy answers of the age?

This series of biblical commentaries was born out of the conviction that dogma clarifies rather than obscures. The Brazos Theological Commentary on the Bible advances upon the assumption that the Nicene tradition, in all its diversity and controversy, provides the proper basis for the interpretation of the Bible as Christian scripture. God the Father Almighty, who sends his only begotten Son to die for us and for our salvation and who raises the crucified Son in the power of the Holy Spirit so that the baptized may be joined in one body—faith in *this* God with *this* vocation of love for the world is the lens through which to view the heterogeneity and particularity of the biblical texts. Doctrine, then, is not a moldering scrim of antique prejudice obscuring the meaning of the Bible. It is a crucial aspect of the divine pedagogy, a clarifying agent for our minds fogged by self-deceptions, a challenge to our languid intellectual apathy that will too often rest in false truisms and the easy spiritual nostrums of the present age rather than search more deeply and widely for the dispersed keys to the many doors of scripture.

For this reason, the commentators in this series have not been chosen because of their historical or philological expertise. In the main, they are not biblical scholars in the conventional, modern sense of the term. Instead, the commentators were chosen because of their knowledge of and expertise in using the Christian doctrinal tradition. They are qualified by virtue of the doctrinal formation of their mental habits, for it is the conceit of this series of biblical commentaries that theological training in the Nicene tradition prepares one for biblical interpretation, and thus it is to theologians and not biblical scholars that we have turned. "War is too important," it has been said, "to leave to the generals."

We do hope, however, that readers do not draw the wrong impression. The Nicene tradition does not provide a set formula for the solution of exegetical problems. The great tradition of Christian doctrine was not transcribed, bound in folio, and issued in an official, critical edition. We have the Niceno-Constantinopolitan Creed, used for centuries in many traditions of Christian worship. We have ancient baptismal affirmations of faith. The Chalcedonian Definition and the creeds and canons of other church councils have their places in official church documents. Yet the rule of faith cannot be limited to a specific set of words, sentences, and creeds. It is instead a pervasive habit of thought, the animating culture of the church in its intellectual aspect. As Augustine observed, commenting on Jeremiah 31:33, "The creed is learned by listening; it is written, not on stone tablets nor on any material, but on the heart."[8] This is why Irenaeus is able to appeal to the rule of faith more than a century before the first ecumenical council, and this is why we need not itemize the contents of the Nicene tradition in order to appeal to its potency and role in the work of interpretation.

Because doctrine is intrinsically fluid on the margins and most powerful as a habit of mind rather than a list of propositions, this commentary series cannot settle difficult questions of method and content at the outset. The editors of the series impose no particular method of doctrinal interpretation. We cannot say in advance how doctrine helps the Christian reader assemble the mosaic of scripture. We have no clear answer to the question of whether exegesis guided by doctrine is antithetical to or compatible with the now-old modern methods of historical-critical inquiry. Truth—historical, mathematical, or doctrinal—knows no contradiction. But method is a discipline of vision and judgment, and we cannot know in advance what aspects of historical-critical inquiry are functions of modernism that shape the soul to be at odds with Christian discipline. Still further, the editors do not hold the commentators to any particular hermeneutical theory that specifies how to define the plain sense of scripture—or the role this plain sense should play in interpretation. Here the commentary series is tentative and exploratory.

Can we proceed in any other way? European and North American intellectual culture has been de-Christianized. The effect has not been a cessation of Christian activity. Theological work continues. Sermons are preached. Biblical scholars produce monographs. Church leaders have meetings. But each dimension of a formerly unified Christian practice now tends to function independently. It is as if a weakened army has been fragmented, and various corps have retreated to isolated fortresses in order to survive. Theology has lost its competence in exegesis.

8. *Sermon* 212.2.

Scripture scholars function with minimal theological training. Each decade finds new theories of preaching to cover the nakedness of seminary training that provides theology without exegesis and exegesis without theology.

Not the least of the causes of the fragmentation of Christian intellectual practice has been the divisions of the church. Since the Reformation, the role of the rule of faith in interpretation has been obscured by polemics and counterpolemics about *sola scriptura* and the necessity of a magisterial teaching authority. The Brazos Theological Commentary on the Bible series is deliberately ecumenical in scope because the editors are convinced that early church fathers were correct: church doctrine does not compete with scripture in a limited economy of epistemic authority. We wish to encourage unashamedly dogmatic interpretation of scripture, confident that the concrete consequences of such a reading will cast far more light on the great divisive questions of the Reformation than either reengaging in old theological polemics or chasing the fantasy of a pure exegesis that will somehow adjudicate between competing theological positions. You shall know the truth of doctrine by its interpretive fruits, and therefore in hopes of contributing to the unity of the church, we have deliberately chosen a wide range of theologians whose commitment to doctrine will allow readers to see real interpretive consequences rather than the shadowboxing of theological concepts.

The Brazos Theological Commentary on the Bible endorses a textual ecumenism that parallels our diversity of ecclesial backgrounds. We do not impose the thankfully modest inclusive-language agenda of the New Revised Standard Version, nor do we insist upon the glories of the Authorized Version, nor do we require our commentators to create a new translation. In our communal worship, in our private devotions, and in our theological scholarship, we use a range of scriptural translations. Precisely as scripture—a living, functioning text in the present life of faith—the Bible is not semantically fixed. Only a modernist, literalist hermeneutic could imagine that this modest fluidity is a liability. Philological precision and stability is a consequence of, not a basis for, exegesis. Judgments about the meaning of a text fix its literal sense, not the other way around. As a result, readers should expect an eclectic use of biblical translations, both across the different volumes of the series and within individual commentaries.

We cannot speak for contemporary biblical scholars, but as theologians we know that we have long been trained to defend our fortresses of theological concepts and formulations. And we have forgotten the skills of interpretation. Like stroke victims, we must rehabilitate our exegetical imaginations, and there are likely to be different strategies of recovery. Readers should expect this reconstructive—not reactionary—series to provide them with experiments in postcritical doctrinal interpretation, not commentaries written according to the settled principles of a well-functioning tradition. Some commentators will follow classical typological and allegorical readings from the premodern tradition; others will draw on contemporary historical study. Some will comment verse by verse; others will highlight passages, even single words that trigger theological analysis of scripture. No reading strategies are proscribed, no interpretive methods foresworn. The central premise in this commentary series is that doctrine provides structure and cogency to scriptural interpretation. We trust in this premise with the hope that the Nicene tradition can guide us, however imperfectly, diversely, and halt-ingly, toward a reading of scripture in which the right keys open the right doors.

R. R. Reno

ABBREVIATIONS

Old Testament

Gen.	Genesis	Neh.	Nehemiah	Hosea	Hosea
Exod.	Exodus	Esther	Esther	Joel	Joel
Lev.	Leviticus	Job	Job	Amos	Amos
Num.	Numbers	Ps. (Pss.)	Psalm (Psalms)	Obad.	Obadiah
Deut.	Deuteronomy	Prov.	Proverbs	Jon.	Jonah
Josh.	Joshua	Eccl.	Ecclesiastes	Mic.	Micah
Judg.	Judges	Songs	Song of Songs	Nah.	Nahum
Ruth	Ruth	Isa.	Isaiah	Hab.	Habakkuk
1–2 Sam.	1–2 Samuel	Jer.	Jeremiah	Zeph.	Zephaniah
1–2 Kings	1–2 Kings	Lam.	Lamentations	Hag.	Haggai
1–2 Chron.	1–2 Chronicles	Ezek.	Ezekiel	Zech.	Zechariah
Ezra	Ezra	Dan.	Daniel	Mal.	Malachi

Deuterocanonical

1–2 Macc.	1–2 Maccabees	Wis.	Wisdom (of Solomon)
Tob.	Tobit	Sir.	Sirach

New Testament

Matt.	Matthew	John	John	1–2 Cor.	1–2 Corinthians
Mark	Mark	Acts	Acts	Gal.	Galatians
Luke	Luke	Rom.	Romans	Eph.	Ephesians

Phil.	Philippians	Titus	Titus	1–2 Pet.	1–2 Peter
Col.	Colossians	Philem.	Philemon	1–3 John	1–3 John
1–2 Thess.	1–2 Thessalonians	Heb.	Hebrews	Jude	Jude
1–2 Tim.	1–2 Timothy	Jas.	James	Rev.	Revelation

General and Bibliographic

ACCS — *Ancient Christian Commentary on Scripture: Colossians, Thessalonians, Timothy, Titus, Philemon*. Ancient Christian Commentary on Scripture 9. Edited by Peter J. Gorday. Downers Grove, IL: InterVarsity, 2000.

ACW — Ancient Christian Writers

ANF — *The Ante-Nicene Fathers: Translations of the Writings of the Fathers down to A.D. 325.* Edited by Alexander Roberts and James Donaldson. 10 vols. New York: Christian Literature, 1885–87. Reprint, Peabody, MA: Hendrickson, 1994.

AT — Author's translation

Bon. conj. — Augustine, *De bono conjugali / On the Good of Marriage*

CCC — *Catechism of the Catholic Church: With Modifications from the Editio Typica.* 2nd ed. New York: Doubleday, 1997.

CD — Karl Barth, *Church Dogmatics.* 4 vols. Edinburgh: T&T Clark, 1956–75.

CDH — Anselm, *Cur deus homo / Why God Became Man.* Translations cited: *Anselm of Canterbury: The Major Works,* translated by Janet Fairweather, edited by Brian Davies and G. R. Evans (Oxford: Oxford University Press, 1998); and *Why God Became Man,* translated by Jasper Hopkins and Herbert W. Richardson (Lewiston, NY: Edwin Mellen, 1974).

CIC — *Codex Iuris Canonici*

Civ. — Augustine, *De civitate dei / City of God.* Translations cited: William Babcock (New York: New City, 2018), Marcus Dods (*Nicene and Post-Nicene Fathers* series 1, vol. 2; New York: Christian Literature, 1887), and John Healey (London: Griffith Farran Okeden & Welsh, 1610).

CL — Cyril of Jerusalem, *Catechetical Lectures* (*NPNF²*, vol. 7)

COQG — Christian Origins and the Question of God (N. T. Wright)

DA — John Henry Newman, *Discussions and Arguments on Various Subjects.* Vol. 2. London: Longmans, Green, 1907.

DC — Anselm, *De concordia / The Compatibility of God's Foreknowledge, Predestination and Grace with Human Freedom*

DCD — Anselm, *De casu diaboli / On the Fall of the Devil*

DEC — *Decrees of the Ecumenical Councils.* Edited by Norman Tanner. 2 vols. London: Sheed and Ward, 1990.

Demo. — Irenaeus, *Proof of the Apostolic Preaching.* Translated by Joseph P. Smith. ACW 16. New York: Newman Press, 1978.

DFR — Ambrose, *De Fide Resurrectionis / On Faith in the Resurrection* (*NPNF²*, vol. 10)

DH — Vatican II, *Dignitatis Humanae / Of the Dignity of the Human Person* (*DEC* 2:1001–11)

Dial. — Justin Martyr, *Dialogue with Trypho*

Enchir.	Augustine, *Enchiridion / Handbook of Christian Doctrine*
Exc.	Ambrose, *De excessu fratris sui Satyri / On the Decease of His Brother Satyrus*
FC	John Paul II, *Familiaris consortio / Letter on the Family*. Available at https://w2.vatican.va/content/john-paul-ii/en/apost_exhortations/documents/hf_jp-ii_exh_19811122_familiaris-consortio.html.
GS	Vatican II, *Gaudium et Spes / Joy and Hope* (*DEC* 2:1069–1135)
Haer.	Irenaeus, *Adversus haereses / Against the Heresies* (*ANF*, vol. 1)
Hom.	John Chrysostom, *Homilies on First and Second Thessalonians* (*NPNF¹*, vol. 13)
Inc.	Athanasius, *De incarnatione Verbi Dei / On the Incarnation of the Word of God*
Inst.	Lactantius, *Institutiones divinae / Divine Institutes*
KJV	King James Version
LG	Vatican II, *Lumen Gentium / Light of the World*. Available at https://www.vatican.va/archive/hist_councils/ii_vatican_council/documents/vat-ii_const_19641121_lumen-gentium_en.html.
LXX	Septuagint. Translated by Sir Lancelot Charles Lee Brenton, originally published by Samuel Bagster & Sons, London, 1844.
Mor. eccl.	Augustine, *De moribus ecclesiae catholicae / On the Morals of the Catholic Church* (*NPNF¹*, vol. 4)
MT	Masoretic Text
NIV	New International Version
NPNF¹	*A Select Library of Nicene and Post-Nicene Fathers of the Christian Church*. 1st series. Edited by Philip Schaff. 14 vols. New York: Christian Literature, 1886–89. Reprint, Peabody, MA: Hendrickson, 1994.
NPNF²	*A Select Library of Nicene and Post-Nicene Fathers of the Christian Church*. 2nd series. Edited by Philip Schaff and Henry Wace. 14 vols. New York: Christian Literature, 1890–1900. Reprint, Peabody, MA: Hendrickson, 1994.
Nupt.	Augustine, *De nuptiis et concupiscentia / On Marriage and Concupiscence*
PG	*Patrologia Graeca*. Edited by Jacques-Paul Migne. 162 vols. Paris, 1857–86.
Phld.	Ignatius, *To the Philadelphians*
PL	*Patrologia Latina*. Edited by Jacques-Paul Migne. 217 vols. Paris, 1844–55.
Res.	Tertullian, *De resurrectionis / On Resurrection*
Retract.	Augustine, *Retractiones / Retractions*
RSVCE	Revised Standard Version, Second Catholic Edition
S.1Th.	Thomas Aquinas, *Super I ad Thessalonicenses / Commentary on 1 Thessalonians*. Translated by Fabian Larcher, OP. Available at https://aquinas.cc/228/230/~1.
S.2Th.	Thomas Aquinas, *Super II ad Thessalonicenses / Commentary on 2 Thessalonians*. Translated by Fabian Larcher, OP. Available at https://aquinas.cc/232/234/~1.
S.Rom.	Thomas Aquinas, *Super ad Romanos / Commentary on Romans*. Translated by Fabian Larcher, OP. Available at https://aquinas.cc/196/198/~1.
ST	Thomas Aquinas, *Summa Theologiae* (Benziger Bros. edition, 1947, translated by Fathers of the English Dominican Province; available with other works by Thomas Aquinas at https://aquinas101.thomisticinstitute.org/st-index)

TCA   Hippolytus, *Treatise on Christ and Antichrist* (*ANF*, vol. 5)

TDNT   *Theological Dictionary of the New Testament.* Brooklyn: New City, 1991.

TR   *Textus Receptus*

Trin.   Augustine, *The Trinity.* Translated by Edmund Hill. Edited by John E. Rotelle. Works of Saint Augustine I/5. Brooklyn: New City, 1991.

VS   John Paul II, *Veritatis splendor / The Splendor of Truth.* Available at http://www.vati can.va/content/john-paul-ii/en/encyclicals/documents/hf_jp-ii_enc_06081993_ver itatis-splendor.html.

WA   *Luther's Works*, Weimar Edition

PREAMBLE

In the front matter of *Confessions of an Inquiring Spirit*, Samuel Taylor Coleridge lays out what he calls the Pentad of Operative Christianity, or "God's hand in the world":

Prothesis
Christ, the Word.

Mesothesis, or
the Indifference,
The Holy Spirit.

Thesis   *Antithesis*
The Scriptures.   The Church.

Synthesis
The Preacher.

Given our present task, we may ask how the theologian fits into this picture. The answer is surely that the theologian stands behind the preacher, who stands at the point of synthesis between the scriptures and the Church that the Spirit makes possible. And what is his task there but to support the preacher by reminding him, as Coleridge himself is doing, that this is precisely where he stands? The theologian's task is to help the preacher discern the word that the Word would have him speak, and to help him articulate it in a way faithful to that which the Church has already heard and received. By "Church" I mean the divine institution referred to as such in the Nicene Creed, to a description of which *Lumen Gentium* is devoted.

The scriptures have no distinct category "theologian," though they know of "experts in the law" and the like. The Church began to identify as theologians those persons whom it regarded as reliable guides in the matter of fitting forms of speech about God (τύποι περὶ θεολογίας, to use Plato's expression). Whether clerical or lay, such persons were steeped in the liturgy and therefore in the living unity of scripture and tradition, interpreting each in the light of the other while bringing both to bear on questions new and old. Their task was at once intellectual and ecclesial, with its own historical, exegetical, philosophical, and spiritual demands. It is not surprising, then, that they formed schools in the cathedrals and monastic houses, the better to pursue their task and to share the fruit of their labor with the presbyterate and the episcopate.

Nominalism, the Reformation, and the modern university, however, have given rise to another kind of theologian: one less certain of the Church and of tradition; one skeptical or scarcely conscious of the Eucharist, in which the Word is touched and handled as well as heard; one who begins to think that the synthesis is grounded in the preaching of the preacher—who perchance even dares to think that it is grounded in the theology of the theologian or expert in the law, who directs the preacher from a standpoint somewhere above both scripture and tradition. (Nothing changes if this theologian prefers the title "historian" or "literary critic.") More problematically, they have given rise to the kind of preacher who has learned to take refuge from the impenetrable and incommunicable mysteries in which he is now trained by making recourse to the banalities of a homespun psychology, such that the audience of his homily is also its chief subject. It is not the Word whom he preaches but rather the inner workings, as he supposes them to be, of the more or less fortunate specimens of humanity seated before him. Thus would he himself usurp, were it possible, the role of the Spirit, only to misdirect his hearers to themselves.

In such a time, the theologian worth his salt will remind the preacher that his primary task is to present Christ, in word as well as sacrament. Does he stand *in persona Christi* at the altar? So in the pulpit it is Christ for whom he speaks and Christ whom he is charged to proclaim, that those who hear may both live in the truth of what they hear and also share in its proclamation to the world. Commentary has no higher purpose than to serve this proclamation, as Christ himself showed his disciples on the Emmaus road. And commentary, where it recognizes and rises to that fact, is necessarily theological. It is marked off from everything that is mere *Religionswissenschaft* by virtue of this service, which does not mean by any lack of concern for historical facts or for human factors in composition, but by its refusal to abstract the act of reading and commenting from the task of bearing witness to Christ.

In reality, of course, there is no such thing as mere *Religionswissenschaft*, nor a-theological commentary, since all science and all commentary (historical or otherwise) rest on premises entailing theological claims. But commentary may be dignified with the adjective "theological" precisely where it means to serve the proclamation of Jesus Christ, the Word of God, and to do so in keeping with tradition. Theological commentary in this sense is not unaware that it needs the light of ancient Near Eastern and Mediterranean studies to make out vital features of the biblical witness to Christ, but neither is it unaware that it needs the light of ecclesiastical and dogmatic studies in order to discover in the text the whole truth to which it points. For the text bears witness to a future as well as a past; it bears witness to "the first and the last, and the living one" (Rev. 1:17–18), who is head of his body, the Church.

Here, however, is a parting of the ways, as Karl Barth made clear a century ago in the opening pages of his commentary on Romans. One does not have to follow Barth entirely in order to distinguish between commentary that takes the path marked out by Reimarus and Lessing and commentary that insists on being theological in the sense just indicated, or to recognize in the latter a more authentic enterprise. One does need to allow that with the appearance of Jesus Christ there came into existence a reality not subject to the laws of transience and decline, that this reality is embodied and manifested in the Church, and that the Church's scriptures are themselves imbricated in that reality. That being so, they cannot be interpreted rightly or adequately by being set over against the Church; that is, by being subjected to a reading that privileges this or that speculative configuration of the circumstances of their composition, or this or that new hermeneutic (be it philosophical or political), over the readings the Church itself has given them in its prayers, liturgies, instructions, and dogmas. For the Spirit is indeed the "indifference" who distinguishes and coordinates along both axes indicated in Coleridge's diagram, causing the Church to yield to scripture and scripture to yield to the Church, such that layer upon layer of meaning is incorporated into an ever-deepening tradition.

▨ Coleridge, it may be remarked parenthetically, has it more or less right in his pneumatological alignment of scripture and Church: "The Scriptures, the Spirit, and the Church, are co-ordinate; the indispensable conditions and the working causes of the perpetuity, and continued renascence and spiritual life of Christ still militant. The Eternal Word, Christ from everlasting, is the *Prothesis*, or identity;—the Scriptures and the Church are the two poles, or *Thesis* and *Antithesis*, and the Preacher in direct line under the Spirit but likewise the point of junction of the Written Word and the Church, is the *Synthesis*. This is God's Hand in the World" (1956: 35). It would nevertheless be better, in correction of his diagram and of his confessions also, perhaps, to put "Tradition" where he has "Church" and to permit the entire pentad to articulate the Church in its character as word (cf. *Haer.* 3.1–5, where Irenaeus lays out the integral relations between Christ, Spirit, Church, scripture, and tradition). Its character as sacrament would require a different schema.

Now, those who object to theologically deliberate readings that take into account the mind of the Church, and not merely the presumed mind of the author and his original readers, are themselves making a theological judgment about the nature of scripture and indeed about the nature of the Church; and these judgments bear directly upon their own readings. They do not agree, in other words, that scripture is not of private interpretation (2 Pet. 1:20–21), whether because they do not agree that the one whom Coleridge calls "the mesothesis" actually moves men to speak from and for God—that is, they reject the vertical axis—or because they do not agree that scripture and Church must be coordinated on the horizontal axis: scripture and empire, perhaps, or scripture and gender, or scripture and economy, or even scripture and "community," but not scripture and Church. But in that case the mesothesis is already the synthesis, and the synthesis the mesothesis. Otherwise put, the genuine trinitarianism of Coleridge has been exchanged for the pseudo-trinitarianism of Hegel, by which the Church is sublated and the whole pentad collapses into the preacher.

That men might speak from and for God is a subject 1 Thessalonians immediately requires us to take up and so, in its place, we shall. Meanwhile we ought to notice that the objection to a churchly reading is sometimes brought as a charge of Marcionism, or at least as a (vaguely Straussian) complaint that ecclesial commentators are too often inclined to forget the Jewish origins of scripture in their rush to import philosophical or theological meaning from other sources. Perhaps they are. The charge is ironic, however, when it comes from the secular academy, for it seems that Marcionism is just what characterizes the latter's scholarship— the Lessingite legacy having long ago cut off the text from its roots in the salvific history that runs from Abraham to Jesus; that is, from any real redemption, answering to an actual fall, embracing an identifiable people. The interpreter is tacitly, if not openly, encouraged to do with the text what he pleases, as Kant put it, for the betterment of the human race generally. He is forbidden to remain in the narrow furrow cut by the plough of divine election, or to give any credence to purported words or deeds of God that are not universally accessible to reason. Yet nothing could lead to taking more liberties with reason than this, save perchance the fanciful genealogies (what Irenaeus called "ropes of sand") spun out by social historians and literary critics in pursuit of an original thesis. Nothing indeed is more inimical to the idea—the very Jewish idea—of scripture as such. At all events, the antidote to the forgetfulness in question is certainly not a self-imposed restriction to historical-critical forms of investigation but rather the learning of that genuine liberty which flows from engagement with the divine realities to which the text points.

That was Coleridge's own antidote to Lessing, and Barth's as well. It is the same antidote that Angus Paddison seeks in *Theological Hermeneutics and 1 Thessalonians*. Paddison wants to approach the text with "the conviction that in 1 Thessalonians we are reading the issue of an apostle," that in it we therefore encounter nothing less than an authoritative word of God in Christ—which makes it "a ceaselessly profound well of meaning" (2005: 10). Paddison draws from that well with the buckets provided by the commentaries of Aquinas and Calvin, lowered and raised by a hermeneutical apparatus put together from various patristic and modern sources. This project, he avers, is "somewhat different from still dominant historical-critical modes of reading the Bible" (14). One may quibble with the "somewhat." In recent literature on Thessalonians Paddison's book marks, or so we may hope, an important turning point. Not because he presupposes that the text arises from, and points toward, a reality greater than anything that can be grasped by way of historical and literary research alone—that presupposition belongs to every ecclesial reader. Nor because, in going beyond the historical-critical and its recent political, social-scientific, and rhetorical variants into the expressly theological, he is not content simply to report on the afterlife of the text: that is, on its "*Wirkungsgeschichte* (history of effects); *Auslegungsgeschichte* (interpretation history); and *Rezeptionsgeschichte* (reception history)" (8). The usefulness of such a report may be judged from Anthony Thiselton's *1 and 2 Thessalonians through the Centuries*. But Paddison is concerned to engage directly, and simultaneously, both the historical and the theological sense of the text—or, as we used to say, the literal sense and the spiritual—and so to make his own contribution to the Church's grasp and deployment of it. In other words, he is engaged, albeit in a different context and in a very different sort of book, in the same broad enterprise in which Aquinas and Calvin were engaged. That is an enterprise in which we too will take part, seeking, without neglecting the literal and historical sense, "the meaning expressed by the biblical texts when read, under the influence of the Holy Spirit, in the context of the paschal mystery of Christ and of the new life which flows from it" ("The Interpretation of the Bible in the Church," Pontifical Biblical Commission, 1993, cited by McCarthy 1998). In that context they must be read separately *and* read together, that they may work together like a multifocal lens. The critic who finds this dizzying might try persevering. Of course, if he thinks Abraham merely a literary or legal fiction invented during a postexilic land dispute, and Jesus largely the product of a more existential sort of "land" dispute after Jerusalem fell to Titus, he has no reason to persevere.

That men might speak from and for God cannot but raise the question, which men? Even Marcion thought Paul such a man, and took both Thessalonian epistles to be from Paul's hand; his truncated canon included the second letter as it did the first. In today's neo-Marcionite setting, however, where the very idea of canon is resisted, things are not quite so simple. The author of 1 Thessalonians is still thought to be the apostle himself, whereas the "Paul" of 2 Thessalonians is widely regarded as a literary artifice. Of what consequence is this for those who wish to undertake a churchly reading of these epistles?

No one will doubt that it is of very considerable consequence in wrestling with authorial perspective and agenda. But the churchly reader will have to deal first with the fact that it is of consequence for the second letter's authority. If it is not from Paul but rather pseudonymous, it might still have the apostolic authority the Church has attributed to it. The Church, that is—ratifying its authority by including it in the canon—might conceivably have sanctioned such an artifice. But it did not do that; rather, it accepted the letter as Paul's. And that was not quite the same as merely supposing it to be Paul's, for 2 Thessalonians specifically claims to be Paul's and, uniquely in the Pauline corpus, does so by pointing to a signature on the autograph. Can such an artifice be regarded as anything other than an attempt to deceive? If not, then it must be understood either that the author is in fact Paul or that the Church itself has been deceived and has canonized a deception.

This sort of reasoning is rejected, naturally, by those who do not concern themselves with the question of authority, who even suppose that such reasoning is the sign of an inability or unwillingness to take historical-critical investigation seriously. For his part, the churchly reader, who does not accept the alternative *either* authority *or* serious historical investigation—who in fact repudiates that alternative as just another form of the faith/reason dichotomy that bedevils modernity—is not at all uninterested in their arguments for taking "Paul" and the alleged signature to be an artifice. He knows that genuine understanding of the text can only be had by wrestling with whatever challenges it presents. He is bound, however, to be suspicious from the outset of any claim that implies that its author is attempting to deceive. For he knows that the hand of God does not deceive, nor he who speaks for God.

We may dispose of the false dichotomy just mentioned by agreeing with Coleridge that faith, so far from being opposed to reason, "subsists in the *synthesis* of the Reason and the individual Will" (*Literary Remains*, 4:437, in Coleridge 1956: 16). Likewise, we may dispose of the fallacious alternative between authority and historical investigation by insisting that authority of some kind is what makes investigation and argument possible. But here is an alternative of which we may *not* dispose, unless of course we wish, with the serpent, to dispose of the authority of God himself: Either an inspired author speaks the truth or his putative inspiration is not from God; if he aims to deceive, he certainly does not speak from or for God.

So what are the arguments for "Paul" rather than Paul? As usual, they can be grouped broadly under three rubrics: literary, historical, and theological. The literary argument concerns itself both with similarities between the two letters that might be taken as evidence of borrowing or emulation and with differences between them that might be taken as evidence of distinct linguistic resources or stylistic habits. The historical concerns itself with circumstances pertaining to the second letter that seem odd in Paul's own day. The theological concerns itself especially with conceptual and perspectival differences in eschatology. This order is an ascending order in the present case, for the literary argument is not very substantial and the historical argument only marginally more so.

To pause briefly with the former, similarities are found in formulaic greetings, prayers, exhortations, and benedictions, as well as in alleged structural elements such as periodic thanksgivings. Dissimilarities include tone, formality, appeals to authority rather than to affection, length or complexity of sentences, and differences of thought where there is overlap of language. With Wrede-like suspicion (and Wrede is at the root of all this), it is posited that the later letter cannot be from the same hand. But is it really so strange that a letter written on one occasion should evince or evoke by way of reminiscence a certain intimacy, and deploy a certain informality of style—tending, say, to shorter rather than longer sentences—and that a letter written on another occasion, with another purpose in view, should adopt a somewhat more exalted style or a different, perhaps more severe, tone? That its vocabulary should vary a little, or a word here and there be used in a different sense than it was before? That it should repeat things that had been said before, while differently deploying them in some instances and simply reinforcing them in others? And which is more likely: that Paul, with the care of many churches on his mind, should develop epistolary patterns that show just such variation and overlap; or that some other "Paul" should go to such trouble, only to show himself now brilliantly deceptive, now transparently clumsy?

▧ It has been pointed out by men of letters far better equipped at such judgments than most biblical commentators that their own authorship would not survive intact the nit-picking analysis that too often passes for critical scholarship today. In the present case, one is almost embarrassed to offer specific illustrations of the literary evidence for 1 and 2 Thessalonians being from different hands. We are to presume that the same person would not write 1 Thess. 1:2 and 2 Thess. 1:3 to a common audience? One may as well say that the same person would not write 2 Thess. 1:3 and 2:13, and so embark on the process of pulling apart each letter individually. Or we are to believe that the variants of Ὁ δὲ κύριος κατευθύναι that appear in 1 Thess. 3:11 and 2 Thess. 3:5 no self-respecting author would deploy in successive letters—that the only explanation for this is the work of a dull-witted imitator who gives himself away by borrowing the language but not the thought? We are to suppose that, having said what is said in 1 Thess. 3:11–13, one would not say what is said in 2 Thess. 2:16–17? That, after writing 1 Thess. 2:9–12, one could not write 2 Thess. 3:8–13? If that indeed is the case, we must conclude that the forger does not know his trade. If it is not the case, the forgery hypothesis falls to Ockham's razor. Why not rather allow, where there is overlap, that Paul was in the habit—the entirely natural habit for someone with his public speaking and writing responsibilities—of producing such variations on his own themes and turns of phrase? Who has not encountered such phenomena, be they deliberate or accidental, numerous times in a given author?

Victor Paul Furnish, who offers a mercifully brief sketch of the authorship question, does not think that the apostle elsewhere "borrows from himself" in this way (2007: 134); but Furnish fails to mention such obvious examples as, say, 1 Cor. 3:16–17 and 2 Cor. 6:14–7:1. He eventually concludes, after considering all three categories, that the second letter's authenticity must at least be doubted. After a more thorough treatment, Abraham Malherbe (2000: 349–74) reaches the opposite conclusion. On his view, there is a paucity of evidence for imitation at the structural and literary level, while variations in vocabulary, tone, or style are not difficult to account for if one is sensitive to context. Malherbe indeed objects to the whole procedure of highlighting variations in this way. "The most serious shortcoming of these linguistic investigations," he protests, "is their purely statistical character. . . . The language of 1 Thessalonians becomes a conglomeration of words, phrases, and sentences to be manipulated to prove a hypothesis" about the second letter's pseudonymity (367f.).

Gordon Fee's complaint that "those who argue most strongly against this letter as authentic have also seldom written a commentary on it" (2009: 238) does not apply to the likes of Furnish, of course, but rather to those such as Wolfgang Trilling (see Weima and Porter 1998: 62f.) who find William Wrede so much more interesting than scripture that they never get around to the latter in its own right. Furnish, however, like Trilling, would have done well to consider the sort of thing that Fee notices in his own sustained, close reading of the second letter—namely, "that its author has a thoroughgoing acquaintance with, and use of, language and terms from the first letter, but knew next to nothing, if anything at all, of the Paul of the later letters" (2009: 240). Fee agrees with those who think that this one fact makes highly doubtful the speculative constructs adopted by adherents of the late forgery hypothesis.

Among the historical reasons, it is said that the signature referred to in 2 Thess. 3:17, as a safeguard against the possible forgeries alluded to at 2:2, has no exact parallel in Paul's other letters. It is added that the very idea of a forgery seems odd at this early period, during which one might with impunity simply disagree with Paul rather than pretend to be Paul. Moreover, there seems already to be in the second letter a definite sense of a Pauline testimony, gospel, or tradition, a sense better befitting the post-Pauline era. The formal, almost impersonal tone of 2 Thessalonians, compared with 1 Thessalonians, reinforces the sense that we are dealing with a pseudonymous author from a later era.

This is the place to mention that in the forgery camp, as in the camp of those who take both letters to be from Paul, there are those who argue for the priority of 2 Thessalonians—a view hardly compatible with the arguments just indicated. Their reasons for doing so are various, and we shall return to them in a moment. Mentioning them here serves no other purpose than to point out that the so-called historical arguments are not really historical at all but purely speculative. What is more, they are developed against the grain of the textual evidence. Not only were handwritten greetings appended to Galatians and 1 Corinthians, but in the former case it would be quite natural to take Paul's interjection—"see with what large letters I am writing to you with my own hand" (Gal. 6:11)—as functioning to deter anyone from questioning the authenticity of that letter, commonly acknowledged to be among the earliest; which makes sense only if the possibility of forgeries was already acknowledged. As for his own quite definite sense of bearing a peculiar testimony and authority, what could be more decisive than the opening gambit of Galatians, "Paul an apostle—not from men nor through man, but through Jesus Christ and God the Father"? Nor is any passage in 2 Thessalonians bolder in laying claim to an authoritative gospel or tradition than Gal. 1:8–10 or 6:17.

Those who concentrate on rhetorical analysis have pointed out that the relation between the two letters has been badly misconstrued by reason of a failure to consider the demands of their respective rhetorical forms. Second Thessalonians approximates deliberative rhetoric rather than following the epideictic, *narratio*-oriented pattern of 1 Thessalonians. That being the case, "we should expect some appeal to authority" in the second letter that we do not find in the first (Witherington 2006: 21ff., here 34). Nor is there any reason to suppose that Paul was unfamiliar with, or incapable of deploying, both rhetorical forms, or indeed of combining them in creative ways. On the contrary, his other letters demonstrate such a mastery. Once the supposition is made, however, that the second letter must be from another hand, what option is left to us but to posit something wholly contrary to the spirit of Paul, and to the personal integrity he belabors in his authentic letters? Take, for example, the speculative reconstruction—it cannot be called historical—of Linda McKinnish Bridges (2008: 216): "The writer of the second letter traces the footprints of the first apostle missionary, Paul, in Thessaloniki, successfully emulating Paul's writing style, and gaining the respect of the believers in the congregation. . . . To Paul's warm affectionate style of pastoral leadership, the author of the second letter adds admonitions for doctrinal purity and ideological room for the apocalyptic imagination of the community." This "new leader remains anonymously cloaked in the image and memory of Paul"; he uses "Paul's reputation and name to gain a hearing in the community, revealing that the author's identity is less important than the care and development of the community." Now, it would be too tedious to spell out the internal contradictions of Bridges's account and it is hardly necessary to remark on its ideological tendencies, which are worn on the sleeve. But it cannot be overlooked that this "new leader," with his backroom tactics, acts in a spirit contrary to Paul's. "We have renounced disgraceful, underhanded ways," says Paul; "we refuse to practice cunning or to tamper with God's word, but by the open statement of the truth we would commend ourselves to every man's conscience in the sight of God" (2 Cor. 4:2). Bridges's account, it may be added, though popular rather than scholarly, is just the sort of thing that historical-critical approaches invite—nay, demand—when they become detached from one or both axes of Coleridge's diagram and from the question of truth and truthfulness.

Let us leave literary and historical concerns to one side, however; not merely because others have treated them as far as they require to be treated but also because the great preponderance of those who argue for pseudonymity do so, in the last analysis, for theological reasons. From J. E. C. Schmidt to Wrede to Trilling, the primary problem has been the perceived conflict between the eschatology operative in 1 Thess. 4–5 and that at work in 2 Thess. 2, especially between the imminence of the parousia in the former letter and its delay in the latter—which also introduces an antichrist motif that is more characteristic of the Apocalypse and the Johannine corpus than of the Pauline. Those who think this conflict artificial, resolvable by patient exegesis, tend also to find the other arguments for pseudonymity individually and collectively unpersuasive. Those who think the conflict irresolvable are generally happy to flank their eschatological arguments with any others that can be mustered. So the whole exercise directs us in the end to the exegetical burden that is also a theological burden: the burden of showing the deep structure of Pauline eschatology as it appears in the Thessalonian correspondence, or of showing that there are different and conflicting structures in play.

Just here, however, we must put again the question of Marcionism, and ask whether distaste for the "Jewish" eschatology of 2 Thessalonians is not also a factor. Judgment, retribution, the mystery and man of lawlessness—none of this was very digestible by the end of the eighteenth century. In 1798 Schmidt argued that 2 Thess. 2:1–12 was an interpolation, an infecting apocalyptic virus, so to say, mysteriously introduced into the Pauline corpus. Wrede saw that it was not tenable to treat the passage as an interpolation, but did not hesitate to follow up with an assault on the authenticity of the entire letter. Perhaps the popularity of his view owes more than a little to a preference for a less apocalyptic Paul? (N. T. Wright 2013: 61 shares this suspicion.) After all, it is easier to dismiss the ideas of a forger, and a forger is precisely what we are talking about. Bart Ehrman puts it bluntly: "The author of 2 Thessalonians, claiming to be the real Paul, warns his readers not to be deceived. Whatever an earlier forger may have asserted, the end had not yet come because there were certain events that had to transpire first" (2008: 384). Deceit upon deceit, in other words—a contest or play of deceits—is what confronts us in 2 Thessalonians (→1:1–2). Let the reader beware!

On the other hand, it may be asked whether those of us who assert the integrity and authenticity of 2 Thessalonians do so just because we are committed to biblical apocalyptic; or at all events because we are committed to the authority of Church and canon. We may take comfort in the conclusions of Malherbe or Witherington, or in the still cogent account provided by I. Howard Marshall (1983: 28–45). We may make every effort to weigh the evidence honestly to the best of our ability. But we can hardly deny that we too have something invested in the outcome. Only those who think Paul and "Paul" equally likely to mislead, or those who at all events do not share the Muratorian Canon's objection to mixing gall with honey, will try to claim otherwise. But their claim, too, may be doubted.

It is to the commentary itself, then, that we must leave the whole business, and to the commentary precisely as a theological commentary that is prepared to wrestle with the eschatology and its implications. Yet we must mark, conscious of the irony, the fact that the Church itself has not entirely encouraged this. For in the lectionary 2 Thessalonians has been quietly hidden away and its most controversial passages elided. While 1 Thessalonians fares a little better, barely half of 2 Thessalonians is read in the churches. The Revised Common Lectionary omits, among other passages, 1:5–10 and 2:6–12. The Catholic Lectionary for Mass (1981 Latin and 1998 USA editions) on Sundays and Major Feasts excludes 2:3–15. On weekdays some twenty-one verses are read, but 2:3b–13 is again omitted. The public reading of the letter is done, then, in such a way as to obscure, if not to distort or suppress, its message. Things are no worse, perhaps, than for many of the psalms and various other portions of scripture, but a correction is needed. Dare we hope that theological commentary will help bring about such a correction? How shall the preacher preach on these things, if he has no assignment to preach and little or no instruction for the preaching? If he gets the sense that the Church prefers among the faithful "their more customary torpor" to any risk of stirring up eschatological fervor (Pelikan 2005: 43)?

To accept the view of the Church in the matter of authorship, asserting that both letters are from Paul, requires us in any case to work out the relation between the two letters without ignoring the difficult parts, and without taking the liberty of positing another and different "Paul" about whom nothing is known and almost anything may be conjectured. But are there grounds for reversing the traditional order of the letters? That, too, is a matter of considerable import for their interpretation, and there is no comparable impediment to the proposal. Were the compositional order in doubt, the longer letter (1 Thessalonians) would likely have been put first by those who gave shape to the New Testament, so the canonical order does not necessarily determine the matter.

▨ The canon's formative period offers few clues. In the Muratorian Canon it is said only that Paul "writes once more . . . to the Thessalonians for the sake of admonition." In *Haer.* 4.29.1, Irenaeus seems to know the letters in their canonical order, but says nothing that would cast light on their compositional order. All that can be concluded is that no evidence emerges from the second century in support of a reversal, or of other, more complex reconfigurations such as that of Walter Schmithals, for example, who posits four genuine letters redacted to two (see Weima and Porter 1998: 67).

Among those who nevertheless attempt to read the second letter first, as Hugo Grotius first recommended, are Thomas Manson and Charles Wanamaker. Manson (1953), defending Acts' account of Paul's mission as well as the authenticity of both letters, took 2 Thessalonians to have been composed in Athens and delivered by Timothy during the visit mentioned in 1 Thess. 3:2. According to both Manson and Wanamaker (1990: 38f.), this makes better sense of several factors: the more definite sense of persecution in 2 Thessalonians that seems (on one reading of 1 Thess. 2:14–16) to be a past problem in 1 Thessalonians; the prior charge to continue working that is mentioned in 1 Thess. 4:11 (cf. 2 Thess. 3:6–12); the introduction to Paul's signature in 2 Thess. 3:17; the "concerning" or "as to" passages in 1 Thess. 4:9, 4:13, and 5:1, each of which touches on questions that could have been raised by the material in 2 Thessalonians; and, in particular, the remark at 1 Thess. 5:1 to the effect that the Thessalonians were already well instructed respecting the end times. Wanamaker allows for the reply that none of these points is conclusive, since each is susceptible to an explanation that does not require the priority of 2 Thessalonians. On the other hand, he thinks the "apparent references" in 2 Thess. 2:2, 2:15, and 3:17 to a previous letter also susceptible of a different explanation, and proposes that 2:15 be read as an internal reference to 2 Thessalonians itself. Malherbe (2000: 362) notes, in addition, Manson's view that the joyful tone of 1 Thessalonians bespeaks a more mature theology than that of the somber 2 Thessalonians, but rightly dismisses this as an arbitrary judgment. Malherbe himself admits that 2 Thessalonians can be read in such a way as to eliminate references to an earlier letter; yet he thinks it very difficult to unpick the knot between Paul's visit and the effort made in 1 Thessalonians to give an account of the intervening period and to develop the relationship established during that visit. Positing the priority of 2 Thessalonians, a letter to which 1 Thessalonians makes no direct reference, seems to him strained. I would say, more than strained.

Arguably, there is no insurmountable problem to be faced by those who wish to read the second epistle first, but neither is there any compelling reason for the reversal. Centuries of reading them *as if* the canonical order were also the temporal order must surely count for something on the hermeneutical scales; nor have those who want them read in reverse order persuaded many that more is gained than lost in doing so. We will therefore allow the ruling on the field to stand, offering a reading that preserves the traditional order. Once again the commentary must help justify the call, however. One of its tasks will be to show—*pace* those who think that 1 Thess. 5:1 makes better sense if the readers already have 2 Thess. 2 in mind—that it is better to view things the other way round. The first ten verses of 1 Thess. 5 seem to lose something of their native power and grace when set against the backdrop of 2 Thess. 2:1–12, whereas the latter passage retains its rhetorical potency when read as counterpoint to the former.

So: we will accept both the traditional ascription of authorship and the traditional order, with the proviso that the grounds for the latter in particular can only be convincingly displayed in the actual attempt at interpretation. Most other matters of introduction may be left to remarks on the first letter's first chapter. We are not quite done here, however, there being one or two further problems to address in advance, beginning with the relation between the Paul of the epistles and the Paul of Acts. For it may be supposed that, even if "Paul" is no artifice in 2 Thessalonians, the Paul that Acts presents *is*—at least in the sense that his character and message, whether in the mission to Thessaloniki (then Θεσσαλονίκη) or elsewhere, are the product of a theological and literary imagination at some distance from the historical reality. Taking Acts to be written by Luke, and Luke to have been one of Paul's intimates, greatly attenuates that difficulty, though it does not much diminish the task of deciding how best to approach Acts—a work that is *sui generis*—even if it narrows considerably the range of cultural and political factors that appear on its near horizon. But that assumption is no longer common in the academy, which tends to frown on appeals to Acts in elucidation of Thessalonians or other Pauline letters. As we will have occasion to make such appeals, a word must be said about this, as also about the Pastoral Epistles, which are widely regarded (even more widely than 2 Thessalonians) as inauthentic.

In *World Upside Down: Reading Acts in the Graeco-Roman Age*, Kavin Rowe takes it for granted that "aside from some basic generalities, we have no idea where Acts was written, or for whom, or at what particular time, or where it was to be sent" (2009: 11). Leaning on Todd Penner's "Madness in the Method? The Acts of the Apostles in Current Study" (2004), he concludes that fascination with the book's provenance has overcome interest in the book itself. "The secondary literature on Acts is no longer full to the brim; it has now burst the dam and threatens to wash away the text of Acts in a torrent of scholarly glossolalia." The threat is real enough, but the adjective "scholarly," I fear, must be taken with a grain of salt. For this literature suffers from the same disorder that we have already encountered with respect to the putative pseudonymity of 2 Thessalonians. Though laden with layers of historical sediment, it is so highly conjectural, and in consequence so thoroughly contradictory, that it is difficult to take seriously. Its authors seem to be splashing about in private ponds; which is to say, "they act like those who bring forward any kind of hypothesis they fancy" (*Haer.* 1.9.4).

One need only peruse Weima and Porter's *Annotated Bibliography of 1 & 2 Thessalonians* to see that this is so with respect to the Thessalonian letters; with respect to Acts the evidence is still more abundant, as Penner's review shows. Penner (2004: 264) is put in mind of the retort of Festus (mistakenly referred to as Felix), "Much learning hath driven thee mad!" But is there much hope that the further methodological reflection he recommends will restore our sanity? Sanity, on Paul's terms, requires belief in the prophets (Acts 26:27), and belief in the prophets, if not actually excluded methodologically, appears to be in very short supply. The Church, which considers itself the custodian of the prophets, may provide the only hope of restored sanity. The Church takes St. Luke to be the author of Acts, something modern scholarship has failed to prove impossible or even unlikely. The "we" passages, which through any fog remain a clear signal that Acts rests upon firsthand accounts and that the reader may approach it as a useful source of information about Paul, the Church recognizes as genuine. While Acts does not offer direct readings of Pauline texts, and we cannot look to it for that, we can still look to it, as the Church does, for help in interpreting Paul and his mission. A canonical reading of either Luke or Paul does not merely invite this; it requires it.

Let us then follow Rowe's advice to take Acts more seriously than we take the recent flood of secondary literature, the twisting torrents of which remind rather of Babel than of Pentecost. More than that, however, let us presume that Luke's Paul and Paul's Paul cohere in Jesus Christ, our one hope of coherence, and so also in fact and history. (By "Paul's Paul" I mean the Paul of Galatians, for example, who is supposed by neo-Marcionites to be at odds with Luke's Paul.) A theological commentary worthy of the label must concern itself, as far as possible, with the whole Paul, the Paul who lives and moves and has his being in the Spirit and within the *communio sanctorum*, who therefore still speaks with his own voice, however refracted in his letters or in other documents of the Church, including Acts. For the same reason, it must also take into account the Pastorals, those allegedly pseudonymous letters to Timothy and Titus in which the Church hears and recognizes Paul. Anyone who supposes this Paul, the Church's Paul, to be mere illusion—the epiphenomenon of a madness driven not by learning but by blind faith—will dismiss the exercise as, at best, a devotional one. But those who recognize in Paul a father in God and a brother in Christ and an apostle with authority in the Church of God, will get on with the task, which is indeed devotional, of thinking theologically in his company. And what the Church includes among those writings which are either directly or indirectly from his own hand, which fill out the resonances of his own voice, they will not exclude.

▨ Douglas Campbell toys with the possibility that the letters to Timothy are indeed written by Paul, but decides against it. The tipping point in his negative judgment is that 1 Tim. 5:18 appears to quote the dominical saying in Luke 10:7 as scripture, something that could only have happened very much later (2014: 361f.). Despite the failure of most other arguments against its authenticity, this "smoking gun" remains. The gun in question is a simple καί, on the strength of which the tradition of the Church is overturned. Then again, Campbell is sufficiently confident in his own judgment as to the provenance of the ten letters he deems authentic to recommend that Bibles be amended to reflect that judgment (2014: 338), which nicely instantiates the posture I think we should not adopt. The alternative, to think in and with the Church, does not require the supposition that in no genre is pseudonymity appropriate, much less the supposition that posthumous editing of a text has not occurred. It does require that Paul not be set against Paul.

Thinking theologically in the company of Paul means, for the moment, letting his Thessalonian letters set the agenda, while allowing the rest of the Pauline literature, and scripture generally, to elucidate it. It means letting others also speak to it, first and foremost those who have standing in the Church, whether towering figures such as Chrysostom, Augustine, and Aquinas, or lesser expositors such as Theodore, Theodoret, Oecomenius, Theophylact, Haimo, and Theitland. Calvin too may have his say, and recent commentators, including those at a distance from the Church. For we need not at all points confine ourselves to those who see and hear Paul with the Church, or to those who agree with Coleridge that "Christianity is fact no less than truth," that it is "spiritual, yet so as to be historical," and that the historical and the spiritual—indeed, the historical and the miraculous, those "*phaenomena* in nature that are beyond nature"—must and do meet (1956: 40). It is not as if no one else, however great their learning, can possibly say anything useful. Nevertheless, this commentary is primarily for those who share the Church's convictions and who therefore take a keen interest in Paul's testimony, both to what is and to what shall be. It is for those who are prepared to take the eschatology of Thessalonians with as much seriousness as they take the Pauline missions in their historic setting.

To let Thessalonians set the agenda is to commit to the task of exegesis (what does the text actually say?) and of exposition (what is the significance of what is said?). These tasks are distinct, but in such a way that neither excuses from the other; they belong to all serious commentary. In theological commentary, however, the task of exposition is expanded. An attempt is made to cast light on matters the text does not itself address, but which in one fashion or another it raises for its readers. Here one does not normally find page upon page of argument about grammatical constructions and semantic or historical possibilities, but may find page upon page of argument about the realities engaged or implied by the text. That entails, necessarily, that the commentator's own agenda will at times intrude on the agenda of the sacred author, which by some will be considered a distraction, even an impertinence. Without denying that it can be either or both, I would deny that it is such in any more egregious fashion than those pages upon pages that alternately delight and horrify the grammarian, the philologist, or the historian. And I would suggest, respectfully, that it is, or at least may be, closer in spirit to the texts themselves.

Otherwise put, a theological commentary will have its own criteria for emphasis and hence for organization, leaving much in the background that other commentaries place in the foreground. It will also venture to connect its commentary topically with other texts that are not even aware that they, too, are commentary of a sort. In doing so, it will not stop short of rendering theological judgment, where such judgment is required of it by the canonical boundaries and authoritative readings that in the Church of God have been recognized and established. Neither will it neglect its proper liberty in drawing out new meanings from old, in the fashion of St. Irenaeus, who knew very well how to trump both Marcionite and Montanist hermeneutics by seeking the deep structures produced in the canon through the Spirit's inspirational art. And while it must try to resist the lure of idle speculation about present as well as past events, it will not altogether ignore those events. Fires were being lit in Thessaloniki even as I began to write, and there are fires being lit all around the world, even, alas, in the Church itself. It would be irresponsible to deny them any examination through the lenses here at hand.

■ A few notes on internal arrangements: As in this preamble, the large-print sections of the commentary can be read consecutively, while the small-print sections provide pauses for annotations, glosses, and excurses. My translation will at times lean to the literal, but some liberties will be taken with a view to filling ellipses and maintaining rather than interrupting rhetorical force, which does not always permit a literal rendering. Clarity and decent English phrasing also require minor additions or adjustments. (That said, it is difficult to do much, for example, about Paul's tendency to overuse the word ἀδελφοί, which is sometimes a rhetorical marker and sometimes just annoying. It is also sometimes aimed at the whole church and, more rarely, at its presbyters, inviting in the latter instance the use of "brothers" rather than "brethren." The word "Church," by the way, will be capitalized where its catholicity is in view rather than its local particularity; on the quality of catholicity, see Cyril, *CL* 18.23.) Much exegetical labor is quietly buried in the translation, with some deleterious effects besides those generated by blunders; namely, a lack of transparency regarding both my own reasoning and debts owed to others. On the more important matters, naturally, and not a few minor ones, that labor stands upright and remains out in the open. As for textual variations, they will be mentioned only where they touch on the meaning of the text. The Greek that appears in the commentary will not always be translated again *in situ*, but this should not much deter the reader without Greek from following. Quotations from biblical texts other than Thessalonians will be from the Revised Standard Version (second Catholic edition) unless they are a fresh translation or another translation is indicated. Capitalization is largely constrained by editorial policy, though a few liberties have been taken here as well (as with "Church" and "church"). It is my own choice to confine myself consistently to a single gender, though I am told that these days one has very many to choose from and that consistency is not required. The word "man," like the word "brethren," is used inclusively of male and female, as it used to be and ought to be. May those famous missionary translators from Thessaloniki, Saints Cyril and Methodius, who were no strangers to controversy, pray for me.

On a personal note, permit me to express my gratitude to McGill University for two sabbatical leaves to work on this project, to those teachers who many years ago enthused me with their love for the Pauline epistles (David Lewycky, Anthony Thiselton, and Tom Wright come immediately to mind), and to the series editor, Rusty Reno, who encouraged me to take up this task and thus to return in more earnest to the kind of activity that is always required of a theologian—even if that theologian lacks the skills and expertise of his erstwhile teachers, not to mention those of his present colleagues in the academy, whose indulgence he also begs. It will be understood by all concerned that what is here offered is not offered in lieu of the more familiar commentary (Malherbe's is most to be recommended, perhaps, though Weima's 2014 tome is a comprehensive wonder) but as a supplement and indeed a complement to it. If nothing else, it will not be denied the merit of being briefer than some exegetical commentaries, whose authors these days think nothing of writing more than a hundred pages on every page of Paul. Of course we theologians have sometimes managed that feat with a single verse, but that's another story.

It remains only to say that I am grateful to the publisher for what is surely a godly patience. This commentary on the first bit of the New Testament was begun, but not finished, in a timely manner. The first looks to be last, or very nearly last. The delay has on some points proved providential, however, and I am grateful to God for that, as for the sobering, even frightening, privilege of writing such a book at all. May what is worthy in it be made fruitful by his grace; and what is not, by that same grace, be discarded without harm. I am aware that the day will come, and perhaps is not now far off, when, as Vladimir Solovyov said in his "Short Tale of the Antichrist," which he set in our century, "the Gospel and Apostolic texts speaking of the Prince of this Age and of the Anti-Christ," and more importantly of the coming of the Messiah and our gathering to him, will for very pressing reasons be "read more carefully and [lead] to lively comments."

Advent 2019

1 & 2 THESSALONIANS

The Earliest Christian Text and Its Sequel

Paul and Silvanus and Timothy, to the church of the Thessalonians in God the Father and the Lord Jesus Christ: Grace to you, and peace.

We always give thanks to God for all of you, constantly remembering you in our prayers, recalling before our God and Father your work of faith and labor of love and steadfastness of hope in our Lord Jesus Christ—knowing, brethren beloved by God, your election, because our gospel did not come to you in word only but also in power and in the Holy Spirit and great assurance; just as you know what kind of men we were among you for your sake.

And you became imitators of us, and of the Lord, having received the word in great affliction with the joy of the Holy Spirit, so that you became a model to all the believers in Macedonia and Achaia. For from you the word of the Lord has sounded forth, not only in Macedonia and Achaia, but also in every place your faith toward God has been publicized, such that it is not necessary for us to say anything. For they themselves report concerning us how well our mission to you was received, and how you turned toward God from the idols, to serve the God who is living and true, and to wait for his Son to appear from the heavens, whom he raised from the dead: Jesus, the one rescuing us from the wrath that is coming.

For you yourselves know, brethren, that our mission to you was not in vain, but though we had suffered beforehand and been shamefully treated (as you are aware) in Philippi, we took courage in our God to proclaim to you the gospel of God amid many hindrances. For our appeal does not stem from error or impurity or guile, but just as we have been approved by God to be entrusted with the gospel, so also we speak, not as those pleasing to men but as pleasing rather to God who proves our hearts.

Translated by D. B. Farrow.

Never did we make our approach with flattering words, as you know, or with some pretext for taking advantage. God is witness. Nor did we seek glory from men, whether from you or from anyone else, our dignity as apostles of Christ notwithstanding. Rather we became gentle among you, like a nursing mother with her children, so solicitous for you that it seemed good to us to share with you not only the gospel of God but our own selves, because you were beloved by us. For you remember, brethren, our toil and trouble—laboring night and day so as not to burden any of you while we preached to you the gospel of God.

You are witnesses, together with God, how piously and properly and indeed irreproachably we behaved toward you who believed; even as you know how we encouraged and exhorted each one of you, as a father his children, and charged you to walk worthily of the God who is calling you into his own kingdom and glory.

And for this also we constantly thank God, that when you received the word of God, heard from us, you accepted it not as the word of men but as it truly is, God's own word, which indeed is at work among you who believe.

For you yourselves, brothers, became imitators of the churches of God in Christ Jesus that are in Judea, for you suffered the same things from your own countrymen as they did from the Jewish authorities, who also killed the Lord Jesus and the prophets and drove us out, who are displeasing to God and hostile to all men—hindering us from speaking to the Gentiles that they might be saved—so as always to heap up their sins. But the final wrath has caught them out.

But we, brethren, being thus torn away from you for a brief moment, in person not in heart, earnestly sought to see your face, with much longing. Hence we determined to come to you—I, Paul, more than once—but Satan hindered us. For who, if not you, is our hope or joy or crown of boasting before our Lord Jesus at his parousia? You yourselves are our glory and our joy.

Therefore, when we could hold out no longer, we thought it best to be left in Athens alone and sent Timothy, our brother and God's coworker in the gospel of Christ, to strengthen you and to rally your faith, that no one be shaken by these tribulations. For you yourselves know that to such we are appointed. Even when we were with you, we were warning you that we are about to suffer tribulation—just as you see also happened. For this reason I, too, when I could no longer bear it, sent to find out about your faith, lest somehow the tempter had tempted you and our labor were in vain.

But now, Timothy having returned to us from you and having told us the good news of your faith and love, and that you always speak well of us, longing to see us even as we long to see you—in all our distress and trouble we were comforted concerning you, brethren, because of this, through your faith. For now we live, if you are standing firm in the Lord. What thank offering can we render back to God for you, for all the joy with which we rejoice because of you before our God, night and day begging profusely that we might see your face and make up any deficiencies in your faith?

May our God and Father himself, and our Lord Jesus, clear our path to you; and may the Lord cause you to increase and abound in love to one another and toward all, as we do toward you, so as to establish your hearts blameless in holiness before our God and Father at the parousia of our Lord Jesus with all his holy ones.

It remains only to say, brethren: We entreat and exhort you in the Lord Jesus that, just as you received from us guidance as to how you must walk to please God—even as you are walking—you should excel still more. For you know what instructions we gave you through the Lord Jesus. This is the will of God, your sanctification: that you abstain from sexual impurity; that you learn how to possess, each of you, his own vessel in holiness and honor, not in the heat of lust like the Gentiles who do not know God; that you not trespass and take advantage of your brother in the matter, because the Lord dispenses justice in all these things, just as we warned you and solemnly testified. For God did not call us to impurity, but for sanctification. So he who dismisses these instructions dismisses not man but God—the God who gives his Spirit to you, his holy Spirit.

But concerning brotherly love you have no need that we should write you, for you yourselves are people taught by God to love one another, and you are doing just that to the brethren in all Macedonia. So again we encourage you, brothers, to excel more, and to strive to live quietly and to mind your own affairs and to work with your hands, just as we instructed you, that you may conduct yourselves honorably toward those outside and have need of no one.

Now we do not wish you ignorant, brethren, concerning those who sleep, lest you grieve for them as others grieve who have no hope. For if we believe that Jesus died and rose, so also we believe that God, through the same Jesus, will bring to life with him those who sleep. Indeed we assure you, by dominical promise, that we who live and remain until the parousia of the Lord shall certainly not precede those who have fallen asleep—that the Lord himself, with a mighty cry, with the voice of the archangel and with the sound of the trumpet of God, shall descend from heaven and the dead in Christ shall rise up first. Then we, the living who remain, shall together with them be caught up "with the clouds" so as to welcome the Lord in the air. And, just so, we shall ever be with the Lord. So comfort one another with these words.

Concerning the times and the seasons, brethren, again you have no need that we should write to you, for you know full well that the day of the Lord is coming like a thief in the night. Just when they say, "Peace and security!"—then suddenly destruction comes upon them, as labor pains come upon her who is with child, and they will by no means escape.

But you, dear brothers, are not in darkness, that the day of the Lord should steal up on you as a thief, for you are all sons of the light and sons of the day. We are not of the night, nor of the darkness. So, then, let us not sleep, like the rest, but rather watch and be sober. For those who sleep sleep at night, and those who get drunk get drunk at night. But we who are of the day should be wakeful and sober, having donned the body armor of faith and love and, as a helmet, the hope of salvation. Because God has destined us not for wrath but for obtaining salvation through our Lord Jesus Christ, who died on our behalf that, whether we should remain on watch or have fallen asleep in Christ, we might live together with him when he comes. So carry on as you are, encouraging one another, each supporting the other.

We entreat you, brethren, to honor those toiling among you and set over you in the Lord and admonishing you on his behalf, holding them exceedingly high in love on account of their labor. Be at peace among yourselves. And we exhort you, brothers, to discipline the disorderly, to encourage the discouraged, to shore up the weak, to be patient with all. See that no one is repaid by anyone evil for evil, but always seek the good for each other and for all.

Rejoice always, pray constantly, in all things give thanks: this is the will of God in Christ Jesus for you. The fire of the Spirit do not douse, prophecies do not despise, but examine all things carefully. Cling to the good; from every form of evil steer clear.

May the God of peace himself sanctify you in your entirety, and your whole spirit, soul, and body be preserved blameless at the parousia of our Lord Jesus Christ. Faithful is the one calling you, who shall also effect that for which he calls.

Brethren, pray also for us. Greet all the brothers with a holy kiss. I adjure you before the Lord that this letter be read to all the brethren. The grace of our Lord Jesus Christ be with you.

✠ ✠ ✠

Paul and Silvanus and Timothy, to the church of the Thessalonians in God our Father and the Lord Jesus Christ: Grace to you and peace from God the Father and the Lord Jesus Christ.

We ought always to render thanks to God for you, brethren, as is fitting in view of the fact that your faith is greatly increasing and the love of each and every one of you for one another is abounding; just as it is fitting that we ourselves boast of you in the churches of God, about your endurance and faith in all your persecutions and in the tribulations that you are bearing. This is proof of the righteous judgment of God, so that you may be counted worthy of the kingdom of God, for the sake of which you also are suffering—if indeed it is right in God's eyes to return affliction to those afflicting you and to provide relief with us to you who are being afflicted, at the disclosure of the Lord Jesus from heaven with his mighty angels in flaming fire, meting out vengeance on those refusing to recognize God and to obey the gospel of our Lord Jesus, who will suffer the penalty due them: eternal destruction, far from the face of the Lord and from the splendor of his might, when he comes on that day to be magnified among his holy ones and to be marveled at among all who have believed. For our testimony to you was believed.

To this very end we pray always for you, that our God may deem you worthy of the call and powerfully fulfill every aspiration to goodness and work of faith, so that the name of our Lord Jesus might be glorified in you, and you in him, according to the grace of our God and the Lord Jesus Christ.

But we beg you, brethren, with respect to the parousia of our Lord Jesus Christ and our assembling before him, that you not quickly be shaken from your senses or disturbed, whether by spirit or by word or by letter, supposedly from us, purporting that the day of the Lord has come. Let no one by any means deceive you, for it shall not come unless the apostasy comes first and the man of lawlessness, the son of destruction, is disclosed—the one taking an adversarial stance and exalting himself over everything said to be deity or an object of reverence, even to seating himself in the temple of God as if he were God. Do you not remember that while I was with you I was telling you these things?

And now you see what is delaying the day of the Lord, namely that the man of lawlessness should be revealed in his own proper time. For the mystery of lawlessness is already at work; only there is one presently restraining it until he shall emerge from the midst of those in whom it works.* And then at last the lawless one will be unveiled, whom the Lord Jesus will destroy with the breath of his mouth and bring down by the display of his own parousia—the one whose parousia is according to the working of Satan, with all demonic power and with false signs and wonders and with every wicked deceit, a parousia unto those who are perishing for want of love of the truth, which they did not receive that it might save them.

For this very reason God sends upon them a deluding influence, that they might credit the lie, so that they should be judged—all those who have not believed

---

* Alternatively, "until that one is ordered to stand down."

in the truth but taken pleasure in unrighteousness. But for you we ought always to render thanks to God, brethren beloved by the Lord, because he selected you as firstfruits for salvation in consecration of spirit and conviction of the truth, unto which he called you through our gospel for possession of glory, the glory of our Lord Jesus Christ.

So then, brethren, stand fast and cling to the traditions you were taught, whether in person or through our letter. And may our Lord Jesus Christ himself, and God our Father, who loved us and in his grace gave us eternal comfort and good hope, encourage your hearts and confirm you in every good work and word.

It remains to say: Pray, brethren, for us, that the word of the Lord may advance triumphantly, just as it did among you, and that we may be rescued from perverse and evil men; for the faith is not the faith of all. But the Lord is faithful, who will steady you and protect you from the evil one. And we are convinced in the Lord about you, that you are following our directives and will continue to do so. May the Lord guide your hearts in the love of God and the constancy of Christ.

And we command you, brethren, in the name of the Lord Jesus Christ, to withdraw yourselves from every brother living in a disorderly manner and not in accord with the traditions you received from us. For you yourselves know how it is proper to imitate us: We were not undisciplined among you, nor did we consume anyone's bread like freeloaders, but were among you rather as those who labored, with toil and trouble night and day, so as not to be a burden to any of you—not that we had no right to impose on you, but we behaved as we did in order that we might make ourselves an example to you, that you might imitate us. For even when we were with you, we were issuing this order, that if anyone refuses to work, neither shall he eat. Yet we hear that some among you are indeed disorderly, doing no work but the work of interfering with others. To such as these, we command and exhort in the Lord Jesus Christ that, working with quietness, their own bread they should eat, not another's.

And you, brothers, we urge not to grow weary in doing good. Should any one refuse to listen to our instruction through this letter, mark that man and do not associate with him, that he might be ashamed. Yet do not regard him as an enemy, but rather discipline him as a brother.

Now may the Lord of Peace himself give you peace in all things and in every way. The Lord be with you all.

Here is the greeting in my own hand, the hand of Paul, which is a sign of authenticity in every letter—this is how I write. The grace of our Lord Jesus Christ be with you all!

1 THESSALONIANS

Commentary on the First Letter

1:1 Paul and Silvanus and Timothy, to the church of the Thessalonians in God the Father and the Lord Jesus Christ: Grace to you, and peace.

When, in the fullness of time, Mary was startled by Gabriel's strange greeting—"Hail, O greatly favored one, the Lord is with you!" (AT)—she naturally wondered what those words might portend. They portended an unprecedented interruption to the lineage of the human race, as to the lineaments of her own life. She had been chosen. She had been filled with grace. She was to carry within her womb the "son" of the God of grace, the Messiah, the King of Israel, the Savior of the world. And she was to do so not by the will of man but by the power of the Holy Spirit, who would hover over her virgin womb, as over the darkness and deep of the unformed world at the dawn of creation, creating life where there was no life.

Thomas Aquinas begins his reading of Thessalonians by adverting to Gen. 7: "The waters increased, and bore up the ark, and it rose high above the earth." "These words," he says—offering allegorical, moral, and anagogical interpretations thereof—"are appropriate to this letter because the Thessalonians stood firm after suffering many tribulations." It is still more appropriate, then, to advert to Luke 1—that is, to the Blessed Virgin Mary as the vessel in which the mediator of the new covenant entered the world—so as to place immediately before us the antitype rather than the type.

When, some fifty years later—the fullness of time not being the end of time—the assembly of Christian converts in Thessaloniki heard a more familiar messenger stand up in their assembly and read out the greetings of Paul and Silvanus and Timothy, it was prima facie a quite mundane event. There was nothing very remarkable about a religious or political community receiving a letter from its founders. Yet they too may have wondered at the portent, for their own lives had been unexpectedly interrupted. They remembered the day, but months earlier, when these men had appeared in their city and disturbed both it and them. Those who were Gentiles had heard strange things about a man named Jesus, from some inconsequential town in Judea, whom the God of the Jews had allegedly raised from the dead and made Lord even over Caesar's realm. Those who were Jews or proselytes remembered the debates at their synagogue—what used to be their synagogue—over his messianic qualifications and about the resurrection of the dead, debates that had gone badly wrong. Gentile and Jew alike recalled the riot that had ensued at city hall, the bond that had been posted, and the hasty departure by night under threat of death. Life is not always welcome even in fertile wombs, nor light in eyes wholly accustomed to darkness. Yet they had welcomed the life and the light. They were the "chosen" of Thessaloniki. Theirs was the assembly (ἐκκλησία) duly constituted by God through his apostolic messengers in the eucharistic presence of the Lord and Savior born to Mary, itself the fruit of a vision in the night (Acts 16:9). Theirs was the task and privilege of shining in the Macedonian darkness, and they too, if not yet full of grace, were being filled for that purpose.

When today we read or hear this letter, the letter that came to them some two thousand years ago, we might well wonder ourselves at its portent. The first literary trace of the life of the Church is what we are reading or hearing. Never before has a document like this appeared—a document addressed to an assembly "in God the Father and the Lord Jesus Christ," a document in the name both of God and of his Christ. The beginning of a new "testament" is what we are encountering, and a new kind of literature to which there is no exact parallel, either in form or in content. It is the literature of annunciation, the literature of interruption, which is how we must receive it if we are to receive it aright.

Among scholars there is considerable agreement, though not unanimity, that 1 Thessalonians is the earliest extant Christian literature, that it comes from Paul himself, and that it was written about AD 50 from Athens or more likely Corinth, perhaps as a follow-up to mission work in Macedonia (→3:1–5; Campbell 2014: 410ff. moves all this ahead by a decade). About the description of that mission in Acts 16 and 17 there is little agreement, Acts being a much-disputed work. Its companion letter, 2 Thessalonians, is equally disputed. A few scholars argue that it was written before 1 Thessalonians and quite a few that it was written long afterward, by another hand. The Church, for its part, regards both letters as

Pauline and takes Luke's account of the mission to be reliable. It does not ignore history in doing so, but judges it differently, in part because it judges differently the character of the authors of this literature. In arranging its canon it does not pay much attention to the order of composition, however, for it does not see that kind of order as fundamental. Narrative order is fundamental, and the Church is not reduced to trying to construct or reconstruct the narrative order by ferreting out the compositional order, because it has known and inhabited the narrative from the beginning.

In the New Testament, the Church therefore places first the Gospels, those four pillars through which it may be found "breathing out immortality on every side and vivifying men afresh" (*Haer.* 3.11.8); followed, since the Council of Trent, by Acts, which tells the story of the advance of the gospel from Jerusalem to Rome; then the Pauline epistles, the longer and the shorter, which come from the man who more than anyone else was instrumental in that advance; afterward the epistles of others, again the longer and the shorter; and last of all, the Apocalypse, which sums up the whole cascade of interruptions that the annunciation set in motion. That cascade finally resolves itself into the healing waters of the new Eden and the peaceful pools of the new Jerusalem, thus completing the story of the coming together of God and man, in fulfillment of the design of creation and of the covenant in Jesus Christ, without which there is no true order.

First Thessalonians has no pride of place, then, even in the Pauline corpus, from a canonical point of view, and the same can be said from a liturgical or lectional point of view. Still, it is worth noticing that 1 Thessalonians appears first, historically speaking, of all Paul's works and indeed of all Christian literature. For the incarnation of the eternal God as Israel's Messiah is an unprecedented affirmation of time that gives new significance to "before" and "after," distinguishing and separating them quite decisively for the benefit of theology, history, hermeneutics, psychology, literature, music, and so forth—even for cosmology and natural science. "Before" and "after" begin to matter after the incarnation in a way they did not matter before. They also begin to be related in a way they were not related before. They are no longer related, as the pagans had all imagined, by eternal recurrence but by recapitulation. Recapitulation means that what came before (Adam) really counts for something, and that what it really counts for is determined by what has come afterward (Christ). Recapitulation means further that nothing comes either before or after Christ that is not subject to Christ. It is recapitulation, then, that makes authentic criticism possible. Of genealogy and tradition, the Old Testament already makes us aware, and this generates a limited form of criticism; of chronology, and hence of a more potent criticism, we become properly aware only when genealogy and tradition are disturbed by the virgin birth.

We may therefore take the chronological priority of 1 Thessalonians—the probability, at least, that it is the first composition of the New Testament—to be of importance in the sense that here we have a window on the earliest period of the development of the mind of the Church as articulated by Paul. To put it this way, of course, is to assume with Paul that there is such a thing as the mind of the Church and that this mind, since it is also and first the mind of Christ disclosed by the Spirit, is self-consistent in its growth and development (1 Cor. 2:11–16; cf. 2 Cor. 1:19–21). The problem with much so-called critical scholarship, unfortunately, is that it neither makes this assumption nor remains conscious of its original inspiration. It is obsessed with before and after, but in a merely genealogical sort of way. It does not recognize any real interruption or believe in anything authentically new. It is essentially Ebionite, if not Arian, in character. In consequence it is constantly scrounging for material in what it fancies the closed realm of mundane cause and effect. Even where it has the appearance of freshness it is betrayed by the odor of decay.

Under these latter conditions, to say that 1 Thessalonians is first historically is not to behold it with a certain wonder but merely to say that its oral or literary precedents are less obvious than most. Nothing really can be made of the fact that here we are handed a letter that is simply unprecedented both in form and in content; that from a literary point of view something *sui generis* appears, "without father or mother or genealogy" in spite of all the recognizable conventions it employs (cf. Malherbe 2000: 101). This Ebionite exercise passes over all too easily into its gnostic counterpart, a speculative fervor that spins out hypothesis after hypothesis, whether more or less fabulous, in pursuit of a smooth transition from before to after. Paul becomes a code to be cracked, his literary corpus a puzzle perpetually pulled to pieces and thrown together again in kaleidoscopic fashion. (In *Framing Paul*, Campbell thinks he's cracked it, and Campbell to his credit is both interested in the theology of Paul and unafraid to reach conclusions that are at times remarkably traditional, offering potent critiques of the Ebionites and gnostics of which we speak; yet, as we observed earlier, he seems to think one can frame Paul without much help from the Church.) As for the recipients of his letters, much is learned in this process about their historical and cultural *Sitz im Leben*, but almost nothing about the fact that they lived in God and Christ (ἐν θεῷ πατρὶ καὶ κυρίῳ Ἰησοῦ Χριστῷ). Criticism of this kind, in other words, helps us with the modifier Θεσσαλονικέων but hardly at all with the noun ἐκκλησία, which already here, at the beginning of the writing of the New Testament, is pregnant with a meaning no mere cultural observation can hope to penetrate—though culture itself would be much changed by virtue of the coming into existence of the Church. It could hardly be otherwise if the Church draws its life from Christ.

"Grace to you, and peace" marks a new departure in epistolary greetings, though the second element was and is standard among Jews. Peace belongs to those who are found in the company of the God of peace (5:23), and grace to those who belong to Jesus Christ (5:28). At 1 Tim. 1:2, grace, mercy, and peace are conjoined as a trio, perhaps under the influence of Wis. 3:9: "the faithful will abide with him in love, because grace and mercy are upon his elect, and he watches over his holy ones." This text may well have been in the back of Paul's mind, for Wis. 3 informs the answer he means to give to the problem set for him by the Thessalonians (→4:13–18). At all events, he presses on immediately to establish their own election. Already they are addressed as an ἐκκλησία, which the Jews among them would have understood as a reference to the people of God gathered in assembly before God, hence as connoting a new covenant reality (cf. Deut. 23:2 LXX). The Gentile converts, who were in the majority, judging from 1:9, would at least have understood that this was no ordinary civic assembly, this "church of the Thessalonians in God the Father and the Lord Jesus Christ." (I take the dative to be locative rather than instrumental, *pace* Malherbe 2000: 99, and to modify τῇ ἐκκλησίᾳ before it modifies Paul's act of address.) However illicit in the eyes of their fellow citizens in the city, as in the eyes of those Jews who had not left the synagogue, this Christian assembly of theirs was a holy synaxis, a coming together as one (ὁμοῦ ἐπὶ τὸ αὐτό, Acts 2:1; cf. 1 Cor. 11:17–20) under the authority of God and his Christ. Its very existence was a sign that something of great political and religious moment was afoot.

N. T. Wright (2002: 89) renders ἐκκλησία as "community," but this fails to communicate either its existing political overtones, on which Wright is often instructive, or the eucharistic and eschatological resonance it acquired (cf. 1 Cor. 5:3–5 and Matt. 16:18–19; see also Zizioulas 1985: 20f.). Gordon Fee's summary is helpful: "Its origins in the Greek city-state as a designation for the assembly of citizens gathered to deal with city affairs, as well as a term for 'societies' of peoples who shared common beliefs, made it the happy choice of the Greek translators of the Old Testament, where it was regularly used to render the Hebrew *qahal*, referring to the 'whole congregation' of Israel. The choice of this word for the community of believers in any given locale was thus a natural one" (2009: 14). The meaning of ἐκκλησία is hardly exhausted, however, whether politically or theologically, by the idea of a community of believers, nor is the meaning of *qahal*. If it were, it could not be used in any but a "congregationalist" sense; that is, in a Radical Reformation rather than a biblical sense. When Paul speaks of "the churches of God in Christ Jesus that are in Judea" (τῶν ἐκκλησιῶν τοῦ θεοῦ τῶν οὐσῶν ἐν τῇ Ἰουδαίᾳ ἐν Χριστῷ Ἰησοῦ, 2:14), or of those in Macedonia and Achaia (2 Thess. 1:4; cf. Rom. 16:4, where πᾶσαι αἱ ἐκκλησίαι τῶν ἐθνῶν refers to the results of Paul's church-planting missions throughout every part of the empire he had by then visited), he has in mind, as later letters make clear, a divinely constituted congregation of the new or renewed Israel, "the Israel of God" (Gal. 6:16), which is manifested in all these places. The churches of God that are in Judea and the churches of the Gentiles are not constitutionally different, though each is distinct. They belong to one common assembly, one common covenant, one common people. Their location and ethnic composition notwithstanding, they are all instantiations of that people in its new covenant configuration, where from Jew and Gentile one new man is being made (Eph. 2:11–3:21). To which we must add, in view of present efforts in some messianic circles to compromise their catholicity by reinstating at least the distinction between those that are predominantly Jewish and those that are predominantly Gentile, that Paul, who was identified by Jesus as "a chosen instrument of mine to carry my name before the Gentiles and [their] kings and the sons of Israel" (Acts 9:15), was not on *two* missions but on one only, a point we will pursue at 2:14–16. Here the point is simply that these "communities of believers" are not self-constituting voluntary societies. They are churches, constituted in Jesus Christ by the Holy Spirit as embassies of his kingdom, as proper civic assemblies belonging to the city of God, with all the privileges and responsibilities appertaining thereto.   ▪

1:2–5 **We always give thanks to God for all of you, constantly remembering you in our prayers, recalling before our God and Father your work of faith and labor of love and steadfastness of hope in our Lord Jesus Christ—knowing, brethren beloved by God, your election, because our gospel did not come to you in word only but also in power and in the Holy Spirit and great assurance; just as you know what kind of men we were [among] you for your sake.**

The exordium seems now to break still more dramatically with literary precedent. So far from being confined to a few polite or expedient lines of praise or gratitude, it goes on and on and does not end until the final verse of chapter 3, such that the actual business of the letter is introduced almost as an afterthought at 4:1. Alternatively, we may say that the exordium passes naturally into a lengthy *narratio* that is punctuated by renewed expressions of praise and gratitude, the purpose of which is to bind authors and recipients to one another and to common values or commitments, in the ordinary fashion of epideictic rhetoric; except that here the purpose is also and primarily to bind them to God. So difficult is it to mark the passing, however—we will mark it at 2:1—that exordium and *narratio* are for practical purposes one.

▪ Witherington (2006: 21ff.) is instructive on the features of epideictic rhetoric and persuasive in his contention that 1 Thessalonians should be seen as such; but it is quite artificial to divide the text at 1:4, as per his outline on page 28. An exordium that extends to 1:10, with the break at 2:1, makes for a more natural reading, both grammatically and rhetorically. ▪

The letter being for the purpose of public reading in the church, it is fitting that the first word after the greeting should be Εὐχαριστοῦμεν, "We give thanks." Giving thanks is what a church does, and what it is for. More generally, it is for prayer. It is a temple or house of prayer, made of men rather than of stones, or rather of people who are "precious stones" (cf. Mark 11:17; Eph. 3:11–22; 1 Pet. 2:4–10; Rev. 21:9–21). Now prayer, whether in the ecclesial assembly or in the company of one or two, as Jesus declared, or even in private, is performed ἔμπροσθεν τοῦ θεοῦ καὶ πατρὸς ἡμῶν, "before our God and Father." To this we must not fail to attend, lest we reduce prayer to something merely private. What are the famous words of Plotinus in *Ennead* 6.9.11? "Such is the life of gods and of divine and blessed men—detachment from things here below, scorn of all earthly pleasures, and flight of the alone to the Alone." But a church's location, not only in Thessaloniki, say, but more fundamentally in God the Father and the Lord Jesus Christ, forbids that characterization of Christian prayer, to say nothing of the life of divine and blessed men (on which see 1 Tim. 6:11–19). Christian prayer is not a flight of the alone to the Alone, for God is not alone. That is, God is not "father" merely in the remote sense intuited by the Greeks, but also in the intimate sense known by the Jews (with Plato, *Timaeus* 28c, cf. Exod. 6:7 and Jer. 30:22) and fully revealed to the world through the birth of Mary's son—who turns out to be God's own Son, ontically as well as messianically. Such a Son has a claim on God that goes beyond that of the creature who gratefully acknowledges his dependence on the Creator. He has a claim that goes beyond even his claim as regent of Israel; that is, as one who has a right and a responsibility to seek God's counsel. In both those senses, the weaker and the stronger, the regent of Israel has a claim on the Father's attention but not on the Father's very being. Jesus, however, does have a claim on the Father's very being, for in his own person he comes from the Father. The Father is not Father, and not God, without him. That is what the Church believes, and what it believes Paul to have grasped, at least to the extent necessary to generate the pattern of trinitarian language that underlies its prayer and its own astonishing sense of entitlement.

▉ How far Paul is thinking ontologically can be questioned. The obvious sense in which God is "father" of Jesus is indeed the messianic sense provided by Psalm 2. It is not clear whether Paul knows of the virgin birth, the implications of which might in any case have stopped just there, as the Ebionites supposed. We are likely several decades short of the ontologizing that is evident in the Gospel of John, and nearly three centuries shy of the Nicene Creed. Yet already for Paul the drawing of Jesus into the confession of God is well and truly underway. The Shema-like statement in 1 Cor. 8:6—"for us there is one God, the Father, from whom are all things and for whom we exist, and one Lord, Jesus Christ, through whom are all things and through whom we exist" (cf. Fee 2009: 16n30)—is anticipated in the present letter by the compound locative of 1:1 (ἐν θεῷ πατρὶ καὶ κυρίῳ Ἰησοῦ), by the regular parallelism that we find again, for example, at 3:11 (Αὐτὸς δὲ ὁ θεὸς καὶ πατὴρ ἡμῶν καὶ ὁ κύριος ἡμῶν Ἰησοῦς), and by the explicit reference to Jesus's sonship at 1:10. Paul simply cannot talk about God without talking about Father, Son, and Holy Spirit, though he is not yet as fulsome or as eloquent in the language of sonship as he will become in subsequent letters. (In the Thessalonian letters, the only explicit use of the title υἱός is here at 1:10. At 1:5, by the way, we need not hesitate to understand a reference to the Holy Spirit, the anarthrous ἐν πνεύματι ἁγίῳ running parallel to ἐν θεῷ πατρὶ καὶ κυρίῳ Ἰησοῦ.) One can only wonder, then, at the naïveté of those who propose that the Church later made an elemental mistake in abandoning, almost accidentally, its messianic "son of God" theology for a new, metaphysical "God the Son" theology. This supposed mistake could only mean that the Church has no such claim on God in prayer as Paul imagines; that its "full conviction" or "great assurance" is an illusion; that it must, if honest, revert to praying to the unknown god of the Athenians, whom Paul put to work in introducing himself on the Areopagus, or, for that matter, to the unknown father of the gnostics.

The sonship of Christ that refines our understanding of the fatherhood of God in a trinitarian direction is the condition of possibility for Christian prayer. For while God knows the thoughts and prayers of all people, and responds as he sees fit, Christian prayer is an approach to God that involves participation in the divine economy as such. The capacity to participate arises from the regeneration of the person in baptism and follows, as Irenaeus says, the steps of Christian initiation rites: "For those who are bearers of the Spirit of God are led to the Word, that is, to the Son; but the Son takes them and presents them to the Father; and the Father confers incorruptibility" (*Demo. 7*, in ACW 16:51f.). That wonderful catechetical passage continues: "without the Spirit there is no seeing the Word of God, and without the Son there is no approaching the Father, for the Son is knowledge of the Father, and knowledge of the Son is through the Holy Spirit. But the Son, according to the Father's good-pleasure, administers the Spirit charismatically as the Father [himself] will, to those to whom He will" (cf. *Haer.* 4.20.5; 5.36, which may likewise serve the homilist well on Trinity Sunday).

The capacity to participate belongs also to the Christian's eucharistic reconfiguration, whereby he acquires the specific character of a *thankful* man, the man whose gratitude is no mere formality, nor a form of flattery, but a delight in both Giver and gift; that is, in God and what in Christ he has received from God. This man's gratitude is not intermittent, nor are his prayers merely occasional. He remembers his brethren before God without ceasing, for he himself is learning to be like God, who cannot forget his children (→2:10–12). Why then is it necessary or even fitting that he should remind God of these children? It is fitting because prayer is a form of participation in the economy of presentation just described. The Spirit, who through the apostles proposes the Son to the Thessalonians as the object of faith and obedience, also enables the apostles to join with the Son in presenting the Thessalonians to the Father as the object of the Father's blessing. The ascension of Jesus into heaven, alluded to at 1:10, is a license to recall "before our God and Father" (cf. John 20:17) the merits of the brethren, past and present, which it would otherwise be presumptuous to recall.

What is recalled here by Paul and Silvanus and Timothy—and of course it is being repeated for the purpose of reinforcement in the Thessalonians—is their "work of faith and labor of love and steadfastness of hope." This is a real manifestation on earth of the kingdom of God, and the occasion therefore both of thanksgiving to God and of petitions for divine benediction. "Work of faith and labor of love" is a hendiadys, specifying one complex activity rather than two. The rhetorical bonding of faith and love, fortified by hope, occurs again at 5:8, where Paul advises the Thessalonians to don "the body armor of faith and love and, as a helmet, the hope of salvation." Faith and love find their mutual expression in work or labor, and Christian works *are* Christian insofar as they are governed by faith and love. Such are the works God has always honored and can be expected to honor. "For righteousness is immortal," and the hope of the righteous "is full of immortality." Those who trust in God, despite their afflictions, "will understand truth, and the faithful will abide with him in love." Their hope is not in vain, nor are their labors unprofitable (Wis. 1:15; 3:4, 9, 11). We shall see that this is so even when the labor in question is simply the labor of earning a living in order to provide for one's family and for the brethren (→4:9–12).

The expression "work of faith" ought to discourage us from reading everything that Paul writes through the lens of the Galatian controversy; or, still more foolishly, through the lens of the Lutheran Reformation. Paul knows very well what answer to give to the question, "What does it profit, my brethren, if a man says he has faith but has not works?" (Jas. 2:14). The very idea of separating faith and works is preposterous. Moreover, the work in question is none other than the labor of love, a very practical love shown to all the brethren without partiality, and indeed to all people. For the work of faith is formed by love, and the labor of love is formed by faith. Love itself is formed by faith and faith by love, as the apostles and fathers all attest.

■ Must we then challenge Luther's claim in *The Freedom of the Christian* that, "when any man is made good or bad, this does not arise from his works but from his faith or unbelief" (*WA* 7:62)? Yes and no. It is certainly helpful, perhaps even necessary at some point, to view all goodness or badness through the lenses of faith and unbelief. But it is equally necessary to view all goodness or badness through the lenses of hope and despair, and especially through the lenses of love and failure to love (Farrow 2018g: 85ff.). What justifies Luther—or Joseph Fletcher, for that matter, whose *Situation Ethics* sequesters love—in isolating the one exercise from the other two? That is not a mistake Paul makes, whether here or anywhere else. The error of the Reformation is not in its *solo Christo*, nor in its *sola gratia*, but in its *sola fide*—which, while combating a false and Pelagian legalism, has the unfortunate side effect of dismembering the triumvirate of theological virtues and thus of rendering strange the phrases that here fall so naturally from Paul's lips.

Let us observe that this famous triumvirate appears fully formed in 1 Thessalonians, seemingly out of nowhere, with faith and hope flanking love. (The more formulaic ascending order, "faith, hope, and love," is established shortly afterward in 1 Cor. 13:13.) To speak of these as virtues is to place Paul among the Greeks, of course. But if virtue "is a habitual and firm disposition to do good" (*CCC* §1833), the follower of Jesus is disposed to the good, as the Greek is not, by something more than a love of justice. He is disposed to do justice to love, to the two great commandments (Mark 12:28–34; cf. Augustine, *Mor. eccl.* 13ff.). Building on Paul and Augustine, Aquinas makes faith- and hope-filled love the very *forma virtutum* (*ST* 2-2.23.8; cf. 1-2.58.3); that is, of all those habits that perfect us in doing good and, just so, in the capacity for happiness. "By charity we love God above all things and our neighbor as ourselves for love of God. Charity, the form of all the virtues, 'binds everything together in perfect harmony'" (*CCC* §1844). Thus are the other virtues, including those related to the simplest work or labor, elevated from the natural to the supernatural. For "the theological virtues dispose Christians to live in a relationship with the Holy Trinity. They have God for their origin, their motive, and their object—God known by faith, God hoped in and loved for his own sake" (*CCC* §1840). ■

The work of faith and labor of love is sustained by steadfastness of hope. No one could mistake this hope for mere optimism, even the kind of optimism that is thought virtuous. For it is hope of a very particular kind; namely, that which both reposes *in* our Lord Jesus Christ (taking τοῦ κυρίου as objective) and is *of* our Lord Jesus Christ (taking it as subjective). Which is to say, it is not only directed toward but also derived from him. Here we may profitably call to mind Gal. 2:20, where Paul claims that his own life is lived by virtue of

Christ living in him, that "he lives by means of the faithfulness of the Son of God, that is, by means of *his* loving sacrifice" (Campbell 2009: 848). So also the Thessalonians. Their faith, love, and hope are an expression of the faith, love, and hope of Jesus Christ himself. Have they faith in God? It is his faith shared with them. Do they love God and hope in God? They do so in and with Christ by the Holy Spirit. In the present context, however, the note Paul means to sound is as much eschatological as soteriological (→5:4–11). The hope in which they persist, the hope that in turn sustains them, has Christ as its immediate object. They expect him to keep his promise. They expect their salvation. They expect him.

Now, the apostolic company is confident in remembering before God the Thessalonians and in seeking the divine benediction on their labor, because it is evident through their works of faith and love that they belong to God's elect, to God's beloved children and family. Everyone is loved by God, for God is love. Everyone who is made is called to seek God and love him in return (cf. Acts 17:27; Mic. 6:8). Everyone who hears the gospel of Christ is called anew and more urgently, for God "desires all men to be saved and to come to the knowledge of the truth" (1 Tim. 2:4). Not everyone is called in the sense that Paul has in mind, however, when he speaks of their election. Among the nations it is Israel and only Israel that is both called and chosen, for its father, Abraham, was called and chosen. This calling and choosing rests on God, as does the calling and choosing of the Twelve who will lead the renewal of Israel. "You did not choose me, but I chose you and appointed you that you should go and bear fruit and that your fruit should abide" (John 15:16; cf. Exod. 19:4–6).

In the salvific works of God, those called are many, but those chosen are few (πολλοὶ γάρ εἰσιν κλητοί, ὀλίγοι δὲ ἐκλεκτοί, Matt. 22:14). This is true even within Israel, for it is but a remnant that becomes the divine instrument, a residuum that becomes the beneficiary. The remnant is reduced eventually to one—"Behold my servant, whom I uphold, my chosen, in whom my soul delights" (Isa. 42:1)—yet all who belong to that one, all who are clothed in the white garment of his righteousness, become heirs to the promises made to Abraham. None will be put to shame of those who are both called and chosen, provided they freely receive what they are chosen for and themselves call on the name of the Lord. And these, though the gate be strait and the path narrow, are not few but many, even if here or there they are but few (with Matt. 7:19, cf. Rom. 5:12–21; 11:30–32). God, in any case, knows those who are his and those who are not (2 Tim. 2:19; cf. John 6:70–71; Rev. 3:4–5).

In all this, the initiative always lies with God, as Paul knew very well from his own conversion. That the initiative lies with God does not negate but enables genuinely free decision, as Mary discovered in saying her *fiat mihi*. What the fall disabled in humanity is restored through union with Christ. For freedom we have been set free, so that with God's help we can now preserve and enjoy freedom (Gal. 5:1; Anselm, *DC* 3.1ff.). Hence Paul's conviction that those who not only hear the gospel, but also receive and live it, give evidence of their having been both called and chosen. The evidence lies in the potency of the word of God among them: "Our gospel did not come to you in word only but also in power and in the Holy Spirit and great assurance" (ἐν δυνάμει καὶ ἐν πνεύματι ἁγίῳ καὶ πληροφορίᾳ πολλῇ).

■ We shall come round to Paul's conversion later (→2 Thess. 3:16). Here I want only to add that these brief remarks on the mystery of election are not intended as a systematic treatment, though the elements of such a treatment are present. Nor are they intended to demystify election, any more than Paul himself demystifies it, whether here or in his most systematic work, the letter to the Romans. It cannot be demystified without being falsified, for the relation between divine freedom and human freedom cannot be grasped from the human side. We must not be surprised to read, on the one hand: "For he says to Moses, 'I will have mercy on whom I have mercy, and I will have compassion on whom I have compassion.' So it depends not upon man's will or exertion, but upon God's mercy" (Rom. 9:15–16). And, on the other hand, that human will and exertion is intended and required: "Note then . . . God's kindness to you, provided you continue in his kindness; otherwise you too will be cut off" (11:22; cf. *DC* 3.9). This mystery is already at play in creation. God makes man, and by co-opting human choices he makes every man who subsequently is made; yet no man chooses to be made, nor does God make or permit to be made every man who might be made. In salvation the mystery deepens. For God saves of his own free will everyone whom he does save, precisely by restoring to them in Christ the freedom they have forfeited, then working with them for a salvation they themselves choose. Therefore "work out your own salvation with fear and trembling; for God is at work in you, both to will and to work for his good pleasure" (Phil. 2:12–13). God does not, however, set every man free or save everyone, though he saves "all Israel" (Rom. 11:26); that is, those from among the Jews first and the Gentiles second whom he desires and requires for the building of the new Jerusalem and the perfection of the new creation. These are those who cooperate with initial graces in such a way as to let grace abound. God will not stop making men, or showing mercy to men, or saving men who will to be saved, until their number is complete. (See Augustine, *Civ.* 14.23, though one cannot do better than to read Anselm's *De libertate arbitrii*, *De casu diaboli*, *Cur deus homo*, and *De concordia*; for Anselm thinks with Paul in fresh ways and quietly refines Augustine.) ■

What is Paul's gospel, and what does he mean when he speaks of it as coming in power and in the Holy Spirit? To the first question: His gospel is simply *the* gospel as entrusted to him (Gal. 1:6–9; 2:7–8). It is the gospel of salvation, both for Zion and for the ends of the earth, which he is under orders to publish as far as he can (1 Cor. 9:16). Deities and Caesars, senators and philanthropists, from time to time publish glad tidings of temporal benefactions. (See, e.g., the Priene Inscription, noted by Witherington 2006: 71, which employs the word εὐαγγέλια.) But Paul and his fellow apostles publish tidings of benefactions both temporal and eternal in the good news that "every one who calls upon the name of the Lord will be saved" (Rom. 10:13; cf. Acts 2:14–40; 17:16–31). The tidings they publish take the form of a report about the coming of the Christ and about his crucifixion, resurrection, ascension, and return in judgment. This report is also an announcement of the kingdom of God and an invitation to become citizens of that kingdom. In other words, it is the gospel preached by Jesus (Mark 1:14–15; cf. Isa. 52:7), coupled with a message about what God has done through Jesus, "who gave himself for our sins to deliver us from the present evil age, according to the will of our God and Father" (Gal. 1:4). In Acts 20, when Paul bids farewell to the Ephesian elders, he reminds them that he has testified "both to Jews and to Greeks of repentance to God and of faith in our Lord Jesus Christ." He speaks of the ministry he received "to testify to the gospel of the grace of God," and of having been among them "preaching the kingdom." All this has, and must have, its place. Using his own shorthand, however, we may refer to it variously as the gospel of God, the gospel of Christ, the gospel of grace, the gospel of peace, and especially the gospel of the kingdom (cf. Wanamaker 1990: 78).

With respect to the second question, we must adduce the analogy of Pentecost. Without the Spirit the gospel is neither preached nor received with full assurance. Without the Spirit there is no faith and no repentance in response to the gospel. Without the Spirit there is no perception of the kingdom, nor any grace that anticipates or advances the kingdom. Without the Spirit there is no Church, either in Jerusalem or in Thessaloniki. For the intervention of the Spirit is the perfection of every divine work, whether in creation or in re-creation, in generating life or in saving life. The power of the Spirit to liberate for life was on display at Pentecost; it was also on display in the Pauline missions. Paul boasts of a "demonstration of the Spirit and of power" (1 Cor. 2:4; cf. 2 Cor. 3:1–4:6). He tells of "what Christ has wrought through me to win obedience from the Gentiles, by word and deed, by the power of signs and wonders, by the power of the Holy Spirit" (Rom. 15:18–19). The intervention of the Spirit, not empty appeals to the

Spirit, is for Paul the *sine qua non* of fruitful evangelism and a necessary condition for establishing the Church on new territory. Recall Acts 19, which tells of the founding of the Ephesian church on some twelve followers of John the Baptist:

> Paul passed through the upper country and came to Ephesus. There he found some disciples. And he said to them, "Did you receive the Holy Spirit when you believed?" And they said, "No, we have never even heard that there is a Holy Spirit." And he said, "Into what then were you baptized?" They said, "Into John's baptism." And Paul said, "John baptized with the baptism of repentance, telling the people to believe in the one who was to come after him, that is, Jesus." On hearing this, they were baptized in the name of the Lord Jesus. And when Paul had laid his hands upon them, the Holy Spirit came on them; and they spoke with tongues and prophesied. (19:1–6)

Hence this, in Paul's letter to the Ephesians: "In him you also, who have heard the word of truth, the gospel of your salvation, and have believed in him, were sealed with the promised Holy Spirit, who is the guarantee of our inheritance until we acquire possession of it" (1:13–14). Irenaeus is only following suit when he says: "For this gift of God has been entrusted to the Church, as breath was to the first created man, for this purpose, that all the members receiving it may be vivified; and the [means of] communion with Christ has been distributed throughout it, that is, the Holy Spirit, the earnest of incorruption, the means of confirming our faith, and the ladder of ascent to God. . . . Where the Church is, there is the Spirit of God; and where the Spirit of God is, there is the Church, and every kind of grace" (*Haer.* 3.24.1, in *ANF* 1:458).

Where the Spirit does intervene—where people are clearly in receipt of the Spirit and the Spirit in receipt of the people—there is proof of election. The Old Testament paradigm is the liberation of Israel from Egypt. The Spirit of Glory who leads the people of God out from bondage, with signs and wonders, claims them as his own. While neither Paul nor Luke mentions such signs and wonders in Thessaloniki as there were in Philippi, the same Spirit has shown his hand in liberating the Thessalonians, who are thus known to belong to God's elect also. Paul wants them to be confident, both corporately and individually, that they too are heirs to the promises, that the divine benediction will not be asked for them in vain.

■ We must not try to parse this confidence by setting the individual against the corporate. In the biblical paradigm, election is patriarchal, which is to say both individual and corporate at the same time. It does not concern individuals qua individuals, but neither is it merely formal or institutional. Rather it is familial and ecclesial, in the sense developed by Paul in Romans and Ephesians. Hence confidence of election can only derive from, and can only be maintained by, participation in the community of the Spirit, which is the community of those foreknown by the Father and chosen in the Son. In just that way, however, it can and does become a personal confidence (witness 2 Timothy, which as it were personalizes Rom. 8:18–39 for Paul himself). For election is not referred to the Father alone, as a strictly inscrutable mystery that repels rather than comforts. Nor is it referred only to the Son, as something priding Israel κατὰ σάρκα or even, as universalists accentuate, humanity generally. It is referred also to the Spirit, who creates a peculiar people and draws particular persons into that people, preparing them for glory. A narrowly patrological (as in Calvin) or even christological (as in Barth) approach to the doctrine of election tends to the supralapsarian error. Only a fully trinitarian approach can avoid that without evacuating the doctrine in some more or less Pelagian fashion.

What we ought to parse is the false confidence of those who wish to domesticate the Spirit, and who for some time have been translating the doctrine of election into a culture of complacency and entitlement. There are more orthodox examples with which to work, but G. E. Lessing deserves mention here. His 1777 essay, *On the Proof of the Spirit and of Power*, asks a pointed question: Can those who live in an age in which miracles no longer happen accept the warrant for Christian faith that the miracles of old are meant to provide? Or are they justified in seeking a different warrant, drawn not from human witness to divine interventions long past but from the present exercise of reason? According to Lessing, it does not matter anymore even whether Jesus rose from the dead. For we have not the event itself but mere testimony to it; and such testimony, however salutary the effect it once had, cannot present itself to us with power or full assurance. It is clear at once, of course, and not only from the essay's ironic tone, that Lessing thinks Paul badly misguided in supposing that his testimony to the resurrection counts, or should count, for anything. On his view even the Thessalonians, if not themselves party to signs and wonders, ought to have responded to Paul as the majority on Mars Hill did. For reason knows nothing of any resurrection, talk of which can only be to it a kind of babbling. What Lessing proposes for us moderns, at all events—absent some never-ending stream of signs and wonders, each confirming what precedes it—is to take from Christianity whatever accords with common sense and no more. Revelation, he argues, we should understand as a form of education; and education, as Socrates shows in the *Meno* dialogue, "gives man nothing which he could not also get from within himself" (Lessing, *The Education of the Human Race* §4). As man advances, then, beyond the primers with which he once worked under the old and new covenants, he is able to dispense with the imperfect forms in which his lessons came to him, arriving at a perfection in which he no longer depends on purported miracles, or on promises of punishment and reward. He is subject to a new and eternal gospel, under which the race as a whole shall find its happy end.

Now, we may want to challenge Lessing's assumption that miracles no longer occur. Or to observe that his alternative basis for faith (as he well knows and does not mean to hide) is nothing but a refusal of faith, since reason may take from faith only what it can recognize as its own. Moreover, after perusing *The Education of the Human Race*, we may wish to point out that Lessing seems only too ready to make universal history do what biblical history is not permitted to do—that is, provide its own "proof of the Spirit and of power"—and to press our doubts as to whether reason can justify this substitution. We may even want to ask (keeping Mars Hill in mind) whether being modern actually has anything to do with all of this. Is the dispute not a very old one? And does Lessing himself not resuscitate the ancient doctrine of reincarnation as the best alternative to the doctrine of the resurrection—asking, quite unconscious of the irony, whether this hypothesis is "so laughable merely because it is the oldest" (*Education* §95)? But it is only necessary here to reckon with the fact that, where the resurrection is disallowed as a meaningful datum and Jesus is ignored as a living reality, the Spirit will inevitably be reduced to "inscrutable Providence" and all particularity of faith dismissed as enthusiasm. Paul is certainly an "enthusiast" in Lessing's sense, since for him miracles do not merely authenticate the apostolic message; they mark out the trajectory of the Spirit and, just so, the path and identity of the covenant people. Lessing, for his part, thinks that one only discovers the Spirit when one advances beyond all that and begins to think instead in terms of universal progress. Hence the complacency (he calls it "patience") and the sense of entitlement to many lives, to multiple tutorials. Hence also the inability to grasp what John Paul II would call Paul's personalism, his refusal to dispose of the individual.

Paul immediately suggests that the Thessalonians can have confidence in him, too, and in Silvanus and Timothy: "You know what kind of men we were among you for your sake." This will receive elaboration along the way of his praise for the Thessalonians, who have followed the same pattern—the Lord's pattern—of deliberately being with and for others in a labor of love. It will also be revisited, more expansively, in 2 Corinthians and other letters, and retrospectively in 2 Timothy: "you have observed my teaching, my conduct, my aim in life, my faith, my patience, my love, my steadfastness, my persecutions, my sufferings" (3:10–11; cf. 4:7). We can turn again to Acts, however, for a glimpse of these men and some understanding of their character. Let us take them in reverse order.

Timothy was the most junior of the three. Hailing from Lystra, he was "the son of a Jewish woman who was a believer; but his father was a Greek" (Acts 16:1). Well spoken of by the brethren in that area, he was seconded by Paul for the mission and immediately proved his character by undergoing circumcision. That mission, of course, under the aegis of "the apostles and elders who were at

Jerusalem" and bearing news of the decisions of the council that had been held there (Acts 16:4), was a mission to the Jew first, then also to the Greek—for the gospel, as Paul says, "is the power of God for salvation to every one who has faith, to the Jew first and also to the Greek" (Rom. 1:16). Whenever possible, a beginning would be made in the local synagogue: "Now when they had passed through Amphipolis and Apollonia, they came to Thessalonica, where there was a synagogue of the Jews. And Paul went in, as was his custom, and for three weeks he argued with them from the Scriptures, explaining and proving that it was necessary for the Christ to suffer and to rise from the dead" (Acts 17:1–3). For such work an uncircumcised son of a Jewish mother was not well suited, even though the council had made clear that circumcision was not a requirement for membership in the ἐκκλησία that would subsequently be formed. No one was more ferocious on that point than Paul, whose controversy with those who thought otherwise had occasioned the council in the first place (Acts 15:1–6; cf. Gal. 5:2; 1 Cor. 7:18–19). Yet Paul nonetheless recognized, as did Timothy, that Timothy's circumcision was appropriate for their sake—that is, for the sake of the Jews to whom Christ was to be preached. As the essential mark of the covenant, circumcision had been superseded by baptism, yes; but as a practical sign of solidarity among the original people of the covenant it continued to have its purpose (→2:14–16). Timothy thus bore in his body a sign, not only of the covenant in its original form but of his character, his embrace of the "for your sake." Paul and Silvanus, who were circumcised as infants on the eighth day, had signs of another kind, the signs of the beatings they had recently received in Philippi.

Silvanus, whom Acts calls Silas—Paul uses the Roman form of his name—was himself an apostle, at least in the sense that he was an official representative of the council as well as a leader among the brethren (Acts 15:22; note the plural ἀπόστολοι at 1 Thess. 2:7). Tradition has him among the seventy sent out by the Lord. In Jerusalem he was deemed worthy by the council to accompany "our beloved Barnabas and Paul, men who have risked their lives for the sake of our Lord Jesus Christ" (Acts 15:25–26). As it happened, Silvanus took Barnabas's place alongside Paul, after the falling out of those two over the question of Mark's fitness for mission (15:39–40). Silvanus had not only Paul's complete confidence but also Peter's, with whom he later served in Rome alongside Mark. In Luke's account—and it is at this point in Acts that the famous "we" passages begin—what Paul does and suffers, Silvanus also does and suffers, though it is clear that Paul is the senior figure. Silvanus himself acquires through his faithful service with Paul a certain seniority in the Church. The first epistle of Peter comes from his pen (διὰ Σιλουανοῦ, 1 Pet. 5:12) and evinces his influence. He is also thought to have been bishop in Corinth for a time. Tradition has him dying a martyr's death in Macedonia, and one of Thessaloniki's early bishops seems to have been given, or taken, his name.

And what shall we say of Paul? Certainly that in him the reality of divine election is immediately clear, as clear as in Peter's own case. Paul is picked out and commissioned by the Lord himself, who makes him a direct witness of the resurrection. Luke, like Paul, is at pains to emphasize this. Three times the great sheet is let down from heaven to persuade Peter that "what God has cleansed, you must not call common" (Acts 10:15–16). And three times the conversion of Paul is recounted, to persuade us that he is God's chosen instrument for reaching those who were common (Acts 9; 22; 26; cf. Gal. 1:12; 1 Cor. 15:1–11). But Luke seems to go even further. Just as David is anointed with the Spirit to wage Israel's battles, with a view to securing a foothold in Jerusalem for the kingdom of God, so Paul is empowered to wage the Church's battles, with a view to securing a foothold for the kingdom in faraway Rome, and for the true King even in Caesar's own house (Acts 28:23–31; cf. Phil. 4:22). Paul is presented to us both as a doughty warrior and as a man truly passionate for God (cf. *Civ.* 14.9). From Luke's depiction a hero emerges who is recognizable as such under the canons both of Hebrew and of Greek biography—a hero a bit like David in his early career but entirely at the service of David's greater son.

▦ Wright (1992: 373–84) points out the Davidic allusions in Luke's Gospel, where of course Jesus, not Paul, is the antitype. The parallels begin with John the Baptist, who, like the prophet Samuel, is born to a woman thought to be infertile, is sent by God to rebuke the leading priests and the reigning monarch, and is instructed to anoint a new "son" whom God has chosen to assume the throne (cf. Luke 1–3 with 1 Sam. 1–16). In Luke 4 this son goes forth, as David did, to fight with Israel's most notorious enemy (cf. 1 Sam. 17). One might expect that enemy to be the hated Roman overlords, against whom Israel was now mustering courage to rebel, but it turns out instead to be Satan himself: the great tempter who seeks by various means, including Israel's fixation on Rome, to gain her allegiance and draw her away from the God of the covenant. Jesus silences this spiritual Goliath with smooth stones from the sling of scripture. The long middle section of Luke (5–18) tells how he gathers his companions for the struggle, how he teaches the people, and how he confronts the lesser agents of Israel's distress, including a jealous Hasmonean/Herodian establishment in Jerusalem (cf. 1 Sam. 18–31 with Luke 11–18). As events begin to reach their climax, Jesus arrives in Jerusalem, where he achieves his greatest victory. Refusing to succumb at last to temptation, he distinguishes himself from David, who at the height of his powers fell into mortal sin, by persevering faithfully in the path marked out for him by God. He himself is enthroned on Zion, only in a gruesome ritual devised by the Romans for rebels. His victory, in other words, comes through identification with Israel in its deepest and most traumatic form of defeat (cf. 2 Sam. 5–12 with Luke 19–23). Vindication arrives in the form of two mighty miracles: his resurrection from the dead and his ascension into heaven—installation on a throne for which David was not fit, from which he fulfills all the promises to David (cf. 2 Sam. 7 with Luke 24 and Acts 1–2). There are still battles to be fought, however, as there were after David's enthronement, only now it is the disciples who will fight them—Paul, above all, who goes from scouring the promised land for any contaminating faith in Jesus to having "turned the world upside down" with his preaching of Jesus (Acts 17:6). Luke devotes much of his second volume to describing the sufferings and conquests of Paul, who eventually, with the blessing of Jesus, sets his sights on Rome. Acts concludes with his arrival in that great city, under imperial guard, where for a time he proclaims the kingdom of Jesus "quite openly and unhindered" (Acts 28:31; cf. 23:11).

It is said that Luke's is a sanitized version of Church history, and in particular that he is concerned to cover up the differences between Petrine and Pauline elements in early Christianity, or between its Jewish and Gentile missions. (His treatment of the Jerusalem Council is offered in illustration, since he avoids the dirty laundry aired by Paul in Gal. 2.) We should decline to exaggerate these tensions, however, recalling the unity between Peter, James, and Paul at the outset of Paul's mission (Gal. 1:13–24) as at the council's conclusion. And when we read in 2 Pet. 3:15–16 of "our beloved brother Paul [who] wrote to you according to the wisdom given him," albeit in letters containing some things "hard to understand, which the ignorant and unstable twist to their own destruction," we may take it that there was in the end a reconciliation both of differences and of feelings. Perhaps it is more to the point, then, to be concerned with pseudo-Pauline and pseudo-Petrine factions in the present time, especially those that betray an interest in undermining apostolic unity that they may undermine apostolic authority also.

Even were the New Testament lacking the book of Acts—something scarcely possible to conceive—we would have to conclude from the Pauline epistles, pseudonymous or otherwise, that Paul attained heroic stature in the Church. But what kind of man was he? Luke's depiction is not Paul's self-depiction, of course, but the same person appears in both, one whose life and works are inexplicable on any other terms than those contained in Jesus's command to Ananias: "Go, for he is a chosen instrument of mine. . . . I will show him how much he must suffer for the sake of my name" (Acts 9:15–16). The entire Pauline corpus is animated by this very conviction, breathing it through every pore. Paul is a man *krank an Gott*, to redeploy Barth's expression, yet every inch (and his inner man far outstripped the outer in stature) alive in Christ. The conformity to Christ that he preached, he also lived, unless we are to disregard his letters as the most fabulous of fictions, full of spiritual tumors and self-deception. But he was known by the churches, and still is. Who can square those letters with the charge that he really is "beside himself" (Acts 26:24; cf. 2 Cor. 5:13)? Or what sublime madness is it that produces passages like this?

> We put no obstacle in any one's way, so that no fault may be found with our ministry, but as servants of God we commend ourselves in every way: through great endurance, in afflictions, hardships, calamities, beatings, imprisonments, tumults, labors, watching, hunger; by purity, knowledge, forbearance, kindness, the Holy Spirit, genuine love, truthful speech, and the power of God; with the weapons of righteousness for the right hand and for the left; in honor and dishonor, in ill repute and good repute. We are treated as impostors, and yet are true; as unknown, and yet well known; as dying, and behold we live; as punished, and yet not killed; as sorrowful, yet always rejoicing; as poor, yet making many rich; as having nothing, and yet possessing everything. Our mouth is open to you, Corinthians; our heart is wide. You are not restricted by us, but you are restricted in your own affections. In return—I speak as to children—widen your hearts also. (2 Cor. 6:3–13)

Yet Paul is judged, if not mad, then "proud, unbending, imperious" (thus Ernest Renan) or otherwise unworthy of his Lord. Adolf Deissmann correctly claims that down through the ages there has "seldom been anyone at the same time hated with such fiery hatred and loved with such strong passion as Paul." This, however, is a testament to his consistency rather than his inconsistency. For the same can be said of Jesus, and it is said of Paul largely because of Jesus. Paul, in fact, is a lightning rod for human reactions to Jesus. These reactions, when negative, are often covered by attempts to divide Paul from Jesus and to set the two at odds; but those who would honor Jesus must heed the advice of Erasmus: "Especially make yourself familiar with Paul. Him you ought to hold ever in your heart, 'day and night he should dwell in your hand,' and his words you should commit to memory." (See Muggeridge and Vidler 1972: 11–16 for these and other nuggets of responses to Paul, some of which are highly amusing.)

1:6–10 And you became imitators of us, and of the Lord, having received the word in great affliction with the joy of the Holy Spirit, so that you became a model to all the believers in Macedonia and Achaia. For from you the word of the Lord has sounded forth, not only in Macedonia and Achaia, but also in every place your faith toward God has been publicized, such that it is not necessary for us to say anything. For they themselves report concerning us how well our mission to you was received, and how you turned toward God from the idols, to serve the God who is living and true, and to wait for his Son to appear from the heavens, whom he raised from the dead: Jesus, the one rescuing us from the wrath that is coming.

To receive the word "with Holy Spirit joy" (μετὰ χαρᾶς πνεύματος ἁγίου), even in the midst of affliction or persecution, is characteristic of the elect. Received in this way, the word—which is preeminently the announcement Κύριος Ἰησοῦς, "Jesus is Lord," accompanied by an invitation to enter his kingdom (cf. Acts 16:6–17:4)—is sure to sound forth again from its recipients, so that they become partners in the apostolic mission. They are imitators in that what they receive they also pass on, not hesitantly but with the same great assurance that characterized Jesus and his disciples in the face of persecution. Thus do they become a model (τύπος) for their brethren throughout the imperial provinces of Macedonia and Achaia, who are likewise charged with proclaiming in those secular jurisdictions the good news of the kingdom of God. They become a model for us also, whose task is no different, since we live as well in temporary, provisional realms whose rulers and whose people require the knowledge that Jesus is Lord, and that the kingdoms of this world have been given to him for his eventual disposal.

If *not* a model for us, then what have we in common with them, with Paul, with our Lady, or indeed with our Lord? "The Lord gives the command; great is the host of those who bore the tidings" (Ps. 68:11; Ps. 67 LXX deploys the future tense: κύριος δώσει ῥῆμα τοῖς εὐαγγελιζομένοις δυνάμει πολλῇ). I mention our Lady again because her Magnificat sounds the first note. No sooner has she received the word from Gabriel than she shares it with Elizabeth; already "the women at home divide the spoil" (Ps. 68:12; cf. Luke 1:39–56). The model in question is not triumphalist. The announcement does not contain any immediate deposition of earthly lords or the reconstitution of their jurisdictions according to divine laws mediated by the Church. The invitation to acknowledge heavenly lordship and law is included, an invitation later taken up in some of those jurisdictions, however defectively. But there is no program in the gospel for "Christendom," nor any "social kingship" theory, even if Christendom, at its best, was a natural fruit of the gospel. The announcement is of a King who has come and will come; let those who were not prepared for his first coming see to it that they are prepared for his second coming, when everything so joyfully foreseen by Mary in the Magnificat will be fulfilled once and for all.

The apostolic mission is ambassadorial. What is publicized or reported respecting Thessaloniki is the apostles' successful entrance (εἴσοδος) into this capital city, bearing their announcement. That announcement was not misrepresented by their enemies, who accused them of "saying that there is another king, Jesus" (Acts 17:7), even if their mission was misconstrued as seditious. They sought no overthrow of the existing political authorities and encouraged no uprising or rebellion. That they were the occasion of riots was not their responsibility but rather the responsibility of those who objected to their announcement and its impact on particular citizens or religious enclaves or the local economy. Nevertheless, they did say that there is another king, Jesus, who has made his εἴσοδος into heaven itself, where God has "exalted him at his right hand as Leader and Savior" or "Founder and Savior" (ἀρχηγὸν καὶ σωτῆρα, Acts 5:31; cf. Heb. 11:10; 13:14). It was on that basis that his ambassadors made their entrances into the cities of Caesar, bearing this announcement, just as they did in the holy city, Jerusalem, where Stephen was slain and Saul sought legal injunctions to stamp out the movement.

▨ The expression ὁποίαν εἴσοδον ἔσχομεν πρὸς ὑμᾶς is difficult to translate, but "how well our mission to you was received" captures the sense of it. Thessaloniki, the object of that mission, was the capital of Macedonia (a Roman province from 146 BC) and a *civitas libera* benefiting from "many commercial and civic privileges, including the right to have its own officials and to mint its own coinage" (Tellbe 2001: 81f.). The city was founded by Cassander in 316 BC, and named for his wife, half-sister of Alexander the Great; its economic and political significance were enhanced by its harbor and its location on the Via Egnatia (cf. Donfried 2002: 35).   ▨

For the rulers of the nations, including today's democracies, it is difficult to know what to do with "ambassadors" from a kingdom not of this world. So long as those ambassadors say only the kind of thing to which Rousseau, for example, tried to limit them—that is, things about another world altogether, the world of the spirit and not of the body, which as body belongs wholly to the political authority—then they are merely a distraction, not a threat. But that is neither what Jesus meant when he said that his kingdom is not of this world, nor what Paul and the others preached. The kingdom of Jesus is "not of this world" because it has its authority from God, not from men, and because its rule involves the total and permanent transformation of this world. It comes into conflict with the kingdoms of this world whenever the latter presume to infringe on, or to restrict, the demands of preparation for its coming, denying the Church "all the freedom of action it needs in order to care for the salvation of humanity" (*DH* 13). And this readily happens as the rulers of transitory realms try to fortify those realms against the ravages of time, investing in them, and in their own offices or even their own persons, powers over body and soul that do not in fact belong to them. The moment they are confronted with this fact by the ambassadors of the eternal kingdom of Jesus, they are confronted with the opportunity for repentance or rebellion. Of this we will hear more in the second letter.

Whatever the case with their rulers, or indeed their neighbors, the people to whom Paul is writing chose repentance and began their preparations. They turned toward God and away from their idols. They began to serve the One who is living and true and to wait for his Son to appear from heaven. Here—in this turning, serving, and waiting—is the very paradigm of Christian conversion. It has no exact parallel elsewhere; which is to say, it is not a general religious concept, though its individual terms have other uses (cf. Malherbe 2000: 119–21; Furnish 2007: 48–49). It corresponds to nothing but the *mysterium fidei*: *Mortem tua annuntiamus, Domine* ("We proclaim your death, O Lord," a death that is the consequence of cleaving to God and spurning the powers of this age), *et tuam resurrectionem confitemur* ("and confess your resurrection," which is no mere resumption of life within the age, but also the taking up of a new and eternal life in which the whole creation shall serve and worship God without ceasing), *donec venias* ("until you come," for your destiny is to appear in glory and so to bring an end to the powers of the age and their supposed *novus ordo seclorum*, which is no such thing; indeed, to bring an end to the *saeculum* as such). Put the other way round, the mystery of faith dictates the proper meaning of conversion, which is not first of all a profound experience of the inner man, though it must also be or become that; but, as with Paul's own conversion, is a public matter involving a change of allegiance, commitments, expectations. It is a response to an announcement, to a proclamation of lordship.

For the Jew, conversion means returning to "the Rock of his salvation" from dalliances with "strange gods" that are no gods, after chastisement by peoples that are not really peoples (Deut. 32:15–22). For the Gentile also, conversion entails renouncing idols: "Then all the Gentiles will turn to fear the Lord God in truth, and will bury their idols" (Tob. 14:6). "We are proclaiming good news," says Paul, "to turn you from these vanities to a living God, who made the sky and land and sea and all that is in them" (Acts 14:15 AT). And what are the idols but projections of man's distorted desires once he has lost sight of the Maker of heaven and earth, who ought to be all his desire (Rom. 1:18–23)?

In Thessaloniki, the idols in question were the gods of the Greeks and of the oriental cults and mystery religions, on the one hand, and the Roman or imperial gods, on the other. Notable among the former were Zeus and Dionysus, of course, but also Isis and Serapis. (Invented for Ptolemy the Savior about the time of Thessaloniki's founding, Serapis took the place of Osiris in Greek realms.) And especially Cabirus, a singular variant of the ancient Cabiri who seems to have captured the imagination of Thessalonian laborers before being co-opted by the ruling class. Depicted on Thessalonian coinage "with a hammer in one hand and a drinking horn in the other," Cabirus was thought to be a source both of virility and of protection; initiations into his cult involved rites with fire, water, and blood, and perchance orgiastic sex.

Robert Jewett (1986: 126ff.) is helpful here. He is not persuasive, however, in proposing that Cabirus was somehow more Jesus-like than other mystery cult figures. We do not know a great deal about Cabirus or his cult. Hippolytus (*Refutation of All Heresies* 5.2) quotes a line respecting his origin: "Lemnus begot Cabirus, fair child of secret orgies." It was not without irony that the ruling class did him homage. Cabirus was murdered by his two brothers, who, presumably to cover their crime, bore his head to Mount Olympus and buried it with a crown and royal trappings. That Cabirus was honored especially by the Macedonians is mentioned by Lactantius (*Inst.* 1.15).

While Cabirus became the main deity of Thessaloniki, the imperial deities were more significant sources of civic blessing. The city worked hard at cultivating Roman favors, historians tell us, and did not stop short of introducing the nascent imperial cult: "Numismatic evidence from as early as 29–28 BCE illustrates that Thessalonica acclaimed Julius as 'god.'" About the time of Jesus a "provincial temple to *Divus Caesar* was established in the city, including a priest and *agonothete* in service of the divine Augustus and Claudius," creating an institution that "seems quickly to have assumed a more prominent status in the pecking order of religious institutions than the local priesthood of 'the gods'" (Tellbe 2001: 84f., following Hendrix 1984; cf. Donfried 2002: 31ff.). Augustus replaced Zeus on the coinage. The honoring of Roma and of Roman benefactors was already a priestly function with an important place in civil religion, but the prominence of the priest in service of the divine imperator (ἱερεύς καὶ ἀγωνοθέτης Αὐτοκράτορος Καίσαρος Θεοῦ υἱοῦ Σεβαστοῦ) at the time these letters were written is noteworthy.

From such gods is it possible to turn without sedition? Was it their perceived rejection not only of the religious bonds of civil society, but also of the political bonds that preserved Thessaloniki's freedom and flourishing, that brought upon these Christians the afflictions to which Paul refers? Was that the reason they were persecuted by their Gentile neighbors, even by civic authorities, from the earliest days of their conversion to the one God whom they regarded as living and true—the God who held his own civic assemblies and refused to share his worshipers with other so-called gods? Were they seen as a threat to the peace of Thessaloniki, quite apart from the agitations of their Jewish opponents? Might they have been accused of breaking their oaths of loyalty to Caesar, who also styled himself "Savior" and "Son of God" (*divi filius*)? Not much is known for certain about their situation, but some or all of this is likely enough.

For Paul, however, the gods are but idols. They are not living and true but lifeless and mute. Yet they are instruments of deception and even of demons. Their worship is to be shunned (1 Cor. 10:14–22). We may add that there are demons, and there are idols, even where there are no such putative gods. For an idol, in the broadest sense, is anything to which we look as if to God, or anything we serve in place of God. To discern the demons and to recognize the idols is necessary for anyone who intends to "abstain from the pollutions of idols" (Acts 15:20). That is the burden of the first ten books of Augustine's *City of God* and our burden again today in the remnants of Christendom, where the gods (under their old names) have been defeated but the new faith has faded, leaving the house swept and empty (cf. Matt. 12:43–45). "When man lives according to man and not according to God . . . he is like the devil" (*Civ.* 14.4, trans. Babcock), and when he is like the devil he is the plaything of demons.

Where shall we begin with this discernment, if not with God "living and true"? This is simply Old Testament bedrock, which became the bedrock of the Christian creed also: "We believe in one God, the Father Almighty, maker of heaven and earth, of all things visible and invisible." Everything that is owes to the living God the fact that it is. Hence no adequate account of it can be given by appeal to nature or the forces of nature, even if the latter are dressed up by theomachy or theosophy. Only by way of appeal to God, who freely brings into existence that which has no existence and who causes life to teem upon the earth, can nature be properly appraised.

All people, including physicians and metaphysicians who rightly seek a scientific understanding of nature, are called to recognize this. Those who fail to recognize it prefer fancies (εἴδωλα) to reality and suffer in consequence a distortion of their own being (Rom. 1:24–32). But the point to be made is not merely that it is wrong to worship nature or the forces of nature, or for that matter human ideologies and power structures, as the Thessalonians did and we also do. We must grasp the positive point that the living and true God, who alone is to be worshiped, is something more than the ἀρχή and αἰτία, the beginning and the cause, of all that is. He is, as Barth puts it, the God who loves in freedom (*CD* II/1, §28). And because he loves in freedom, turning to God from idols means turning from everything servile. We discern the demons when we discern the servile, and we recognize idols when we recognize the logic of servility. Service of the living God *is* freedom. The alternative is always, and inevitably, bondage.

■ "The God who made the world and everything in it, being Lord of heaven and earth, does not live in shrines made by man, nor is he served by human hands, as though he needed anything, since he himself gives to all men life and breath and everything" (Acts 17:24–25). In book four of *Against the Heresies*, Irenaeus takes up this phrase "as though he needed anything" and develops it into a Christian doxology of freedom that stands in stark contrast to the idolatries that darken this world. God, he keeps repeating, has no need of sacrifice. God has no need at all and does nothing out of need. God creates, God loves, God gives in freedom, as the incarnation of the Son amply attests. Whence then the command to Israel to offer sacrifice? Whence the dominical command that the Church offer the Eucharist? Sacrifice is required for our sake, not God's, that we may enjoy God by participating thankfully in the divine economy, giving in return what we have received. But since God has no need of sacrifice, the only fitting sacrifice is that which is offered in pure freedom, as was the sacrifice of Jesus. In him we "follow God without fetters" (*Haer.* 4.13.2). Not that Christian freedom is antinomian, for Jesus does not abrogate the law but rather fulfills, extends, and broadens it so that it truly serves freedom. This is necessary because "the more extensive operation of liberty implies that a more complete subjection and affection towards our Liberator had been implanted within us" (4.13.3, 4.16.5; cf. Ps. 119:96). Freedom, in other words, is found in a deepening synergy of love and obedience— what the Old Testament refers to as the fear of the Lord—which is just what eucharistic participation in the trinitarian economy engenders. "The fear of the Lord is glory and exultation, and gladness and a crown of rejoicing. The fear of the Lord delights the heart, and gives gladness and joy and long life" (Sir. 1:11–12).

With the idols it is otherwise. The idolater is not engaged in an economy of gift but in a barter economy, a remarkably futile one in which he gives up what he cannot get back—his just relation to the Creator—but does not receive anything he does not already have. This is the case even where the idol or idols represent real persons or entities capable of bestowing actual favors (economic, political, sexual, etc.). For idol worship is an attempt to take from God what belongs to God and ascribe it to another, whose power of disposition over it is in fact subject to the judgment and determination of God. What the idolater receives, then, he receives only in the corrupted form of false dependence on, and improper obligation to, a third party. Thus does he fall into bondage. For this third party, whether real or imaginary, demands payment, something God does not do, or not in the first instance. With God the question of payment arises only in response to idolatrous acts that disrupt the economy of gift, a disruption that is not ignored but answered with a still greater gift, the incarnation; after that, if the gift is ignored, payment is demanded (cf. Luke 7:36–50). With the idols, however, payments are constantly being demanded. These payments are psychological and spiritual—distraction, addiction, guilt, fear, etc.—and also material and social, perhaps even to the betrayal of loved ones. While they may in some cases appear voluntary, thus imitating the economy of gift, they prove involuntary in the end.

That idols are not living and true does not mean that they are powerless to entrap and bring into bondage. But their power does not lie in themselves; it derives from our looking to them as if to God. God makes no idols, so nature knows none; but man can make an idol of whatever he will. No sooner, however, does he do so—by fancifully investing in something a capacity for doing what God alone can do—than he becomes its slave. Conversely, when men turn from idols to the living God they are rendered free, like the three friends of Daniel who refuse to look to the image erected by Nebuchadnezzar. In his rage the king casts them bound into the furnace, but to his amazement sees not three but "four men walking around in the fire, unbound and unharmed," the fourth seeming "like a son of the gods" (Dan. 3:25 NIV). For the angel of the Lord has been sent to rescue those who trust in him—no God, observes Nebuchadnezzar, can save like this God! One notes that the Song of the Three, sounding from the depths of the furnace, revisits nothing but the doctrine of creation, which is already sufficient to refute any claim the image can make on them. This song (inserted in the Greek version of Daniel) underscores the observation of Jeremiah on the impotence of idols and on the ignorance of idolaters, who do not seem to know that "the LORD is the true God; he is the living God and the everlasting King." But the appearance of the fourth man echoes Jeremiah's eschatological note: "At his wrath the earth quakes, and the nations cannot endure his indignation. Thus shall you say to them: 'The gods who did not make the heavens and the earth shall perish from the earth and from under the heavens'" (Jer. 10:10–11).

That God is living and true, and altogether unlike the idols, is demonstrated by the fact that he raised Jesus from the dead. The announcement that Jesus is Lord, that the end of the age of the idols is therefore at hand, rests on that same fact. There is no gospel on any other terms, however stubborn and indeed prodigious the effort to produce one, from ancient gnosticism through medieval Islam to modern utopianism. There is no ambassadorial mission that, uncertain of his resurrection, can rightly demand the attention of either Jew or Gentile. Those who turn to God from idols, determining to serve the God who is living and true, do so precisely as those who believe that Jesus—the very man whom Paul himself once regarded as a false prophet and failed messiah—returned to life, departed the grave, appeared to his disciples, and ascended to glory. They serve

God as those who wait for his Son from heaven; that is, for his return in glory (cf. 1 Tim. 3:16; 6:14–15; Titus 2:11–13).

We have already observed that Paul uses "Son" (υἱός) sparingly. Where we do encounter the term, we know that we have come to a climactic point in his rhetoric, as can be illustrated from other epistles. We also discover that it generally appears first in the exordium, where it is already connected with a preliminary statement about resurrection and/or return, for Jesus's revelation as Son is intrinsically linked to those events. This serves to prepare the reader for what is coming later. For example, in Rom. 1:4 we read that Jesus was "designated Son of God in power according to the Spirit of holiness by his resurrection from the dead," while the consequences of this for "the glorious liberty of the children of God" are expounded in Rom. 8. Here in 1 Thessalonians we find something similar in 1:10, followed up at 4:1–5:11. (Cf. 1 Cor. 1:4–9 and 15:1–28; Gal. 1:1, 15–16; 2:20 and 4:4–6 also bear consideration.) We also discover that Paul has constructed the opening of his letter in such a way as to proclaim the triune name, the holy name into which they were baptized:

1:1   in God the Father and the Lord Jesus Christ (cf. 1:3)
1:5   and in the Holy Spirit (cf. 1:7)
1:9   a living and true God.

It is for the living and true God, in the person of the incarnate Son, that they wait. That said, Paul is not directly concerned in Thessalonians to expound sonship as such, except in the sense that Christians are "sons of the light and sons of the day" (→5:5). It is the eschatology rather than the Christology that will occupy him once he has finished his other business, for it is the eschatology that seems to occupy his readers.

Now, the proclamation of the resurrected Jesus has been made over into many things: most often into a parable aimed at the transformation of the human psyche; occasionally (as by Teilhard and his disciples) into a theory of cosmogenesis, a "cosmic Christ," or something equally foreign to the Jewish hope of the resurrection and the παλιγγενεσία or regeneration of all things (Matt. 19:28; cf. Farrow 2007b). It has even been made over into news of the event by which God becomes God, a mistake modern trinitarian thinkers have made by collapsing the messianic and the trinitarian sense of the title "Son," thus introducing a false necessity into the contingent and a false contingency into the divine (see Farrow 1999b; cf. Wright 2003: 719–36). As we find it in Paul, however, the proclamation of the resurrection is a straightforward announcement that God vindicated a dead Jew by restoring him to life, in a great triumph over death that foreshadows the παλιγγενεσία. Was Jesus convicted and executed on the grounds that he made false and blasphemous messianic claims? Then his resurrection is proof of his messiahship and of his right to the whole panoply of prophetic promises, whether Davidic or postexilic, including those with political and cosmic repercussions. It is proof that the Lord reigns, that the glory of the Lord is about to be revealed, that all flesh shall see it together, that reward and recompense are at hand (Isa. 40:5–10; cf. 60–66).

The proclamation of the resurrection, therefore, is like the sounding of *reveille*, a call to vigilance, a warning to expect "wonders in the heavens above and signs on the earth beneath"—portents of the impending day, "the great and manifest day," the day of the Lord. In the background is the prophet Joel:

> Alas for the day!
> For the day of the LORD is near,
> and as destruction from the Almighty it comes.
> . . . .
> Blow the trumpet in Zion;
> sound the alarm on my holy mountain!
> Let all the inhabitants of the land tremble,
> for the day of the LORD is coming, it is near,
> a day of darkness and gloom,
> a day of clouds and thick darkness!
> . . . .
> But the LORD is a refuge to his people,
> a stronghold to the people of Israel. (1:15; 2:1–2; 3:16)

And in the foreground is Zephaniah:

> The great day of the LORD is near,
> near and hastening fast. . . .
> A day of wrath is that day,
> a day of distress and anguish.
> . . . .
> "Therefore wait for me," says the LORD.
> . . . .
> "For I will leave in the midst of you
> a people humble and lowly.

> They shall seek refuge in the name of the LORD. . . .
>   and none shall make them afraid." (1:14–15; 3:8; 3:12–13)

The proclamation of the resurrection of Jesus fills out this scene by asserting that there is one capable of delivering God's people from the destruction which that day of distress will bring (at Zeph. 1:15 the LXX has ἡμέρα ὀργῆς ἡ ἡμέρα ἐκείνη, ἡμέρα θλίψεως καὶ ἀνάγκης, which *pace* Fee 2009: 50n89, connects ὀργή and θλῖψις); by declaring that there is one who will make himself the promised refuge and stronghold, rescuing them from the coming wrath (ἐκ τῆς ὀργῆς τῆς ἐρχομένης) and from death itself.

To the notion of God's wrath we must return, as to the other subjects that Paul has now indicated he intends to treat. We need only note here that there is little point in going on with our reading of Thessalonians if we fancy that we can find out a God without wrath; that is, if we hope with the heretics of old somehow to separate the God of love from the God of justice. "That they might remove the rebuking and judicial power from the Father, reckoning that as unworthy of God, and thinking that they had found out a God both without anger and good, they have alleged that one judges, but that another saves, unconsciously taking away the intelligence and justice of both deities" (*Haer.* 3.25.2, in *ANF* 1:459). Paul will have none of that! Likewise, if we think that talk of a savior appearing from the heavens is merely the stuff of dreams, dreams as dangerous as they are empty, we must dispense with Paul, for that is the plotline to which he is working.

Ἐκ τῶν οὐρανῶν (and its Hebrew equivalent) can be translated "from heaven" or, more literally, "out of the heavens." The former indicates well enough that Jesus will come with divine power and authority, for he himself is ἐξ οὐρανοῦ (1 Cor. 15:47), but the latter suggests in more dramatic fashion a confrontation of cosmic proportions such as the prophets foresaw. (There is nothing else to commend the more literal translation, just as there is nothing to commend at Matt. 6:9 the translation, "Our Father who art in the heavens.") On that day the heavens will open and all humanity will learn that there is more to creation than has hitherto met the eye. Those who enter the new or renewed creation will discover that of which they have not yet even dreamed (1 Cor. 2:9). The earth too will open, that she may give up her dead. For the day of the Lord will be a day of judgment for the peoples, as well as a day of destruction for the demons and the idols. Above all it will be a day of relief and vindication for the faithful, for the Lord waits to be gracious to those who wait for him (Isa. 30:18). The prayer of the psalmist (68:1–3) will be fulfilled:

Let God arise, let his enemies be scattered;
  let those who hate him flee before him!
As smoke is driven away, so drive them away;
  as wax melts before fire,
  let the wicked perish before God!
But let the righteous be joyful;
  let them exult before God;
  let them be jubilant with joy!

2:1–4 For you yourselves know, brethren, that our mission to you was not in vain, but though we had suffered beforehand and been shamefully treated (as you are aware) in Philippi, we took courage in our God to proclaim to you the gospel of God amid many hindrances. For our appeal does not stem from error or impurity or guile, but just as we have been approved by God to be entrusted with the gospel, so also we speak, not as those pleasing to men but as pleasing rather to God who proves our hearts.

The *narratio* now expands on 1:5, "you know what kind of men we were among you for your sake." Their time together had been short—Acts leaves the impression that it was just a few weeks—and the circumstances at the end were these: What had happened in Philippi happened again, albeit less dramatically, in Thessaloniki. False accusations were made to the authorities, a public disturbance was manufactured, and it was deemed best that Paul and his company depart the city. This time the accusers were Jews, for the mission was launched at a synagogue. There was no beating or imprisonment by hasty public officials, though of hindrances (beginning perhaps with the wounds they still bore) and of opposition there was no shortage. The departure was by night, secretly, rather than by day after a formal apology. And there was no earthquake to show that they were approved by God, if not by man. Any verdict in Thessaloniki would have to be reached on the merits of the message itself and of the messengers. As usual there were two conflicting verdicts. The synagogue was divided. Some Jews and a good many God-fearing Greeks were persuaded; others were not, pursuing them even to Beroea, to stir up more trouble for them there (Acts 17:1–15). The latter party doubtless delighted in pointing out that Paul and friends had fled Thessaloniki by night before they could be brought to trial, making them out to be both heretics and scoundrels. So what, on sober reflection, should be made of these messengers and their mission?

It is characteristic of Paul, as of Jesus, to take the question of the messenger seriously. In Jesus's case, the messenger is the mission and the mission the messenger.

The one cannot even be conceived apart from the other. Of course it is otherwise with Paul, who is but an ambassador. Just so, however, he knows himself to have a holy calling, to be "a minister of Christ Jesus to the Gentiles in the priestly service of the gospel of God, so that the offering of the Gentiles may be acceptable, sanctified by the Holy Spirit" (Rom. 15:16). He knows that he will be judged as such by God, that it is possible to preach to others while yet disqualifying himself (1 Cor. 9:27), and that men will inevitably judge his mission and message at least in part by his own person. He therefore takes great pains, both during and after his missions, to present himself also to man as a person of integrity and as "a workman who has no need to be ashamed" (2 Tim. 2:15). Because he is an ambassador, speaking to issues of life and death, it matters how he comports himself in their presence and what they think of him.

▨ Witness his great *apologia* in 2 Corinthians, beginning at 2:17: "For we are not, like so many, peddlers of God's word; but as men of sincerity, as commissioned by God, in the sight of God we speak in Christ." Surely this ought to be the concern of every preacher, particularly those who share in the apostolic vocation through holy orders as well as baptism. For they too are ministers of Christ Jesus "in the priestly service of the gospel of God," with a view to the preparation among the nations of an offering acceptable to God. They too speak—or fail to speak—in the sight and hearing of God. The question, not only of understanding but also of integrity and courage, is put to them as to Paul. Are they mere peddlers of God's word, or for that matter of God's sacraments? Or are they people of integrity, worthy of their calling? "This is how one should regard us, as servants of Christ and stewards of the mysteries of God. Moreover it is required of stewards that they be found trustworthy" (1 Cor. 4:1–2). While the verdict as to whether they are indeed trustworthy must be rendered by him whose ministers they are, this does not alleviate the need for mutual trust between the ministers and their charges. To cultivate that trust is always the point of Paul's apologetics, as of his manner of life: "Have you been thinking all along that we have been defending ourselves before you? It is in the sight of God that we have been speaking in Christ, and all for your upbuilding, beloved" (2 Cor. 12:19). Obviously there can be no upbuilding, and no ministry of reconciliation, without trust. "Therefore, knowing the fear of the Lord, we persuade men; but what we are is known to God, and I hope it is known also to your conscience" (2 Cor. 5:11). ▨

"We took courage in our God," says Paul, "amid many hindrances." One thinks of Cicero, who also knew what it was like to face many hindrances or much opposition (a good alternative translation) and to persevere. Yet it was from exile in Thessaloniki in 58 BC that Cicero penned these dolorous lines to his dear friend Atticus, lines that conjure up an image almost the exact reverse of St. Paul: "Your pleas to me not to think of suicide have one result, that I refrain from laying violent hands on myself; but you cannot make me cease to regret our decision and my existence. What is there for me to live for, especially if I have lost even that hope I had when I set out? I will forbear to mention all the miseries into which I have fallen through the villainous machinations not so much of my enemies, as of those who envy me, for fear of arousing my grief again, and provoking you to share it by sympathy. But this I will say, that no one has ever suffered such a misfortune, and no one ever had more right to wish for death. But I have missed the time when I could have died with honour. At any other time death will only end my pain, not heal it" (*Letters to Atticus* 3.7, in Cicero 1912: 1:203f.).

Cicero, who eventually lost his head to an imperial swordsman in Italy, died courageously enough but never knew Paul's confidence that "to live is Christ, and to die is gain" (Phil. 1:21). Would that he had known Paul's God! Would that he had known the fear of the Lord in which Paul was raised. For knowing the fear of the Lord and taking courage in God are pretty much the same thing. Paul's experience, on the way to a fate like Cicero's, was that of the psalmist:

> The Lord is my light and my salvation—
>   whom shall I fear?
> The Lord is the stronghold of my life—
>   of whom shall I be afraid?
>
> When the wicked advance against me
>   to devour me,
> it is my enemies and my foes
>   who will stumble and fall.
> Though an army besiege me,
>   my heart will not fear;
> though war break out against me,
>   even then I will be confident. (27:1–3)

Paul knew what it meant to be "afflicted in every way, but not crushed; perplexed, but not driven to despair; persecuted, but not forsaken; struck down, but not destroyed" (2 Cor. 4:8–9; cf. 11:22–33). He knew what it meant to hold the treasure of the word of God in an "earthen vessel" without losing heart and how to persevere amid much opposition. For if the fear of the Lord is a bulwark against error (πλάνη), it is also a bulwark against cowardice and despair (cf. Ps. 119:105–20, where the psalmist says, οὐκ ἐπλανήθην, "I strayed not," 118:110 LXX).

That Paul regarded courage as a necessary condition for apostolic ministry is evident in his dispute with Barnabas over Mark, who seemed to him lacking just here (Acts 15:38–40; but cf. 2 Tim. 4:11). Then again, even fools may be bold, and scoundrels too. But Paul and Silas and Timothy were neither. Their summons (παράκλησις) to the Thessalonians, their appeal to them to recognize, as Jesus himself put it, that "the time is fulfilled, and the kingdom of God is at hand" (Mark 1:15), their invitation to repentance and faith, was not based on some presumptuous folly. Nor was it a clever bit of trickery to prise from their audience some favor, sexual or financial or political. Their minds were clear and their motives pure. They remained that way because they aimed not at pleasing men, who could only guess at their motives, but at pleasing God, who was perfectly capable of weighing them with a precise measure.

2:5–9 Never did we make our approach with flattering words, as you know, or with some pretext for taking advantage. God is witness. Nor did we seek glory from men, whether from you or from anyone else, our dignity as apostles of Christ notwithstanding. Rather we became gentle among you, like a nursing mother with her children, so solicitous for you that it seemed good to us to share with you not only the gospel of God but our own selves, because you were beloved by us. For you remember, brethren, our toil and trouble—laboring night and day so as not to burden any of you while we preached to you the gospel of God.

The task of pleasing men is for politicians and performers. Cicero was both and knew well how to make an approach with flattering words, just as he knew how to write his philippics. One sees many traces of such skills in Paul. He works just as hard at persuasive effect, encouraging and criticizing and prodding by turns. Certainly he is conscious of the dignity of his office and does not shy from mentioning that he might with justice have wielded authority in a more burdensome fashion (to offer a more literal rendering of δυνάμενοι ἐν βάρει εἶναι ὡς Χριστοῦ ἀπόστολοι). But such is not his way. He prefers rather the way of the Lord Jesus, who became poor that we might become rich. He is not without ambition, and his rhetoric serves his ambition; yet his ambition is as different from Cicero's as the kingdom of God is from the republic of Rome.

"Nor did we seek glory from men": the whole difference is just here. Rome was never about anything else, nor for that matter was Cicero's campaign for the consulship, with its short-lived privileges. But the kingdom of God, the kingdom than which none greater can be conceived, derives its glory from God. To receive glory from God is to receive "the crown of righteousness, which the Lord, the righteous judge, will award . . . on that Day, and not only to me but also to all who have loved his appearing" (2 Tim. 4:8). To seek glory from men so ill befits an apostle and ambassador of that kingdom that it amounts almost to an abdication of office, spiritually speaking, and certainly to a foolishly premature cashing-in of the promise of glory. "Truly, I say to you, they have their reward" (Matt. 6:5).

How many apostles or ambassadors of Christ, including those who have sat in Peter's seat as *servus servorum dei*, have thus abdicated spiritually what they have gained juridically by seeking glory from men? How many indeed, vainly guarding their transitory glory, have refused to rebuke the treachery of the treacherous, betraying even the little ones among their flock to ravenous wolves? How many have failed to hear what Peter himself says? "To the elders among you, I appeal as a fellow elder and a witness of Christ's sufferings who also will share in the glory to be revealed: Be shepherds of God's flock that is under your care, watching over them—not because you must, but because you are willing, as God wants you to be; not pursuing dishonest gain, but eager to serve; not lording it over those entrusted to you, but being examples to the flock. And when the Chief Shepherd appears, you will receive the crown of glory that will never fade away" (1 Pet. 5:1–4 NIV).

What then is the dignity of the apostolic office, and how might Paul and company have brought to bear their weight as apostles? The dignity, if we are speaking in the broad sense in which Silas and Timothy are also to be included— Paul defends elsewhere (Gal. 1–2) his own special dignity as one called directly by the Lord in a fashion analogous to that of the Twelve—lies in the commission from the Spirit of Jesus, confirmed by the Church, to proclaim Jesus as Lord, to announce the kingdom, and to deliver "to them for observance the decisions which had been reached by the apostles and elders who were at Jerusalem" (Acts 16:4). Were Caesar's messengers possessed of dignity when sent out to some city with his good news (εὐαγγέλια) about favors to be bestowed or indeed about punishment to be meted? How much more the messengers of Jesus! They also carried not only promises and instructions but also the power to command. Was their dignity lessened because they were generous with the former, stingy with the latter? Not at all, though their dignity had always to be defended among those who found dignity only in the power to command.

Ironically, it was Paul's exercise of the latter in Philippi, commanding a demon to depart when it kept putting their dignity on parade—"These men are servants of the Most High God, who proclaim to you the way of salvation" (Acts 16:17)— that had landed these apostles in prison. That was because the authority of Jesus brought them into conflict with the authority of Mammon—a much subtler and more powerful force than any soothsaying spirit—which in turn brought them into conflict with the local magistrates. Delivered by Jesus, the apostles were not about to lend any credence to Mammon by demanding that those who acknowledged their gospel provide them the financial hospitality befitting their status as apostles. No, they would earn their own living so as to eliminate any hint of compromise with Mammon, while using their workshop, along with the home of Jason, as a base for evangelizing and catechizing (cf. Weima 2014: 29f.). They were hindered in Philippi by someone's private commercial interests; they were hindered in Thessaloniki by factional interests in the synagogue. But for their part they would put no obstacles in anyone's way, even by perfectly legitimate demands or expectations. Combining voluntary support from Philippi (cf. Phil. 4:14–16) with physical labor, they would see to their own needs without burdening the Thessalonians, though we may perhaps assume that some of the converts among the "leading women" in the city were not unhelpful (Acts 17:4; cf. Luke 8:1–3).

Jason, at all events, was very helpful, opening his home to them and their mission. Providence had placed him there for that purpose. Tradition has it that this Jason is the one who appears in Rom. 16:21 as Paul's kinsman and collaborator, that he himself came from Tarsus and afterward was made bishop there, and that with Sosipater he later evangelized Corfu. He is regarded as a saint and numbered by the Orthodox (from the early third century) among the seventy apostles. For these claims we have no corroborating evidence. To judge from Acts 17, however, Paul's host in Thessaloniki was a Jewish man of means, who apparently needed no introduction. Paul, curiously, does not mention him in the Thessalonian correspondence, as we might have expected; but then neither does he mention Demas, who may have been from that city (cf. 2 Tim. 4:10), or Secundus and Aristarchus, who certainly were (Acts 20:4; 27:2)—despite the fact that Aristarchus appears at Col. 4:10 and Philem. 24, having by then become one of Paul's closest companions. It is possible that the early second-century *Dialogue of Jason and Papiscus*, an extant fragment of which describes Jason as a *hebraeus Christianus*, may have been modeled on the Jason of Acts 17 and/or Rom. 16 (see Lawrence Lahey, in Skarsaune and Hvalvik 2007: 585ff.; cf. 6, 164). It was not uncommon, by the way, for Jews named Yeshua to take a Greek name such as Jason (or Justus, as in Col. 4:11).

It was love, not necessity, that dictated this course of action. They behaved with the quiet dignity of the mother who, purely out of love, spares by hard work the children she suckled from labors they might otherwise have to undertake, so that they might delight rather in their freedom to explore the world now opening up to them; who also humbles herself to join them in their play or to read them their stories, so that they might connect that world, and their own curiosity about it, with the comforts of hearth and home. "Wheresoever I open St Paul's epistles," cried Donne, "I meet not words but thunder, and universal thunder, thunder that passes through all the world" (Muggeridge and Vidler 1972: 12; cf. 2 Cor. 10:10). This characterization is true in its way, but it is not large enough to capture the man or his writings. It does not reckon with his motherhood.

▨ The ἤπιοι/νήπιοι debate in v. 7 need not detain us. Whichever word Paul used, the idea is gentleness and lack of pretentiousness, not infancy per se, and (*pace* Weima 2014: 180–87) the textual uncertainty recommends the rendering that makes the best literary sense. Aquinas, who has *facti sumus parvuli* (though the Vulgate has *lenes*) handles it nicely: "Then when Paul says, 'but we were gentle [as children] among you,' he makes two points: first, that he is not desirous of human glory; secondly, that he does not wish to appear avaricious (2:9). In handling the first point Paul does two things. First, he gives evidence of his humility; secondly, he shows his concern by a simile (2:7). Paul makes the first point by saying that 'we were as children,' that is, humble. 'If they make you master of the feast, do not exalt yourself; be among them as one of them' (Sir. 32:1). Then he employs the simile saying, 'like a nurse taking care of her children,' who bends down to an infant and speaks to the stammering child, so that the child may learn to speak; the nurse even makes use of gestures: 'I have become all things to all men' (1 Cor. 9:22). 'As babes in Christ, I fed you with milk, not solid food' (1 Cor. 3:1)" (*S.1Th.* 2.1.33–34). ▨

2:10–12 You are witnesses, together with God, how piously and properly and indeed irreproachably we behaved toward you who believed; even as you know how we encouraged and exhorted each one of you, as a father his children, and charged you to walk worthily of the God who is calling you into his own kingdom and glory.

Paul, who took no wife and had no children, was both mother and father to them. In his spiritual fatherhood he was no more remote and detached than in his motherhood. What belonged to his fatherly role was admonition and encouragement. In point of fact, both παρακαλέω and παραμυθέομαι can mean either to exhort and inspire or to comfort and console, and these are not gender-specific roles; but Paul is now emphasizing the fatherly, and adding the element of admonition. He and his colleagues took care to neglect neither side of their responsibility and to neglect no one in either respect. Bishops and presbyters, like the prophets and apostles in whose ministry they share, are called to this parental *imitatio dei*, this constant dialectic of admonishment and encouragement, of instruction and inspiration, of correction and consolation. Whether they belong to the Latin tradition, which has made the prudential judgment that clergy should follow the example of Paul rather than of Peter, remaining single and without natural children for the sake of the spiritual children committed into their care, or to some other tradition that does not require this, all have the high and holy duty of seeing that parental attention is directed faithfully to each one. "Strange!" remarks Chrysostom: "In so great a multitude to omit no one, neither small nor great, neither rich nor poor" (*Hom.* 3). Perhaps it is not so strange, however, if each is regarded as a member not only of the kingdom but also of the royal family; yet there may be the makings here of an argument against oversized churches and dioceses, in which personal attention is all but impossible unless there are presbyters in abundance.

Now, both sides of the dialectic must also appear in preaching the gospel of God, just as in the confessional or in the conduct of pastoral life, where the sincerity of the preacher is tested and proven. As Aquinas observes, "something is sound because it serves its nature," and "preaching is sound when someone teaches in that manner in which Christ taught" (*S. 1 Th.* 2.1.28). That Christ's own preaching was fatherly and motherly, neglecting neither admonition nor encouragement, is evident from his poignant reflection on those who were impervious to both: "O Jerusalem, Jerusalem, killing the prophets and stoning those who are sent to you! How often would I have gathered your children together as a hen gathers her brood under her wings, and you would not! Behold, your house is forsaken and desolate" (Matt. 23:37–38).

The preaching of those set over that house had long been suspect. Consider Eli the priest, who had charge of the temple and the ark of God. He was willing to admonish the people, even individually, as he did Hannah, though in her case his admonishment was well wide of the mark (1 Sam. 1:12–16). Occasionally he would admonish his own sons, but these "were worthless men [who] had no regard for the LORD" (2:12). Perhaps he had failed to inspire them as youths or had never charged them to walk worthily of their God? Did he neglect his own sons while he was busy pastoring others? Was he prey to a false and sentimental compassion that in reality was not compassionate at all? Was he altogether out of touch, the last one to know what was going on? Or did he seek to avoid scandal by covering up his sons' actions until the tide of scandal overwhelmed him? What seems clear enough is that he left serious admonishment until much too late (2:22–25) and that he had not, either as natural parent or as father in God, labored diligently at the dialectic of admonition and encouragement. His sons shared his responsibility for the household of God, but because of their collective failure the promised kingdom receded from view, the ark was lost, and their own priestly house was left forsaken and desolate (2:27ff.). Paul, who inherited a share of the new priesthood in Christ, set a very different standard for his spiritual son, Timothy: "I charge you in the presence of God and of Christ Jesus who is to judge the living and the dead, and by his appearing and his kingdom: preach the word, be urgent in season and out of season, convince, rebuke, and exhort, be unfailing in patience and in teaching" (2 Tim. 4:1–2). He himself adhered to this standard throughout his ministry, even from these early days in Thessaloniki. Why is it that in so many churches today the example of Eli prevails over the example of Paul? Why is it that preaching is so often anemic, anecdotal, unserious, unsound, not serving its nature? Wherever such is the case, that house too is in danger of being left desolate and forsaken.

What does it mean to "walk worthily of the God who is calling you into his own kingdom and glory"? To walk worthily can only mean, in the first instance, to keep the commandments. Nothing has changed in that respect from the very beginning, when God called the first humans out of the animal kingdom by making them rational souls, permitting them to share in his own Logos, to be made after his own image and likeness, to mediate his divine lordship to their fellow creatures. "The LORD God took the man and put him in the garden of Eden to till it and keep it. And the LORD God commanded the man, saying, 'You may freely eat of every tree of the garden; but of the tree of the knowledge of good and evil you shall not eat, for in the day that you eat of it you shall die'" (Gen. 2:15–17). Nothing has changed from the time of Moses, when God called Israel out of Egypt, his son out of slavery. "You have seen what I did to the Egyptians, and how I bore you on eagles' wings and brought you to myself. Now therefore, if you will obey my voice and keep my covenant, you shall be my own possession among all peoples; for all the earth is mine, and you shall be to me a kingdom of priests and a holy nation" (Exod. 19:4–6). Nothing has changed, in that respect, with the coming of our Lord: "'Teacher, what good deed must I do, to have eternal life?' . . . 'If you would enter life, keep the commandments'" (Matt. 19:16–17). Or more personally: "If you keep my commandments, you will abide in my love, just as I have kept my Father's commandments and abide in his love" (John 15:10; cf. 1 John 5:3–4). The path of life is still marked out by commandments, whether summarized by ten Words or by two (Exod. 20:1–20; Matt. 22:36–40).

But wait. Didn't Paul himself make a change, or rather recognize a change made by God, when he went on to argue in Galatians and Romans that "by works of the law shall no flesh be justified" (Gal. 2:16; cf. Rom. 3:28)? Yes, in the sense that justification is a function of the cross, by which we are released from the condemnation of the law. No, in the sense that justification is never without sanctification, and sanctification is a process that engages us with the substance of the law. What has changed, in other words, is not the existence of commandments or their goal—"I charge you to keep the commandment unstained and free from reproach until the appearing of our Lord Jesus Christ" (1 Tim. 6:14)—but the freedom in which that goal is sought and reached (Rom. 8:1–17). "The chief element in the evangelical law," says Aquinas, is "the grace of the Holy Spirit bestowed inwardly." As for the other elements in this *legem evangelii*, "namely, the teachings of faith, and those commandments which direct human affections and human actions," they are secondary (*ST* 1-2.106.2). The secondary is not abrogated by the primary, however, such that the gospel is without law. Rather the law, or he who would keep the law, is quickened by the Spirit so that its commandments are now internal rather than external to his being. What *is* abrogated is the function of the law of Moses in demarcating the people of God as such (Gal. 5:2–6). The demarcation now is baptism into Christ, not circumcision on the eighth day, though some are circumcised, and "faith working through love," not the observance of fast days and feast days, though there are fast days and feast days. For in the font one passes with Christ into the eighth day of creation itself—that is, into the new creation—and in the Eucharist one feasts already on the manna of the world to come (1 Cor. 10:1–21; cf. Rev. 1–5).

▉ We should not be sidetracked here by debates about justification, particularly since δικαιόω and its derivatives do not appear in Thessalonians—that language and discourse features only in Galatians and Romans. We may observe, nevertheless, that Paul had not the slightest intention of encouraging antinomianism. This is evident from the context in which he places his maxim, "But if you are led by the Spirit you are not under the law" (Gal. 5:18). For what precedes and follows that maxim shows that the Spirit/law contrast is one and the same with the Spirit/flesh contrast. It is the law *deployed as a fleshly attempt to overcome the flesh* to which he is objecting, not the law as such (Rom. 7:4–25). Hence there can be no appeal to the Spirit against the objectives of the law, but only against the objectives of the flesh. "Walk by the Spirit, and do not gratify the desires of the flesh.... The works of the flesh are plain: immorality [πορνεία], impurity, licentiousness, idolatry, sorcery, enmity, strife, jealousy, anger, selfishness, dissension, party spirit, envy, drunkenness, carousing, and the like. I warn you, as I warned you before, that those who do such things shall not inherit the kingdom of God" (Gal. 5:16–21). Otherwise put: "Walk worthily of the God who is calling you into his own kingdom and glory." Some manuscripts, by the way, have the past tense—"called" for "calling"—but the present is more dynamic, reminding us that justification has a past, a present, and a future dimension. To be called is to be numbered with the righteous, for only the righteous will enter the kingdom, and to be numbered with the righteous is already to be justified. Yet to enter the kingdom, where no unrighteousness dwells or can dwell, it is necessary actually to be righteous. The calling that justifies is one and the same, then, with the calling that sanctifies, for without sanctification no one is finally justified, nor will they see the Lord (1 Cor. 6:9–11; cf. Heb. 12:14). We shall take this up at 1 Thess. 4:3. Meanwhile, the summary provided by the *Catechism of the Catholic Church* (§2020) suffices: "Justification has been merited for us by the Passion of Christ. It is granted us through Baptism. It conforms us to the righteousness of God, who justifies us. It has for its goal the glory of God and of Christ, and the gift of eternal life. It is the most excellent work of God's mercy."

It is indeed a kingdom to which we are called, a kingdom that will commence "with a cry of command" (→1 Thess. 4:16). But what marks off this kingdom, God's own kingdom and glory, from the kingdoms that seek to mimic or supplant it? The latter glorify man as if he were God, albeit only a few men (Augustus, e.g., whose statue in Thessaloniki suggests his divinity; cf. Weima 2014: 19f.). The former glorifies God so as to glorify man in God, every man who takes seriously the vocation to "seek first his kingdom and his righteousness" (Matt. 6:33). "For as those who see the light are within the light, and partake of its brilliancy; even so, those who see God are in God, and receive of his splendor" (*Haer.* 4.20.5). And that being the case, to walk worthily means also to walk in the company of God and his Christ. After all, to be with the Lord always is the goal of walking worthily (→1 Thess. 5:17; cf. 2 Cor. 5:1–10).

On the mount of transfiguration those two worthy friends of God, Moses and Elijah, appear talking with Jesus, Tabor serving as their tent of meeting. This, perhaps, they were accustomed to doing, though Peter, James, and John were obviously unaccustomed to the fact that the one with whom they conversed daily was able to converse also with people of diverse times and places, being himself the Lord of time and place. Exodus 33:7–11 and 34:29–35 already hint that invitations to the tent of meeting are to become universal among those who walk worthily. That is what Paul takes up in 2 Cor. 3, and Irenaeus in *Haer.* 4.20: "For it is not possible to live apart from life, and the means of life is found in fellowship with God; but fellowship with God is to know God, and to enjoy his goodness. Men therefore shall see God, that they may live, being made immortal by that sight, and attaining even unto God; which . . . was declared figuratively by the prophets, that God should be seen by men who bear his Spirit, and do always wait patiently for his coming. As also Moses says in Deuteronomy, 'We shall see in that day that God will talk to man, and he shall live.' . . . For the glory of God is a living man; and the life of man consists in beholding God" (*ANF* 1:489f.).

2:13 And for this also we constantly thank God, that when you received the word of God, heard from us, you accepted it not as the word of men but as it truly is, God's own word, which indeed is at work among you who believe.

One receives the call to glory by hearing the word of God with faith. The word of God is, at one and the same time, a word about God by faithful witnesses, a word that is from God and thus is God's, and a word that becomes the vehicle of God's actual presence and power. All three senses are present in this verse, τοῦ θεοῦ functioning in the first instance as an objective genitive, in the second as a subjective or possessive genitive, and in the third (where it is only implicit) as a genitive of apposition. Paul and Silas preach and write, and what they preach and write is the word of man to man, having an account of God and the kingdom of God as its matter or substance. There can be no dispute about that, though there be much dispute about the truth of their account, particularly where it concerns the ῥῆμα Χριστοῦ or preaching of Christ (Rom. 10:17). But Paul and Silas claim to speak and write under commission, on God's behalf. God stands behind what they say, as if he had said it himself. Those who hear with faith acknowledge that to be the case; they take these words as God's own (the semantic structure invites us to render λόγον θεοῦ as "God's own word"; Farrow 1987: 51ff.). That, for the apostles, is a great cause of thanksgiving, for it is proof that they have not spoken in vain. God is working salvation through their preaching. He is quickening their words, which are also his words, so that they become "spirit and life" (John 6:63). God's mediated word is at work because God himself is immediately at work in it, generating faith and faithfulness among the residents of Thessaloniki.

When this theology of the word—the word that is both human and, in the two senses indicated, divine—is developed by the Church, it naturally incorporates a doctrine of faith, for faith is the only proper response to the word of God (Heb. 11; cf. *Haer*. 5.19.1, which contrasts the response of Mary with that of Eve). Faith, as we have already observed, is a mode of knowing in which there is a synthesis of reason and will, indeed of reason and love. That synthesis, we learn here, is stimulated by God, who makes himself the very milieu of faith, the milieu in which the human being not only hears but also receives and grasps and abides in his word.

God does this quite literally in the incarnation, his own Son and Word adopting the proper human posture of absolute faith in God that the serpent taught man to reject. That posture his Spirit has already begun to teach Enoch, Abraham, Moses, Elijah, Anna, Simeon, and all who frequented the tent of meeting and longed for his coming. But Mary alone—she whose very womb was to serve as a tent of meeting—is taught to perfection. She is taught *ab initio* and from her own conception delivered from the serpent's grasp through the merits of her Son (Pius IX, *Ineffabilis Deus*). In her, Eve's bent back is straightened, that she might receive the Word and receive him freely. It is the Word himself who, seeking her out and approaching her a second time, does this. "'Woman, you are freed from your infirmity.' And he laid his hands on her, and immediately she was made straight, and she praised God" (Luke 13:12–13).

According to Anselm, expanding in *De conceptu virginali* his argument in *Cur deus homo* that Mary was cleansed by faith in her Son, this straightening was not necessary for the Word's own sake. It was not necessary, that is, in order for him to enter into solidarity with Adam's race without contracting, through his mother, sin's contamination—as if he *could* be contaminated by sin, as if he were not himself the remedy for sin and the author of that straightening power that would be exercised from his miraculous conception, in which he assumed our created nature without the agency of a human father and was made like us in all things *except* sin (thus Chalcedon; cf. Heb. 2:17 and 4:5), through to his glorious ascension on our behalf to the right hand of his Father in heaven. He, after all, is the source of her liberation, not she of his! "Keep joyful holiday, sweet Mother, joyful and unending in the peaceful vision of thy Jesus, the Author of thy immunity from sin" (Anselm 1872: 85). But it *was* necessary for Mary, whose assent to all this could not otherwise be free assent (*CCC* §490). The Word does not lay hold of her womb by deception or by force, but in such a way as to lay hold of her entire life, enabling her to share in his freedom from her own conception through to her assumption into heaven with him (Pius XII, *Munificentissimus Deus*; cf. Farrow 2011: 82ff.). It is for freedom that we have been set free, and Mary is the first to be fully freed. In her preservation from the power and stain of sin for the purpose of free assent, we can and should find the most potent illustration of prevenient grace—indeed, of both operative and *co*operative grace—without any hint of separation from the true source of grace: the incarnate Son (→5:23–24).

God does this also, through Christ, in the Church. Being the temple of the Lord, the new tent of meeting, the Church itself becomes the divine milieu of faith. Hence it is said in the missal, at the exchange of peace, "Look not on our sins, but on the faith of your Church." Hence it is said as well, with Augustine,

that "there is nothing more wholesome in the Catholic Church than using authority before argument" (*Mor. eccl.* 47); and, with Aquinas, that "science is not
more certain than faith, nor is anything else" (*ST* 2-2.4.8). For faith is a mode of
human knowing that reposes in God, while God himself is active in it (John 15;
cf. Augustine, *De Praedestinatione Sanctorum* 1.40).

Just as naturally, this theology of the word incorporates a doctrine of scripture
and the infallibility of scripture. If God commissions and inspires and deploys the
word of his servants, he also stands behind it; and if he stands behind it, it carries
his own authority. It is true and not false, for God himself is true and not false.
It is fully reliable because God is fully reliable. "In Sacred Scripture, the Church
constantly finds her nourishment and her strength, for she welcomes it not as
a human word, 'but as what it really is, the word of God'" (*CCC* §104). "The
inspired books teach the truth. 'Since therefore all that the inspired authors or
sacred writers affirm should be regarded as affirmed by the Holy Spirit, we must
acknowledge that the books of Scripture firmly, faithfully, and without error teach
that truth which God, for the sake of our salvation, wished to see confided to
the Sacred Scriptures'" (§107). A qualification follows, but it is a qualification of
the Christian religion, not of the Christian scriptures: "Still, the Christian faith
is not a 'religion of the book.' Christianity is the religion of the 'Word' of God,
a word which is 'not a written and mute word, but the Word which is incarnate
and living.'" This qualification underlines the importance of holding all three
senses together: "If the Scriptures are not to remain a dead letter, Christ, the
eternal Word of the living God, must, through the Holy Spirit, 'open minds to
understand the Scriptures'" (§108).

The doctrine of scripture must not be overinflated, however, as if God himself
had in scripture assumed creaturely form. Scripture, like Mary, is venerated not
worshiped. It is not another incarnation that confronts us here but rather an effect
of the one and only incarnation. That men really should speak from God and for
God is possible only because God himself has determined to speak with a human
voice. Their speech is called into his service as and because he makes himself, in
the person of the incarnate Son, both its object and its authentic hermeneutic.
And what is that service? "Every passage of scripture is *theopneustic*, profitable for
teaching, reproof, correction, and training in righteousness, so that the man of
God may be adequate, equipped for every good work" (2 Tim. 3:16–17 AT). In
this sense, scripture cannot be nullified or broken (John 10:35). What it intends
to say or show to the people of God can be relied upon for just these purposes. Its
inspiration does not forestall or eliminate all literary and historical imperfections.

■ This distinguishes the Christian view of scripture from the Islamic and even (much less sharply) from the Jewish. Jesus is the perfect man, and to him the scriptures bear witness; but the Holy Bible is not the perfect book, if indeed there could be such a thing as a perfect book. Neither the Torah nor the Gospels are the blueprint for creation, though the true nature of creation can be discovered when both are read together. As for the Qur'an, which is said by Muslims to be an actual "recitation" of God's own words, transmitted by Gabriel to Muhammad, of whose status as "the Prophet" it is the greatest proof, none of these claims can be admitted by Christians. Nor are these claims analogous to Paul's. Paul purports to have heard things in the presence of God that he cannot repeat among men (2 Cor. 12), but what he does say among men has not been dictated to him. His words, when handed over to the churches in written form as an exercise of his apostolic authority, are understood, like the rest of the scriptures, to be θεόπνευστος or God-breathed (Farrow 1987: 86–97); but that is a matter of being moved by the Spirit to speak, in his own peculiar fashion, from and for God (with 2 Tim. 3:16, cf. 1 Pet. 1:12; 2 Pet. 2:3; 3:15–16) and above all to bear witness to Jesus Christ, which of course the Qur'an does not. Coleridge was right, in his *Confessions*, to criticize any view of the Christian scriptures that equates inspiration with dictation. ■

Yet it is not the case that scripture is infallible only insofar as God deigns to use it in particular times and places and persons, only insofar as he puts it to work among those who believe. It is infallible already as that human word which God has called forth, made his own, and appointed for the instruction and edification of his covenant people. The great danger today, alongside sheer ignorance of scripture and of the apostolic preaching, lies in the temptation to detach the third sense of "the word of God" from the first two senses, privileging, as it were, the genitive of apposition. It is highly convenient, for anyone wishing to skirt round what scripture actually says, to shift attention to what God may wish to accomplish through it among (secretly disbelieving) believers. That move is mirrored in moral theology by those who bypass the primary question about the inherent goodness or badness of an act in order to take up instead secondary questions about intentions and consequences (*VS* 71ff.).

But there is a second danger, or perhaps it is the same danger in another form, which is the temptation to set ourselves up as authorities over the sense and meaning of scripture and of the preaching of Christ, as if this belonged to us individually or to our own movements and guilds. There are those "approved by God to be entrusted with the gospel" (1 Thess. 2:4), and while that category may include the humblest priest or deacon or religious or lay missionary, it includes first of all Peter, then James and John and Paul and the whole college of the apostles, and their legitimate successors. In short, it includes preeminently those burdened with the teaching office or magisterium of the Church. Which means that scripture and tradition are, asymmetrically but in their mutuality, the common source feeding the Church and governing the faithful. "All those things are to be believed with divine and Catholic faith which are contained in the Word of God, written or handed down, and which the Church, either by a solemn judgment or by her ordinary and universal magisterium, proposes for belief as having been divinely revealed" (Vatican I, *De Fide* 3, in Manning 1861; cf. *DEC* 2:807). "For Sacred Scripture is the word of God inasmuch as it is consigned to writing under the inspiration of the divine Spirit, while sacred tradition takes the word of God entrusted by Christ the Lord and the Holy Spirit to the Apostles, and hands it on to their successors in its full purity, so that led by the light of the Spirit of truth, they may in proclaiming it preserve this word of God faithfully, explain it, and make it more widely known" (Vatican II, *Dei Verbum* 9; cf. *DEC* 2:975).

Coleridge was wrong, then, to begin with "what *finds* me" in scripture, as he searched for the answer to the riddle of biblical authority. He knew that "as a Christian, I cannot,—must not—stand alone" and warned against the "presumptuous spirit in the negative dogmatism" of those who think—let biblical commentators beware!—they can simply "take up the Bible as they do other books, and apply to it the same rules of interpretation" (1956: 42, 48). Nevertheless, his Protestant sensibilities made it difficult for him to reckon fully with the role of the Church in determining and interpreting the canon, holding together the three senses of the word of God. Coleridge was an astute student of the creed as well as of scripture. But the authoritative witness to Christ, buttressed by the gift of infallibility, is not confined to scripture and creed. If the Church had not its own magisterial authority, there would be neither canon nor creed, nor could they abide as such.

At the dawn of the Reformation, during the 1519 Leipzig Debate, there was a pivotal moment when Johann Eck appealed to 2 Maccabees in support of the doctrine of purgatory. Luther replied that Maccabees could lend no support because it wasn't really scripture. By thus taking refuge, not only in the *sola scriptura* thesis but in the narrower canon of rabbinic Judaism, he opened the door for a progressive retreat to the redoubt of this or that canon within the canon—he himself was soon doubting James as well, which did not "find" him at all—and eventually to an all-out assault on the very idea of a canon. Which is also, of course, an assault on the very idea of the Church. For if it is true to say "no Church, no canon," it is also true to say "no canon, no Church." Ironically, the very passage we are considering is thought by many to be an interpolation—a corruption of some purer Pauline text—that may therefore be discounted as having no authority, canonical or otherwise. But let us proceed in our reflection on this putative interpolation, which extends to 2:16.

2:14–16 For you yourselves, brothers, became imitators of the churches of God in Christ Jesus that are in Judea, for you suffered the same things from your own countrymen as they did from the Jewish authorities, who also killed the Lord Jesus and the prophets and drove us out, who are displeasing to God and hostile to all men—hindering us from speaking to the Gentiles that they might be saved—so as always to heap up their sins. But the final wrath has caught them out.

Whatever may have happened since the apostles' hasty departure from Thessaloniki, the attack on the house of Jason that precipitated it—which was instigated by the leading Jews (οἱ Ἰουδαῖοι), who had not accepted their message as the word of God, and which also involved hired louts from the agora (Acts 17:5)—had set the stage for persecution. It had produced a motley alliance of Jews and Gentiles, backed by the crowds and the city authorities, that in its way mimicked the alliance in Jerusalem that sent Jesus to his cross. But if the harassment of the churches in Judea had its analogue in Thessaloniki, so, happily, did their faithfulness, on which Paul now remarks further.

In the first chapter he commended the Thessalonians for their imitation of himself and his team, and spoke of others in Macedonia and Achaia imitating the Thessalonians in turn (→1:6–10). Here he draws their attention to the fact that their mutual experience belongs to a pattern woven into the very fabric of salvation history. It is not merely the product of an unfortunate misunderstanding, or of the peculiar personalities in their local synagogue, or of the abundance of hooligans presently available for hire. Rather it is all of a piece with the experience of the prophets and of Jesus himself. It is exactly what Jesus alluded to in the parable of the vineyard's wicked tenants, by which he deliberately provoked his enemies at the beginning of his final, fateful week in Jerusalem.

On Mark 12:1–12, see Wright 1996: 497–501. On the variety of meanings of οἱ Ἰουδαῖοι, which at its narrowest refers to the leaders in Jerusalem—that is, to "the chief priests and the scribes and the elders" (Mark 11:27; cf. John 1:19), of whom Paul was first an agent and then a persecuted opponent (Acts 8:3; cf. 2 Cor. 11:24)—and at its broadest to all who are Jewish, see also Wright 1996: 542 and 2013: 1145f. "Jewish authorities," as I have translated it, situates this usage near the narrow end of the spectrum, in line with Mark 12.

The ownership of God's vineyard is contested and the contest is bloody. It did not end with the crucifixion of Jesus or the persecution and scattering of his followers, in which Paul himself once participated. The gospel may be "the power of God for salvation" to the Jew and the Greek, but to those who reject the gospel the ingathering of the Gentiles is a great offense, and to no one is it more offensive than to those who have seized the vineyard for themselves. In defending what they have seized and refusing to share it with others, they only heap up their sins like the Gentiles who once occupied the land on which this vineyard was built. As that land was taken from the latter, however, it will be taken from the former also. For, as Jesus made clear in his parable, wrath has been readied for them: "What will the owner of the vineyard do? He will come and destroy the tenants, and give the vineyard to others" (Mark 12:9). They have gone too far. Their sin is willful and stubborn, but their project is dead. Their verdict on Jesus, carried out by Rome, has been rendered null and void by his resurrection. They have dug a pit for him and fallen into it themselves. The trap they set for him, God has sprung on them. They have been caught out by the coronation of the great King and Heir, and by "the wrath that is coming" against all who have set their face against him—wrath εἰς τέλος, the final wrath, the wrath that will utterly consume the enemies of God.

"It was necessary for the Christ to suffer and to rise from the dead" (Acts 17:3), and so he has. Because he has, the final wrath is ready, just as the final and ultimate salvation is ready. Neither can be stopped now. Paul does not mean that the divine wrath has already fallen, but that the divine decision has already been delivered. He desires the Thessalonians to understand this so that they may understand as well the situation of persecution in which they find themselves. Some of the remaining gaps in their understanding will be filled in later in the present letter; others, as we shall see, in his second letter.

▓ There are three main reasons for regarding 2:13–16 as an interpolation; the others are all trivial and can safely be set aside. The first is that it seems to interrupt the flow of the letter, which reads quite nicely if one simply omits these verses. The same could be said of other passages, of course; hence that observation can in no way be decisive. The second is that it seems to contain a Gentile slur (cf. Tacitus, *Historiae* 5.5) against the Jews that is difficult to square with Romans. But read as we are reading it, it is actually a very Jewish "slur." Even in chapters 9–11, where Paul proposes that God will turn the evil of Jewish rejection of the Messiah to the good of the Gentiles and so eventually to the Jews' own good, is he not conceding that unbelieving Jews make themselves hostile to all men? Such slurs, which are in fact sober assessments, are frequently found in the Old Testament. They run the gamut from the Song of Moses to the ironies of the book of Jonah. Second Chronicles 36:15–16 would seem to be immediately in view, for Paul as for Jesus: "The LORD, the God of their ancestors, sent persistently to them by his messengers, because he had compassion on his people and on his dwelling place; but they kept mocking the messengers of God, despising his words, and scoffing at his prophets, until the wrath of the LORD rose against his people, till there was no remedy." As for the difficulty of explaining such things to Gentiles, it should be recalled that many of the new converts were already God-fearers (Acts 17:4) and not entirely in the dark about the Jewish scriptures.

The third reason, then, is the real reason: One could easily take ἔφθασεν δὲ ἐπ' αὐτοὺς ἡ ὀργὴ εἰς τέλος (the aorist verb having, as it does, the force of the perfect tense) to refer to some dramatic punishment already meted out by God in Judea. This is a quite natural reading if we translate, with the RSVCE, "But God's wrath has come upon them at last!" The only punishment that obviously qualifies, however, is the one prophesied by Jesus when he takes up Judaism's internal critique (Matt. 23:37–24:2); namely, the fall of Jerusalem in AD 70. Is this statement, then, a marginal gloss that, after the city fell, made its way into the text? Or might the whole paragraph be a deliberate interpolation from that time? There is no support for either thesis among the manuscripts. Moreover, the latter (which raises again the issue of forgery discussed in the preamble) does not account for Paul's concern to clarify the nature of the tension between those who accept the announcement of God's kingdom and those who reject it. It leaves aside a key piece of the puzzle, a piece required by the Thessalonians to make sense of what was going on in their own city.

But what of the former thesis, that a short marginal gloss has entered the text at the end of 2:16? The RSVCE rendering can be read retrospectively, in that way, but it can also be read proleptically, as I think it should. My own rendering, "The final wrath has caught them out," captures the proleptic sense a little better, perhaps, or we might consider a more expansive paraphrase: "The wrath of God has anticipated them right to the bitter end." While φθάνω normally indicates either precedence (to anticipate or come before) or reach (to attain or arrive at), the context, together with the unusual combination of prepositional phrases, invites us to retain both senses in a configuration not unlike that which appears in Matt. 12:28, where Jesus says, ἄρα ἔφθασεν ἐφ' ὑμᾶς ἡ βασιλεία τοῦ θεοῦ, "then the kingdom of God has come upon you." There, the Pharisees charge Jesus with casting out demons by the prince of demons. "And what," he responds, "if I cast them out rather by the Spirit of God? Then the kingdom of God has taken you unawares" (AT). Which is to say: It has come and is coming, though you do not recognize it. And because you do not recognize it, you are and will be excluded from it (cf. Isa. 6:9–13; Acts 28:25–28; Asiedu 2019: xv).

Does this not capture the sense of that passage? Here in Thessalonians something very similar is being said. The kingdom both has come and is coming, and with it the wrath of God. The former has caught up believers, whether they be in Judea or Macedonia, in preparation for the parousia; the latter has caught out their opponents, who do not yet grasp the gravity of their situation. This proleptic or eschatologically suspended sense allows us to give εἰς τέλος its due, as referring to the final or ultimate judgment (cf. Marshall 1983: 80–83), of which AD 70 provides only a foretaste. (Cf. Chrysostom, *Hom.* 3: "But the wrath is come upon them to the uttermost. What is 'to the uttermost'? These things are no longer like the former. There is here no return back, no limit. But the wrath is nigh at hand. Whence is this manifest? From that which Christ foretold.") It also allows us to reject unnecessary speculation about glosses or interpolations.   ▧

The opponents, Jewish or Gentile, whom the Thessalonian Christians now face are on the backside of history, so to say. They may seem to be in control, but they are not. The end has already anticipated them, for the Christ whom they oppose has risen from the dead and ascended to glory, whence he shall come to judge the quick and the dead and to winnow from his kingdom all who do evil. We will hear much more of this anon. It is necessary meanwhile only to remark that it is not the Jewish people as such who are on the backside of history— God forbid!—but rather those people, Jewish or Gentile, who set themselves stubbornly against God's Christ. The Christ is from the Jews and for the Jews, though not for them only, even if Israel κατὰ σάρκα is in part, and for a period, hardened against him (Rom. 11:25; cf. 3:4). As for Israel κατὰ πνεῦμα, it now comprises Jew and Gentile alike in the one body of Christ, and in that body the Jew is still the natural member while the Greek is the adopted member. Those who make of the present passage a condemnation of Jews generally—who lean on it as a crutch for their harsh supersessionism, as if the Mosaic covenant were abrogated in such a fashion that its former beneficiaries, despite being descendants of Abraham, were no longer the people of God but rather a people united only by an impending wrath eagerly anticipated and even brought forward by the Gentiles—have no choice but to regard it as an interpolation. For Paul, as Romans 9–11 makes clear, held the very opposite of such a view. If Paul was a supersessionist at all, he was a supersessionist in just the same sense that Jesus was, and in no other: The kingdom of God would be torn away from those who thought they had it in their grasp and given instead to those who were worthy of it. It would belong to "the Israel of God" (Gal. 6:16), not to those determined to take it by force (Matt. 11:12). The Israel of God, to be sure, would comprise both Jew and Gentile. It would not be defined by genetic or ethnic markers. But that it would be purified from everything Jewish, that Jews would have no place in it, that the divine promises to Jews would be null and void—nothing could be further from the mind of Paul or closer to the mind of Satan.

▧ There are Jewish and there are Gentile ways of trying to seize the kingdom by force. The Israel of God, which in the days of the apostles was opposed by οἱ ἄρχοντες and οἱ Ἰουδαῖοι alike, acting σὺν ἔθνεσιν καὶ λαοῖς Ἰσραήλ (Acts 4:27), naturally became a target of this violence, both from without and also, as the apostles frequently warned, from within. Harsh supersessionism is one of those ways (Farrow 2018g: 220–24). It completely obscures the fact that the Church is grounded in the Jewish flesh of Jesus and in the election of Israel κατὰ σάρκα for Jesus's sake. It overlooks the fact that the Church, which is called together from Jews and Gentiles (*LG* 9), has roots that are undeniably Jewish and that there is a Jewish "vine" to which every branch, natural or grafted, is attached. The animus against those roots, as Karl Barth pointed out in the run-up to World War II, is an animus against the vine itself. If that animus (which was already simmering in the pot of late-medieval Europe and boiled over after Luther took the lid off Christendom) is a feature of modern history, it is a feature herding the nations into the cauldron of God's wrath. Every trace of it must certainly be eradicated from the Church. *Pace* Barth (*CD* II/2, 259ff.), who did much to eradicate it, we should not even say that, within the Church, it is the peculiar role of the Jewish people to disclose the meaning of the cross rather than the resurrection. There is no warrant for that distinction, if the people of the new or renewed covenant are one people, with one witness to the faithfulness of God. Nor should we forget that the faithfulness of God will be revealed fully only when the hardened part of Israel κατὰ σάρκα has been overcome by his grace, such that "all Israel" may be saved (Rom. 11:25–26), and that this overcoming will certainly take place in the context of the mutual suffering of the Jew and the Gentile Christian.

These days, of course, it is necessary to defend Paul's thinking about the Israel of God both from the hard supersessionists and from the antisupersessionists. The latter accuse the Church itself of trying to seize the kingdom by force, through its talk of *perfidi Iudaei* and its periodic bans on Judaizing practices such as religious circumcision, together with other restrictive or penal actions that helped poison the culture against Jews. They try to read the New Testament very differently from how it has been read, taking the baptism of Timothy, for example, as a sign that Paul thought Jewish followers of Jesus bound to be Torah-observant in the old Mosaic rather than the new eucharistic sense. The Jerusalem Council is said to have assumed precisely that; and, by assuming it, to have established it as Christian orthodoxy, an orthodoxy the Church later abandoned. Paul's vow-taking in Jerusalem after his meeting with James and the elders, just prior to his arrest in the temple (Acts 21), is regarded as another such sign. Everything he says in his epistles to the contrary is alleged to have been directed exclusively to Gentiles. It is even claimed that there are two distinct peoples of God—Jews, whether they believe in Jesus or not, and Gentile believers— hence also that there are within Christianity two churches, an *ecclesia ex circumcisione* and an *ecclesia ex gentibus*. The new covenant, it is claimed, applies quite differently to each, since it neither releases the former from their obligations under the old covenant nor transfers those obligations to the latter. All of this is posited so as to repudiate as thoroughly as possible the Marcionite tendency that, in their eyes, has marred Christianity for nearly two millennia and implicated it in the Holocaust.

To this several things must be said in reply, if we are not to nullify Paul's critique of the Jewish authorities and their allies who made themselves enemies of the gospel. First, just as it is a mistake to read Paul through the lenses of Reformation law/gospel dualism—the antisupersessionists are right to think it a mistake, though they are wrong to project that mistake back into the patristic era—so it is a mistake to read Paul through the lenses of Holocaust guilt. Second, the Holocaust was a neo-pagan phenomenon that cannot fairly be charged against Christianity, though many historic abuses of Jews can be charged against Christians. Third, Paul is not wrong but right to attack faithless Jews for their faithlessness and to warn them of judgment, just as he warns faithless Gentiles; nor is the Church wrong to pray for "*perfidis Iudaeis*"—Jews who lack faith in *Yeshua Hamashiach*—even if, for fear of being misunderstood, it no longer uses that expression. Fourth, trust in Torah in opposition to trust in Jesus is indeed a form of faithlessness, if Torah truly is ordered to and fulfilled by him. Fifth, the Church is correct to say, as Paul has said, that there is but one Lord, one faith, one baptism—one Israel of God, with one path to salvation. Sixth, the old Mosaic form of the covenant with Abraham is superseded by the new, eucharistic form it has been given through the self-offering of Jesus Christ, who himself supersedes every mediator who came before him, including Moses and Aaron. There has been a change in the mediation and in the priesthood, hence a corresponding change in the law (Heb. 7–10), a change not confined to cultic law. Seventh, the supersession of the Mosaic form of the covenant does not mean that Israel κατὰ σάρκα, insofar as it remains outside the Church, ceases either to be elect or to be obligated by Torah. It does mean that it cannot be saved without being led by Torah to Jesus and that, being found in him, it is liberated eucharistically from the stewardship of the law of Moses for life according to the perfect law, the royal law, the law of liberty. While God wills Israel κατὰ σάρκα to continue to exist and preserves it as such— the whole batch remaining holy, as Paul explains in Rom. 11, because of those who have believed or shall believe—God does not will it to live outside the freedom of Christ but always invites it into that freedom. Eighth, this liberty means freedom for the Jewish believer, like Paul, to become all things to all people, so that by all means he may help to save some (1 Cor. 9:19–23). It means that Timothy may be circumcised, though not that he must be circumcised; that converts to Jesus in Jerusalem at the time of the protocouncil might carry on living much as they were accustomed to living, not that there was in perpetuity to be an *ecclesia Iudaeorum* alongside an *ecclesia Gentium*. "For we are the circumcision—we who worship by the Spirit of God and boast in Christ Jesus and put no confidence in the flesh" (Phil. 3:3 AT). This "we" cannot be divided along ethnic lines, not only because the epistle is addressed to "all the saints in Christ Jesus who are at Philippi" but because every fiber of Pauline theology forbids it.

Is this nothing, however, as the antisupersessionists charge, but a closeted form of anti-Semitism? Nothing, that is, but a mandate for Jews to be assimilated to a basically Gentile reality? Absurd! For the Church is not basically Gentile. The Church is a *tertium quid*, or rather (as even the pagans quickly grasped) a *genus tertium*. It is a new humanity, made *ex Iudaeis* and *ex gentibus*, in which all come together as one new man in Christ. Where the Church appears basically Gentile, it is not because of a numerical predominance of Gentiles, to whom Jews are being assimilated, but because the Church itself, Jew and Gentile, is being assimilated falsely to the world. And what shall we say to that? Better a non-Christian Jew, striving to keep Torah without knowledge of Christ, than a Christian Jew who does not know what it means to be Christian. Better even a non-Christian Gentile than a Christian Gentile who has forgotten what it means to be Christian; for that one, as Erik Peterson has said, is capable of almost anything, including the Holocaust (Peterson 2011: 65ff.). He is capable of becoming the man of lawlessness, whom we will meet when we come to 2 Thessalonians.

2:17–20 But we, brethren, being thus torn away from you for a brief moment, in person not in heart, earnestly sought to see your face, with much longing. Hence we determined to come to you—I, Paul, more than once—but Satan hindered us. For who, if not you, is our hope or joy or crown of boasting before our Lord Jesus at his parousia? You yourselves are our glory and our joy.

The nurse himself becomes the orphan when torn away from his beloved children in the Lord, from those whom God has given him as spiritual progeny. He sees them not; they cannot converse face to face. He is deprived of them, however, in person not in heart, outwardly not inwardly. They remain drawn to each other at the deepest possible level.

Some three centuries later, in the thick of the trinitarian debates, this word πρόσωπον ("person" and "face") would attract the word ὑπόστασις as a synonym, stealing it away from οὐσία, so that the idea of the person might have ontological and not merely phenomenological weight. The personal would be what is innermost, what runs deepest, not what is on the surface, what makes an appearance. Person and heart would then mean much the same thing. But this weight, this gravitational force of the heart, is already being felt. If we are not yet at the idea of personhood, with Paul we are beginning to discover a new basis for spiritual kinship and so for the person as such. We are beginning to discover fellowship (κοινωνία) and spiritual friendship as something still more fundamental than we already knew it to be—something at once more instant and more lasting, more intimate and more remote, more spacious and more capable of growth, than we imagined. Why? Because of a perichoretic capacity granted by the Holy Spirit—as much mocked as mimicked by our modern technological prowess and virtual communities, where faces appear everywhere and persons nowhere (→4:13–18).

77

It is not only those who have known him face to face who have felt this gravitational force in Paul, and been attracted by it, for the force is not Paul's alone, but the Spirit's. It is a curvature in the divine Love, particular to the persons in question. Anyone who is well educated may know that Paul's voice "passes like thunder through all the world." But who longs for Paul? Who returns his affection? Who feels deprived of his presence, as he felt deprived of the Thessalonians? Those who know him in the Lord as their father in faith.

> O St Paul, where is he that was called
> the nurse of the faithful, caressing his sons?
> Who is that affectionate mother who declares everywhere
> that she is in labour for her sons?
> Sweet nurse, sweet mother,
> who are the sons you are in labour with, and nurse,
> but those whom by teaching the faith of Christ
> you bear and instruct?
> Or who is a Christian after your teaching
> who is not born into the faith and established in it by you?
> And if in that blessed faith we are born
> and nursed by other apostles also,
> it is most of all by you,
> for you have laboured and done more than them all in this.

Thus Anselm, in his *Oratio ad Sanctum Paulum* (2006). One gets the sense that Paul, were he able to do so, would come as urgently and as earnestly to Anselm, or to us, and indeed that he does so both in his letters and, by the grace of God, in the *communio sanctorum*. For he desires to encourage our hearts and to be encouraged by us. Why do we ask the intercession of the saints, except that we know them to maintain this friendship in the Spirit, for Christ's sake, even with those whom they have not met or whose friendship they no longer require? One can have great affection for a poet like Virgil or a philosopher and statesman like Cicero, but one cannot know that it would be requited. It is otherwise with Paul and the saints, and with everyone whose friendship is grounded not in natural affections alone but in the Lord. We love Paul, as Augustine says (*Trin.* 8.9), for his just soul; but we love him also for his passionate love, through which we glimpse Christ's own love.

▨ Chrysostom's peroration on friendship at 2:7–8 might well have been placed here instead, for Paul is now speaking all at once as nurse, soul mate, and friend, as one who in the Lord loves deeply and is deeply in love—if by love we mean the charity that includes and does not exclude φιλία, *amicitia*, but sets it on a higher level. "What is a friend," asks Ambrose (*De officiis* 3.134), "but a partner in love, to whom you unite and attach your soul, and with whom you blend so as to desire from being two to become one; to whom you entrust yourself as to a second self, from whom you fear nothing, and from whom you demand nothing dishonourable for the sake of your own advantage?" Spiritual friendship, the kind Chrysostom considers, is the kind that emerges where grace permeates and elevates this wonderful human capacity, and also liberates it from its privacy and exclusiveness (that is, from the potential flaw that concerned C. S. Lewis in *The Four Loves*). Grace in the Holy Spirit, who in God is the very *vinculum amoris*, makes it possible for one to have many such friendships and to have them even without all the conditions that normally attach to them on the natural level. Grace also makes it possible for one to be "as careful of his friend's soul as of his own" (*Hom.* 2) and to be more gratified in doing good to the friend than in receiving good from him; or indeed, as Chrysostom observes and Aquinas also (cf. *ST* 1-2.4.8 and 2-2.23), to do good to the friend that the friend may be more able to do good himself, to enter more fully into that divine economy of giving about which we spoke at 1:6–10, the economy in which one is always "counting out the increase" that accrues to the Lord through the other (*Haer.* 3.17.3).

In all of this Paul is beyond his own personality, even his literary personality. He is beyond the classic treatments of friendship in Aristotle and Cicero, about which he is not even thinking. No doubt he is well aware, as they were, that genuine friendship is a school of virtue, indeed, *the* school of virtue; that it is a divine blessing that helps keep us on the path to happiness. Conversely, he knows that virtue is essential for genuine friendship (Cicero, *Laelius de Amicitia* 27), especially friendship in Christ. But he also knows and has experienced something they did not know. He knows what Augustine would later discover, that real friendship is possible only where the highest virtue, love for God, is shared in common. He has already anticipated Aquinas, who marveled at the divine expansion of friendship to include unequals: Moses is the friend of God; Mary, Martha, and Lazarus are the friends, the intimate friends, of the Son of God; John leans on the bosom of him who dwells in the bosom of the Father! He has learned what Anselm and Aelred, among others, would learn from him, to love in truth and to be truthful in love. If his epistles are passionate in just this way, it is because he suffers a longing placed in his heart by God, a hunger for spiritual unity, which means also for the unity of faith, for "complete accord on all subjects human and divine" (Cicero, *Laelius de Amicitia* 6). "A great thing is friendship, and how great, no one can learn, and no discourse represent, but experience itself." It is for want of this friendship that the heresies appear, remarks Chrysostom, which through pride disrupt and divide the faithful (*Hom.* 2; cf. John 17; 1 Tim. 6; 2 Tim.). It is for the sake of this friendship that Paul moves back and forth, with such ease, from doctrinal instruction to professions of love.

How long Paul was in Thessaloniki before being forced to depart in secret, one step ahead of the police, is not known, but it was long enough to win a large number of converts from among the God-fearing Gentiles, set an example of honest work, and receive support more than once from Philippi (cf. Weima 2014: 26). It was long enough also to see serious opposition form among those Jews who would not follow their brethren into the kingdom he was preaching, nor indeed accompany those Gentiles whom they had themselves brought near to the kingdom, of whom they now became jealous—jealous enough to pursue Paul to Beroea, as we have already noted. On the other hand, it was not long enough to complete the mission he had in view, so perhaps it was only a couple of months. Jason and his fellows were forced to post bond when the apostles could not be found, and Paul was doubtless anxious about their fate.

Perhaps this bond was among the hindrances that kept Paul from returning? He and Silas—not young Timothy, apparently, who later did return—were charged with "acting against the decrees of Caesar" (Acts 17:7; cf. Weima 2014: 34f.), and accomplices such as Jason were implicated. Which decrees is not specified, though "saying that there is another king, Jesus," would certainly seem to qualify. Jason and others had to give some assurances, including monetary ones, that it was not their intention to violate any imperial decrees, and this may well have included assurances that Paul and Silas would not reappear in their midst preaching this other king. Whether they made any attempt to explain that the king in question had another sort of kingdom, and that his followers were not revolutionaries who denied Caesar's temporal authority, we don't know. This explanation would not have been easy and, if made, may not have been very persuasive, as the apostles did in fact preach a king who can command what Caesar cannot command and who can overrule Caesar, if he pleases. In short, it was not the case then, nor is it now, that Κύριος Ἰησοῦς stood in no competition with Κύριος Καῖσαρ.

▨ The Jason who evangelized Corfu (→2:5–9) would not escape imprisonment by the king of that island, nor would his early converts escape martyrdom. Even the king's daughter would be martyred, after King Jesus inspired her (through their example) to sell her jewelry and give the proceeds to the poor. That part of the Jason legend may serve to remind us of this competition, which even in Christendom remained a competition, because temporal and eternal interests do not always coincide. If in our time and place we think we have managed, through the separation of church and state, to minimize the competition, we ought to recall Leo XIII's observation: "The Almighty, therefore, has given the charge of the human race to two powers, the ecclesiastical and the civil, the one being set over divine, and the other over human, things. Each in its kind is supreme, each has fixed limits within which it is contained, limits which are defined by the nature and special object of the province of each. . . . [Nevertheless] one and the same thing—related differently, but still remaining one and the same thing—might belong to the jurisdiction and determination of both" (*Immortale Dei* 13). Which is to say, the kingdom of King Jesus and the kingdom of Caesar or of Corfu do not exist in splendid isolation, one from the other. Neither the princess nor her diamonds could claim to be wholly in the one and not at all in the other, and hence immune from all conflict. Likewise with ourselves, and with our health or education systems, with marriage and public morals, with civil liberties, and so forth; there are many spheres that occasion serious disagreement between the city of God and the city of man. The gospel proclaimed in the former is often quite alien and even threatening to the latter. Where that is so, the posting of bonds or other legal action does not usually resolve the problem, but represents at best a temporary truce.

Whatever hindrance Paul was alluding to, whether at law or elsewhere, he put it down ultimately to ὁ σατανᾶς, the great adversary of the gospel and accuser of the brethren. This adversary was the same whom Jesus had faced and overcome, though not without posting his very life as a bond; for in the wisdom of God the author of death was conquered "by the death of the author of life," whom, "though there was nothing deserving of death in him," Satan had killed all the same (*Trin.* 13.23; cf. Mark 4 and 14 with Zech. 3; Heb. 7–10). Satan would kill Paul as well in due course, doubtless with much evil delight, since Paul, or Saul as he was then, had once been in his service, setting out to "lay waste" the Judean churches before being intercepted and claimed by Jesus (Acts 8:3). Paul knew full well that the adversary hated him and was determined to thwart his new mission wherever and however he could. If Satan had marshaled all his forces against Jesus, and against the apostles and prophets in Jerusalem, trying to prevent the mission from getting underway at all, would he not do the same as the mission moved into Gentile territory?

Paul also knew that Satan's cause was a lost cause. Death itself had been defeated and was no longer able to hold its prey. Like Stephen, the protomartyr whose death Paul had approved, he himself had caught a glimpse of Jesus standing at the right hand of God in heaven. His life work was to give witness to that one irrepressible fact (→2 Thess. 3:16). Yet he was well aware that Satan could not and would not sue for peace. Satan's fall was irrevocable, his situation irrecoverable. His place in heaven was lost, but his place on earth remained. As John would later write, "When the dragon saw that he had been thrown down to the earth," he became angry and made war against "those who keep the commandments of

God and bear testimony to Jesus" (Rev. 12:13, 17). That included Paul, perhaps especially Paul.

The devil, since the enthronement of Jesus in heaven, has been bound to earth. Through the success of the gospel of Jesus, he has been bound even on earth—consigned to the infernal realm of those whose hope has already been extinguished. He is no longer free to deceive the nations at will, now that life and immortality have been brought to light (2 Tim. 1:10). But he is able to harass and hinder the emissaries of the gospel, and to stir up strife among the nations. From his bunker he still wages war. Eventually he will be permitted to mount one last, unrestrained offensive (Rev. 20:1–10). The stage for that is now being set.

Today's emissaries, therefore, must like Paul anticipate many hindrances. They will know both protection and violation. They will rise and they will fall, and they will rise again. They will appear to have failed, but they will triumph, just as Jesus appeared to have failed but triumphed. Meanwhile, they must be careful that Satan does not steal a march on them, stirring up strife in the Church itself. And how does he do that? By exploiting their own sins and carelessness; by noticing when they have strayed after him (1 Tim. 5:15), like prey foolishly trailing the beast of prey, which at the right time turns to devour them. By exploiting their hardness of heart also, and their refusals to forgive (2 Cor. 2:10–11). By disguising himself as an angel of light so as to gain access to the Church. By teaching others, not least among the clergy and the theologians, to disguise themselves, the better to pervert the faith and to sear consciences (2 Cor. 11:1–15; cf. 1 Tim. 4). For Satan is both "a liar and the father of lies" (John 8:44). If he can no longer deceive the nations freely, then he will seek to deceive the people of God and so destroy their light to the nations (*VS* 1). He will claim synagogues for himself, and churches also. Where he dares to appear, he must be rebuked and driven out. That is a vital feature of the mission of Jesus, who will not share the people whom God has given him with the great adversary of his Father's will (Acts 10:38; 1 John 3:8). It belongs also, then, to the mission of the Church. The followers of Jesus cast out demons and tread upon serpents. They are those who conquer, who overcome, by standing fast in the faith (Luke 10:17–20; Rev. 2–3).

■ "Your adversary the devil prowls around like a roaring lion, seeking some one to devour. Resist him, firm in your faith" (1 Pet. 5:8–9). "Although you see the devil thwarting you ten thousand times, never fall back" (Chrysostom, *Homilies on the Statutes* 1.30, in ACCS 9:71). Very good advice, for every faithful witness of Jesus will experience temptations and hindrances, and not a few will encounter what can only be considered the work of the adversary himself. Yet a word of caution is in order. We must be well prepared, not flippant, lest our lot be that of the sons of Sceva (Acts 19:11–16). And we should not be like Luther, who saw in all that opposed him, even all who disagreed with him, the activity of Satan (Eire 2016: 185ff.). That is to aggrandize both ourselves and Satan, who is certainly not omnipresent, though he has a myriad of servants and devices in support of his cause. We should not be lulled into thinking he is sulking in his bunker rather than hard at work. Neither, however, should we become fixated on one who has, after all, been cast out of heaven—something he wishes us to forget. His destiny is the lake of fire. He is already a vanquished foe, a lesson in futility. Where we do encounter his minions or recognize his enterprise or suffer from his successes, we should learn patience and humility and firmness of faith. In our own successes we must not become puffed up. For the devil is a judo master, as capable of using our strengths against us as our weaknesses. In our failures or our suffering we must not become discouraged. For God permits such "messengers from Satan" precisely to keep us from thinking too highly of ourselves (2 Cor. 12:7), Satan's own vice. Certainly we must never let our fear of him or of those who do his bidding get the best of us. "Do not fear those who kill the body but cannot kill the soul; rather fear him who can destroy both soul and body in hell" (Matt. 10:28). "Fear not, I am the first and the last, and the living one; I died, and behold I am alive for evermore, and I have the keys of Death and Hades" (Rev. 1:17–18; cf. Wis. 16:13). Those who, for Christ's sake, suffer the worst the enemy is capable of doing, shall, with Christ, emerge to eternal life and eternal glory. They participate in the binding of Satan (Rev. 20:1–6). They cannot be bound by him or by death itself—so long, that is, as they keep the faith and a good conscience, and "wage the good warfare" even unto death (1 Tim. 1:18–20; 2 Tim. 4:6–8).

We may pause to consider how Satan became the adversary, the better to avoid becoming anything like him ourselves. Anselm's *De casu diaboli* remains the best account, and it begins where we must begin; that is, with the question, "What do you have that you have not received?" If it is pride that goes before a fall (Prov. 16:18), it is the kind of pride that is rooted in ingratitude. Anselm reminds us straightaway that "no creature has anything of itself," but has its being and its goodness (for God makes nothing that is not good) as a gift. For rational creatures, this gift includes rectitude of will and the power to preserve it. It includes the capacity to pursue justice as well as happiness, that they may have a hand in their own advance toward God. No one can deprive them of this justice, though they themselves can choose to abandon it: which they do the moment they perversely deny the gift-nature of their being, the moment they refuse to lift up their hearts to the Lord in humble gratitude. Thus it is with Lucifer, when he begins to will independently of God, to will as if his will were strictly his own, as if he had it from himself, as if it were autonomous and subject to no one—a prerogative of the divine will alone (*DCD* 4). It is not in willing to be like God that Lucifer falls, but in willing to be like God in such a way as to be "God" to and for himself; in willing to will autonomously in that sense, which is not possible.

What he was willing concretely at the time, we do not know. Perhaps, like Eve, whom he later deceived, he was willing something that God also willed but willing it wrongly, out of time, out of sequence. It does not matter. He willed in such a way as to do a fundamental injustice to the great Giver. He willed ungratefully and placed himself outside the economy of giving and receiving that, by the grace of God, is the whole foundation of creaturely life. He willed as if he himself were God, and so set himself over against God as the adversary. Everyone who wills like that partakes of his perversity. Everyone who wills like that commits the sin of covetousness, which is the opposite of gratitude. Covetousness is idolatry (Col. 3:5), not merely because it sets something up as being more desirable to possess than God himself, but because it sets up the will of the one who desires it as a will equal to, indeed greater than, God's own will. It remains only to add that in this sacrifice of justice for the sake of some imagined happiness, both are lost; for there is and can be no happiness without justice, as Anselm further explains in *Cur deus homo*.

It is not uncommon today to demythologize the devil by regarding him as "shorthand for evil at its most potent" (Hastings 2000: 166); that is, as a literary or conceptual distillation from the acts, structures, and psychology of evil. This will not do. The problem here is not nominalism, which doesn't really know how to say anything more about "evil" than about the devil. Nor does the difficulty lie entirely in that skepticism about the supernatural that bedevils the modern scientific mindset. It does not lie in the historian's skepticism either; that is, in the peculiar fact that a figure that barely appears in the Old Testament is so prominent in the New. There are, after all, other critical elements of the New Testament—belief in the resurrection of the dead, for example—that only come to the fore in the intertestamental period. Nor yet does it lie in the tension internal to the New Testament, the tension between the great power of Satan as "the ruler of this world" and his impotence as a defeated foe. For the already/not yet of Christian eschatology applies just as much to the defeat of the devil as to the defeat of death, through fear of which the devil holds all men in bondage (Heb. 2:14–15). Again, the problem with recognizing the devil does not lie in the wildly conflicting images cast up by the Christian imagination. Is he the theatrical buffoon of the late Middle Ages or the noble if tragic figure of *Paradise Lost*, in whom the modern autonomy ideal begins to take shape? Surely he is neither, even if in some sense he is both, for in the moral sense he is a proper fool. No, the problem lies in the utility of anonymity, in the depersonalization of the devil and so also of evil, our own evil.

The devil is no mere shorthand for a larger, more mysterious something called evil. Evil is not in fact something, but always and only a willed turning from what is or ought to be, from what has being and goodness. Its effects on what has being and goodness are real enough, however, and these effects may be called evil, just as those who habitually attack what has being and goodness may be called evil, together with the organizations and structures they put in place to perpetuate evil. The devil, who inaugurates and afterward incites such a turning, is most certainly real. He is called by Jesus "the evil one" (ὁ πονηρός,

Matt. 5:37; 6:13; 13:19, 38), the one from whose grasp we need to be delivered and should pray to be delivered. "Lead us not into temptation but deliver us from the evil one" (καὶ μὴ εἰσενέγκῃς ἡμᾶς εἰς πειρασμόν ἀλλὰ ῥῦσαι ἡμᾶς ἀπὸ τοῦ πονηροῦ): rhetorically this sends us back to Jesus's πειρασμός in the desert after his baptism by water and forward to his πειρασμός in the garden before his baptism in blood. In both cases he is the victor. We also are victorious with his help, then, but we rightly ask God to lead us along paths less perilous than that which our champion trod (cf. Ps. 23). We do not take the evil one lightly, even as a defeated foe.

At 1 Thess. 3:5, Satan is referred to as "the tempter" (ὁ πειράζων). He is already known as such in the book of Job, where, operating only in the background, he is allowed to try that putatively righteous man, inviting him to despair of life and goodness, to curse God and die. If in the New Testament Satan is suddenly thrust into the foreground, it is because a righteous man has arrived on the scene whom he *must* try, whom he can by no means ignore. Poor Job knew nothing of Satan, who orchestrated the destruction of his wealth and health and family, hoping thus to destroy also his soul. But Jesus is another matter. Jesus has come quite specifically to effect the destruction of Satan and all his works (1 John 3:7–8). In the presence of Jesus, Satan can no longer remain hidden or anonymous. He is outed as a personal agent who is driven by envy, "a thing foreign to God" (*Haer.* 5.24.4). He is disclosed as a covetous and malefic spirit who seeks, with other such spirits, to dominate man.

Those who treat the devil as a mere cipher for something else—or, as some would have it, for nothing at all, for an illusion or a bad dream—tend to refer their own evil to something else. They merely reproduce in another form Eve's canard, "the devil made me do it." They also overlook the fact that they are entrenching the very dualism that Christianity is at pains to repudiate (cf. Hastings 2000: 164f.). For if evil is not a reality rooted in persons, a quasi-something generated by their willful perversion of the gift of reason and volition (*DCD* 11)—if it is not the product of those who have "arrogated to themselves a false likeness to God" in opposition to his Son and Word (*CDH* 2.9)—then evil is either something God did not make and cannot overcome, for it preexisted even the creation of persons, or it is something God *did* make because God himself is not pure, not simple, not wholly good. Alternatively, though this is really just another way of putting the latter option, it is a dream that God himself has while he is generating the world. So either God's adversary is invincible, and "the true likeness of the Father" has come in vain, or God is his own adversary. Such is the dilemma faced by those who do not recognize the serpent in Gen. 3 as a cipher for the devil and instead suppose the devil to be a cipher for something else, or for nothing.

That modern man is thus deceived, even after that prototypical thug or "strong man" has been exposed and "bound" by the Son, testifies to the fact that he does not want to acknowledge his own fall. Instead, he has doubled down, adopting as the very standard of his personhood the devil's idea of autonomy, willing as if his will were subject to no one. In so doing, he has set himself against reason, against the scriptures, and against the Church (*Trin.* 4.10). He is no longer "in his senses" but has reverted to the state of the Gadarenes (cf. Matt. 8:28–36; 12:22–29). We will discover later, in treating 2 Thess. 2, that Paul expected something like this to develop. Anselm, arguably, saw it coming (Farrow 2018g: chap. 7). He also knew the antidote, for Augustine had already observed that the devil is defeated by justice, not by power. One learns justice by learning to want nothing wrongly, thus following the Son rather than the serpent (*Trin.* 13.6ff.; cf. Matt. 4:1–11). The hindrances of the latter, like other ills of the age, can be redeployed as means by which to defeat him—to defeat him in the same way Christ defeated him, by thankful persistence in doing the will of the Father under trial and so by training oneself for life in that kingdom where power has been added to justice. This does entail seeking power now, but only to use "in an odd way" against oneself for oneself, so that one may become truly good (*Trin.* 13.17; cf. Col. 1:9–14). It entails seeking the Lord by prayer and fasting and by means of the Holy Eucharist, where he may always be found. For when the Great Thanksgiving is rendered through, with, and in the Just One (ὁ δίκαιος, Acts 22:14), so is the proper retort to the ingratitude of the evil one. "Let us give thanks to the Lord our God. It is right and just!"

The enemy had not only contrived to force Paul and Silas from Thessaloniki. He had managed to block the road by which they might return, to make it for the moment impassable, perhaps through a network of watchful opponents. Paul looks forward to its clearance (→3:11), to the restoration of face-to-face communion with the Thessalonians. Meanwhile he wants them to know that, far from moving on and forgetting about them, he longs for them. Their futures are bound together in Christ. They themselves are the proof of his service to Christ, of the success of his mission. They will be his "crown of boasting" when the Lord appears and his stewardship is assessed. Whether this wreath or crown is an image drawn from the games or from some other political arena hardly matters, except to say that this is neither a game nor a political scheme of some kind. What becomes of them is by no means a matter of indifference to him. They need not fear that he is merely an agitator, spreading a novel and dangerous theopolitical doctrine, then leaving them behind to foot the bill. They themselves, whose faith has made them ready to welcome the Lord at his arrival, are his true delight and his hope of glory. That they should stand approved before the Lord Jesus, when he comes, is both what Paul hopes to offer the Lord and to receive back from him as a reward. That goes for the Philippians as well (Phil. 4:1) and for the rest of Paul's converts.

He is going to say more about the parousia, to which he has already alluded at 1:10. If 2:19 contains the first extant Christian use of that word, it is plainly

formulaic from the outset, and in his letters to the Thessalonians Paul uses it liberally, more liberally than it is used in any other canonical text. Almost as plainly,
it is deployed by analogy with the imperial parousia, not a remote prospect in a
city such as Thessaloniki, which from time to time could hope for a royal visit of
one sort or another (or fear one, for that matter, as when Theodosius notoriously
sent his troops to massacre some 7,000 of them over the Butheric affair). Did
Paul expect, within their lifetime, *the* royal visit, the *adventus personalis, visibilis,
beatificus, terribilis, et gloriosus* of the one appointed by God to "judge the world
in righteousness" (Acts 17:31)? Was the day fixed by God for that grand assize,
which Paul proclaimed also in Athens, a day that belonged to their own generation? Or did Paul expect his and their mutual glorying in the advent of Christ
to take place only by way of the resurrection of the dead (cf. Tertullian, *Res.* 24)?
Let us wait and see what he says that may cast light on that question, noting in
the meantime that, while communion in person is what is longed for as regards
the Lord himself, there will be no such communion without passing through the
crucible of judgment.

Whenever and however we appear before the Lord, whether at the Eucharist or at the
hour of our death or at the parousia and resurrection, there is a reckoning that takes place
(Rom. 14:7–12; 1 Cor. 3:12–15; 4:5; 11:17–34; 2 Cor. 5:1–10; 2 Tim. 4:1–8; cf. Matt.
25; 1 Pet. 4). So "we make it our aim to please him" and we beg the prayers of those who
have pleased him: "Hail Mary, full of grace . . . pray for us sinners, now and at the hour of
our death." Though, as we commune with Christ in his passion, we look for the parousia,
the hour of our own death does not cease to concern us. For should that hour intervene,
we know that we will come before God, the judge of all men, in the interiority of the
naked soul. We know that in the very fact of our death his judgment is confirmed (Gen.
2:17), and we know also that this judgment is not merely general but rather peculiar to
each of us. We are already known by him in every particularity, and every particularity
will be accounted for (cf. Ps. 139; Eccl. 12:13–14). Just so, we will be consigned, as the
Old Testament hints and Jesus in the parable of Dives and Lazarus confirms, to the fate
prepared for us, though that fate in its fullness awaits the last day, the day of the Lord and
his grand assize.

Of these things also Paul will speak further anon, but what shall we say here of the parousia? The word itself has the sense either of arrival or of presence, or of both, and is often
used nontechnically (e.g., at 1 Cor. 16:17 or 2 Cor. 7:6–7). As a technical term, referring
to royal visits with all their pomp and ceremony, its background is Hellenic, not Hebraic.
One might, however, think in Hebrew terms of the cloud of the Presence descending
on Sinai, on the tabernacle, on the temple of Solomon, and on the new creation. Or of

the high priest, descending from the holy place on Yom Kippur, carrying the blessings of God for the people waiting in the temple courts (Sir. 50). Conversely, one might think of David, arriving with the ark at Mount Zion (2 Sam. 6). Or of the parousia of the Son of Man in heaven, his appearance before the Ancient of Days, as foretold in the vision of Dan. 7, that he might receive dominion over all things and inaugurate the new creation. That indeed one must think of, for it lies in the background of Matt. 24, where παρουσία is used by Jesus (or by Matthew in translation) four times, in such a way as to correlate the power given to the Son of Man in heaven with his eventual display of that power on earth, which will bring about the close of the age. (Matthew 24:21–22 is expanded in graphic detail in Rev. 16, and the allusions in Matt. 23:37–39 and 24:32–35 to the impending fall of Jerusalem that frame this discourse are extended to "Babylon" in Rev. 17–18, with Dan. 7 still in view.) One also finds the word occasionally in the general epistles, where it is used in a technical sense at Jas. 5:7–8; 2 Pet. 1:16; 3:4; and 1 John 2:28. In Paul it crops up as a technical term only at 1 Cor. 15:23 and here in Thessalonians: four times in the first letter (2:19; 3:13; 4:15; 5:23) and three times in the second (2:1, 8, 9, including one application to the man of lawlessness). Ἀποκάλυψις is used at 1 Cor. 1:7 to refer to the same event as "the revealing of our Lord Jesus Christ," while the verb ἀποκαλύπτω is used several times, analogously, of the man of lawlessness in 2 Thess. 2. Ἐπιφανεία is deployed in the Pastorals to emphasize the majesty of his coming, for with him there will not be, as with Augustus, the mere suggestion of the divine! (See, e.g., 1 Tim. 6:14–16; cf. Luke 17:24, 30. On all three terms, see further Milligan 1908: 145–51.)

Of that majesty a foretaste is already on display, of course, in the events described in the Gospels, which Ignatius refers to as "the parousia of the Savior" (*Phld.* 9; cf. Justin, *Dial.* 32). The Orthodox emphasis on the transfiguration reflects a keen awareness of that. Unfortunately it also tends in certain quarters to a conflation of two distinct displays of majesty: that which 2 Pet. 1 refers to as "the power and coming" (δύναμιν καὶ παρουσίαν) on the holy mountain and that which 2 Pet. 3 refers to as "the promise of his coming," a future coming at which the very elements will melt. (The glory of the cross and the glory of the resurrection likewise suffer conflation, then; cf. Raith 2018: 10–22, 36–47.)

"We preach not one advent only of Christ, but a second also," says Cyril of Jerusalem, "far more glorious than the former. For the former gave a view of his patience; but the latter brings with it the crown of a divine kingdom." Paul hopes to wear a crown as well, a crown of converts, of willing subjects who will welcome the returning King; who will say, as was said in Jerusalem, "Blessed is he that comes in the name of the Lord!" These converts, however, need to remember that Christ's comings are indeed two. "In his first coming, 'he endured the cross, despising shame'; in his second, he will come attended by a host of angels, receiving glory" (*CL* 15.1, in *NPNF²* 7:104). To be ready for the second, they must have a share in the first. They must learn endurance. And about this, Paul has already a word to say, as he begins to draw toward the conclusion of his *narratio*.

3:1–5 Therefore, when we could hold out no longer, we thought it best to be left in Athens alone and sent Timothy, our brother and God's coworker in the gospel of Christ, to strengthen you and to rally your faith, that no one be shaken by these tribulations. For you yourselves know that to such we are appointed. Even when we were with you, we were warning you that we are about to suffer tribulation—just as you see also happened. For this reason I, too, when I could no longer bear it, sent to find out about your faith, lest somehow the tempter had tempted you and our labor were in vain.

There is a certain irony in the fact that neither Paul's colleagues, nor he himself, can endure the uncertainty to which separation has exposed them. What is happening in Thessaloniki? Are the jewels in their crown firmly fixed, or are they beginning to drop away? Is the love that bound them to the apostles, and to one another, losing its ardor? Has persecution driven them for refuge to the relative comfort of their former communities, whether Jewish or Greek? Have they been able to withstand the pressure, or have they begun abandoning their profession of Christ? The tempter tempts, and sometimes he tempts by attempts at coercion. He managed, after all, to drive out the apostles and prevent their return—has he also managed to deceive their converts and persuade them to fall back in line? Is it possible that Paul and Silas have sown on rocky ground, gaining only those who receive the word of God with joy but, having no root in themselves, endure a short while, then, "when tribulation or persecution arises on account of the word," immediately fall away (Matt. 13:20–21)? Being human, and themselves imperfect in faith, they are troubled by the thought that their work may have been in vain after all. Timothy, they conclude, must go back and find out, though it is apparent that Paul is loath to part with him.

Their torment, we may safely assume, is the torment of love; the same that is known to anyone who cares more for the beloved than for themselves. Despite talk of a crown of boasting, it has little to do with their own prospects at the parousia and everything to do with the prospects of their Thessalonian brethren. Not their immediate prospects of escaping attempts at coercion by the authorities—we must always put it this way, for no one *can* be coerced to compromise faith or conscience; they can only be punished for refusing to do so—but rather their future prospects, indeed their eternal prospects, as determined by their faithfulness to the Lord, to the one true Savior and Judge of all.

Luke says nothing of Timothy's clandestine mission to Thessaloniki, and the timetable seems a bit tight; nevertheless, it must have been managed. Acts 17 tells us that Paul was run out of Beroea also, by the same network of Jewish opponents using the same techniques, but that Silas and Timothy were able to remain while Paul went on to Athens to wait there for the rest of his team. It appears from Luke's account that they did not actually join him again until Corinth (Acts 18:5), but Luke may be simplifying things to keep his narrative flowing. Timothy's return to Thessaloniki, of which we learn here, certainly took place during this period. The most natural reading of 1 Thess. 3:1 is that Silas and Timothy did indeed come to Paul, however briefly, in Athens, Paul and Silas being left alone there as soon as Timothy departed on his solo mission. He could have reached Thessaloniki by sea in just a few days (Campbell 2014: 193). In that scenario, Silas perhaps waited with Paul until Timothy returned, the letter was dispatched, and they parted company again on individual missions or errands until they were reunited in Corinth. We might also posit, however—given that Luke's account shows no trace at all of any teamwork in Athens—that Silas departed to Philippi or some other destination about the same time that Timothy left for Thessaloniki (Weima 2014: 208). Or that they were never together in Athens at all, Paul signaling by courier to Beroea his approval of Timothy's solo mission. (That would account for his "I, too" remark at 3:5, requiring only that we read 3:1 as suggesting that Paul had expected Silas to arrive shortly in Athens, whereas Silas waited instead for Timothy in Beroea before they embarked together for Corinth to catch up with Paul.) On either of the latter two scenarios, the letter would have been written from Corinth immediately upon their reunification there. (Malherbe 2000: 68f. supports Corinth as the place of writing, while Campbell, in an ambitious reconstruction of Paul's itinerary undertaken without the same regard for Acts, supports Athens.)

Timothy is now praised as συνεργὸν τοῦ θεοῦ, God's own coworker (unless we render it in the weaker sense of Rom. 16:21, where he appears as "my coworker," taking τοῦ θεοῦ to mean God-given). He has proved himself in his apostolic role, and the three of them together are fellow workers in service of the gospel and of the kingdom announced in the gospel, as indeed are all those who set out for Christ's sake, laboring in and for the truth (3 John 8; cf. Col. 4:11). He was sent not only to find out how they were faring but to encourage them in their faith, which is sure to be tested further. They must learn not to be shaken by tribulation and persecution, because God has appointed them, with the apostles, to a witness that the enemies of the gospel, the opponents of the kingdom, resist. Are they a city of believers set on a hill? A light for their countrymen, raised upon a lampstand rather than carefully shielded, like the lights of brigands and thieves (Matt. 5:15; cf. Eph. 5:11–14)? Then they must expect attempts to conquer them, to snuff them out, lest like Jesus himself they draw too many into the light and that light begin to shine on those who prefer darkness. Moreover, they must understand that the persecution they are already experiencing presages a greater tribulation to come. Of this they were forewarned and are warned again. (We should read προελέγομεν ὑμῖν ὅτι μέλλομεν θλίβεσθαι in such a way as to preserve the import of the present tense of μέλλομεν.) For tribulation may be sporadic, times of peace sought and hoped for. But tribulation is not anomalous, nor will it inevitably decrease with time—quite the contrary, as the second letter will elaborate and explain. Paul remains concerned that the Thessalonians should prepare themselves.

In times of persecution there is, of course, a need for the clandestine, as the Christians of the catacombs and Christians today in China and North Korea, or in Muslim lands, knew or know very well. Timothy would have slipped in and out of Thessaloniki as quietly as possible. Paul may have taught him a thing or two about that before letting him go (cf. Acts 9:23–25), for prudence does not compromise the witness to Christ, even when it requires extraordinary measures. (Immoral measures are another matter, for it is never licit to do evil that good may come.) Christ himself did not do at first the things he did at last, such as ride into Jerusalem on the foal of a donkey, or drive the money-changers from the temple. Only when he knew his hour had come did he forsake all caution. He did expect that hour, however, and prayerfully discern it. And he did not shy from it when it came (John 12:27; cf. 2:13–25).

3:6–10 But now, Timothy having returned to us from you and having told us the good news of your faith and love, and that you always speak well of us, longing to see us even as we long to see you—in all our distress and trouble we were comforted concerning you, brethren, because of this, through your faith. For now we live, if you are standing firm in the Lord. What thank offering can we render back to God for you, for all the joy with which we rejoice because of you before our God, night and day begging profusely that we might see your face and make up any deficiencies in your faith?

Faith and love are the very light of life, according to Paul. To live and thrive, to breathe freely and flourish—thus we may understand the hyperbolic ζῶμεν in 3:8—is to share faith and love before it is anything else. It is to share faith and love in spite of everything else, tribulations included. Their beloved converts are standing firm; therefore the apostles have a spring in their step! Unlike Cicero, they have something to live for. There is something quite natural about this, but also something supernatural. In God we all have our common source of life: "in him we live and move and have our being," as Paul had just reminded a pagan audience in Athens (Acts 17:28, quoting Epimenides). But the Christian way of doing so is unique. Christians have not merely a common source but a common life. They live not only from God but to God, as we saw earlier (→1:2–5). Because the Spirit of God lives and moves in them, they are not individuals but persons in communion. "With Christ I have been crucified. I live—yet no longer I, but Christ lives in me. The life I still live in the flesh I live by faith, the faith of the Son of God, who loved me and gave himself on my behalf" (Gal. 2:19–20 AT; cf. 3:2). This is liturgical language, such as we find in 1 Cor. 11. It is also ontological language, as John Zizioulas points out in *Being as Communion*. It is ethical language as well, for such persons live by a kind of participation in the other, by dwelling simultaneously in Christ and the neighbor, by being *for* Christ and the neighbor, as Luther observes in *The Freedom of the Christian*. If one flourishes, so does the other. If one is distressed, so is the other. They need not be together for this to be so, for the Spirit unites what is separated in time and space. Yet humans are bodily creatures who do desire to be face to face and side by side. And Paul—who may well have had some doubts about the hasty departure from Thessaloniki that was urged upon him as prudent—is quite naturally relieved to discover that the desire is still mutual, that they still think and speak well of him. Despite his failure to return and accompany them in their troubles, their remembrance (μνεία) of him is only good. No doubt they remember him by name whenever they remember the Lord in their eucharistic anamnesis. That, at all events, became the custom of the churches, which developed litanies for the purpose of mutual remembrance and reciprocal rejoicing before the Lord. Which is just where Paul begins when he takes up his pen to respond (→1:2–3; cf. Phil. 1:3–11).

It is through hearing of their faith and love, particularly their faith, that the apostles are comforted, for this is what will make the Thessalonians ready to greet the Lord when he comes. People standing firm in the Lord is a cause of great jubilation to them. They know that they are not themselves the source of the perseverance—that is a work of the Spirit—and in their jubilation they know themselves to be deeply indebted to God. What thanksgiving (εὐχαριστία) shall they return to him? While the question is rhetorical, Paul hopes and intends, God permitting, to render a thank offering that consists in making up the remaining deficiencies in the faith of the Thessalonians; that is, in their knowledge of God and his purposes. He wants to impart to them, as to all his converts, "the whole counsel of God" (Acts 20:27), a process for which there has not been time. That they do not lack the faith by which God is known, the *fides qua*, he has been reassured; it is otherwise with the *fides quae*, the faith or doctrine of God's holy Church, which they have received only in part. He implores God for the opportunity to resume the process of instructing them, and in the remainder of the letter he will make a start on that.

In the present pericope the *todah* (תּוֹדָה) tradition of Leviticus—which distinguishes the people of God from the heathen who neither honor God nor give thanks (Rom. 1:21)—again comes to the fore. In that tradition, the offering of a gift goes hand in hand with a "sacrifice of praise" (θυσία αἰνέσεως, Lev. 7:13 LXX). The latter is often formalized in a psalm or hymn displaying the divine comedy that catches up the person or people delivered from distress (see Exod. 15; 1 Chron. 16 and 29; 2 Chron. 29:30–36). The habit of thanksgiving, and the psalms that allow it articulation, have been incorporated into the eucharistic life of the Church and into the *communio sanctorum* (Eph. 5:19; Heb. 13:15; cf. Gray 2002; Pitre 2016: 56). Paul himself has been delivered from distress and he gives thanks, much as David gave thanks in Ps. 16, for example: "As for the saints in the land, they are the noble, in whom is all my delight. . . . I have a goodly heritage. . . . My heart is glad, and my soul rejoices. . . . You show me the path of life." Paul is also ready to present a further gift (cf. Ps. 116:12), both to God and to the Thessalonians, by showing them that path.

3:11–13 May our God and Father himself, and our Lord Jesus, clear our path to you; and may the Lord cause you to increase and abound in love to one another and toward all, as we do toward you, so as to establish your hearts blameless in holiness before our God and Father at the parousia of our Lord Jesus with all his holy ones.

The long exordium (*cum narratio*) now comes to an end, with this final punctuation point that appeals to God the Father and the Lord Jesus Christ, in whom and because of whom they are "the church of the Thessalonians" (1:1), from whom and for whom both they and the apostles live and thrive. The longed-for visit is in God's hands, as are the Thessalonians themselves. He it is who will make their "work of faith and labor of love" (1:3) increase and abound, who will see that their faith is formed by love and their love by faith. He it is who will make them advance in both, until in due course they are granted what Irenaeus calls that "faculty of the uncreated" (δύναμιν ἀγεννήτου) by which they may enjoy eternal life. He it is who will ready them for the judgment to be effected at the parousia, by way of which they may enter eternal life.

> [For] in all things God has the pre-eminence, who alone is uncreated, the first of all things, and the primary cause of the existence of all, while all other things

remain under God's subjection. But being in subjection to God *is* continuance in immortality, and immortality is [partaking in] the glory of the uncreated One. By this arrangement, therefore, and these harmonies, and a sequence of this nature, man, a created and organized being, is rendered after the image and likeness of the uncreated God—the Father planning everything well and giving His commands, the Son carrying these into execution and performing the work of creating, and the Spirit nourishing and increasing, but man making progress day by day, and ascending towards the perfect, that is, approximating to the uncreated One ... [until] being glorified, he should see his Lord. (*Haer.* 4.38.3, in *ANF* 1:521f., emphasis added)

Such is the divine economy by which God counts out the interest on what he has lent us, by which he causes faith and love to grow together, so that when Christ comes with his holy angels for the brethren he has redeemed and made holy, we and the whole Church may be found rich in virtue and blameless in holiness, to the glory of God. Those who participate in that economy now are those who will stand then, with a clear conscience, before God and his Christ, unashamed at the coming for which the whole creation eagerly longs and waits.

▪ Linguistically, Paul is leaning on Zech. 14:5, "Then the LORD your God will come, and all the holy ones with him"; but for "the LORD your God" (MT, "the LORD my God") he has substituted "our Lord Jesus" (see Fee 2009: 134f., who observes that Paul has no difficulty making such substitutions since he clearly regards Jesus as God). Cf. Rom. 8:18–39; 1 Cor. 1:4–9; and Titus 2:11–14.   ▪

4:1–8 It remains only to say, brethren: We entreat and exhort you in the Lord Jesus that, just as you received from us [guidance as to] how you must walk to please God— even as you are walking—you should excel still more. For you know what instructions we gave you through the Lord Jesus. This is the will of God, your sanctification: that you abstain from sexual impurity; that you learn how to possess, each of you, his own vessel in holiness and honor, not in the heat of lust like the Gentiles who do not know God; that you not trespass and take advantage of your brother in the matter, because the Lord dispenses justice in all these things, just as we warned you and solemnly testified. For God did not call us to impurity, but for sanctification. So he who dismisses these instructions dismisses not man but God—the God who gives his Spirit to you, his holy Spirit.

The letter's first goal has been accomplished. The relationship between the apostles and the believers in Thessaloniki has been clarified and confirmed. Now begins the paraenesis, in which the doctrinal instruction on things eschatological is also to be embedded, completing the letter's work. The paraenesis develops the theme of sanctification by giving specific moral instructions, especially important for Gentile converts, then as now, since they have not been brought up by Torah and may not even recognize in religious conversion a need for moral conversion (Malherbe 2000: 133).

Paul and Silas doubtless carried with them a copy of the letter from the Jerusalem Council that established the minimum standards of the sanctified life, making clear to those converts that Christianity was incompatible with idolatry and with the consumptive and sexual habits associated with idolatry. This would have been presented to the Thessalonians as instruction from God himself "through the Lord Jesus," whose decree it was. The church, then, has heard that the community of the new covenant, like that of the old, has definite moral boundary markers established by divine authority. Paul means now to reinforce all this. For being blameless in holiness, though it is indeed a matter of the heart, is also a matter of conduct. It is both inward and outward. It touches desire and choice, intention and action, the ordering of acts to their proper ends and the repair of what is disordered. It concerns the integrity of the community as well as the person.

The Church is a moral community. It may be more than that, but not less than that. Its doctrine about God and his Christ drives its teaching about sanctification, which bears on human well-being in both the present world and the world to come. Sanctification, in the final analysis, *is* preparation for the world to come— for deification, for dwelling with and in God, the immortal and thrice-holy God. Those who suppose that doctrine can be divorced from morals, or faith from fidelity, have no grasp at all of the aims or purposes of the gospel, which concern readiness for God and the kingdom of God. Paul therefore counsels the Thessalonians how to live with the parousia in prospect, and he starts where the conciliar encyclical leaves off, with abstention from unchastity, from πορνεία (Acts 15:29).

What is *porneia*? Broadly speaking, it is any sexual violation of love, love (ἀγάπη) being the fundamental vocation and determining feature of image-bearing creatures. It is the dishonoring of bodies and persons out of disordered sexual desire (ἔρως), whether in the passion of lust (ἐν πάθει ἐπιθυμίας) or in its more deliberate determinations. It is the perversion of the right order of love, through preference for the lower at the expense of the higher, the immediate at the expense of the ultimate, the body at the expense of the soul. We must put it this way because the lower is good in its place, the immediate in its time. The body is good in itself and good sexually, too, though it may be sexually quiescent without ceasing to be good. In fallen human beings, however, the body strives against the spirit; the lower competes with, rather than serving, the higher. That is why Paul tells us to master our own vessel in sanctification. For the body, conjointly with the mind or spirit, is ultimately for God. It too is intended to be in receipt of the Holy Spirit and, just so, of eternal life. (Cf. Ezek. 37:14 LXX, which Paul is all but quoting: δώσω πνεῦμά μου εἰς ὑμᾶς, καὶ ζήσεσθε, "I will put my Spirit in you and you will live.") To that life it is ordered. *Porneia* or fornication, sexual uncleanness of any kind, is a refusal of that ordering, an all too common refusal.

▨ "Learn how to possess (κτᾶσθαι), each of you, his own vessel (σκεῦος) in holiness and honor": Shall we understand "vessel" as "wife"? Perhaps that is possible if we read this text together with 1 Cor. 7, though σκεῦος is not employed there. It would fit well enough with Paul's allusion to the commandment against adultery that appears in verse 6 with the word ὑπερβαίνειν, here rendered "trespass." (See Malherbe 2000: 224ff. and Witherington 2006: 114ff. on σκεῦος as "wife" and on Paul's view of marital sanctification; cf. Tob. 4:12–13, which may lie in the background, as Aquinas thinks, but only deep in the background.) The phrase "each of you" militates against this reading, however, since not all have wives and in 1 Cor. 7 Paul actually encourages singleness. In any case, it is a restrictive reading. Σκεῦος can refer to the body as such—cf. 2 Cor. 4:7 and 1 Pet. 3:7, on which latter text the commentators are often mistaken; σκεῦος there does not refer to the wife but to the *body* of the wife as weaker than the body of the husband—and the verb κτᾶσθαι can refer to self-mastery or self-possession rather than to acquiring or possessing or commanding someone or something else. If "his own vessel" (τὸ ἑαυτοῦ σκεῦος) refers to the body of each, then guidance is given to each, as Theodoret says (2001: 115), and emphasis is placed on the fact that sexual morality begins with self-control. If, on the other hand, the meaning is "acquire his own wife," we must posit advice only to the unmarried, and rather strange advice at that since pagan men acquired mistresses for passion and acquired wives, by family arrangement, for reproduction (Fee 2009: 148; Weima 2014: 269). Or if the meaning is "possess his own wife," then the advice is only for the married and, more particularly, for those given to domestic abuse or to adulterous relations.

In short, a case can be made for "possess his own wife" but not for "acquire his own wife." A much better case can be made for "possess his own body," against which there is no very telling objection. On the other hand, reading σκεῦος euphemistically as a reference to genitalia (as Bruce, Fee, and Weima are inclined to do) invites the very serious objection that Paul has allowed the phallic cults to determine his frame of reference and to draw his rhetoric down to that level. Weima tries to keep the whole body in view along with the genitalia, as if Paul were employing σκεῦος with a kind of double entendre, but this won't do. Paul may have been conscious of that possibility in the Hebrew text of 1 Sam. 21:5 (as his readers certainly were not) or of profane texts that played on the term (as his readers likely were), but his own text is debased by this proposal. Of course, possessing one's body in holiness and honor involves mastery over its most unruly parts; no one is in doubt about that. But to find "the force of σκεῦος" (Bruce 1982: 83) in a direct reference to the penis is crass and, from a literary standpoint, rather perverse. By contrast, Nathan Eubank wisely sends us to a late Pauline text, 2 Tim. 2, which makes its own allusion to holy vessels: "If anyone cleanses himself from these things, he will be a vessel for honorable use, consecrated, useful to the master, ready for every good work. Flee youthful desires and pursue justice, faith, love, and peace, along with those who call on the Lord from purity of heart" (2019: 88, emphasis omitted).

That everyone is called to pursue personal sanctification seems almost to require the broader reading, "possess his own body," not "possess his own wife." We, at all events, require it; that is, we require instruction in biblical anthropology, just as they did. Such instruction must first of all be frank and without dissimulation, as it is in this pericope. As opportunity permits, it must also be elaborated patiently and systematically, while altogether free of crassness. That is what John Paul II (1997) attempts in his Wednesday audiences on the subject, though exponents of his "theology of the body" sometimes concern themselves too much with sexual union and too little with the wholeness of the person qua person, allowing ἔρως to displace ἀγάπη and the communion for which everyone is made to be overshadowed by conjugality. Biblical anthropology is not dualistic. A false flight from the body cannot be corrected by a false fascination with the body; the focus must always remain on whole persons. It helps to bear in mind that in this anthropology, even as refined through engagement with Greek philosophy, "soul" (ψυχή, *animus*) is used as shorthand for more than one dimension of the human person. The human soul is not a spiritual substance trapped in a body like a genie in a bottle, but is rather the unifying and quickening form or principle of the whole embodied person; that is, of the man or woman as such, who is both an intellectual being, like an angel, and a bodily being, like other animals. Which is to say, the human soul is not opposed to the body any more than it is opposed to the mind or spirit; it is the ordering principle of both in their unity. Hence, in the shorthand at 2:8, τὰς ἑαυτῶν ψυχάς means "our own selves." Or, in the longhand at 5:23, Paul can say, "may your whole spirit [πνεῦμα], soul [ψυχή], and body [σῶμα] be preserved blameless." Or in Augustine's mixture of shorthand and longhand, man can be defined as "a rational soul with a mortal and earthly body in its service" (*Mor. eccl.* 52, "rational soul" standing for both spirit and soul). This is not just pedantry. It reveals something about the proper order the soul is meant to maintain. In this unique creature, the human person who is at once animal and intellectual, there is a unique responsibility to rule its passions, including its sexual passions, by the determined application of reason. The body is servant, not master. It is to be mastered, to be under command, to be possessed in a fashion that aids the sanctification of the whole person and, indeed, sanctifies and honors the body itself (cf. *Civ.* 14.5ff.).

"For by the hands of the Father," says Irenaeus, "that is, by the Son and the Holy Spirit, man, and not merely a part of man, was made in the likeness of God" (*Haer.* 5.6.1). The mind or spirit is not the man; the body is not the man; the soul that unites them is not the man, but the whole man is all three at once. So man must learn to love with body, soul, and mind (Deut. 6:5). Ultimately, to be perfected and attain immortality, he must learn to do that in the power of the Holy Spirit. Vivified by the Spirit, he himself becomes spiritual, a truly living man, because he lives in and by the divine Love itself. He is spiritual in body, soul, and mind, like Jesus Christ, who has already become "a life-giving spirit" (1 Cor. 15:42–50; cf. 2 Cor. 5:1–5). Irenaeus, like Augustine, is following Paul. He knows where this anthropology is going. It is going to a Christian morality that regards the body in an entirely different light than paganism is capable of casting on it. Paul, he says, "declares that those are the perfect who present unto the Lord the three without offense," by the Spirit having preserved themselves blameless both inwardly and outwardly. Whereupon he turns (*Haer.* 5.6.2) to 1 Cor. 6:12–20: "Now the body is not meant for *porneia*, but for the Lord, and the Lord for the body. . . . So glorify God in your body."

If the Spirit is to possess the whole man as a temple to the Lord, that man should begin now to possess what he has been given in such a way as to honor the Lord (1 Cor. 6:19). And who is this Lord? Certainly not some god of the Greeks but rather the God of the Jews, and the God of the Jews as known through Jesus Christ. At the opening of the paraenesis Paul appeals again to the threefold name of God into which the Thessalonians were baptized, the holy name he invoked at 1:1–10. The Lord he is talking about, here as in 1 Corinthians, is the living and true God, Father, Son, and Holy Spirit: the God who makes the body, who himself takes a body, and who raises the body. Those who do not understand that the body is for the Lord—that it also, as constituent to the human person, is in receipt of the Spirit—are in no position to grasp the ethics of sanctification. The better pagan writers knew that the cardinal virtues applied to sexuality, but the theological virtues were unknown or opaque to them because God himself, the triune God, was unknown or opaque to them. Therefore they did not know how to think virtuously about sex in any very profound way. As for the better pagan emperors, that their laws in support and protection of marriage did not well succeed cannot, perhaps, be held against them (cf. Weima 2014: 262). Christian rulers would later do somewhat better, though all that they achieved is now being swept away in a tidal wave of *porneia* and pornography, as the cults of Cabirus and Dionysus, or our own local versions thereof, are resuscitated.

What are the virtues but habits of the soul that order the things of the body to the things of the mind or spirit, and the whole person to the things of God? And what are the vices but habits of decommissioning, of isolating the body from the mind or the mind from God? The latter isolation leads inevitably to the former, as Paul remarks in Rom. 1:16–32. For virtue in sexual matters begins, like every other kind of virtue, in thanksgiving. It is because people will not render thanks for the goodness of the Creator and of the created order, showing gratitude in word and deed and self-discipline, that they are given over "in the lusts of their hearts to impurity," to degrading passions, unnatural relations, "shameless acts," and "the dishonoring of their bodies among themselves," thus "receiving in their own persons the due penalty for their error" and corrupting their relations with others on virtually every level. The damage (as Paul makes abundantly clear) cannot be confined to the sexual but redounds on the whole of human life. People become "foolish, faithless, heartless, ruthless," spurring each other on to still more destructive behavior, just as they are today in a land that, having grown ashamed of the gospel, is now ashamed of virtually nothing else (cf. Wis. 14:22–31).

Porneia is viciously destructive, individually and collectively. By perverting the order of being, it serves death rather than life. God therefore calls his people to chastity, to virtue in sex. He calls them to purification; that is, to the process of sanctification (ἁγιασμός) and to the life of holiness (ἁγιωσύνη). He calls them to genuine love, in which they spur one another on to good deeds, not evil deeds. *Porneia*, even at its romantic best, where its baseness is least evident, cannot be justified in the name of love. Love is rather the remedy against it, as Chrysostom says. Faced with incredulity at his claim that love and fornication are incompatible, he insists that the one who loves truly will draw the beloved away from fornication; for "there is no sin, none at all, that the power of love, like fire, cannot consume" (*Hom.* 4).

God does not justify without also glorifying, and sanctification is a *sine qua non* for glorification (Rom. 8:30). But there is no sanctification of the soul without a corresponding sanctification of the body of which it is in fact the soul. "Or do you not know that the unrighteous will not inherit the kingdom of God? Do not be deceived: neither fornicators, nor idolaters, nor adulterers, nor male prostitutes, nor sodomites, nor thieves, nor the greedy, nor drunkards, nor the blasphemous, nor the rapacious will inherit the kingdom of God. And such were some of you. But you were washed! But you were sanctified! But you were justified in the name of the Lord Jesus Christ and in the Spirit of our God!" (1 Cor. 6:9–11 AT; cf. 5:11). The vessel of the body, like the liturgical vessels (τὰ σκεύη τῆς λειτουργίας) used in the Eucharist, must be holy, sanctified, set apart for the Lord. Hence those who indulge in *porneia* are excluded from the Eucharist. For the Church itself is, par excellence, "the temple of the living God" (2 Cor. 6:16; cf. 1 Cor. 5).

These things require to be said in the Church in every generation and in every culture, but especially in our culture, shaped as it is by the advent of "the pill" and the subsequent normalization of artificially sterile sexual acts, acts that deny the ordering of copulation to procreation, and by the elevation of sexual pleasure above all other sexual goods. Among the consequences of this disorder are a rise in disease, a decline in population, rejection of the natural family as the fundamental unit of society, alienation from the body itself, and a subsequent search for identity in sexual habits or sexual psychology or even through the denial of sex. With these consequences go others, of course, including loss of confidence in the value or even the possibility of a morally well-ordered life and increasing reliance on the state to provide such order as may be possible.

Between sexual libertinism and political bondage there is a deep connection, fostered by the state's assumption of almost all pedagogical responsibility and more than its share of economic responsibility. Responsibility for reproduction is, as Huxley foresaw, just around the corner. Meanwhile, the state itself comes under duress through the difficulty of maintaining borders, whether moral or jurisdictional, and with borders the rule of law. Globalism of one sort or another seems the only solution, but globalism also serves to break down identity and, indeed, requires the breaking down of identity. It necessarily cultivates a soulless bureaucracy inimical to the maintenance of homes and of homelands, subjugating the Shire, as it were, to something orcish and Mordor-like (Farrow 2018d). These too are the results, just a few of the results, of refusing to order sexual capacities to copulation and copulation to procreation, of preferring pleasure to higher sexual goods and *porneia* to purity. In other words, we are not talking here only about a private purity code briefly held over, like rules about eating or washing, from a minority religion beholden to controversial biblical texts and bent on preserving its own distinctive character. We are talking about a way of life proper to the people of God, hence about the need for that people to "come out from them and be separate" (2 Cor. 6:17; cf. Isa. 52:11). But we are also talking about divine design for human life and welfare—all human life and welfare.

Such is the design, a design over which humans have no rightful authority, that to be unitive in principle the conjugal act must also be procreative in principle. It can be procreative in principle without being procreative in practice, of course, as will be the case whenever one or both spouses are infertile; but where it is in principle nonprocreative, through contraception or sterilization, it is in principle nonunitive as well, for the unitive cannot successfully be extracted from the procreative in defiance of divine design. The pleasure and emotional comfort copulation affords, when detached from the other goods that providence intends and from the disciplines that virtue in sex demands, are beguiling but lack integrity. They are shallow, transitory, addictive. The path of sanctification is not being trod when they are pursued in detachment. It is the path of *porneia* that one is on. Which makes it difficult, if not impossible, to help steer the spouse, or indeed anyone at all, from that path.

Elizabeth Anscombe (1993) cogently observed fifty years ago, at the outset of the great *Humanae vitae* controversy, that if contraceptive sex is morally permissible so are other forms of sterile sex, including virtually all the pagan practices that Christianity had repudiated and to a significant extent marginalized. In this she was prescient, predicting the process that led to same-sex marriage and the whole series of related demands that no sexual vice be left behind in the bid to normalize what had been condemned or marginalized, even that much smaller category of practices rejected as *porneia* by the pagan world. How difficult it actually was for Christianity to achieve the moral and legal marginalization of deviant sexual practices can be seen, for example, by perusing Peter Damian's eleventh-century treatise on clerical homosexual practice. Alas, it is still more difficult today, now that those gains have been undone, undone even in the Church, about which a new *Book of Gomorrah* must be written. (More edifying reading, in aid of those seeking the right path, can be found in Pruss 2013, for example.)

The in-principle connection between sex and procreation is a moral given; that is, a divine plan for human welfare rather than a brute fact of nature, like a crevasse to be spanned or a hill to be leveled by some feat of prowess. The plan can be rejected by man, but where it is rejected penalties are incurred that bear both on the person and on society at large. Nietzsche warned us that the death of God is like a sponge that wipes away the horizon. The loss of the connection in question is that sponge at work, removing the possibility of moral distinctions in matters of sex—removing indeed the very concept of sex, which is being replaced by the fluid, horizonless notion of "gender." Reproduction, meanwhile, is being handed over to technicians, as if it were but a technicality. That rational animals have been given sexual capacities for the sake of partnership with God in the begetting of rational animals—that is, of animals with a vocation to live freely by and through love, rather than in the bondage of mere appetite satisfaction—is now all but unthinkable. So, then, is the doctrine that offspring be sought by natural means and that human life should not be produced *in vitro* or by technological means: not because God is opposed to technology, though technology is often opposed to God; nor merely because the use of technology inevitably means the creation of embryos for storage, experimentation, and destruction; but because every child, if called by God to love and to holiness, is called *ab initio* through an act of love in which two become one and, only so, three or more. That is the divine design, viewed from the other side, which we violate at our great peril. However the violation takes place, and there are many ways for it to take place, it cannot change the human vocation nor preclude its being fulfilled, thanks be to the redemptive work of God in Christ. Yet it does disadvantage, even where it does not kill. For in the rejection of love, or the triumph of technology over love, a grave wrong is done, and such wrongs are never without consequence.

See further *Dignitas Personae*, the 2008 Instruction from the Congregation for the Doctrine of the Faith, which addresses the fact that when the unitive is abstracted from the procreative, inevitably the procreative is also abstracted from the unitive, with equally disastrous effects. Among those effects is that the state assumes responsibility for children and the education of children, as for marriage itself. For if marriage is not procreative, it is not educative either. Instructing society's young in matters sexual has thus become the prerogative of the state, which seems determined to create a "moral community" altogether different from that at which the Church aims, or at which parents ordinarily aim.

It is pastorally urgent that these things be said, both in the Church and in the world. A Christian analysis must go beyond the doctrine of creation, however, and take into account the doctrine of re-creation, which forbids any idolization of conjugal union and the natural family. Knowledge of the Holy Family already warns us away from that, for the Holy Family is not a natural family. Moreover, Jesus himself tells us that in the resurrection there will be no marrying or giving in marriage (Matt. 22:30). Why? Because the city of God will then be complete. Conjugal union is primarily for procreation and child-rearing, which will not be required in the world to come. The natural family is not an end in itself, but a means to a higher social end that is an end in itself. It is ordered to the appearance and health of the city of man, thence to the appearance in the city of man of the city of God, and finally to the eschatological kingdom of God. By that city and kingdom it is in some sense subverted, not merely relativized (Farrow 2007a: 69–76). The eternal, not the temporal, provides the standard by which we must judge.

This bears directly on our sanctification in matters sexual. If marriage were eternal, then families and tribes and distinctions between Jew and Gentile and population balances, and so forth, would also have eternal implications. What is that but patriarchalism writ large? If, on the other hand, sexual differentiation itself were to disappear in the world to come, as Origen supposed, then sanctification in this world would mean as far as possible—Origen himself, it is said, took this quite far—the suppression of one's sexuality and of one's capacity for reproduction. The Church, however, knows better. Sexual differentiation is permanent; marriage is not. Therefore what is demanded is chastity, or virtue in sex, for both the married and the unmarried. Chastity matters, and it matters to everyone.

Against Origen et al., Augustine insists that sexual differentiation will not disappear, for it belongs to the nature of man, to his goodness as both male and female (*Civ.* 22.17; cf. 14.23). Nevertheless, in the kingdom man will no longer be reproductive, the full complement of those who are to enjoy God having already been reached (*Civ.* 20.1; cf. Anselm, *CDH* 1.16–18). Neither then will man be copulative or governed by marriage. In the city of perpetual peace, conjugal union can no longer serve as the foundation for society, a society both human and angelic. (Plato intuited that in the *Republic* but couldn't make sense of it, not knowing about the resurrection.) In that city, conjugality cannot serve even to enhance the unitive good, as it does presently. It would falsely constrict the communion that belongs to our deification. Marriage is for this present world, and even in this world it is not the highest form of human life, though it is quite rightly the most common. Likeness to Jesus, which is preparation for the world to come, determines the highest, "for the form of this world is passing away" (cf. 1 Cor. 7:31ff. with Matt. 10:34–39; 12:46–50; 19:12). Is that not the point of a celibate clergy and of religious vows? The option for virginity serves, in Marian fashion, as a reminder that the ways proper to this world are rightly grasped only when they are referred to, and qualified by, the inbreaking of the life of the world to come.

But what then will be the utility or value of sexual differentiation in that world? In answering that question we must begin with continuity of identity; for man is and will remain an animal, a sexually differentiated animal. He is made male or female and this distinction, which is not merely biological but also social and spiritual, belongs to his goodness. Reestablished in the resurrection, humans will not *become* angels, though they will become *like* angels in the sense that they will neither marry nor be given in marriage but share rather in an incomparably higher kind of communion and happiness (Augustine, *Civ.* 22.17). Sexual sanctification now, whether through marriage or virginity, prepares us for that sharing, the mode of which will still, for humans, be twofold, for humans are twofold. God made them male and female. The Church, because it is neither Origenist nor Manichaean in its eschatology, and because it is Irenaean rather than Marcionite in its approach to scripture, faithfully affirms this, though she is now vilified for doing so.

Here, however, we enter upon the eschatological problem of continuity and discontinuity to which we will come later in treating the resurrection. For now we need only notice that the modern attack on natural marriage through the promotion of contraception and abortion and homosexuality, together with the attack on sacramental marriage through the blessing of divorce and remarriage and on spiritual marriage through the rejection of religious vows—all this represents, among other evils, a falsely realized eschatology, an eschatology that does not so much posit the anticipation of the ultimate within the penultimate as the ultimacy *of* the penultimate. We would be like angels now; we would be gods before our time (*Haer.* 4.39.2). We do not need marriage. We do not even need our bodies. We are already so "sanctified" that we may decide our own gender, or become genderless. But in fact we are like fallen and depraved angels, coveting strange flesh and mocking sexual self-control, instructing our youth to experiment with their bodies in every conceivable way and to abort any accidental product of conception. Even among Christians, alas, it is as if the virginity of Jesus, of Mary, or of Paul for that matter, were somehow strictly anomalous and scarcely worthy of theological attention; as if copulation, or its sterile *simulacra*, were the very standard of what it means to live humanly; as if virtue in sex were simply more sex. Which is thoroughly heretical, pastorally fatal, and in the offense it gives to children, never mind to God, damnable (Matt. 18:6). ◾

Sanctification in matters sexual begins, practically, by following dominical instructions. It begins, intellectually, with understanding sex as a capacity given to humans for the sake of partnership with God in the begetting of other humans; that is, of young who have a vocation to love and holiness. If we do not begin there, we are already on the road to *porneia*. The reason why the Church insists on chastity in marriage—meaning, among other things, that sexual acts not be made artificially sterile or performed in lust—is that sex, to be virtuous, to contribute to sanctification, must be an act of authentic love, love that is fully open and committed to the spouse, fully open to the Creator and his design of the human person, fully open to the offspring that (when both spouses are fertile) may result from the act. And the reason it insists on chastity outside marriage, which involves a still more complete continence, is that sexual acts outside marriage are not and cannot be true acts of love. Though there be an aspect of love in them, they stand in contradiction to the order of love. Appeals to what is "natural," or (worse) to "what is natural to me," do not justify such acts but only condemn the agent, who calls natural what is in fact a parody of the natural. When Paul advises the Thessalonians or the Corinthians to pursue holiness and shun immorality, he is not advising them to abandon nature for the sake of some alien supernature, but to allow the grace of God to restore and perfect nature.

◾ Unfortunately, there is a bone to be picked here with Augustine, who encouraged the view that the only thing natural about the conjugal act is its procreative function; that morally it is permissible on that account, despite the inevitability of venial sin that now attaches to it in that it is performed by disordered partners who are unable perfectly to govern their bodily passions. Augustine believed marriage to have three natural goods, not one: *proles, fides, et sacramentum*. Marriage is not merely for procreation. It is a school of faithfulness and chastity, and of human unity, of the bond between male and female that grace affirms and elevates into a sacrament of the bond between Christ and his ecclesial bride. He would not have disagreed with Aquinas (*ST* 3.49.3) that the unitive good is the chief good of marriage, or at least that is where he begins in *De bono conjugali* (cf. §1, 21, and 32). His line of thought about the conjugal act, however, rests on the premise that it is unitive only indirectly and cannot be justified in that connection: "For they are joined one to another side by side, who walk together, and look together whither they walk. Then follows the connection of fellowship in children, which is the one alone worthy fruit, not of the union of male and female, but of the sexual intercourse" (*Bon. conj.* 1, in *NPNF¹* 3:399). This leads him to conclude that the conjugal act should not be performed except for purposes of procreation or, by way of concession to human weakness, in rendering the conjugal debt to the weaker partner (*Bon. conj.* 6; *Trin.* 13.23; cf. Aquinas at *ST* 3.49.5). Both the premise and the conclusion are faulty, however, and the mature thinking of the Church does not confirm them (see *CCC* §2360–63).

It has been observed that Augustine himself called them into question in his later attempt to walk a fine line between the old Manichaean and the new Pelagian heresies, defending marriage against both the "detestable censure" of the former and the "cruel praise" of the latter (*Nupt.* 2.9; see *Retract.* 2.53, which contextualizes *De nuptiis*, and Banner 1999: 20–26, 55–60). In pointing out the Pelagians' quiet incorporation of concupiscence into the goods of marriage, he had to distinguish more carefully between lust and sexual love, the pleasure of which can be honorable—or rather, might have been honorable in paradise, where it would have been a calm rather than a passionate pleasure, unencumbered by disorderliness of body or soul, by any shame or need to hide, by any guilt or transmission of guilt to offspring (cf. *Nupt.* 2.14, 22, 37, 52–55). At the same time, he thought it would not do to allow that there is nothing amiss with the conjugal act as we know it. For if there is nothing amiss it is difficult to see how original sin, the sin incurred by way of our origin (*Trin.* 13.16), is transmitted. This had obvious implications for the Pelagian debate and seemed to threaten Christian faith in the need of every human being, even an infant who has committed no sin, for the Savior, which was of far greater concern than sex, for it went to the core of the gospel (*Nupt.* 2.42). Certainly it is the gospel that must control our view of sex, not our view of sex the gospel. Grace does not only elevate nature; it first restores it and thus reveals it for what it is. And the gospel makes clear that our nature is not now what it once was, that there is such a thing as inherited fault and inherited guilt. Augustine was not wrong to deduce from this that sexual union, if it transmits a fault, must also in some way be implicated in the fault. But it does not follow that there is no good and proper use of the conjugal act unless it be performed in the service of *proles* or, if necessary, *fides*—that it has no (or no other) unitive function among its proper uses. Even in his mature work, Augustine does not back away from this claim. "Marriage," he says, "was instituted not for the purpose of sinning, but of producing children" (*Nupt.* 2.42). Yes indeed, but not only for the purpose of producing children, as he himself has made clear already at the outset of *De bono conjugali* and in developing his idea of the three goods. If the conjugal act can be justified by its service to two of them, why not by its service to the third and chiefest good? Making that allowance would not in any way praise concupiscence or even minimize the problem of concupiscence. In some sense it magnifies it, by forcing us to ask again what concupiscence means in matters sexual, and therefore also what sanctification means.

So where exactly is the problem? It lies, we may suspect, in his notion that we would still be as we were intended to be "if the organs of generation were not obedient to lust, but simply to the will, like the other members of the body." In our diseased condition, says Augustine, we cannot achieve this; hence our shame and desire for secrecy in sex (*Nupt.* 2.53, 55; see also *Civ.* 14.16–26 and cf. Aquinas, *ST* 2-2.151.4). This seems a half-truth that does not do justice either to the created nature of man or to the *posse non peccare* of his present situation. We need to probe it a little, with the help of his literal commentary on Genesis, for in *De nuptiis* itself he is better at demolishing the false optimism of his Pelagian opponent than he is at rounding out his own view of human sexuality. According to the eleventh book of that commentary, it is not by way of sexual desire that the fall transpires (as, say, in Hendrick Goltzius's portrayal in the painting that now hangs in the National Gallery in Washington) but rather by idle curiosity and impatience and prideful ambition, presumably in some other connection (an actual apple, say, in keeping with a literal rendition of the story). Sexual union is intended by God from the beginning for the sake of procreation, but sexual desire is aroused only after the fall, expressing itself unbidden and thus inducing shame. It is in facing each other rather than the future and in looking down rather than ahead—in the opening of their eyes to their aroused genitals, to their animal sexuality and their lack of self-control, to the rebellion of their bodily members that follows on their own willful rebellion against the command of God—that Adam and Eve discover the consequences of their prior disobedience. It is thus that they taste the bitter fruit of a knowledge of good and evil wrongly acquired. It is in sex, or rather in the unbidden hunger for and anticipation of sex, that they realize they are no longer covered by grace and decide to cover their rebellious bodies with fig leaves instead.

Genesis 2–3 is tricky hermeneutical business, and there's something to be said for Augustine's conduct of it. But is this really quite right? Does it do justice to the goodness of romantic love and of sexual union? Is there any place here for the Song of Songs and the Edenic intimacy to which it alludes? Why is that work fit for use in describing the soul's attraction to God if it is not fit for use in developing a rich account of sexuality? Suppose we suggest rather (in the tradition to which Goltzius belongs, though not quite like Goltzius) that the curiosity and impatience and pride that brought about the fall may very well have had its occasion in their sexuality; that the fruit-bearing tree in the midst of the garden is a reference to their own bodies and that its fruit—as the fruit of sexual union prematurely sought, disobediently and without the requisite graces—proved not the joyful expansion of life but rather, as they were warned, a harbinger of death. We might even assume that in their premature sexual union they hoped and intended to procreate, demonstrating their own native fecundity outside and apart from any partnership with God. We are not told (though see Gen. 4:1, where partnership with God is expressly noted) and it hardly matters. What matters is that they did not abide in the grace in which they were created and therefore began to experience their own bodies, whether as instruments for relating to one another or to the whole world or to God himself, in a new and disconcerting way (John Paul II 1997: 68ff.). Among other consequences, lust began to replace love, and fear to drive out the love that remained. The sentence of death began, as Augustine says, to take on meaning. There was soon fratricide and other strife, and eventually there was old age and the failure of life itself.

There is no need, for present purposes, to argue the toss between the more and the less literal readings, for both can be turned this way or that. It seems, however, that Augustine prefers the literal because he finds it more congenial to his view of the unitive good of marriage as a good to which sexual union is but a distraction—a dangerous distraction if it is not kept in mind that its only proper harvest is procreation. The task at which Augustine fails, ironically, is the task of keeping all three goods of marriage not merely in view but in mutual relation. None of the three should be allowed to stand alone or apart from the other two, whether morally or socially or legally or in any other way. For God makes things whole. Let us be clear, in that very connection, that the dispute is not about pleasure in sex. Pleasure is not a good of marriage but a good that accompanies other goods when properly pursued, a good that disappears whenever it is made the very thing pursued. That is what concupiscence is: the pursuit of pleasure for pleasure's own sake, or even (if we are speaking of that inherited concupiscence of which we are only indirectly culpable) the inclination to pursue pleasure for pleasure's sake. Certainly there can be no sanctification where concupiscence rules. Sanctified sex is not concupiscent sex but sex that simultaneously respects the three goods of marriage, doing service to one or more of them and disservice to none. Sanctified sex has a place for eros, however: the eros that is both a spiritual and a physical desire for unity. It even has a place for that which the mind and will do not fully determine, a place in which they are humbled before the body—their own body and the body of the spouse. This is a place where the soul, as that which holds body and mind together and is unafraid of their togetherness, recognizes with rejoicing the mystery of a communion that belongs to it precisely as it unreservedly gives itself to the other and unreservedly receives the other in return, thus also receiving itself back with and from the other. It is a place, in this life perhaps *the* place—apart of course from the Eucharist to which it points, the Eucharist in which the unmarried also share, the Eucharist that exceeds it in every way—in which that which mediates, the human soul, is itself mediated.

Into this place, where husband and wife are intended by God not only to be side by side but face to face, mortal sin may enter. Indeed it will enter if the sexual union and communion is not in accordance with the justice of marriage and with justice in marriage. Into this place, we must also allow (cf. Aquinas, *S. 1 Th.* 4.1), venial sin regularly creeps just because, under the conditions of the fall, we come so short of unreserved self-giving and thus leave ourselves prey to lust and/or insensibility, to displays of concupiscence. There is room here, theologically speaking, for something like Augustine's notion of the transmission of original sin. Only humans who are perfectly God-like in their self-giving, which we are not, can hope to have God-like offspring. But the concupiscence in which we partake and which we transmit is not located in passion qua passion. It is not located in the quiescence of reason, so long as reason does not fail to do the work of maintaining justice. If the unruliness of our members is one sign of failure, if it is a sign of injustice and concupiscence, it is not the thing itself. The thing itself is the failure to give, the withholding or reserve of the self-enamored soul, which means also of the fearful soul, the soul that lusts after what it can never obtain because it is ungodly and does not know how to give and receive. The union of two such souls, not merely as friends but as one flesh, or rather as one flesh without true friendship, cannot but yield (if it does yield) fallen offspring, whether they walk with God like Enoch or wander with the devil like Cain. But that does not make the conjugal act into an act whose sole good lies in procreation, in generating potential members of the city of God. The conjugal act is ordered to the unitive as well as the procreative, and it is rational to use it as such, even if the procreative end is the primary end (that is, if *generatio et educatio prolis* must be judged the controlling purpose of marriage and so also of the conjugal act, a judgment reinforced by Pius XI in *Casti connubii* 17 and by Pius XII in his *Address to Midwives*).

Augustine, when he allows *fides* alongside *proles*, even *fides* without *proles*, as a justification for the conjugal act, recognizes after a fashion that there is a unitive dimension to the act. He does it little justice, however, and to that extent falsifies its nature. He ought to have allowed *sacramentum* or bonding (in the natural rather than the supernatural sense) as a proper use of the act, though not of course contraceptively in contradiction of *proles* and indeed in self-contradiction, since contraception is a refusal to give unreservedly. Which is also to say that the fight against sexual sin, whether venial or mortal, and the struggle for sexual sanctification, requires both ascesis and enrichment, as St. John Paul II emphasizes in the final audiences comprised by *Theology of the Body*, which treat side by side, in dialectical tension, the Song of Songs and *Humanae vitae*. That correlation is a deliberate shock to the system, and well placed, for John Paul II grasps in a way Augustine never quite did that "the human body in its masculinity and femininity is interiorly ordered" to the *communio personarum* of the spouses and not simply to procreation (1997: 319).

Briefly put, Augustine is right in what he roundly rejects—namely, the approach to sex that, substituting pleasure for happiness, mires itself ever more deeply in the mud of "laudable lust" (*Nupt.* 2.59), like Dostoevsky's depraved Fyodor Karamazov though often without his excesses or his self-knowledge. Yet Augustine would have done well to make a little more room for the fact that creation includes, within its order and not against it, the irreducibly contingent, an element of the chaotic. Why should this not apply, *mutatis mutandis*, to the order in man, in whom there is a legitimate place for passion? We need not make the mistake of a Böhme or a Berdyaev, tracing the chaotic back into God, in order to consider this feature of man (both male and female) in a positive light and to avoid the hyper-rationalism to which Latin theology did sometimes succumb, including the assumption that the conjugal act necessarily involves venial sin despite the fact that it is not itself sinful. That said, we should not be too hard on Augustine, who in the last analysis knows well enough that "the good and proper use of passion is not a passion" (*Retract.* 2.22). His basic point stands, and today is the more important point: *Marriage does not license concupiscence.* For the human being is structured in such a fashion that the body is servant, not master, and the will is responsible for and to the intellect, which is responsible in turn to the mind and purposes of God. Where sexual drives are not ordered to the good, where the body with its passions—treacherous as they are under the conditions of our fall—is not subdued by the spirit and brought under control (1 Cor. 9:27), where indeed the body is not regarded as a temple of the Holy Spirit and made an instrument for the glorification of God, the human being is fundamentally disordered. Its sin will certainly not remain venial but inevitably become mortal. Therefore "shun immorality" (φεύγετε τὴν πορνείαν, 1 Cor. 6:18).

Shunning immorality is not just for the unusually devout. It is what the sixth (seventh) commandment requires of everyone when it says, "You shall not commit adultery," and the ninth (tenth) when it says, "You shall not covet your neighbor's wife." Paul surely has these commandments in view, the one forbidding a sin of the flesh and the other a sin already embedded in the soul, when he warns his readers not to trespass or take advantage of one another. Sexual sanctification does not reduce to following these two commandments, of course. The *Catechism of the Catholic Church*, however, rightly develops around them a whole treatise on sexual sanctification, concluding at §2548 with "I want to see God." For they stand at the heart of the matter by protecting chastity and conjugal faithfulness as the basic form of sanctified sexual relations. Paul's way of putting the sixth commandment includes not only the adulterer, who is violating the marital vow, but also the unmarried, who may initiate or cooperate in the violation (cf. Chrysostom, *Hom.* 5). He may also have in mind the abuse of minors and of servants. Jesus warns even against the lustful look with all the seriousness with which Moses warns against adultery itself. Why? Because the lustful look is incompatible with the two great commandments—to love God with all the heart, soul, and mind and to love the neighbor as oneself. On this twofold love "depend all the law and the prophets" (Matt. 22:40). On it depend eternal life and the city of eternal peace, from which fornicators (πόρνοι, Rev. 22:15) are excluded precisely because by their fornications they break the first commandment, as well as the sixth and ninth. They are idolaters of the self, refusing to yield up to the healing love of God their private yearnings for gratification. Adulterers and fornicators remain unfit for true communion with God or neighbor, which is why they cannot enter the city. Without repentance and restoration to the path of life, they will never arrive there. They will never see God, whom they do not love.

Once upon a time, the Church was not afraid to say this. Witness, for example, the scene in the tympanum of the twelfth-century cathedral of Saint Lazare in Autun, created by Gislebertus. The Blessed Virgin is seated to the right of Jesus Christ. On his left, lower down and close behind Satan, the accuser of those being brought before his judgment seat, stands Luxuria with her children, who suckle at her snakelike breasts. The message is stark and clear. If you enter the cathedral you enter the home of Mary, mother of purity. The children of Luxuria ought not to enter, unless they mean to repent. They belong outside, which is where they shall find themselves on that great day of judgment when the door to the kingdom is finally shut, its last guest safely inside (cf. Gal. 5:19–21).

Once upon a time, the Church was not afraid to say that the path of lust, the vice most closely associated with concupiscence and most obviously opposed to chastity, can be mapped pretty much as Aquinas and Dante mapped it in the thirteenth and fourteenth centuries—that it can be traced down, as Gislebertus hints in the architrave, into the very bowels of hell. The Church was not afraid to speak of sins against nature as well as sins against God, and about "unnatural vices" as the greatest vices of all just because they defy divine order in the world at its deepest roots (anal sex, for example, which parodies the face-to-face inter-course for which the body is designed). All this was intended to warn and deter people from the broad road that leads to destruction. It was the definite "No" contained in the great evangelical "Yes." The revenge of modernity, however, which was already being prepared in the days of Gislebertus and Aquinas and Dante, was gradually to abandon the idea of "nature" and to replace it with a free-floating concept of autonomy (→2:17–20). This has left many scratching their heads in puzzlement, not only at talk of hell but at the apparent irrelevance of the whole moral tradition from Moses to Paul to John Paul II, which (as in

John Paul's incisive encyclical, *Veritatis splendor*) sharply distinguishes between moral freedom and moral license.

Sanctification, it bears repeating, is a feature of justification, for justifying grace does not stop short of making man just, of enabling him to play a part in his own God-likeness and salvation. Man cannot see God by himself, but neither can he see God in spite of himself. Chastity is that form of sanctification that makes the embodied person fit for communion. More specifically, it is that virtue by which we learn, in matters of sex, to present our bodies "as a living sacrifice, holy and acceptable to God" (Rom. 12:1). Chastity belongs to our spiritual worship as sexual beings. It is therefore a condition of, not a barrier to, our happiness. For the human person either "governs his passions and finds peace, or he lets himself be dominated by them and becomes unhappy" (*CCC* §2339). Lust, on the other hand, begins where love leaves off, where love for God is absent and obedience to God has ceased. It is, as Aquinas says, a capital vice; that is, a vice "that has a very desirable end, so that through desire for that end, a man proceeds to commit many sins" (*ST* 2-2.153.4). Besides adultery, we may list among those sins pornography, masturbation, contraception, sexual relations between the unmarried or the falsely married—"fornication" in that narrower sense, whether heterosexual, homosexual, or polyamorous—incest, rape, bestiality, and the like (cf. *ST* 2-2.154.11); and, of course, incitement to any of these things, whatever motivates that incitement. All such activities and illegitimate sexual partnerships deny the basic principle of sanctified sexuality, which is that the body is for the Lord and the Lord for the body.

The body cannot be presented to the Lord in holiness unless it is chastely kept, meaning that its sexual function is reserved for the man-woman partnership, the monogamous not polygamous partnership that belongs to the divine design for man, the partnership that is in principle fecund and reproductive. Chastity always involves continence, then, in one fashion or another, a continence that begins with the spirit, guides the eyes, and governs one's words and deeds. This chastity and continence do not desexualize the body or rob it of its sexual goodness. They do not imply that conjugal union is somehow shameful, or in the framework of the present world lacking in its own wonder, power, and secret glory. They do not Platonize all sexual desire, or all readings of the Song of Songs. The person who clings to chastity is quite capable of acknowledging the joy and beauty of sexual union. But he knows what kind of union he is talking about: the union that is capable of sanctification and is in fact sanctified, the union that pleases God, the marital union that perfected by grace is capable of pointing to the mystical union between Christ and the Church.

▪ We are now in a position to explain why Jesus not only brought the people of God back to the monogamy of Gen. 2 but also disallowed the serial monogamy of their and our culture (Matt. 5:31–32), and why divorce and remarriage was forbidden in the Church, as a grave offense that incurs excommunication. Marriage, whether natural or sacramental, is indeed partnership with God in the task of bringing new human beings into the world and introducing them to the school of personhood, whose master is Christ, "the personalizing Person" (Torrance 1992: 67f.). A union closed to that possibility, not by reason of the physical frailties belonging to the curse but by deliberate intent, is no marriage, be it heterosexual or homosexual. A union open to it, if ratified through marriage, is always holy by nature and is never violated without grave sin, for the love of God and the love of neighbor must begin at home and prevail at home. Where it does not prevail, the solution is not to profane the partnership by regarding the union as disposable and replaceable but rather to sanctify it afresh through forgiveness and reconciliation—or where that is not possible, by sexual continence and devotion to the care of existing offspring. The former course, disposal and replacement, belongs to the school of betrayal, not the school of personhood. It depersonalizes the discarded spouse and children. One must not commit adultery, because adultery already profanes the marriage and tends to its destruction; it is already a deep betrayal of God and of the spouse-neighbor and child-neighbor. But one must not divorce either, of one's own accord, for that tends to adultery even where adultery does not yet exist. What often follows divorce—namely, remarriage—merely throws the cloak of civil law over the sin of adultery.

On one reading of the dominical warning against divorce and remarriage as it appears in Matt. 5—the exception made there for cases involving *porneia* is lacking in Mark 10:11–12 and Luke 16:18—the man cannot make of his wife an adulteress if she already is such, so he may then divorce her. If she is not, however, the divorce puts her in a position where out of need or desire she is likely to become one, with her new partner sharing in her adultery, for she is not released by God from her marital obligation just because she has been released by her husband, who indeed cannot release or dismiss her without grave sin. On another reading, the exception clause is taken to refer to the unchastity of a union that was said or thought to be marriage but was not, making divorce a moot point. Whatever is made of the exception clause, the dominical warning itself and the sacramental view of marriage as a partnership with God, not only naturally in the matter of children—one notes that in Mark the dominical warning is immediately followed by the blessing of children—but also supernaturally in witnessing to the union of Christ and the Church (Eph. 5:21–33), led the Church to ban divorce and remarriage altogether where the baptized are concerned. The unfaithfulness of a baptized but unrepentant spouse might justify separation and singleness of life, or even divorce under civil law should the spouse demand it, just as other kinds of violence might do so; but it does not justify remarriage, which assumes release from one's own obligation. In the case of a valid sacramental marriage, that obligation is permanent and is not annulled by the sins of either partner; remarriage is not possible while the spouse lives (cf. 1 Cor. 7:15, 39).

The Church thus draws a distinction between natural marriage, which though designed to be permanent is not altogether indissoluble under the conditions of the fall—if it were, Moses could not have permitted divorce—and sacramental marriage, which, fortified by the grace of God given in baptism and in holy matrimony, is indeed indissoluble, having become among the redeemed a token of the indissoluble union between Christ and his Bride. When a natural marriage is broken and unrepairable, it may under some circumstances be replaced. When a sacramental marriage is broken, and the mutual will to allow grace to repair it is lacking, it is not thereby dissolved and it may not be replaced (*CIC* 1141–55; cf. Augustine, *Bon. conj.* 17). In the turmoil of our times the teaching of Jesus, as enunciated and applied at the twenty-fourth session of the Council of Trent during an earlier period of turmoil, stands out like a beacon of light: The perpetual bond of matrimony, established by God at the beginning of the human race, because of the grace merited by Christ which serves to "perfect natural love, strengthen the unbreakable unity, and sanctify the spouses," has been raised to the level of a sacrament and rendered binding while both spouses live. Those who violate it, and will not desist from their violation, set themselves against Christ and cannot approach holy communion in a state of grace. Eucharistic anticipation of the vision of God is closed to them (*DEC* 2:753–55; cf. *FC* 84).

"You know what instructions we gave you through the Lord Jesus." Following these instructions, once received, is necessary in order to see God, and must never be subordinated to the prevailing culture or to so-called discernments of conscience—as if conscience were anything other than the human capacity to recognize them as applicable and binding, be they written into nature only or recorded and elaborated, as here, in holy scripture. Conscience, whether it accuses or acquits, refers one to the judgment of God, who is greater than the conscience (cf. 1 Cor. 4:4; 1 John 3:19–24). The conscience must be conscientiously trained to do its work of referral well, through an ever better grasp of the truth, a process greatly enhanced by genuine knowledge of God and of man through Jesus Christ. For "it is always from the truth that the dignity of conscience derives" (*VS* 63). In the business at hand, then, it is not what we suppose to be true about sex or marriage that matters, but what is actually true. It is not what we decide to include in or exclude from the category *porneia* that matters, but what God has included. Conscience "compromises its dignity when it is culpably erroneous" (*VS* 63), that is, when natural and divine law are habitually ignored.

Paul now bids us remember that the Lord himself is the ἔκδικος (cf. Rom. 13:4), the dispenser or executor of justice, hence also the avenger of wrongs done

by sexual disobedience. There is no impunity in matters sexual just because we
are animals with animal instincts. For we are rational animals, with the capacity
to direct our bodies and control our passions by offering them to God in the
spiritual worship of obedience, a capacity vitiated in Adam but restored to us
in Jesus. The one who rejects dominical instructions flouts not only the law of
Moses or the law of the Church, but God himself. He shall not escape judgment,
however successfully he has deformed or silenced his conscience. His judgment
has already begun the moment he refuses the Spirit of holiness in which he has
gained a share, for the Spirit of holiness and the Spirit of life are one and the same
(cf. Rom. 1:4). Paul's solemn warning and testimony to the Thessalonians calls
to mind a still more sobering text: "A man who has violated the law of Moses
dies without mercy at the testimony of two or three witnesses. How much worse
punishment do you think will be deserved by the man who has spurned the Son
of God, and profaned the blood of the covenant by which he was sanctified, and
outraged the Spirit of grace? . . . It is a fearful thing to fall into the hands of the
living God" (Heb. 10:28–31).

The preacher who either does not believe these things or is afraid to preach
them perforce preaches a different gospel. Does he prefer mercy? What he calls
mercy is a very cruel mercy that causes others to stumble and fall, suffering the
penalties that accrue to the disobedient both in this life and (where repentance
is lacking) in the next; for when the ἔκδικος arrives, with his holy ones and for
his holy ones, those who thought their disobedience a small thing, who forgot
that the virtue of obedience is in its way "the mother and guardian of all virtues"
(*Civ.* 14.9), will not be ready and will not be able to stand. Does he prefer "accompaniment" to anything that might be deemed harsh or judgmental? But if
accompaniment means a gradualness of the law (the weak being excused from
its demands) rather than a law of gradualness (everyone learning to excel more
and more on the path of holiness), it is accompaniment in the wrong direction
and to the wrong destination. Those who hope to stand before the Lord when
he comes cannot "look on the law as merely an ideal to be achieved in the future:
they must consider it as a command of Christ the Lord to overcome difficulties
with constancy" (*FC* 34).

4:9–12 But concerning brotherly love you have no need that we should write you, for
you yourselves are people taught by God to love one another, and you are doing just
that to the brethren in all Macedonia. So again we encourage you, brothers, to excel
more, and to strive to live quietly and to mind your own affairs and to work with your

hands, just as we instructed you, that you may conduct yourselves honorably toward those outside and have need of no one.

Love is not only, or even primarily, sexual (cf. Luke 20:34–36). Love is the life of all those who truly live. And here the Thessalonians are, in a word Paul may have coined, θεοδίδακτοί, those taught by God, not merely by the apostles (Malherbe 2000: 244). They are those taught by God to love, which in the last analysis is something that only God can teach. The apostles know something of love, just because they know something of God. They themselves are developing the virtue of love, which is the form of all the virtues, the very form of godlikeness. But God alone, who does not have the virtue of love but rather *is* love and the source of love, is perfect in love. And only God can reveal God. That is why Paul, when he sees the godliness of love in the Thessalonians, knows they have been taught by God himself.

▌ "All your sons shall be taught by the LORD" (Isa. 54:13a). This is a new covenant reality, on the basis of which we speak of the *sensus fidelium* or "supernatural appreciation of faith on the part of the whole people" when, together with their bishops, "they manifest a universal consent in matters of faith and morals," adhering to the faith, penetrating it "more deeply with right judgment" so as to apply it "more fully in daily life" (*LG* 12). It includes a divine guarantee. "The entire body of the faithful, anointed as they are by the Holy One, cannot err in matters of faith." For the truth that sanctifies the faithful, setting them apart from those who do not know or believe God, is also the truth that unifies them. It unifies them in and for God, who is truth. It unifies them in and for God, who is love. To love in truth and to speak the truth in love: that is the ground of unity, the path of sanctification, and the evidence of having been taught by God (John 17). Yet we should not overlook the fact that Paul deploys this new term θεοδίδακτοί, the eschatological tenor of which Weima (2014: 288f.) rightly stresses, quite precisely in connection with love for the brethren. For if there is an apostolic magisterium for faith and morals, there is only a divine magisterium for love. Perhaps Isa. 54:13b was as much an inspiration as 13a. Because they are taught by God himself to love, "great shall be the prosperity [LXX εἰρήνη, peace] of your sons."

The chief sign of being God-taught is not consent in matters of faith and morals, as vital as that is, but the peace that flows from loving as God in Christ loved. (See 1 John 4:7–10, a passage even Paul cannot match for its simplicity and power, unless perhaps at 1 Cor. 13 or 2 Cor. 5:13–15.) Just as there can be no question of divorcing doctrine from morals, or faith from fidelity, there can be no question among the God-taught of divorcing truth from love, because in the perfection of God there is a complete harmony of attributes. God indeed does not have attributes but is his attributes. Truth and love and goodness and beauty and being itself—all these are, only as and because God is. They must be learned from God in communion with God, as Anselm argues (or rather illustrates and demonstrates) in his *Proslogion*. And in this learning, as in any attempt to articulate what has been learned, we must allow love to hold the central place. Love is the anchor.

> Aseity (God is from and for himself and absolutely self-sufficient)
> Simplicity (God, being the only cause of himself, is not composite)
> Freedom (God is just as he wills to be, altogether without hindrance)
> Ineffability (God is inscrutable, in his greatness beyond human ken)
> Immutability (God is *actus purus*, hence eternal, changeless, impassible)
> Omniscience (God comprehends everything, all at once and perfectly)
> Omnipotence (God has perfect power over all things, times, and places)
> Love (God is love, the love of Father and Son and, just so, embracing Spirit)
> Goodness (God is goodness itself, the source of all being and goodness)
> Truth (God is his own guarantor, and the measure of all creaturely rectitude)
> Faithfulness (God is always true to himself, hence true or constant toward us)
> Mercy (God is for us, even if we are against him and so also against ourselves)
> Justice (God is impartial, resolute in upholding the good order he has willed)
> Holiness (God is incapable of corruption and cannot be compromised)
> Glory (God is happy, and beautiful in the display of his happiness)

Love is the anchor. That is why theology and philosophy, and preaching and teaching, are nothing of consequence except as a God-taught form of love. However the theologian or preacher wishes to arrange things in attempting to speak of the divine perfections, love must remain at the center, as in the very imperfect attempt above. Here love alone is not paired, or rather is paired with each pair (omnipotence and goodness, etc.). For "he who does not love does not know God" (1 John 4:8), even in the ways he thinks he knows him. To know God, he must know the love that God is. Is that not why Jesus said, "No one knows the Son except the Father, and no one knows the Father except the Son and any one to whom the Son chooses to reveal him"? (Of this key synoptic saying, found in Matt. 11:27 and parallels, the Gospel of John is an extended exposition, reaching a climax pedagogically in chapters 16–17; see esp. 16:12–15.) The Spirit personalizes us through love, precisely by engaging us in the mutual life of the Father and the Son. "All your sons shall be taught by the LORD, and great shall be the prosperity of your sons."

To enter the divine love, one has to be God-taught. That the Thessalonians are θεοδίδακτοί is evident in the way they treat their brethren in sister churches, as well as one another. Paul has already praised them for the way their faith and joy have inspired other believers throughout Macedonia; now he remarks on their love, having in mind, no doubt, reports of their hospitality and generosity. That he uses the verb ἀγαπάω (which runs the gamut from offering welcome to loving dearly, but tends to the practical) alongside the noun φιλαδελφία (love for kinsman or friend), and that he speaks of the whole of Macedonia, suggest this; likewise the fact that he immediately offers advice about living quietly, minding their own affairs, earning a living, and not placing themselves unnecessarily in debt to others, especially outsiders, lest hospitality and generosity be abused.

Abuses of hospitality were likely enough, and the Thessalonians may well have inquired about that. What do we do when someone comes to us who has been socially or professionally disenfranchised by conversion and remains among us in a fashion that seems to take advantage of us? What are the obligations of fellowship in Christ? There may also have been questions about the norms of Christian friendship and the nature of Christian community, about the degree of separation in matters political, social, and economic, and about what Christians were to say to their neighbors about their own concept of the ideal life, since the pagans had vigorous debates about such things. Paul does not indicate whether he is responding to questions, but he sketches quickly some of the basic principles, using language that would have been familiar to them from those debates or from the great philosophers.

In a well-ordered soul or a well-ordered city, each faculty or person or class is to perform its own task and mind its own affairs, says Plato (*Republic* 4.441–43)— sometimes with a certain quietism, if necessary, the just man "standing aside under shelter of a wall" to weather a storm of lawlessness, thus keeping himself, at least, free from iniquity (*Republic* 6.496d). There is something of that in Paul's own advice. But was his counsel to "make it your ambition to live quietly" an ironic reference to the Epicurean rejection of ambition, as Malherbe suggests (2000: 248f.)? Was he trying to distinguish the Christian life as a more responsible form of quietism? Perhaps, but there is a danger here of over-reading the text in terms of contemporary debates about the good life or, for that matter, in terms of friendship codes or patron/client relations and the like, just as there is a danger of overfreighting the eschatology that might favor an unobtrusive and unencumbered life. We can say with much more confidence that Paul sought to inculcate in the Thessalonians, both by instruction and by example, a combination of responsible self-sufficiency under God, which leaves one free of unnecessary entanglements and obligations (cf. 1 Cor. 7); respect for the dignity of manual labor, as part of God's design for man; and a spirit of open generosity like God's own (cf. 2 Cor. 8–9). That, as Witherington notes (2006: 123), rules out both the parasitic and the sycophantic in human relations. It also invites the admiration rather than the animosity of neighbors, even if those neighbors have some reservations about Christian detachment from certain civic or social or religious affairs, or look down on what they regard as menial labor (→2 Thess. 3:11–12; cf. John Paul II 1981: 26).

Striving to live quietly does not mean shirking public responsibility. If we are to pray for those in authority, in hopes of leading "a quiet and peaceable life, godly and respectful in every way" (1 Tim. 2:2), we must also be willing to assume some authority and responsibility, when and where appropriate, as Christians have a long and distinguished record of doing. Nor ought we to stand aside under shelter of a wall in a storm, should we have opportunity to rescue others from that storm. What is said to the Thessalonians in their own particular context, as they begin to establish a Christian presence in Thessaloniki, serves as a general guide to prudence for any church community seeking the sort of internal and external relations that would make it attractive to neighbors. It does not serve as a general mandate for political quietism, as if the city of God bore no responsibility at all, except in prayer, to contribute to good order in the city of man. That is not Paul's concern here, however, nor would it become a major concern until such time as the empire itself threatened to collapse in a storm of lawlessness. His primary interest is good order among the people of God and preventing them from erecting false barriers to their ambassadorial mission. They were precariously situated, having turned from the idols to a form of life unfamiliar to their countrymen. They had a rather tenuous dual citizenship. Prudence demanded that they live a quiet and peaceable life as far as possible.

Beyond all this, Paul wished to remind them that the God-like give freely, not out of need. The faith they have adopted and the witness with which they are charged must not be corrupted by any indigence induced by laziness or presumption. To have need of no one and to be ready to give to everyone—that is a worthy aim that might be pondered also in dealing with our own situation under the conditions of the modern welfare state. How much distortion has the gospel endured on account of its witnesses becoming dependent on the state in one sphere of life after another? The divine economy of gift serves the Church best when it is not corrupted by dependency on those whose economy is based only on calculation.

Paul will have more to say about orderly and virtuous behavior in his concluding exhortations, but he is ready now to return to his eschatological framing and to take up the third burden of his letter: a doctrinal elaboration intended to help the

Thessalonians prepare for the royal parousia that is their great expectation, and to guard against any sense of futility or despair that might meanwhile overtake them. That will require addressing the situation of those whose quietness is the quietness of death.

4:13-18 Now we do not wish you ignorant, brethren, concerning those who sleep, lest you grieve for them as others grieve who have no hope. For if we believe that Jesus died and rose, so also [we believe] that God, through the same Jesus, will bring [to life] with him those who sleep. Indeed we assure you, by dominical promise, that we who live and remain until the parousia of the Lord shall certainly not precede those who have fallen asleep—that the Lord himself, with a mighty cry, with the voice of the archangel and with [the sound of] the trumpet of God, shall descend from heaven and the dead in Christ shall rise up first. Then we, the living who remain, shall together with them be caught up "with the clouds" so as to welcome the Lord in the air. And, just so, we shall ever be with the Lord. So comfort one another with these words.

In Paul's day the majority of people, being uncertain about life after death or what it might hold and focusing primarily on the present life—lacking, moreover, belief in *creatio ex nihilo* and the sense of divine providence cultivated among Jews and Christians by that belief—were inclined to be quite fatalistic. Taking comfort in the face of death meant accepting what could not be reversed and seeking such consolation as could be had among the living. Hope of reuniting with loved ones in the netherworld or some higher world was not altogether absent and might be sought through philosophical or religious means, but for the most part either abandonment to grief or a stoic suppression of grief were the options. Increasingly that is the case again now. But not for Christians. Christian hope is neither vague nor blind, any more than Christian faith is vague or blind. For we know him in whom we have believed and are persuaded that he is well able to keep until that day what has been entrusted to him (2 Tim. 1:12): to keep us, the baptized, if we in turn keep until death what has been entrusted to us; namely, the obedience of faith. We therefore expect the resurrection of the dead and the life of the world to come.

That is our firm hope, and the reason for it is simply and eloquently stated by Augustine: "He died, but he killed death! In himself, he put an end to what frightened us. He caught it and he killed it. Like the mightiest hunter, he seized and slew the lion. Where is death? Search in Christ, for it is not; but it was, and it died there. (O Life, the death of death!) Be of good cheer; it will die in us also. What happened first in the head will be rehearsed in the members. Death will die in us also. But when? At the end of the world, at the resurrection of the dead, in which we do believe and of which we have no doubt" (*Sermo* 233, *PL* 38:1112–15, AT). (Levering 2019 attempts to treat the doubts of those who doubt the resurrection of Jesus himself, something Augustine also does, though Paul does not. Paul is a witness, not an apologist.) *Quod praecessit in capite, reddetur in membris*—that indeed is the principle on which our hope rests. He rose and we shall rise. "Nor is Christ only the pattern," adds Aquinas (*S.1Th.* 4.2.95). "He is also the efficient cause of our resurrection, for the things done by Christ's humanity were done not only by the power of His human nature, but also by virtue of His divinity united in Him. Just as His touch cured the leper as an instrument of His divinity, so also Christ's resurrection is the cause of our resurrection, not merely because it was a body that arose, but a body united to the Word of life." But Aquinas points in the wrong direction when he says that "the Word made flesh revives our bodies, while the Word as such revives our souls." Rather the Holy Spirit, who unites us to Christ, body and soul, quickens us together with him for eternal life, as the Spirit quickened Christ himself. As for his suggestion that the angels will also play a role, as soldiers of Christ and servants of the living God, there is no reason to deny it.

The particulars of our rising we cannot know except as the Lord, who does know, reveals them. We depend on dominical teaching, on λόγοι κυρίου, instruction or promises from the Lord. Paul assures the Thessalonians that the Lord has made known what he now tells them, though when and to whom he made it known is not said. We should remember, of course, that the one speaking is no stranger to the word of the Lord. Indeed, he is one who later claimed to the Corinthians that he had, fourteen years earlier—not long before he wrote the present letter, then—been caught up (the verb in 2 Cor. 12:3 is the same as that used here at 4:17: ἁρπάζω, to seize or snatch up) into the third heaven, into paradise, where he learned things that cannot be told; as also, presumably, things that must be told. At all events, what he tells them now he tells them on behalf of the Lord. When the last trumpet sounds, its immediate effect will be to wake the righteous dead.

The resurrection of the righteous at the end of the age was not a new doctrine. From his youth Paul had known it and in his Pharisaical training in Jerusalem he had doubtless given it some thought, for it was one of the points that distinguished the Pharisees from the Sadducees (Acts 23:6–11). We may surmise that some of the converts from the synagogue also believed it before they were converts. Paul is not simply following convention, however, in giving them this assurance (*pace* Witherington 2006: 107). Nor, for that matter, is he merely paraphrasing Old

Testament texts by incorporating sayings of Jesus such as we find in the Gospels, though he is doing that. He has things to say to the Thessalonians that he, like the other apostles, has received from the risen Lord, things only the risen Lord could know.

Now, the Thessalonians had very likely queried him on the subject through Timothy (cf. Malherbe 2000: 208ff.). We ought not to read too much into that query about their sense of the imminency of the parousia. There is no basis for supposing—indeed it is rather silly to suppose—that they only thought of the question because some among them had died and they hadn't anticipated such a thing happening. Paul's response to the related question about "times and seasons" at 5:1–11 makes clear that he had already explained to them that the precise timing of the parousia is not predictable; he even thinks it necessary to underscore the need to be watchful and ready. Nor should we suppose that they already knew all about the resurrection and were preoccupied only with the question of precedence in honor, like the disciples whom Jesus more than once rebuked for that sort of thing, or (*pace* Thiselton 2011: 181; Weima 2014: 322) with the finer points of who gets to enjoy what. No, their question about their dead was likely a simpler and more natural one: "Are they really included in the salvation that the parousia will bring? How so?" That it had not been posed and addressed earlier was due, no doubt, to the interruption of Paul's stay with them (*pace* Malherbe 2000: 284; cf. Witherington 2006: 130; Fee 2009: 164f.). He had already mentioned the resurrection of the righteous, but even his Jewish converts did not yet know just how to connect that with the parousia. As for Gentile converts, they were more deeply puzzled by it all and perhaps still clinging to their old ways of lamenting the dead. Paul's response is unequivocal. The dead in Christ will rise up at the last day, and they will rise up first. They will be party to everything that happens.

Chrysostom extends Paul's line of thought by taking into account the saints of the old covenant. Just as the latter could not be perfected without us, he says, appealing to Heb. 11:40, neither shall we be perfected without them. Paul does not attempt here to address the relation between those who fell asleep before Christ and those who have fallen asleep since Christ (cf. Rom. 5; Gal. 3:6ff.; 1 Cor. 15:29). Nor does he speak of the general resurrection that precedes the judgment of the nations (Matt. 12:41–42). Here, as in 1 Corinthians, his first concern is to establish firmly the resurrection of the righteous dead and the transformation of the righteous living, that both may greet the Lord together. (Augustine, *Civ.* 20.20, and Aquinas, *S.1Th.* 4.2.101–3, call the latter transformation a kind of death and resurrection, inasmuch as the living require an equally radical change; cf. Calvin 1961: 365f.) Given the principle on which Paul is working in both texts, the head-and-members principle, we may read διὰ τοῦ Ἰησοῦ ἄξει σὺν αὐτῷ as indicating that God will bring the dead to life with and through Jesus, though we must supply the "to life." Support is lent by 2 Cor. 4:14: "He who raised the Lord Jesus will raise us also with Jesus and bring us with you into his presence." That through Jesus God will bring the dead with Jesus, as many translations have it, is awkward in every way, even if it arrives at the same point; namely, that when Jesus returns in glory so will the righteous dead.

We have already observed that the mighty host that accompanies Jesus is the army of angels that will do his bidding, announce his presence, and effect his rule. As Jesus himself says, "the stars will fall from heaven, and the powers of the heavens will be shaken; then will appear the sign of the Son of man in heaven, and then all the tribes of the earth will mourn, and they will see the Son of man coming on the clouds of heaven with power and great glory; and he will send out his angels with a loud trumpet call, and they will gather his elect from the four winds, from one end of heaven to the other" (Matt. 24:29–31; cf. 25:31 and Fee 2009: 135). This dominical saying Paul surely knew and had in mind. Nor will its allusion to Dan. 7:12–14 and 7:26–27 have been lost on him, as it is perhaps on us. The parousia of Jesus Christ is the revelation on earth of what has already happened in heaven, the witnessing on earth of the judgment made in heaven, and hence its effecting in full.

In his ascension, the Son of Man is presented before the Father, coming to him "with the clouds of heaven" (μετὰ τῶν νεφαλῶν τοῦ οὐρανοῦ, 7:13 LXX), in the presence of the myriad hosts of heaven, to receive dominion over all things. That is his heavenly parousia, the terminus toward which his ascension moves (Eph. 1:15–23). His earthly parousia is not something altogether different. He came to us in humility, carrying out his Father's will. He returned to his Father in triumph, appearing before him in great glory. When he appears again before us, what will that appearance be but the manifestation of his glory? It is the opening of heaven, not merely to a seer such as Daniel or to an apostle such as Paul or to a eucharistic celebrant such as John ἐν τῇ κυριακῇ ἡμέρᾳ (Rev. 1:10), but to all the earth and all who have ever inhabited the earth. "Behold, he is coming with the clouds, and every eye will see him, every one who pierced him; and all tribes of the earth will wail on account of him" (Rev. 1:7; cf. Zech. 12:10–13:1, which specifies a redemptive mourning for the tribes of Israel). Jesus Christ, in his presentation before God, will be presented by God before us also, and we shall be brought visibly under his dominion through the agency of the angels who minister to him. We shall all witness what Daniel and Paul and John, in their different ways, witnessed. We shall all find ourselves present and accounted for at the parousia "of our Lord Jesus with all his holy ones." Then the righteous will be enrolled with the holy ones and the unrighteous with the legions of the damned (→2 Thess. 1:5–12).

■ "God has gone up with a shout, the LORD with the sound of a trumpet" (Ps. 47:5; cf. Fee 2009: 176f.). That divine triumph is realized in principle when the God-man ascends to begin his heavenly session; it is realized in practice when he descends with glory to claim his earthly kingdom. The latter event begins a new and distinct movement in what can be called "the anaphoric work of Christ," by which the whole creation is presented to God in and with Christ (Farrow 2011: 158). We must distinguish the heavenly parousia from the earthly, the ascension from the second coming, recognizing in that distinction a time between the times, a eucharistic time, a pause in which the Church has its own anaphoric work to do, especially on the Lord's day. But it is equally important to see that Paul is thinking these two events together, as movements that ultimately coincide in God's one great work of exalting Jesus, and us with Jesus. He wants the Thessalonians, like the Philippians, to reach out with him "for the prize of the upward call of God in Christ Jesus" (Phil. 3:14). In 1 Thess. 4:17, he speaks of their being caught up ἐν νεφέλαις εἰς ἀπάντησιν τοῦ κυρίου εἰς ἀέρα. In the background stands Dan. 7:13–14; by reading with Daniel's help we can understand what Paul is saying. The holy ones on earth, like the holy ones in heaven, will follow Christ in his train of glory as he is presented before the Ancient of Days and takes his seat at the right hand of the Almighty. To be "caught up 'with the clouds' so as to welcome the Lord in the air" means to join the heavenly host in receiving the King of Creation. For the movement of the ascension, the enthronement of Jesus Christ, is not complete until the heavenly host is complete. Hence the mission of the Church. Hence the Eucharist itself, which in a provisional and preparatory way is a kind of catching-up to glory (Corbon 2005: chap. 4). The faithful on earth belong to that host and at the parousia shall be made part of it, not provisionally but finally.

In Daniel's vision, as later in John's, the seer is caught up to heaven to see what cannot yet be seen on earth, except prophetically and eucharistically. But what they see in heaven will eventually be seen on earth—the Son of Man coming on or with the clouds of heaven to receive dominion and glory. What they hear being determined in the divine court will be carried out on earth. Earth will be made subject to heaven. Heaven and earth will become one. The trumpet will sound and God's triumph will be complete. And the Thessalonians will be there to celebrate it, even if they have to be gathered from the grave and not merely from the ground. But must we be content, then, if we are reading with Daniel's help, to read only metaphorically? If so, what world-historical meaning should we attach to what Paul is saying? There are two mistakes to avoid here, that of the literalist who will not read metaphorically and that of the symbolist who sees only religious states of mind or ordinary historical events invested with an exalted meaning to which they can never quite attain. N. T. Wright rejects both errors when he protests that this passage is treated "with astonishing literalness in popular fundamentalism and critical scholarship alike to suggest that Paul envisaged Christians flying around in mid-air on clouds." He wants us to understand that Paul, like Daniel, is employing metaphors to speak about the real and actual vindication of God's suffering people, a vindication that "will consist, for those already dead, in their resurrection; for those still alive, in their transformation so that their body is no longer of the corruptible sort" (2003: 215f.). Paul, he contends, is blending images drawn from Daniel with images drawn from an imperial visit, or even from a triumphal procession in Rome, to produce a "spectacular" text that is none the worse for its blending of images and mixing of metaphors. Neither we nor Paul are in a position to work out the details nonmetaphorically; that will have to await the event in question. But Paul is proposing to us that we understand the upward call to greet our Lord and King in terms analogous to "a meeting outside the city, after which the civic leaders escort the dignitary back into the city itself." The image we should have in mind is that of Jesus surrounded by the faithful "as he comes to inaugurate God's final transformative, judging-and-saving reign on earth as in heaven" (2003: 218). Daniel's "clouds," which Paul incorporates, signal that when this event happens it will be the fulfillment of the divine reign through a true union of heaven and earth.

This seems about right, though the blended imagery, particularly the cloud imagery, is rather thicker than this. The basic point is that Paul desires the Thessalonians to recognize both themselves and their dead as those happy subjects who will throng to Christ at his parousia. Perhaps he also wants them to remember who really "rides on the clouds": not the *baalim* of this world, not even him whom Jesus calls "the ruler of this world" and Paul ἄρχων τῆς ἐξουσίας τοῦ ἀέρος, "the prince of the power of the air, the spirit now at work in the sons of disobedience," but rather the Lord God and his enthroned Christ (Eph. 1:15–2:7; cf. Deut. 33:26–27; Isa. 19:1–2; Ps. 104, etc.); hence those, too, who belong to Christ. Be that as it may, as soon as we think of thronging together, and of cloud imagery in that context, we are forced to think not only of Daniel but also of Moses—to think of the Shekinah and the Sinaitic paradigm, of which mention was made in passing at 2:19 and of which more will be said anon.

At his earthly parousia the Son of Man will be presented not only to the living but also to the dead, and presented in such a way as to bring them back to life in the body, just as he himself lives in the body. Of this eventuality the dead under the old covenant were put on notice when Jesus, after the cross and before his resurrection, undertook his descent *ad inferos* to preach the gospel in spirit only, which was the only fashion in which they could receive it (1 Pet. 3:18–19). The dead under the new covenant have already been put on notice, of course, though they will hear more of it from Jesus in what is called their particular judgment, a judgment with purgatorial effects. Both will be ready, then, for that great day. And by the power of God the souls of the righteous dead, having already been perfected and admitted into the presence of God for Christ's sake, will appear with him when he appears, by taking up again the bodies they have laid aside, bodies now made new and glorious and immortal. (What is described in Matt. 27:51–53 seems to foreshadow this.) So in that sense Jesus does come with the whole company of heaven, the eucharistic company, the company of angels *and* of saints, the company of the faithful dead. He comes as he is pictured by Michelangelo in the Sistine Chapel, with Mary already, like himself, in the body, while the rest of the dead arise at the angels' bidding, the saints of both covenants first and the unrighteous dead afterward. Then will all their works be tried and proved publicly, and the works of the angels too, in the judging of which the purified Church will share.

Thus 1 Cor. 6:3; cf. Matt. 25:31–46; 1 Cor. 3:11–15; 2 Cor. 5:1–10; 2 Tim. 4:8; and by analogy 1 Cor. 4:14–21, where Paul warns of his own future coming to Corinth to test their works in person. The general idea is already in place in the Wisdom of Solomon, though its clarification had to await direct knowledge of the Christ, knowledge which was not long in coming: "But the souls of the righteous are in the hand of God, and no torment will ever touch them. In the eyes of the foolish they seemed to have died, and their departure was thought to be an affliction, and their going from us to be their destruction; but they are at peace. For though in the sight of men they were punished, their hope is full of immortality. Having been disciplined a little, they will receive great good, because God tested them and found them worthy of himself; like gold in the furnace he tried them, and like a sacrificial burnt offering he accepted them. In the time of their visitation they will shine forth, and will run like sparks through the stubble. They will govern nations and rule over peoples, and the Lord will reign over them for ever" (Wis. 3:1–8; cf. Rev. 21–22, the visions of which Corbon 2005: 82f. wrongly draws into the present age).

There is no real need, then, to debate the translation of 4:14. Christ comes or appears with his angels. He also comes or appears with the souls of the righteous dead, that he (or God through him) may bring them to life again in the body. What we must be sure not to lose sight of in any rendering of this text is the head-and-members principle. What God has effected for Jesus—namely, his own resurrection from the dead—he will effect also for us, through the merits and authority of this same Jesus, when he appears in glory. Paul insists on complete consistency here: "Now if Christ is preached as raised from the dead, how can some of you say that there is no resurrection of the dead? But if there is no resurrection of the dead, then Christ has not been raised; if Christ has not been raised, then our preaching is in vain and your faith is in vain" (1 Cor. 15:12–14). The head-and-members principle is deployed in reverse, but to the same effect. If it doesn't happen to the members, it didn't happen to the head. But it did happen to the head and so it will happen to the members (cf. 6:14; 15:23–24). The head will be followed by the members, and it will not matter whether those members are dead or alive at the time. So certain is the resurrection of the dead, he tells the Corinthians, that it is rather the living who ought to wonder what exactly will happen in their own case. "Behold! I tell you a mystery. We shall not all sleep, but we shall all be changed, in a moment, in the twinkling of an eye, at the last trumpet. For the trumpet will sound, and the dead will be raised imperishable, and we shall be changed. For this perishable nature must put on the imperishable, and this mortal nature must put on immortality" (15:51–53).

This perishable nature, not some other! Why is it perishable? Because it has life, not from itself but from God. Why is it actually perishing? Because, in its sin, it is alienated from God. And when does it perish? When the soul can no longer hold body and spirit together; when we have not a proper man but only the shade of a man, bound for Hades. Yet it is not now bound for Hades, or not necessarily, because Christ has harrowed Hades (the realm of the dead, not the hell created for Satan and his ilk) and opened the gates of paradise to the faithful. "The spirits of just men made perfect" already behold his face in glory, though they do not yet inhabit glory as Christ inhabits it (Heb. 12:22–23). For that they await the parousia and the resurrection of the dead, when they shall be fully conformed to Christ. That there is a shade, rather than nothing at all, is a consequence of the fact that the rational creature is made uniquely for God; for what is made uniquely for God is, by the will of God, incapable of not existing. Man is by nature perishable, then, and because of sin does now perish, but in perishing he does not, like other creatures, cease to exist. He only quits the nature proper to him, his embodied nature. And that will be restored on the last day, whether for glory or for ignominy, for bliss or for punishment. If for punishment, then at the command of God; for every man will appear, not merely as a shade but as a man among other men, before the judgment seat of Christ. And if for bliss, then through a share in Christ's own glorious resurrection; for "that most faithful mediator between God and man, Jesus Christ," as Tertullian says, "shall reconcile both God to man and man to God, the spirit to the flesh and the flesh to the spirit" (*Res.* 63; cf. Augustine, *Civ.* 9.15).

In this double reconciliation the Good Shepherd restores the soul and grants it green pastures. He leads it to a bliss even the saints in heaven do not presently enjoy, since they enjoy the vision of God by quiet waters, so to say, but do not yet enjoy it as the men they are meant to be. That they do already enjoy it, as the best of that "far better" of which Paul spoke in Phil. 1:23, was settled in the time of Pope John XXII, who was not mistaken to wrestle with the question. We must wrestle with it still, for while there can be no doubt that seeing God is sufficient for perfect happiness, we know that it is not yet the full man who is doing the seeing. He is with Christ, in whom and through whom he sees God. His soul, however, though alive in God, is not yet able to hold spirit and flesh together, as the soul of Christ does. Nor in any case are the conditions for his full happiness met, for the justice of God and his Christ has not yet triumphed on earth, as the souls "under the altar," the souls of the martyrs, bear witness (Rev. 6:9–11). The flesh, like the world, is lagging behind, then, but it will catch up; or rather it will *be* caught up when Christ returns in judgment and sets the world to rights. "Be not disquieted, O flesh and blood, with any care," admonishes Tertullian. "In Christ you have acquired both heaven and the kingdom of God" (*Res.* 51). Or as Isaiah exclaims at 26:19, "Your dead shall live, their bodies shall rise. O dwellers in the dust, awake and sing for joy!"

Just here we must return to the dialectic of continuity and discontinuity, a dialectic to be applied to spirit and flesh alike; that is, to the whole man. Of the body, Paul says: "What is sown is perishable, what is raised is imperishable. It is sown in dishonor, it is raised in glory. It is sown in weakness, it is raised in power. It is sown a physical body, it is raised a spiritual body" (1 Cor. 15:42–44). It will be the same, yet it will not be the same, for the body that follows and obeys the soul, when the soul follows and obeys God, is a body capable both of living in nature and of living beyond nature, like the rational soul itself, which is not merely a product of nature but contains the breath of God (cf. Lactantius, *Inst.* 2.13). In the regeneration of all things, that is what the body will do, for it will belong to a soul capable of commanding the wind and the waves. It will do the soul's bidding, without hindrance, and properly image the soul.

That it will be body and not soul is not in question, at least not in 1 Thessalonians. That it will be active and not merely passive (*pace* Aquinas; cf. Farrow 2018g: 47ff.) is the assumption of the prophets and apostles and fathers. But how shall it come to be the body that it then will be? The creative power of God, says Augustine, working swiftly and wonderfully (*miro atque celerrimo, Civ.* 22.14), will recall into being the bodies of the righteous and render them fit for life eternal. "In the resurrection every man and woman shall arise with the same body that he or she had, or would have had in fullest growth, in all comeliness, and without deformity of any the least member" (*Civ.* 22.20, trans. Healey). That body will be light, not cumbersome, slave to no necessity, having "the substance of the flesh, yet quite exempt from all fleshly corruption" (*Civ.* 22.24; cf. 22.19 and, behind all this, book 13, which points out that it is not the body as such that weighs down the soul, but rather the body as corrupted by the sinful soul). "The bodies of the saints will therefore rise again free from every defect, from every deformity, as well as from every form of corruption, encumbrance, or hindrance. In this respect their freedom of action [*facilitas*] will be as complete as their happiness [*felicitas*]; and for this reason their bodies have been called 'spiritual,' though undoubtedly they will be bodies and not spirits. . . . Harmony between the flesh and the spirit will be so perfect, the spirit quickening the subordinated flesh on which it is no longer dependent, that within our own selves there will be no conflict any longer. As we shall then not have to cope with any enemy from without, so we shall not have to struggle within against ourselves" (*Enchir.* 91, in ACW 3:86f.; cf. *Civ.* 19.13).

■ The power that shall bring all this to pass is the same that makes the body and blood of Christ from the bread and wine of the Eucharist, says Irenaeus (*Haer.* 5.2.3), implanting in us the seed of Christ's own immortality, that our perishable bodies may inherit imperishability. Thus, in the perishing and inheriting, will we know both our own deficiency and God's efficiency, our own weakness and God's power. To that Isaiah already testifies, in words more than able, when backed by the resurrection of Jesus and the sacrament of the Eucharist, to comfort us in the face of death: "On this mountain the LORD of hosts will make for all peoples a feast of fat things, a feast of choice wines—of fat things full of marrow, of choice wines well refined. And he will destroy on this mountain the covering that is cast over all peoples, the veil that is spread over all nations. He will swallow up death for ever, and the Lord GOD will wipe away tears from all faces, and the reproach of his people he will take away from all the earth, for the LORD has spoken. It will be said on that day, 'Behold, this is our God; we have waited for him, that he might save us. This is the LORD; we have waited for him; let us be glad and rejoice in his salvation'" (25:6–9).   ■

But what shall we say of the mind or spirit? The very same dialectic is required, as Tertullian knew when he argued that "changes, conversions, and reformations will necessarily take place to bring about the resurrection, but the substance will still be preserved safe" (*Res.* 55). This is as true of the spirit as of the flesh. The former, unlike the latter, deals in things that do not change as well as things that do. That does not make it eternal, however. Only direct participation in God can make it eternal, for only God is eternal. The spirit requires *gratia elevans* if it is to live eternally. It requires an ever-new conversation with God (*Haer.* 5.27.2, 5.36.2), and for this it must be fitted by the Holy Spirit. Moreover, it has been corrupted by the fall, and like the body needs transformation by the *opus dei mirum*.

The Greeks were wrong about the immortality of the rational soul because they were wrong about its divinity, which it does not have in itself but only from God, as the old man pointed out to Justin (*Dial.* 4–6). They were wrong, too, about the fate of the body, as were the Sadducees, because they knew neither the scriptures nor the power of God (Matt. 22:29). Both body and spirit are capable of immortality because God can and will give it to both; neither is capable in and of itself. Changes, conversions, and reformations there must be, then, yet the substance will indeed be preserved in both cases. In discontinuity there must be continuity, in change identity. "For it cannot be believed that the mind, or the memory, or the conscience of existing man is abolished by putting on that change of raiment which immortality and incorruption supplies; for in that case all the gain and fruit of the resurrection, and the permanent effect of God's judgment on soul and body, would certainly fall to the ground. If I remember not that it is I who have served him, how shall I ascribe glory to God? How sing to him 'the new song,' if I am ignorant that it is I who owe him thanks?" (*Res.* 56).

▨ Tertullian allows that these changes are so decisive as to seem almost "a complete destruction of the former self"; nevertheless, they introduce a radical discontinuity into "our condition, not our nature" (*Res.* 56; cf. *Haer.* 5.9.4, 5.36.1). Both the nature—that is, our humanity—and the person remain the same. If they do not remain the same, then either Christ himself does not remain the same or the head-and-members principle fails. But what is a person? We must think about this if we want to understand the continuity and the discontinuity.

According to Boethius in *De persona et duabus naturis*, a person is an individual substance of a rational nature, *naturae rationabilis individua substantia*. As Gilles Emery points out, this involves three things: an intellectual nature, entailing free will; individuality or indivisibility; and a proper act of existing through itself and for itself, being subsistent rather than constituent in something else (2011: 993ff.; cf. Aquinas, *De potentia* 9.3; *ST* 1.29.2–3, 3.16.12). But must we not also say that to be subsistent as a person is to be through and for oneself precisely by being through and for the other? For personhood belongs to the Father first of all—the Father who is never without his Son and their Spirit—and only analogously, by participation in God, to creatures, be they angelic or human. (In *De potentia* Aquinas works from the creaturely to the divine, but of course the creaturely is derived from the divine, not

the divine from the creaturely, and the analogy must therefore undergo trinitarian revision.)
Now the human being, which exists as a unity of mind and body maintained by the soul,
is a person—a who, not a what—by virtue of the fact that he exists through and for God,
particularly through and for the Son of God who takes human nature, and just so for the
Father himself and also for the neighbor. Being of an intellectual nature (*natura rationalis*)
belongs to this existence through and for God and is essential to creaturely personhood,
as is irreducibility and subsistence, but it is not sufficient to approach personhood merely
by reference to this intellectual nature. That is the mistake of the rationalist, who assumes
that volition arises from reason alone (an assumption Scotus was right to challenge) and,
more dramatically, the mistake of the artificial intelligence community, which having lost
sight not only of divine personhood but of the very idea of subsistence cannot understand human personhood and therefore cannot distinguish properly between humans and
machines. The corresponding error is that of the preference utilitarians, who distinguish
between humans, as between persons and nonpersons, on the basis of their ability to plan
and pursue life-projects.

To guard against the rationalist tendency, whether medieval or modern, we must be
guided by trinitarian and incarnational insights, especially by recognition of the divine
persons as subsistent relations in the one being of God. The fatherhood of the Father and
the sonship of the Son and the procession of the Spirit are constitutive of their persons, not
mere qualifications thereof, just as these three persons *are* the one God rather than com-
ponents in God (thus the tritheists) or characteristics of God (thus the Sabellians). In this
light, we may emphasize, with Emery, that "the human person is not a 'rational individual,'
but a *subsisting* being of a rational nature" (2011: 1001). This stress on subsistence allows
a proper focus, learned christologically, on "the will and freedom of action" that belongs
to rational nature (2011: 997), whether divine or human or angelic. But I think we must
go further in our attempt to overcome rationalism, improving on the Boethian definition
through a more adequate triangulation: *a human person is self-subsistence in a rational nature
by participation in the relation of the Son to the Father*. For personhood is a possibility generated for us by God, first by *gratia creans* and second by *gratia elevans*, mediated in view of
the fall by *gratia sanans*; that is, by baptism.

On this explicitly theological definition all humans are persons and have the metaphysical
or ontological dignity pertaining to persons, though it is recognized that not all humans
are or will be fully personalized. Which is to say, all share in the *imago dei*, but not all will
be glorified through advance in the mysteries of God, through which both the person and
the nature are perfected (see *Haer.* 2.25–29, 4.33ff., and book 5). In that advance our condition changes greatly while our nature, as embodied rational souls in receipt of the Spirit,
remains the same and our persons remain self-identical. What renders our nature mortal
(deficiency as yet in receipt of the Spirit) and what causes us actually to perish (resistance to
the Word and the Spirit) is overcome and disappears. That is the change in our condition,

put negatively. Positively, we become *non posse peccare* and *non posse mori* through a higher form of participation in the three-personed God and so in the divine nature as such, a nature which *is* personal (cf. *Civ.* 22.30).

Did I say "theological"? I meant also "liturgical," for this definition derives from baptism, in which radical discontinuity of condition, and even (for adults) a change of name to mark the transition from the old man to the new, means restoration of nature and person through liberation from autonomous self-enclosure to a mode of existence that is through and for the other. In union with Christ, the great danger in the high and holy privilege of being self-subsistent—namely, that one might attempt to be self-sufficient, to be through and for oneself only, thus corrupting both person and nature—is overcome. Overcome how? By reinsertion, so to say, in God's own way of being personal. (See again *Demo.* 7, quoted above at 1:2–5; cf. Rom. 8.)

Grappling with the problem of continuity and discontinuity as it pertains to the person inwardly rather than outwardly, to the rational soul rather than to the body, leads to a number of difficult questions that Paul does not attempt to address. Brief comments on a few of them are nevertheless in order. Plainly Paul does not think the sleep of death a state of oblivion, since to depart this world, he says, is to be with Christ, a condition far better than living here (Phil. 1:23; 2 Cor. 5:6–8). Here we are clothed only with the rags of our mortal bodies and lack, despite Christ's eucharistic presence (1 Cor. 10:1–22), the full intimacy with him that Paul anticipates experiencing after death. But what is this "far better" experience of being with Christ? Shall we call it heaven? And is it preceded by a personal judgment of some sort? By a process of purgation? Those who go to sleep in Christ can expect to rise at the last day, but what should they expect meanwhile? What can "meanwhile" mean? Christians are bound to ask such questions, whether or not the Thessalonians had yet thought of posing them.

Asking is one thing, of course, and answering another. There is no biblical declaration about a particular judgment at death, whether in Paul or anywhere else. (Texts such as 2 Cor. 5:10 and Heb. 9:27 seem rather to refer to the last judgment.) Nor do we find anything about a purgatorial process. That there is a determination of destiny at the time of death can be inferred from a variety of texts, however, as can belief in an intermediate state, whether blessed or cursed. (With the texts just mentioned, cf. 2 Macc. 7:35–36; Luke 12:13–20; 16:19–31.) Though some have doubted, it is the settled mind of the Church that there is an intermediate state that is not pure quiescence or soul-sleep, and hence that there is also a determination of destiny made known to the soul at death. It is a very short step from there to some doctrine of purgatory, though that step was not taken formally until the Council of Florence, since to whatever degree the soul is aware of its union with Christ it is aware also of its need to be perfectly centered on Christ and to be free, not merely from penalty but also from the perversion that gives rise to penalty. It is also the settled mind of the Church that those who are properly centered on Christ enjoy with him the vision of God, that they no longer see as in a mirror dimly but face to face, that they know as they are known (1 Cor. 13:12).

▨ Anselm states the obvious: "God cannot raise up to a state of blessedness anyone who is to any extent bound by the indebtedness arising from sin" (*CDH* 1.21); that is at once a matter of the justice of God, the good order of the universe, and the requirements of happiness itself. God can, however, raise up those who are unbound through their union with Christ: "Take me and redeem yourself" (2.20). There is no deficiency in what is being offered, either to us or to God! But in us there may be a deficiency in the personal capacity to receive and enjoy the exchange by which we are redeemed and raised up. The doctrine of purgatory, properly understood, is about the rectification of that.   ▨

The doctrine of purgatory can be put simply: "All who die in God's grace, but still imperfectly purified, are indeed assured of their eternal salvation; but after death they undergo purification, so as to achieve the holiness necessary to enter the joy of heaven" (*CCC* §1030). Or still more simply: "purification through fire in the encounter with the Lord, Judge and Saviour" (Benedict XVI 2007: 48). It is as inconceivable that the rational soul undergoes no refining fire, that it receives no purification or liberation from the ways and consequences of its spiritual corruption, as it is that the body undergoes no reconstitution and liberation from the ways and consequences of material corruption. "Though our outer man is wasting away," say the baptized, "our inner man is being renewed every day. . . . Slight momentary affliction is preparing for us an eternal weight of glory" (2 Cor. 4:16–17). Yet not all are equally prepared when this life comes to an end, not all are ready for that weight of glory. Shall he who has begun in us a good work not bring it to completion, burning away the dross to reveal the glory (Phil. 1:6; cf. Rom. 8:18–30)?

But what sort of fire burns the soul that is absent from the body? How does the soul that, despite its sacramental preparation, perchance even its martyrial preparation, suffers still from imperfect virtues and remaining vices, come to be perfected once it has left the body? How does the person, the inner person, insofar as this is not yet the case, come to be through and for himself precisely as one who is through and for the Son and, just so, for the Father? The fire in question is already burning in the soul while it is still in the body, and the brighter it burns the more one attains readiness for the resurrection of the dead, counting "everything as loss because of the surpassing worth of knowing Christ Jesus" (Phil. 3:7–11). The widespread notion that purgatory is a place to which we go in order to pay for post-baptismal sin is semi-Pelagian. Purgatory is the whole process of learning by grace the surpassing worth of Christ.

In ordinary usage, however, the term references only that part of the process that takes place at or after death, when the soul stands naked before him, unable to blame the body, or the neighbor, or the serpent, or in any other way to hide from the truth about itself and its deeds in the body. But that is only the negative side. The positive side is that the soul that stands naked before Christ and without any possibility of further dissimulation is, by that very fact, known to itself truly. Moreover, Christ is known to it truly, and for both reasons able to be loved by it truly, to be preferred in every way above everything. Purgatorial fire burns uniquely in and for each soul according to its remaining need of knowledge of God in Christ and knowledge in Christ of itself. The soul cannot love perfectly what it does not know perfectly, but neither can it know perfectly what it does not love perfectly. God will show himself to the soul, that the soul may know and love God. God will show the soul itself, so that the soul may truly despise what it was apart from Christ and truly love itself as made new in Christ. God, in other words, will see to it that the soul is able to fulfill the great commandments.

The doctrine of purgatory ought to cause both holy fear and holy rejoicing, for the fire of purgatory is the fire of truth and love, the divine fire. It is also a fire that has already been kindled in us, a fire that belongs to us in Christ. It is not a fire that burns by divine fiat only but also by the human *fiat mihi*. The body will rise up and walk when it is instructed to do so at the last day. It will do exactly what it is told, by God and by the soul, when it is no longer alienated from the soul. But how is the soul itself delivered of all alienation from God? How does it live in the immortal light of God? How is it deified? The soul cannot simply be told to "rise and walk." In being told, it must make reply, for that is its nature. It cannot simply be commanded, it must consent. It must not only consent, it must love, for it is proper to a person to love. There must be discontinuity—a miraculous transformation of soul, as of body, in union with Christ—but there must be continuity also. To reject Pelagianism is not to reject that! To know as we are known, we must love as we are loved. I myself must love and love truly, or

I shall never enter the kingdom of love or sing the new song of joy that is sung in the city of God. I shall never enter the joy of my Lord. "I live, yet not I, but Christ lives in me"? Just so. But that is now, not then. Then I shall live in Christ as fully as Christ lives in me. That is the great mystery of deification, of the unspeakable glory at which we aim. "Beloved, we are already children of God, and it does not yet appear what we shall be. We know that when he appears we shall be like him, that we shall see him just as he is. And every one having this hope in him purifies himself, even as he is pure" (1 John 3:2–3 AT). All this a doctrine of purgatory must try to say.

We ought to dispense with two impediments to a proper understanding of this doctrine, one cosmological and the other juridical. The former arises from supposing the time of the intermediate state to be our own secular time, or its analogue in a sort of parallel aeon or world suspended between earth and heaven. This derives originally from the *exitus/ reditus* scheme of the Platonists. Origen tried to reiterate that scheme within Christianity as a purgatorial process that requires many aeons. Though this was viewed as heterodox, it survived in the simplistic version that posits one such aeon. That was justified by an overly literal reading of Jesus's parable of Dives and Lazarus, to which was added, quite without warrant, a distinct fiery realm, not separated from paradise by an uncrossable gulf but open upwards. (Dante eventually gave this a powerful poetic form, which also has been read too literally.) The latter or juridical impediment reinforces the cosmological. It arises from thinking of purgatory not in terms of completing conversion to Christ but rather in terms of completing a sentence handed down, of suffering the temporal penalties accruing to post-baptismal sin. This is what Joseph Ratzinger objected to when he criticized Tertullian for imagining "some kind of supra-worldly concentration camp where man is forced to undergo punishment in a more or less arbitrary fashion." We ought instead to think of purgatory as "the inwardly necessary process of transformation in which a person becomes capable of Christ, capable of God and thus capable of unity with the whole communion of saints" (1988: 230). We may add that the time of purgatory, of this inwardly necessary process insofar as it is still necessary after death, is whatever kind of time a soul can have through its participation in the descent and ascent of Jesus Christ. It is still eucharistic, in other words, and from the perspective of secular time can take place in the twinkling of an eye. Attempts to measure it in secular time, the time of bodily motion in the present world, arise from a basic category mistake.

Unfortunately, though not surprisingly, there remained much confusion about this through the patristic period and into the medieval era. Correcting that confusion does not mean rejecting the very idea of purgatory, as Protestants did, or claiming that we who inhabit the *saeculum* should not pray for the dead or do penance for the dead, as in 2 Macc. 12:38–45 (a practice taken up by the Church, unlike the practice of being baptized for the dead). Still less does it mean that we cannot seek the intercessions of "the angels in festal gathering" and "the spirits of just men made perfect" (Heb. 12:22–23), another early form of Christian piety that suffered collateral damage in the Reformation. This we can do and should do, since our time and our lives intersect with theirs in the Eucharist, as the author of Hebrews is plainly saying. It does mean, however, that there is pastoral benefit in clearing up the confusion as far as possible, on which we can make a start by pausing again with Augustine for a moment.

In book 21 of *The City of God* Augustine undertakes to correct those Christians who posit with the Platonists that all penal sufferings are remedial, a notion linked to the pagan doctrine of eternal return. Only those sufferings incurred before the last judgment are possibly remedial, he insists. Remedial punishments "are suffered by some in this life only, by others after death, by others both now and then; but all of them before that last and strictest judgment." Of those who suffer after death, some are and some are not "doomed to those everlasting pains which are to follow that judgment," because in some cases what has not been remitted in this world will be remitted in the next (21.13, *NPNF¹* 2:463ff.). Remedial or otherwise, there are "pains proper to the spirits of the dead" (21.24.2). Perhaps there are pains proper to the body too, he allows, though rather hesitantly: "But if it be said that in the interval of time between the death of this body and that last day of judgment and retribution which shall follow the resurrection, the bodies of the dead shall be exposed to a fire of such a nature that it shall not affect those who have not in this life indulged in such pleasures and pursuits as shall be consumed like wood, hay, stubble, but shall affect those others who have carried with them structures of that kind; if it be said that such worldliness, being venial, shall be consumed in the fire of tribulation either here only, or here and hereafter both, or here that it may not be hereafter—this I do not contradict, because possibly it is true." All this, he speculates, may belong to the trajectory of death to which the body itself succumbs, "so that the time which follows death takes its color in each case from the nature of the man's building" (21.26.4). At all events, purgatorial pains are certainly to be distinguished from the pains of eternal punishment.

What Augustine did not attempt to correct or clarify, unfortunately, is the relation between punishment and remediation. This left an opening for the idea that justice requires that every sin be accounted for by a punishment, condign not arbitrary—if not in this life, then in the intermediate state where souls await the last judgment. Purgatory thus continued to take on a juridical hue, retributive rather than remedial justice coming to the fore. Construed in that way, the doctrine eventually suffered a great many abuses that, a millennium later, had no small part to play in the Protestant schism. And all quite unnecessarily, for what Augustine himself aimed at is what the doctrine ought to aim at; namely, an account of the importance, indeed the necessity, of learning to love and prefer Christ above all things, and so to wage war against vice with all keenness by delighting in true righteousness (21.16). The keynotes of Augustine's response to those "perversely compassionate persons" who, like the Platonists, could not bring themselves to acknowledge the reality of hell ought also to be the keynotes of any doctrine of purgatory. One is the note of freedom and, hence, responsibility; the other is the note of grace and salvation. "'How great is the abundance of Your sweetness, Lord, which You have hidden for them that fear You!' . . . Let us then seek that sweetness of His, which He perfects to them that hope in Him, not that which He is supposed to perfect to those who despise and blaspheme Him; for in vain, after this life, does a man seek for what he has neglected to provide while in this life" (21.24.5). Again: "We shall then ascertain who it is who can be saved by fire, if we first discover what it is to have Christ for a foundation" (21.26.2). And who is it who has Christ as a foundation but the one who, in the last analysis, prefers Christ to all else? Purgatorial fire is permitted the baptized precisely for the purpose of exposing the true foundation of a person and making clear to him the source of divine sweetness. In that respect it is all of a piece with tribulation in this life and unnecessary where the foundation and source have already become clear.

Augustine knows, with Paul, that there is but one possible foundation for the happy life. He knows that whatever we have built in this life—if in any sense we have built on Christ— will be disclosed on the day of the Lord. The wood, hay, and stubble produced in pursuit of carnal pleasures will go up in smoke; the silver, gold, and precious stones of spiritual virtues and spiritual works will survive as material for the kingdom (1 Cor. 3:11–15). He knows that our readiness for the day of the Lord requires purgatorial suffering before and sometimes after death to completely center us on Christ, and he is especially conscious of the suffering that will accompany the Church in the last days to effect its collective readiness. He does not view purgatorial suffering primarily in terms of the tabulation of sins and penalties for sin, but in terms of the capacity to see, to rest upon, and to incarnate the grace of God. He reminds us that without holiness no one will see God or take part in the kingdom of God and that, if we do not seek holiness in this life at all, we cannot hope to seek or find it afterward (→2 Thess. 1:3–10). If we do seek it in this life, we shall find it afterward, however we find it. He reminds us also that what we are seeking is the righteousness of Christ, in which we may share, not a righteousness of our own apart from Christ. The former is sought by those in whom perfect love is casting out fear; the latter by those motivated only by an ungodly fear. We may conclude, then, quite in keeping with Augustine, that any doctrine of purgatory that promotes ungodly fear is a false doctrine, just as any doctrine of justification that sets aside the need for full and perfect sanctification is a false doctrine—false for want of godly fear. Doctrines of purgatory focused on satisfaction for post-baptismal sin through punishment tend to the former; doctrines denying any need for purgatory at all tend to the latter (see Farrow 2018g: chaps. 3–4). ▪

Entering the joy of the Lord is the goal of Christian living and Christian dying. "Blessed are the pure in heart, for they shall see God" (Matt. 5:8). It is in view of that goal and in reliance on that promise that the fathers at Florence asserted in their decree of union that "the souls of those who have incurred no stain of sin whatsoever after baptism, as well as souls who after incurring the stain of sin have been cleansed whether in their bodies or outside their bodies, . . . are straightaway received into heaven and clearly behold the triune God as he is, yet one person more perfectly than another according to the difference of their merits" (*DEC* 1:527f.). No one, of course, whatever their merits, sees God without God, as we have already observed; for only God can see God, and only God can make the creature see God (cf. *ST* 1.12.4, 1.12.6). When Paul cries out, "Wretched man that I am! Who will deliver me from this body of death?" (Rom. 7:24), he makes the only possible response, the eucharistic response: "Thanks be to God through Jesus Christ our Lord!" It follows that the mystery we are talking about, in relation to soul or body, must for now remain a mystery, like the eucharistic *conversio* itself. It is not for us to resolve the problem of continuity and discontinuity, but only to press on toward the goal, to keep reaching for the prize. Yet some, like Schleiermacher (1989: §157ff.), have stumbled at this problem, even to disbelieving the biblical narrative about the parousia and the resurrection of the dead, while others have distinguished themselves by much foolishness in apocalyptic speculation. Both deserve the rebuke Jesus directed at the Sadducees for their ignorance of the scriptures and of the power of God. We must strive rather with the fathers to strike a judicious balance between what can and can't be said, knowing what it is that will happen without pretending to know how or in precisely what order (*Civ.* 20.30.5). Regarding the appearing of Jesus—this very same but oh so different Jesus—he himself has told us what will happen.

When the enthronement of the Son of Man in heaven is fully disclosed on earth, when the fanfare of heaven is heard on earth, when the cleansing of the heavenly realm is repeated on earth, all this will be centered on Jerusalem (Farrow 2011: 122ff.). But Jesus will not be taking a room at the Ramada or a suite at the King David Hotel. He will not be coming as once he came, riding on a donkey, with a crowd shouting praises they did not understand or did not really mean. He will come in all his glory, and his coming will be like lightning that flashes to the ends of the earth (Matt. 24:27). "On that day the LORD will punish the host of heaven, in heaven, and the kings of the earth, on the earth" (Isa. 24:21; cf. Exod. 32:17ff.). His faithful ones will flock to him in the midst of the two, as he comes to "reign on Mount Zion and in Jerusalem" and to display his glory "before his elders" (Isa. 24:23; cf. Rev. 4).

Besides the Synoptic accounts drawn from Jesus, we have no better description of his coming than what Paul provides here in 1 Thessalonians. Even the Apocalypse offers us, at the last, only an image Caesar would quickly have recognized had he bothered reading that coded work: a ruler Faithful and True, seated on a white steed, ready to ride up triumphantly when his armies have done their furious work routing the forces of a corrupt contender (Rev. 19:11–16). The rest is left to our imagination. Paul's vision (which in 2 Thessalonians will be explained further) is a bit more explicit, drawing as it does on Exodus and Daniel and Matthew, and on whatever special knowledge Paul may have received. Michelangelo's famous painting brings to the surface the Sinaitic layer that underlies the imperial imagery in both authors, particularly the allusions to Exod. 19 and 32, where the descent of God to be greeted by his people and the descent of Moses to winnow them with the sword together foreshadow the glorious and terrible descent of the God-man. When the latter appears from heaven, from the Glory-cloud that once again will hover over the holy mountain—now Zion, not Sinai—he will not come by foot, as Moses did. He will not come like Caesar either, on horseback or by carriage. He will not come by announcements posted in taverns along the road, followed by hoofbeats and the voice of imperial trumpets. He will come after the mighty deeds and sober warnings of his two witnesses—this is John's addition—and he will come suddenly, with the voice of the archangel and the sound of that divine *shofar* that the Israelites could not stand (cf. Theodoret on 4:15), the sound that now shall pierce every corner of creation, reaching even the remains of the faithful dead, beginning with those on the side of Jerusalem that looks toward Olives. The living will not rush out ahead of the dead, but the faithful dead and the faithful living, wherever they may be, will be snatched up to him as he returns to Jerusalem and will greet him together, accompanying him into the holy city. In that very snatching up they will be conformed to him and so be assured of being forever with him. They will swell the ranks of the heavenly host to the size and array required for the bliss and glory of the new Jerusalem.

No apology need be made for this riot of biblical images in which the Sinaitic and Zionist allusions ultimately overwhelm the imperial. At Rev. 11:15–19 John brings them to order when he writes: "Then the seventh angel blew his trumpet, and there were loud voices in heaven, saying, 'The kingdom of the world has become the kingdom of our Lord and of his Christ, and he shall reign for ever and ever.' And the twenty-four elders who sit on their thrones before God fell on their faces and worshiped God, saying, 'We give thanks to you, Lord God Almighty, who are and who were, that you have taken your great power and begun to reign. The nations raged, but your wrath came, and the time for the dead to be judged, for rewarding your servants, the prophets and saints, and those who fear your name, both small and great, and for destroying the destroyers of the earth.' Then God's temple in heaven was opened, and the ark of his covenant was seen within his temple; and there were flashes of lightning, loud noises, peals of thunder, an earthquake, and heavy hail." And if it be objected that all this is too earthbound, too salvation-historical, that neither Paul nor John have any interest in the geography of salvation—Fee (2009: 181f.) maintains that rather Marcionite thesis with respect to Paul—it may be replied that a Jew without geography is no Jew, even if he be a Christian Jew.

No apology is necessary either, in a theological commentary, for thinking about Paul and John together, particularly where they are united by appeal to Sinaitic cloud imagery. It is in the preceding verses of Rev. 11 that John introduces the two olive trees or two witnesses who have Moses- and Elijah-like powers to punish the earth's inhabitants and who, after martyrdom, hear the heavenly trumpet that wakes the dead, going up to heaven like Jesus ἐν τῇ νεφέλῃ, which we may take to be a reference to the cloud of the Presence (Exod. 13:21–22; cf. Acts 1:9). Paul, for his part, has just declared by dominical authority that the destiny of all the faithful is to greet the Lord in the air, to meet him in the pillar of cloud and fire when he comes to judge and to save, there to offer him the royal welcome (ἀπάντησις) he deserves. The command heard by the two witnesses, "Come up here," is one that will be heard by all who are "on the LORD's side" (Exod. 32:26, a text, as Ambrosiaster [Thiselton 2011: 125] remarks, that strikes an ominous note; cf. Rev. 14:14).

Michelangelo means to encourage the righteous but also to warn the unrighteous, as does Chrysostom in his treatment of these final verses of chapter 4. "If sudden death," writes the latter, "or earthquakes in cities and threatenings [such as were foretold in Matt. 24] terrify our souls, when we see the earth breaking up and crowded with all these [the dead whom God is calling forth], when we hear the trumpets, and the voice of the Archangel louder than any trumpet, when we perceive the heaven shriveled up, and God the King of all himself coming near, what then will be [the state of] our souls? Let us shudder, I beseech you, and be frightened as if these things were now taking place. Let us not comfort ourselves by the delay! For when it must certainly happen, the delay profits us nothing" (*Hom.* 8). Chrysostom then undertakes a long discourse designed to disabuse us of any conceit that the events of which Paul is speaking will not lead to the ultimate discontinuity, the irreconcilable discontinuity, between heaven and hell. Though God is indeed "full of love to man," it is incumbent upon man to take heed of the choice before him, as Jesus also taught (Farrow 2020b).

Who is on the Lord's side? The question cannot be avoided, nor can the consequences of its answer. So there is false comfort and true. The false arises from vain appeals to the love or mercy of God that seek to evade the question. The true belongs to those "of highest station"—the faithful who will go out of the city to greet the King with gladness "while those accused of crimes await the arrival of the judge inside." The former will comfort one another in the meanwhile, and "bear nobly the troubles of the present age" (Theodoret 2001: 118). For they know that they too shall "be caught up in the Spirit" at the close of the age and ride upon the clouds. "Lo the chariot of Elijah, lo the fire, though not seen are prepared, that the just may ascend, the innocent be borne forth, and thy life may not know death" (Ambrose, *DFR* 94, in *NPNF²* 10:189).

A word must now be said about death and grieving. Death, as Ambrose insists, "was no part of man's nature, but became natural; for God did not institute death at first, but gave it as a remedy" (*DFR* 47). Death, he tells us, is threefold: spiritual death, "when we die to sin, but live to God"; natural death, "when the soul is set free from the bonds of the body"; and eternal death, the death of punishment, when "not only the flesh but also the soul dies" (*DFR* 36–37). But this analysis is marred by too positive a view of "natural" death, which has a penal as well as a remedial element. Augustine's fourfold analysis is more helpful: "The death of the soul occurs . . . when it is abandoned by God, just as the death of the body occurs when it is abandoned by the soul. And the death of the two together— that is, the death of the whole human being—happens when the soul, itself abandoned by God, abandons the body. For, in that case, neither does the soul draw life from God, nor the body from the soul. This death of the whole human being is followed by . . . the second death. This is the death to which the Savior referred when he said, *Fear him who has the power to destroy both body and soul in hell*" (*Civ.* 13.2, trans. Babcock). Since death can only happen to those who are evil—that is, to those whose souls have ceased to draw their life from God—death cannot be good. Like everything else, however, it can be used for good by God and by those who are good (13.3–8).

Death is a kind of mercy to fallen man, certainly. Yet death is not man's friend, since it marks the dissolution of the unity between soul and body that man is and ought to be (Tolkien 1993: 303–66). Death is good, given the fall, for it is good that there is a limit both to sin and to suffering. Yet death remains a judgment on man's condition, not a solution to it. It remains an enemy, even where it is a friend. As Paul says, it is the last enemy, but also an enemy now overcome (1 Cor. 15:26; cf. Farrow 2018f). We have good reason, then, to grieve death, which separates body from soul and friend from friend. As Ambrose himself says: "Not all weeping proceeds from unbelief or weakness. Natural grief is one thing, distrustful sadness is another, and there is a very great difference between longing for what you have lost and lamenting that you have lost it" (*Exc.* 1.10, in *NPNF²* 10:162).

Those who grieve with the knowledge that what has been lost, or who has been lost, is not lost to God but kept safe in Jesus Christ to be found again at the last day, grieve, but not as those who have no hope. They long, but do not lament.

What, though, of grief over those who are not known to be in Christ? If, as Ambrosiaster says, we are not to lament "those who depart with the sign of the cross" (*Commentarius* 3.226, in Thiselton 2011: 124f.), what of loved ones who depart without that sign? There is a temptation here to pretend, to suppose that a Christian funeral or memorial is sufficient to impose that sign. It is true that only God knows, in the last analysis, those who are his, those whom he will bring to life with Christ on the last day. We are sometimes mistaken in hope about those who depart with the sign of the cross and mistaken in doubt about those who do not. The certainty of our hope is in Christ, not in ourselves. Thus the sphere of hope for the dead is not definitely delimited by visible signs of faith or even by the sacraments and rites of the Church, though the latter must be reserved for those who in faith have sought them (cf. *CCC* §1680–90; *CIC* 1183–85; on suicide, *CCC* §2280–87). Nevertheless, though in the transition from the old covenant to the new there was briefly such a thing as baptism for the dead, if baptism and baptismal faithfulness mean anything at all—if the difference between a confessor and a denier of Jesus Christ, between a martyr and a *traditor*, means anything—there is a difference, a most profound difference, between those who go to sleep under the sign of the cross and those who do not (1 Cor. 15:29–34). So what, then, of grief over the latter? The answer is still that we must not grieve like the rest, who have no hope. For even if we have very little hope in the salvation of the loved one, yet we have much hope in God, who sustains us despite our grief, and whose judgment of the deceased will be just and true. We cannot grieve as the rest because all our relationships and all our loves, if from our side they are true loves, are held within and not apart from the love of God, to whom both the lover and the beloved always belong qua creatures capable of love. Nor should we ever forget that the fate of the beloved rests on how, in the end, he is disposed to the love of God. One who is not disposed to, and therefore by, the love of God for eternal life cannot be disposed to or by our love either. Therefore we must not cling to what we have lost or to the one whom we have lost. Our grieving may be more painful, something closer to lament, but it cannot be the untempered lament of those who do not know the love of God, any more than it can be the stoic shrug of those who merely recognize their impotence before the unfeeling hand of Fate. We must learn to grieve as God grieves, who "desires all men to be saved" (1 Tim. 2:4) but whose eternal joy is not, by reason of the refusal of some, in any way blighted or diminished. Of this we are not ourselves capable, to be sure, since as creatures we are passible, not impassible. But elevating grace can make us capable, and for that we should pray, lest by inordinate attachment to a loved one, we fall into distrustful sadness. ▪

5:1–3 Concerning the times and the seasons, brethren, [again] you have no need that we should write to you, for you know full well that the day of the Lord is coming like a thief in the night. Just when they say, "Peace and security!"—then suddenly destruction comes upon them, as labor pains [come] upon her who is with child, and they will by no means escape.

Paul, for his part, knows full well (however he knows it) the eschatological teaching of Jesus, just as he is well versed in the prophetic texts on which Jesus drew. He has already passed on to the Thessalonians the general gist of that teaching. Of the chief practical point, that the world will not be ready for the Lord's coming and that they themselves must be, the Thessalonians have a sound grasp. They have learned the fundamentals accurately (ἀκριβῶς). The present exchange about times and seasons, about people crying "peace" when there is no peace, about a thief in the night and sudden destruction, is based on the dominical discourse later recorded in Mark 13, Matt. 24, and Luke 21. Paul's mission in Thessaloniki may have been cut short, but not so short that he has failed to share with them the exhortation of Jesus to read the signs of the times and to be prepared for what is coming. So he can cut straight to the chase, as indeed he does.

▨ "It is not for you to know times or seasons which the Father has fixed by his own authority," says Jesus (Acts 1:7; cf. 17:26). The expression χρόνους ἢ καιρούς should be read hendiadically, as at Dan. 2:21 LXX, which has καιροὺς καὶ χρόνους. It references the eras, arrangements, and movements that lead in due course to the end of history, for secular history will come to an end. Like the phases of the moon or of earth's relation to the sun and stars, the times and seasons are fixed by God; but unlike those phases, they are not, or not precisely, predictable by man. Neither man nor angel, but only the Father in heaven, knows them with any exactitude. Only from the sanctuary of God, at God's good pleasure, are orders issued to those who enforce the boundaries (cf. Rev. 14:14–16). Hence we cannot know when the day of the Lord will come and his kingdom appear, for no one knows that except the Father (Mark 13:32). It follows that Christians must not be drafters of eschatological timelines. It does not follow that they can afford to ignore the character and course of the present age, or the dénouement toward which it moves. If they don't know about that, they won't know how to live in the present age, or how to "take heed, watch and pray" (Mark 13:33). Those today who are as quick to dispense with the knowledge Jesus and Paul took such trouble to share, and the Evangelists to record, as they are to excoriate those who proffer speculative timelines, have missed the point—most likely because they don't mean to watch and pray.   ▨

Paul has spoken of the end to which the Church looks, of what it longingly awaits. He speaks now of the end to which the world does not look, the end that will take it quite by surprise. This is not the end for which God made it but the end to which it is nonetheless coming insofar as it persists in its opposition to the purposes of God, insofar as it seeks its end outside of God. For what did God establish the human race? For what did he establish the whole creation, including the angels? That all rational souls should flourish, each in the way proper to it, in "that most orderly and harmonious society to be enjoyed with God and mutually in God" (*Civ.* 19.13.1 AT), enjoying "eternal life in peace, or peace in eternal life" (19.11.1). But not all seek the city of God; many prefer the city of man. It too seeks peace, and sometimes supposes itself to have found it. Peace and security (εἰρήνη καὶ ἀσφάλεια is also hendiadic) were promised by the empire and its officials, and frequently said to have been delivered (Witherington 2006: 146f.; Weima 2014: 350f.). Such peace is partial and transitory, however, and always contains the seeds of its own destruction. The security it affords comes at a high cost in freedom. Moreover, the nearer the city of man comes to something with an air of permanence, the nearer it comes—as Babel, rising up and up like Noah's ark, unknowingly did—to its final judgment. Though its denizens say, "at last we have found peace and security," destruction comes upon them because this peace and security is based not on God but on man himself in his attempt to usurp the place of God. At the last, it will come very suddenly, because that destruction will not be the destruction brought on naturally by the decline of right reason, the destruction history has witnessed so many times before. It will be the supernatural destruction brought about by the parousia of the man God has appointed to judge the world in righteousness. It will take them unawares, like the flood, and it will be a universal destruction that none can escape, save those who have chosen the city of God over the city of man (Matt. 24:36–44; cf. Amos 9:1).

The tower of Babel was built after the flood. It was to reach to heaven, in defiance of any future flood, yet it came to nothing. The tower of Techno-Man— the man who makes and manages himself and his world without reference to God—that we are now building we are building in dismissal of the judgment that overtook Jerusalem in AD 70, and of the Crucified One whose death sealed Jerusalem's fate. Its architects continue to plot in vain against the Lord and his anointed (Ps. 2). They utter delusions and promulgate lies and say "peace" when there is no peace (Ezek. 13:8; cf. Amos 6). Their tower is not visible to the eye, like a single great ziggurat against the horizon. It is slowly wrapping itself around the whole world, which will soon be inside rather than outside. What will it look like when it is done? Who will stand on its commanding heights? What regimen will it enforce? We do not know, but we know that the judgment that overtakes it will not be like the judgment that overtook the builders of Babel. It will be like the judgment that overtook Jerusalem, the judgment so graphically predicted by the prophet Amos—complete, universal, overwhelming judgment, with not one stone left upon another. "Flee to the mountains," advised Jesus; but at the end will there be anywhere to flee? For his own, perhaps, for his eye is on the sparrow; but not for those taken by surprise when the lightning of his parousia flashes out from Jerusalem to the ends of the earth. His angelic legions will gather to him the faithful, from among the living and the dead, having already gathered against him, for destruction, the unfaithful.

As with the head, so with the members? Yes, and as with faithless Israel, so also with the faithless nations. They will quarrel over the city of man, as Sadducees and Zealots quarreled over the holy city, until they are united by their opposition to the holy city itself; or rather, to the Jews who are regathering there and to their messianic brethren, Jew and Gentile, in the city of God that is spread round the world. And just when they suppose that they are in year one of the kingdom of man, as Bar Kokhba once imagined he was in year one of the kingdom of God, their destruction shall come upon them suddenly.

We may ask here, parenthetically, whether faithless Israel will then still exist. The question is difficult to answer. According to Paul, "all Israel will be saved." By that he seems to mean "the Israel of God" (Gal. 6:16; cf. Amos 9:8–15), the Israel that is joined to Jesus by the Spirit, the Israel that is not merely of Abraham κατὰ σάρκα but κατὰ πνεῦμα, the spiritual Israel that includes both the righteous remnant and baptized Gentiles; in short, the Church. But in this Israel of God Paul also seems to envision, at the time of the end, most of ethnic Israel, which he does not believe God has abandoned or will abandon (Farrow 2018c). How Israel κατὰ σάρκα will be drawn more fully into Israel κατὰ πνεῦμα he does not say, beyond insisting that the gospel is for the Jew first and appealing to the faithfulness of God, who will eventually make many more Jews jealous of the benefits that Gentiles, disproportionately, have derived from the gospel.

Dare we speculate, without any pretense that the speculation is Pauline, that the work of the two witnesses may, at the last, have something to do with that? We need not confine ourselves, as Joseph Mangina (2010: 134–41) does, to the idea that they are only a prophetic type referring to "the oil of testimony" that in the Church never runs dry. Perhaps they are that, but why not also individuals? In the passage on which Rev. 11 builds, Zechariah thrice asks the angel to identify the olive trees or witnesses, and is twice teased by the reply, "Do you not know what these are?" His profession of ignorance finally elicits the counterintuitive explanation, "These are the two anointed who stand by the Lord of the whole earth" (Zech. 4:14). John has them coming to do battle with "the beast that ascends from the bottomless pit" (Rev. 11:7) in the final week of years, that "broken seven" (in Mangina's terminology) that is divided in two by their martyrdom, just as all of history, itself figuratively a week, is divided by the cross of Christ (→2 Thess. 2:1–5). There may be something to the tradition that names the witnesses as Enoch and Elijah, who were snatched away, without yet dying, and told to stand by the Lord of the whole earth until further notice (cf. Wis. 4:10–15). At all events, there is likely something to the notion that Israel κατὰ σάρκα is still to witness in its midst, just when it most needs it, a deeply disturbing testimony through which many will be convicted of the truth of the gospel and readied to greet the Lord when he comes (Matt. 23:39; cf. Farrow 2018a).

5:4–11 But you, [dear] brothers, are not in darkness, that the day [of the Lord] should steal up on you as a thief, for you are all sons of the light and sons of the day. We are not of the night, nor of the darkness. So, then, let us not sleep, like the rest, but rather watch and be sober. For those who sleep sleep at night, and those who get drunk get drunk at night. But we who are of the day should be [wakeful and] sober, having donned the body armor of faith and love and, as a helmet, the hope of salvation. Because God has destined us not for wrath but for obtaining salvation through our Lord Jesus Christ, who died on our behalf that, whether we should remain on watch or have fallen asleep [in Christ], we might live together with him [when he comes]. So carry on as you are, encouraging one another, each supporting the other.

"Awake, O sleeper, and arise from the dead, and Christ shall give you light" (Eph. 5:14; cf. Mal. 4:1–3; Luke 1:76–79). The Thessalonians are among those on whom the light of Christ has already fallen. Since they belong to the day, they have no reason to be caught off guard. Still, that remains possible, as Jesus warns the church in Sardis. "If you refuse to awake, I will come like a thief and you will certainly not know at what hour I will come upon you" (Rev. 3:3 AT). Paul doesn't know of Sardis, but is solicitous of Thessaloniki. A master of the mixed metaphor, he has joined here, under the "nighttime" motif that binds them together, images of the thief who strikes in the wee hours and of the army that creeps up under cover of darkness. The day of the Lord is the thief, the heavenly host is the army. Those who sleep spiritually are the target of the former, whether they are carrying on as if there were to be no day of the Lord, stubbornly refusing to acknowledge such signs as are given, or whether by debauchery they are defrauding themselves of the salvation it will bring. The faithful are the target of the latter, for the heavenly host will effect their rescue. So are the nations that oppose them, which will be brought under the rod of judgment, final and irreversible judgment.

▪ Sleep, in the present sense, need not be a purely passive condition. It may be filled with ardor, even moral ardor, in passionate pursuit of utopian dreams wherein, as in natural dreams, one thing does not properly connect with another—where rights are detached from right, freedom from fidelity, love from the gift of life, peace from the God of peace. To sleep spiritually is not necessarily to deny all spiritual interests, preferring material goods and comforts only. It is, more essentially, to be oblivious to the Holy Spirit, who pursuant to the ascension comes to convict the world regarding sin and righteousness, to expose it to judgment along with the ruler of this world. (In John 16:8, ἐλέγξει does not mean "convince," as the optimistic translator would have it; since Jesus is the bearer of the Spirit, his departure to the Father does not mean a greater measure of the Spirit for the world at large, but rather for witnesses to Jesus in the world.) It is to prefer a private or a popular judgment to the judgment of God, submission to which would require faith in the raising up of Jesus to God's right hand and the casting down of Satan from heaven. To sleep spiritually is to be content with Satan's deceptions. These, as the Thessalonians will discover, can as easily be apocalyptic as utopian or progressivist, though the latter are more common and are in view here.   ▪

Now, the martial imagery eventually prevails, as Paul urges the Thessalonians to arise early, put on their armor of faith, love, and hope (cf. 1:3), man the watchtower, and encourage their fellow watchers right round the walls. The army of God is coming to bring relief to them and to their embattled fortress. They long to see the banners of that friendly host appear with the dawn. They must not give up hope of rescue or suppose the night to be endless. A long night it may be, and some of their number will cede their watch and sleep in the ground before the dawn arrives; but all will rise to greet it, as Paul has already explained. "For it was not merely for those who believed on Him in the time of Tiberius Caesar that Christ came, nor did the Father exercise His providence for the men only who are now alive, but for all men altogether, who from the beginning, according to their capacity, in their generation have both feared and loved God, and practised justice and piety toward their neighbors, and have earnestly desired to see Christ, and to hear His voice. Wherefore He shall, at His second coming, first rouse from their sleep all persons of this description, and shall raise them up, as well as the rest who shall be judged, and give them a place in His kingdom" (*Haer.* 4.22.2, in *ANF* 1:494).

Donning this helmet of hope is especially important for watchmen. Hope may not be as high a virtue as love (cf. 1 Cor. 13:13), but this is its very own business. It is vital that they not gradually lose hope and begin to despair. They must "remember the predictions of the holy prophets and the commandment of the Lord and Savior" (2 Pet. 3:2), refusing to be daunted by the scoffing of those who prefer to follow their own passions and so make fun of the very notion of a coming dawn or a day of judgment, a day of recompense and reward.

▓ Among the many prophetic texts that Paul may have had in mind, Isa. 59:14–19 deserves mention (Fee 2009: 195f.), for it applies in Thessaloniki as in Jerusalem, and in the modern world as in the ancient:

> Justice is turned back,
>   and righteousness stands afar off;
> for truth has fallen in the public squares,
>   and uprightness cannot enter.
> Truth is lacking,
>   and he who departs from evil makes himself a prey.

Such was their own experience, as increasingly it is ours. God himself, however, in his displeasure, will "put on righteousness as a breastplate, and a helmet of salvation upon his head," that he might get victory over liars and evildoers, repaying them according to their deeds, while bringing salvation to his elect. As for the elect, their breastplate must be faith and love, and their helmet hope in God, who will indeed "come like a rushing stream, which the wind of the LORD drives" (59:19).

Second Peter also deserves mention here, because Peter has Paul's own text or texts in mind, along of course with the Olivet Discourse on which both are dependent. The connection Jesus makes (Matt. 24:36–39) between the universal judgment by water in the days of Noah and the coming judgment by fire is developed by Peter in a way that fortifies Paul's argument, and he explicitly comes to Paul's defense at 3:15–16. He adds features of his own by emphasizing that Noah, before the deluge, was the object of scoffing, and by reaching back behind Noah to the primeval fall of angels, rendering the entire history of the world a history suspended under signs of impending judgment. (Tolkien, in the *Ainulindalë*, does the same.) He also adds a lengthy warning about a fifth column, so to say, operating within the Church. The telltale mark of this fifth column is that it spurns the call to holiness and sanctification of the flesh emphasized by Paul (2 Pet. 2:1ff.; cf. 2 Tim. 4:1–8). Both Peter and Paul link the dominical teaching that "the day of the Lord will come like a thief" (2 Pet. 3:10; Matt. 24:43–44) very closely to the call to holiness, which in Peter is reinforced by remarks about the dissolution of the present world. Both take the conclusion to the Olivet Discourse as their own: "Watch therefore, for you do not know on what day your Lord is coming" (24:42).

The *signs* of his coming we do know. Of these we will say more in connection with 2 Thessalonians. It suffices for now to say that they are not like the chiming of a clock.

The hour of dawn is approaching—of that there is no doubt—but it does not approach in predictable increments. Nevertheless, "you know what hour it is, how it is full time now for you to wake from sleep. For salvation is nearer to us now than when we first believed; the night is far gone, the day is at hand. Let us then cast off the works of darkness and put on the armor of light; let us conduct ourselves becomingly as in the day, not in reveling and drunkenness, not in debauchery and licentiousness, not in quarreling and jealousy" (Rom. 13:11–13).

That his readers are destined for salvation, not for wrath, is the theological *Grundmotif* of Paul's Thessalonian letters. Who is Jesus, if not "the one rescuing us from the wrath that is coming" (1:10)? And how does he do that? First, by dying and rising, then by returning in such a fashion as to claim his own and to punish their enemies. The next letter will deal with that, but the present one, referencing Jesus's death directly for the first time—albeit only in a qualifying clause: τοῦ ἀποθανόντος ὑπὲρ ἡμῶν ἵνα . . . ἅμα σὺν αὐτῷ ζήσωμεν, "the one having died on our behalf that . . . we might live together with him"—invites us to touch on Paul's understanding of that death and its effects.

Paul does not find it necessary in this letter, as in his first letter to Corinth, to preach again "Christ crucified" (cf. 1 Cor. 1:23; 2:2). Perhaps he thinks the Thessalonians have already a firm grasp on that, both theologically and ethically, and that their immediate challenge lies rather in eschatology. At all events, he now specifies that the head-and-members principle, as we are calling it, applies to the crucifixion as to the resurrection, but with a vicarious element: Christ dies *on our behalf* that we might live with him. Punctuated editions of the Greek text differ here, some placing a comma after ὑπὲρ ἡμῶν, thus reading "destined us not for wrath but for obtaining salvation through our Lord Jesus Christ, who died on our behalf, that whether we should remain on watch or have fallen asleep we might live together with him." This connects living-together-with-Christ directly to being destined to salvation and only indirectly to Christ's vicarious death. How Paul would punctuate we do not know. We do know that he sees deliverance from wrath as a necessary condition of the life that is to come and that he understands Christ's vicarious death as the first phase of that deliverance. Christ dies that we might live, and this principle appears more readily if we omit the comma.

I have omitted it, though in my rendering of the passage a comma is required after "that" (ἵνα). I have also used the expression "remain on watch"—that is, on duty—so as to extend the military analogy and eliminate confusion about the kind of watching and the kind of sleeping presently in view.

It is in Romans, of course, that Paul most thoroughly develops this. He speaks there of "Jesus our Lord, who was put to death for our trespasses and raised for our justification" (4:24–25), going on in the following two chapters to expound a theology of baptismal participation in Christ. "We were buried therefore with him by baptism into death, so that as Christ was raised from the dead by the glory of the Father, we too might walk in newness of life. For if we have been united with him in a death like his, we shall certainly be united with him in a resurrection like his" (6:4–5). While we cannot treat either Romans or Corinthians here, the present text demands some account of the vicarious nature of Christ's death and its atoning effect, without which there could be no deliverance from wrath or destiny to salvation, nor any sacrament of baptism by virtue of which what is done vicariously is made participatable and hence effective for salvation.

How is it that we have peace with God? As a gift of divine grace, certainly, that freely justifies. More specifically, "through the redemption that is in Christ Jesus, whom God put forward as a propitiation, through faith, by means of his blood." This redemption displays God's righteousness, making sense of his forbearance in passing over former sins, showing him now "to be just and the justifier of the one who lives by faith," the same faith or faithfulness by which Jesus lives (Rom. 3:24–26 AT; cf. Wis. 11:23). God's righteousness is manifested in two ways, then. If he has overlooked sin, he has done so neither from careless indulgence nor from necessity, but only with a view to dealing with sin decisively and effectively. Second, in treating sin effectively through the offering of Jesus, he is able also to generate by his Spirit true repentance and a lively faith, so that by both objective and subjective means he justly justifies his people. Thus does God make good on the covenant guarantees, on his promises and his warnings, proving his own faithfulness.

How much of this Paul had already formulated and communicated to the Thessalonians is difficult to say, but his own mature reflection tells us what we need to know. Take, for example, Eph. 5, where he is again encouraging both the holiness and the watchfulness that befits children of light: "Therefore be imitators of God, as beloved children. And walk in love, as Christ loved us and gave himself up for us, a fragrant offering and sacrifice to God" (5:1–2; cf. 5:25). An offering of love, pleasing and acceptable to God—that is how sins are expiated, the righteousness of God demonstrated, and peace with God achieved. Jesus offers himself to God as we ought to and have not and by ourselves cannot. He does so on our behalf, as an act of divine love embodied in human form and rendered to God for man. And his offering is received. Having been received, it not only turns aside the divine wrath from those for whom it is received—that is, from those who avail themselves of it and live accordingly (5:3–20)—but fully justifies their deliverance from the destructive consequences of sin and their rescue from the judgment that is about to fall on the whole world.

One of the best exponents of Paul in this respect is St. Anselm, though his theology of atonement has often been distorted beyond recognition, by friend and foe alike (e.g., Stump 2018; cf. Farrow 2020a). The chief distortion is to find here a theology of atonement by punishment, which is not how Anselm sees things at all. He sees the death of Jesus just as he sees his life—in Paul's words, as a fragrant offering freely rendered to God. Every man owes God his life, of course, for he owes God all he is and has. But Jesus not only gives his life, as we sinners do not, he gives his death, which after a sinless life he does not owe. He dies in the place and condition of the Godforsaken, though not as the Godforsaken die. He dies freely not of necessity, and faithfully not faithlessly, continuing to offer himself "without blemish" to God "through the eternal Spirit" (Heb. 9:14, which with John 16:32 and Ps. 22 must inform our reading of Mark 15:34 and parallels). All this he does for our sake, in concert with the Father, who far from punishing an innocent man lovingly welcomes his offering despite the Godforsaken place from which it comes. By his death Jesus renders to God a gift of infinite value, a gift that restores man to a position of justice before God. Thus does he conjoin justice and mercy, which in God are one, by averting punishment for all who receive him and make his offering their own.

Cur deus homo is a masterful distillation of the theologies of atonement at work in Paul and Hebrews and the Gospels themselves. It wants, to be sure, a fuller treatment of Paul's doctrine of union with Christ in the Spirit, but it ably expounds his claim "that God was in Christ reconciling the world to himself" (2 Cor. 5:19 AT), that Christ died ὑπὲρ πάντων "that those who live should no longer live for themselves but for him who both died and was raised on their behalf" (5:15 AT). One thing Anselm makes especially clear, subsequent distortions notwithstanding, is that the death of Christ is not the reconciliation of God to God through punishment of the Son by the Father, but the reconciliation of man to God through the self-offering of the Son that releases man from the threat of punishment through superabundant satisfaction; that is, through the fulfilling of all righteousness (Matt. 3:13–17; cf. Heb. 5:7–10). Anselm does not shy away, however, as so many of his critics do, from the teaching of Paul and of Hebrews that "a fearful prospect of judgment, and a fury of fire which will consume the adversaries," awaits those who spurn the grace to be found in Christ (Heb. 10:5–31; cf. 2 Thess. 1:7–8).

Reminders of the coming dawn, and of deliverance from the coming wrath, are to be shared freely among the Thessalonians, each doing his part to build up (οἰκοδομεῖτε, "support" or "strengthen") the other, to restore flagging spirits, to maintain esprit de corps. It is not the dead who concern Paul, in other words, but the living; not those who sleep in Christ but those who seem to be only half awake. Unavoidably, "sleep" is deployed as a metaphor for both death and spiritual dullness. Those content with spiritual dullness have lost track of the fact that the gospel narrative, as it applies to the individual Christian, has a beginning, a middle, and an end. The beginning (justification as a declaration of good standing, for those who turn to the living and true God) is indispensable. The middle (sanctification as confirmation in that standing, for those who are tractable to the teaching of God) is equally essential. But the beginning and the middle lose their meaning and their power to motivate where the end is ignored: actual salvation, effected by the parousia of Jesus, "the one rescuing us from the wrath that is coming" and granting us access to the kingdom of God, to the harvest of eternal joy his self-offering has reaped. That is something of which we need constantly to remind one another, says Paul, persevering by virtue of "our hope of sharing the glory of God" (Rom. 5:2; see 5:1–11). If we do not persevere, neither do we obtain the salvation for which we are destined.

The sequence of Rom. 8:30—predestined, called, justified, glorified—is the sequence by which God relates to his people, corporately and individually. It is the summary of God's history with us, a summary underwritten by Jesus Christ, who is chosen before the foundation of the world as its chief actor and as the guarantor of its outcome (Eph. 1:1–2:10; 1 Pet. 1). From this, however, one ought not to draw the supralapsarian conclusions either of the universalists or the double predestinarians, which militate against finding meaningful human decision in anyone other than Christ. We also are agents who will and who act, and we can, having begun the journey to our proper destiny in Christ, abandon it if we so choose, just as our parents abandoned it in the garden of Eden. We cannot begin that journey or remain on it without the prevenient and subsequent grace of Christ and the Spirit, through whom we are now new creatures, creatures *posse non peccare* and capable of perseverance. But we are not yet, since we are not glorified, creatures *non posse peccare* or incapable of apostasy. Hence obtaining or possessing our salvation means also "attaining to" our salvation (on περιποίησις, cf. Richard 1995: 255f.; see further Augustine, *Civ.* 11.11–12.9, 14.11–13, and 22.30, though it is Anselm, in *DC* 3, who makes the best sense of it).

The end will have to be elaborated in the next letter, at least in its secular dimension as the dramatic reappearance in human history of our Savior and Judge, but the apostles have a few more reminders for the Thessalonians pertaining to the middle, to their sanctification, as the present letter draws to a close. So they resume, in conclusion, its third task, beginning with an appeal to good order through proper respect for authority in the church and through patient pastoral care.

5:12–15 We entreat you, brethren, to honor those toiling among you and set over you in the Lord and admonishing you [on his behalf], holding them exceedingly high in love on account of their labor. Be at peace among yourselves. And we exhort you, brothers, to discipline the disorderly, to encourage the discouraged, to shore up the weak, to be patient with all. See that no one is repaid by anyone evil for evil, but always seek the good for each other and for all.

The word ἀδελφοί is repeated and, modern commentators notwithstanding (e.g., Weima 2014: 390f.), we may with the fathers take the first instance as addressing everyone and the second as addressing those brothers who are doing the admonishing or disciplining, noting that the verb Paul chooses for that (νουθετέω, "to reason with" or "correct") is also repeated. In other words, he addresses the faithful first and then their presbyters. The final command in this paragraph, forbidding acts of retaliation while calling for reciprocity in acts directed to one another's welfare and to the common good, is again addressed to everyone, though the burden of oversight falls on the presbyters. About each of these cryptic exhortations a few words of elaboration are in order.

First, regard for those in authority: The local church is a community of the baptized, of brothers and sisters in Christ who worship and witness together. But it is not a self-constituting community, much less a mere collaboration of believers pursuing their own private interests in a more or less congenial atmosphere (which is how Western courts and governments today view it, in the hyper-Protestant fashion learned from John Locke that conveniently deprives it of certain corporate rights and freedoms; perhaps soon, even freedom from taxation). No, it is ambassadorial in nature. It derives its existence and its mandate from elsewhere. It belongs (even what the Catholic Church calls an "ecclesial community" of "separated brethren" belongs in its way) to the Church in its wholeness, and just so to a city that comes down from above, not to one that arises from below, whether by force or by consent of the governed. In that city, which is a kingdom, not a republic or a democracy, the universal authority committed by God to the ascended and enthroned Jesus is publicly acknowledged. Where that city or kingdom has, in the *saeculum*, its embassies, however modest or grand, it bears witness through them to his authority. In this witness every baptized person participates in one fashion or another. Each is specifically equipped by the Holy Spirit to do so. (Is that not what the sacrament of confirmation is about?) Yet each is subject to the lines of authority and to the jurisdictions established by Jesus.

A church, if it is a church, is more than a mentoring community, free to organize itself however it wishes. It is a community with authority and under authority. "Obey your leaders and submit to them; for they are keeping watch over your souls, as men who will have to give account" (Heb. 13:17). On the other hand, there is in it no force of compulsion other than that which belongs to God and his Christ. It has its law, yes, and it shares episcopally in the exercise of the keys. It can admonish the disorderly and dispense or withhold sacramental graces (→2 Thess. 3:6–12). But it cannot compel and it ought not to ask the state to compel for it, as it sometimes has done. It ought not to act as if its pastors, even its pope (for in Catholic ecclesiology, the pope is a pastor of each church as well as his own church), were vicars of Christ in any sense other than this: that they are responsible for the ministry of word and sacrament vouchsafed to the Twelve (as later to Paul) in the Great Commission, and for the doctrinal and liturgical discipline, *cum Petro et sub Petro*, that belongs to the exercise of this ministry. It ought not to lose sight of the fact that all its members, from the least to the greatest, are invited to become friends of Jesus and not subjects only (cf. John 14:21; 15:15). How then can it be otherwise in their relations with one another? Friendship and authority are not mutually exclusive in the army of the Lord. The Thessalonians are entreated or implored (the verb is ἐρωτάω) to honor those who are over them in the Lord, both because that honors the Lord himself and because it befits their own honor as friends of the Lord. For the same reason, they are entreated to keep peace among themselves. Christians, their leaders included, are to be subject to one another for Christ's sake (Eph. 5:21). There is to be love between them, as well as honor and obedience. And in that love, the practical love (ἀγάπη) that sees to actual needs, those who are set over them and toil hard among them are to be held exceedingly high; not as those who lord it over others—to facilitate that is to share in the hellish idolatry that put Christ on the cross (Matt. 23)—but as those who, in their service to all, must fare well if a church is to fare well.

▓ Malherbe (2000: 312f.; see 307ff. and 322ff.) is mistaken to see here, in these early days, only a mentoring community, a church of psychagogy without hint of hierarchy. He is not mistaken to observe that nothing is said explicitly about presbyters or the presbyterial office. He interprets προϊσταμένους (those presiding) quite informally and treats the church in Thessaloniki by analogy with philosophical communities that practiced psychagogy or mentoring relationships that we might call spiritual direction. The analogy is apt, even if some of the arguments for it aren't, but hierarchy and psychagogy are not incompatible. That Paul only discovered the importance of overseers and deacons sometime later is a hypothesis very difficult to defend, partly because it runs counter to the clear witness of Acts and partly because they are already in place in Philippi by the time he pens that letter. The concerns of Acts 14, it should be noted, run closely parallel to those of 1 Thess. 5. "Strengthening the souls of the disciples, exhorting them to continue in the faith, and saying that through many tribulations we must enter the kingdom of God" is in Acts seen to be preliminary to a process of prayer and fasting that leads to the appointment of "elders for them in every church" (14:22–23). The latter process sometimes took place, as Acts 14 indicates, during a second visit; hence Titus, for example, is elsewhere reminded of his charge to "amend what was defective, and appoint elders in every town" (Titus 1:5). So it is quite possible, given Paul's aborted stay, that Thessaloniki itself was defective in not yet having had presbyters formally appointed. Was this, perhaps, one of the things he and his colleagues had in view when they prayed that they might return to rectify what was still lacking among them? If so, we must also posit that certain brothers there had been given authority *pro tempore*.

Whenever and wherever King Jesus is proclaimed, his friends and subjects rejoice, recognizing that the prophetic gift is bestowed more liberally than the prophetic office. Legitimate authority to represent the King and to speak for him, however, is communicated apostolically. It is magisterial, not spontaneously generated or privately assumed. Likewise, legitimate authority to mediate to a church the high-priestly ministry of Jesus, to conduct on earth his heavenly liturgy (Heb. 8:1–3) that the people may participate in it. This authority must come from above through holy orders. For the "one, holy, catholic, and apostolic Church" to which each local or particular church belongs is not a heavenly reality only, hinted at by the appearance here and there of earthly simulacra, constructed to the best of men's ability or by the occasional bestowal of special graces. No, it is also an earthly reality, with actual institutional lineaments (*LG* 8). Authoritative proclamation, accompanied by right doctrine and right worship—by orthodoxy, in other words, in which *lex credendi* and *lex orandi* cohere as one law for the people of God—are also inherited apostolically, not invented locally. That is why Paul begins his first letter to Timothy, in which he will elaborate on these things, with "Paul, an apostle of Christ Jesus by command of God our Savior and of Christ Jesus our hope, to Timothy, my true child in the faith." Discipleship is a function of particular people in local churches, but the law of faith and the law of prayer and the canon of scripture are no more subject to the determination of local churches than is the privilege of ecclesial being itself. For ecclesial being is dominically instituted as well as pneumatically constituted. Were it not so, it could not possibly be characterized as one, holy, catholic, and apostolic. Its institution (by virtue of which it has its definite authority) and its constitution (by virtue of which this authority is not merely the inherited weight of tradition but light and life in the Holy Spirit) coincide epicletically in the real presence of Jesus Christ, through which in the Holy Eucharist his ecclesial body is fully realized in a given time and place together with the gift of his own body, soul, and divinity (cf. *Haer.* 1.10, 3.2–4, 4.17, 4.26, 4.32, 4.36, 5.1f.; see Zizioulas 1985, chap. 3, which offers a view of these things from the standpoint of the epiclesis or invocation of the Spirit).

This is the deep background of proper regard for those in authority, a regard that belongs first of all to the bishops as members, by inheritance, of the apostolic college, gathered round the successor of Peter in his role as keeper of the keys (Matt. 16:19), and by extension to the other presbyters. That Paul says nothing here about such things, and knows little or nothing of the later institutional lineaments that would develop in manifestation of the Church's unity and catholicity, is no objection. For Christ is the center of everything ecclesial and the ground of everything proper to the churches (Rev. 1:4–20). In him the Church itself coheres from father Abraham, even father Adam, to the last "fathers in God" left standing. Paul certainly knows something of the Petrine ministry and of the apostolic college, in which he participates (Acts 15). He speaks of the Church as being "built upon the foundation of the apostles and prophets, Christ Jesus himself being the cornerstone" (Eph. 2:20). When necessary, he is zealous to defend his own apostolic authority (cf. Gal. 2; 1 Cor. 3–4) and he urges apostolic gravitas on those, such as Timothy and Titus, to whom he communicates that authority through the laying on of hands. He can be gentle or fierce, as the occasion demands. He knows that the Church is to judge the world and even the angels, though it is presently under the watchful eye of the angels. The vision of Jesus, adumbrated in the Apocalypse, in which the Church is set forth as the city of God, with twelve gates and twelve thrones of judgment in those gates, is not something foreign to him (with Matt. 19:28 and Rev. 21:12–14, cf. 1 Cor. 6:1–11 and 1 Tim. 5:21). Indeed, he prepares the groundwork for later adumbrations by way of his own high doctrine of the Church as the instrument through which "the manifold wisdom of God might now be made known to the principalities and powers in the heavenly places" (Eph. 3:10; cf. 4:1–13).

His present concern, however, is a simpler one. He merely points out to the Thessalonians that their leaders labor hard for their welfare, having been set over them in the Lord (προϊσταμένους ὑμῶν ἐν κυρίῳ) for that purpose. Their faithful toil will earn what eternal reward is due them, but here and now it should also earn the loving support of their charges, of the flock committed to their care. For a letter such as this, the focus of which lies elsewhere, it suffices to say: Hold your leaders in esteem; offer them your loving support and be generous to them; do not disregard their authority to admonish and correct you. In 1 Tim. 5:17 he speaks in the same vein, linking honor and honoraria: "Let the elders who rule well be considered worthy of double honor, especially those who labor in preaching and teaching."

■ The deep background should reinforce for us what is in the foreground: namely, mutual love between presbyters and people and between the people themselves. "This I command you, to love one another" (John 15:17). When things are going well in a particular church, that is not too difficult a command to follow, as regards the pastors at least; likewise when things are going well in the universal Church. But if, as too often, such is not the case—if our leaders are weak or confused or even dishonest and immoral—what then? We may still esteem the office, indeed we must do so (Matt. 23:2–3; cf. John 15:16), and show charity to its occupant. "He who loves Christ," comments Chrysostom, "whatever the priest may be, will love him [also], because through him he has obtained the awful Mysteries" (*Hom.* 10). Nevertheless, that love, if genuine, may have to take an odd form: admonishing the admonisher, who is never himself above admonishment or correction, even if his office admits none higher. Paul knew about this, having had on one occasion to confront Peter (Gal. 2:11). But do we know it? Or has love grown cold as our concept of honor and rank has grown more worldly, more idolatrous?

The toleration of corrupt popes, prelates, and priests, of pastors and shepherds who devour their own flocks financially, even sexually, who despise liturgical and doctrinal discipline, who despise and abuse their own offices, who traffic in the sheep—this is neither love nor respect. With all its ruinous consequences, is it not rather a judgment from the Lord? That periods of ungodly tolerance of the intolerable come and go, that they often precipitate dire warnings on an apocalyptic scale accompanied by dubious claims to revelations and curious spiritual or liturgical obsessions, should not blind us to the fact that they are indeed judgments. Or to the fact that they have a cumulative effect, generating conditions that, despite intervening reforms, must finally provoke the great and terrible day of the Lord. Because "the LORD of hosts cares for his flock," his anger waxes hot against the shepherds, clerical and political, who will be punished (Zech. 10:3). Woe to them! But woe also to the flock "doomed to slaughter," woe to the people for complicity in their sins. "For behold, I am raising up in the land a shepherd who does not care for the perishing, or seek the wandering, or heal the maimed, or nourish the sound, but devours the flesh of the fat ones, tearing off even their hoofs" (11:4–17). In our time this note, too, must be sounded.

Second, the exhortation to care for the weak: Disciplining the disorderly (ἄτακτος) is the first step here, because the disorderly are a threat to the peace of the whole community. "We do not abstain from admonishing for fear lest by rebuke a person should perish," says Augustine. Quite the reverse. The unruly must be rebuked, the disorderly admonished, *lest* they perish or cause others to perish (*Rebuke and Grace* 16.49, in ACCS 9:96). And who are the disorderly? Perhaps they are those who cannot endure sound teaching or do not abide by sound morals. Perhaps they are those who disrupt the liturgy, competing to be seen or heard in it or to have their own way with it (cf. 1 Cor. 11–14; 1 Tim. 2:8–10; 2 Tim. 2:14ff.). Perhaps they are those who refuse to work with their hands so as to provide for themselves and those who depend upon them. Or perhaps, since idleness tends to other forms of evil, they are those who make themselves busybodies, disturbing the minds and homes of others (1 Tim. 5:13). These seem to be especially in view (→4:9–12 and 2 Thess. 3:6–12), but we should not confine our attention to them. Those who are misled by the love of money—thus attempting the impossible, to serve two masters (Matt. 6:24; cf. Mark 10:17–25; 1 Tim. 6:17–19)—are also among the disorderly. So is everyone in whom the passions rule rather than the virtues, or whose tongue is "an unrighteous world" (Jas. 3:6). There are in fact a great many ways to bring the gospel into disrepute, to undermine the mission, to disrupt the peace of the community. Do not be so feeble, so small-minded, as to be unable to bear an insult, says Chrysostom (*Hom.* 10), for that too is a way. And do not be involved in schism, which is disorderliness carried to the point of rupture.

Of schism Paul does not speak here, having no need, though he begins to broach the subject in his treatment of dissension in 1 Corinthians. We need not speak of it either, except to say that schism is often justified by schismatics as an attempt to restore a lost order, unless perchance it is justified by appeal to some new revelation. (Luther provides an example of the former, Montanus and Muntzer examples of the latter.) The problem with both justifications is that those who offer them make themselves, or their own private judgment, the principle of order. They have rejected the advice of St. Ignatius: "See that ye all follow the bishop, even as Jesus Christ does the Father, and the presbytery as ye would the apostles; and reverence the deacons, as being the institution of God. Let no man do anything connected with the Church without the bishop. Let that be deemed a proper Eucharist, which is [administered] either by the bishop, or by one to whom he has entrusted it. Wherever the bishop shall appear, there let the multitude [of the people] also be; even as, wherever Jesus Christ is, there is the Catholic Church. It is not lawful without the bishop either to baptize or to celebrate a love-feast; but whatsoever he shall approve of, that is also pleasing to God, so that everything that is done may be secure and valid" (*To the Smyrnaeans* 8, in *ANF* 1:89f.). Or if they be themselves bishops, they have neglected the warning of Irenaeus against "all those who, in whatever manner, whether by an evil self-pleasing, by vainglory, or by blindness and perverse opinion, assemble in unauthorized meetings"; against those who depart from "that tradition derived from the apostles" and safeguarded by "the very great, the very ancient, and universally known Church founded and organized at Rome by the two most glorious apostles, Peter and Paul," with which "every Church should agree" (*Haer.* 3.3.2, in *ANF* 1:415). To recall this advice and this warning is not to say that we must follow our own bishop, or even the bishop of Rome, into some harmful practice or into erroneous opinions at odds with tradition. It is to say rather that we must, if necessary, persist in admonishing the admonishers until the tradition with whose preservation they are charged is again honored in their own lives and teaching, or until they themselves are properly succeeded by more worthy holders of their office. That is what faithful love requires, a love that is not disorderly.   ◼

The disorderly are loving neither God nor neighbor as they ought. The pastor or other responsible person who fails to discipline the disorderly is not loving God or neighbor either, and his failure, even more than that of the disorderly, puts the whole community at risk. Perhaps the most poignant example in all of scripture is the one mentioned earlier (→2:10–12), the case of Eli and his sons, who in their dissipation and corruption and spiritual presumption led the entire people of God down the path of destruction. Eli's mild and ineffectual remonstrations did not qualify as real discipline and he himself, though an otherwise good man, met a sad fate through the discipline of God. David's failure to rein in his beloved son, Absalom, is another tragic example. Alas, we have our own examples in the Church today, on the same scale and with consequences likely to be no less serious. While they go untended, it is idle even to speak of admonishing the idle or of disciplining the disorderly.

Care for the weak also includes care for the discouraged or fainthearted, and for all who need shoring up in faith or godliness. The emphasis falls here on bolstering flagging spirits and encouraging struggling brethren to let the light of the gospel narrative dispel the gloom they feel about their own personal or communal narratives. "Count it all joy, my brethren, when you meet various trials, for you know that the testing of your faith produces steadfastness," writes James, who does not mince words in an epistle devoted to the disciplining of the disorderly and the encouraging of the weak. The key he offers to everyone who is struggling, and to everyone who would help the struggling, is prayer (cf. Jas. 1:2–5; 5:13–20). Chrysostom, commenting on 1 Thess. 5:9, is eager for this: "Do not despair of yourself, O man, in going to God, who has not spared even His Son for you. Faint not at present evils. He who gave His Only-Begotten, that He might save you and deliver you from hell, what will He spare henceforth for your salvation?" (*Hom.* 9). Some of the fainthearted are timid, others just tired; still others ill. Many have been wounded by life experiences and are not yet healed. Some wrestle with doubt and confusion, or with powerful temptations. Each needs a helping hand and the word that sustains the weary. That word is the word of Christ. For real encouragement does not come from telling our own stories and being affirmed in the telling, as so many today imagine. It comes rather from learning properly the story of Jesus and letting him "who loved me and gave himself on my behalf" live in me. Once that lesson is properly grasped, the next lesson follows. "For the sake of Christ, then, I am content with weaknesses, insults, hardships, persecutions, and calamities; for when I am weak, then I am strong" (2 Cor. 12:10). To be patient with all is to find the best way to help them learn these lessons, despite the impediments that present themselves.

Third, the exhortation to be concerned for the common good, which has a negative and a positive component: "See that no one is repaid by anyone evil for evil, but always seek the good for each other and for all." Or, as Hebrews has it: "Let us consider how to stir up one another to love and good works, not neglecting to meet together, as is the habit of some, but encouraging one another, and all the more as you see the Day drawing near" (10:24–25). "See to it that no one fail to obtain the grace of God; that no 'root of bitterness' spring up and cause trouble, and by it the many become defiled" (12:15).

Evils will be done, even among the people of God. But returning evil for evil is a denial of Jesus, who returned good for evil and asked us to do the same (Matt. 5:38–48). Doing evil plants a root of bitterness; returning evil causes it to spring up. Returning good for evil plucks it up. When Paul expands these same exhortations in Romans, he is careful to stress this very point: "Never flag in zeal, be aglow with the Spirit, serve the Lord. Rejoice in your hope, be patient in tribulation, be constant in prayer. Contribute to the needs of the saints, practice hospitality. Bless those who persecute you; bless and do not curse them. Rejoice with those who rejoice, weep with those who weep. Live in harmony with one another; do not be haughty, but associate with the lowly; never be conceited. Repay no one evil for evil, but take thought for what is noble in the sight of all.

If possible, so far as it depends upon you, live peaceably with all. Beloved, never avenge yourselves, but leave it to the wrath of God; for it is written, 'Vengeance is mine, I will repay, says the Lord.' No, 'if your enemy is hungry, feed him; if he is thirsty, give him drink; for by so doing you will heap burning coals upon his head.' Do not be overcome by evil, but overcome evil with good" (12:11–21).

Those who always seek the good for each other and for all are like God, who desires all to be saved, and like their Lord, who gave himself for us. Paul sharpens the positive side of this dialectic in his first letter to the Corinthians: "Let no one seek his own good, but the good of his neighbor" (10:24). Are we, each of us, a rational soul with a body in its service? And are we governed by the two great commandments, the second of which tells us to love our neighbor as ourself? Then we must seek, for the neighbor also, both the good of the body (which Augustine, *Mor. eccl.* 48–56, calls medicine) and the good of the soul (which he calls discipline). Moreover, as with the self, we must love the soul and nurture the mind first, before the body, lest that which is merely in service be treated as if it were master. In doing so, we must help the neighbor on toward God, who is the neighbor's highest good as he is our own highest good. To seek the good of the neighbor is, in the last analysis, to join with the neighbor in loving God above all things. Nothing less will do, though many lesser things be done in the process. For no one is or can be saved without learning to love God above all things.

▨ "He has showed you, O man, what is good; and what does the LORD require of you but to do justice, and to love kindness, and to walk humbly with your God?" (Mic. 6:8). If the linkage of these three is not to be overlooked, and if the common good is not to be overlooked, a word must also be said about justice. More specifically, a word about retributive justice, which is not doing evil but doing good, if done in the right way, at the right time, by the right agent. Paul's concern here, as in the Romans passage cited above, is not to deny retributive justice—the logic of the second letter rests on the rightness of retributive justice—but to deny our own agency in it. There is a place in the city of God for commutative justice (as in Acts 6:1–7 or 1 Cor. 6:1–7) and for restorative justice (as in acts of penance), but not for retributive justice. For the city of God witnesses in and to the city of man that retributive justice belongs ultimately to God, who will exercise it himself at the right time, after which it will no longer be needed. This does not mean that it is not needed now, in the city of man, or that human agency is not required; quite the contrary (Rom. 13:1–7). It does mean that the Church is not the agent and that the Christian, qua Christian, is not the agent.

Here is another reason to regard the two witnesses as individuals who appear at the end, arriving in the city of man out of another dispensation, so to say, as a final warning;

for they have power to repel and even to slay those who would harm them, and power to shut the sky and "to afflict the earth with every plague, as often as they desire" (Rev. 11:5–6). The Church has no such power and should not desire it. James and John desired it and were rebuked by Jesus (Luke 9:51–55; cf. 22:49–51). The Ananias and Sapphira episode in Acts 5 is no exception, particularly when we compare it with the martyrdom of Stephen in Acts 7. Stephen was questioned, condemned, and executed by the men of the Sanhedrin, who wrongly supposed themselves to be exercising divine justice. Ananias and Sapphira were questioned by Peter before the elders in Jerusalem, only when they came to them of their own accord. Found to be false, they also were put to death. Their sentencing and execution, however, were acts of God, not acts of the Church, which has no retributive mandate or function.

When in Christendom efforts were made to get round this fact by handing heretics over to the state for retributive justice, the limits of the Church were being recognized. Unfortunately, they were also being transgressed. Despite everything that can and should be said about the value of cooperation between churches and states in seeking the common good and about the fact that the state has an obligation to exercise retributive justice—albeit with the modesty and mercy that arise in learning from the Church that the state itself stands under and ought to anticipate the final judgment and justice of God (cf. O'Donovan 1996: 146ff., 219; 2005: 98)—it does not follow that the Church may act as the juridical, and the state as the penal, arm of society. Retributive justice simply does not belong to the Church, which is why it does not engage in war. Nor do its members, though they may without contradiction do so qua citizens in the city of man, if the war is just and justly conducted. (Calling a war a "crusade" only confuses the issue.) The Church, unlike the state, has nothing even to protect, as Augustine points out, since what it has that is really worth protecting is inviolable (*Civ.* 22.6; cf. Col. 3:1–4). If only we had a firmer grasp on that principle, how different would be our relation to the state itself! Disaster after disaster of ecclesial *Ostpolitik* could have been, and would be, avoided.

The Church does have its own law and its own "penal" sanctions (laicization of an abusive priest, for example). These are not retributive, however. Even its ultimate sanction, which ought not to be exercised except in consideration both of the good of the individual and the common good of the Church, is not retributive. Excommunication is the last resort for dealing with the disorderly (→2 Thess. 3:13–15), by committing them to Satan—that is, to the realm of retribution, often malign rather than just, that exists outside the city of God—in hope that lessons learned there will lead to their repentance and so to their salvation on the day of the Lord. (See 1 Cor. 5:5, in which it must be noted that the σάρξ/πνεῦμα contrast is not a body/soul or σῶμα/ψυχή contrast. Neither is it the σῶμα/πνεῦμα or Πνεῦμα distinction drawn at 5:3. It is a contrast between the fleshly man and the spiritual man. The man who is obedient to the Spirit is spiritual in body and soul; the man who is disobedient is carnal in body and soul. He is fleshly and does the works of the flesh, as specified in Gal.

5:16–26. So to the realm where those works rule, he must go.) Excommunication, which recognizes juridically one's de facto defiance of God, removes one from the sphere of the Spirit's sacramental graces. It consigns one to one's own resources, but not to one's own dominion, for one has no such dominion. The options are only two: the dominion of Christ or the dominion of Satan, Christ's defeated foe (cf. Mark 9:40; Matt. 12:30). Consigned to the latter, one either covets lost graces and returns to them, like the prodigal son, or one lives and dies in the far country.

5:16–22 Rejoice always, pray constantly, in all things give thanks: this is the will of God in Christ Jesus for you. [The fire of] the Spirit do not douse, prophecies do not despise, but examine all things carefully. Cling to the good; from every form of evil steer clear.

Many seek the particular will of God for their own life, as indeed they should, but this is the will of God for us all—that with which the beginning, middle, and end of our sundry life stories should be bound up, if by baptism they are bound up with Jesus Christ: to rejoice always, to pray constantly, and in all things to give thanks. Such are the anchors of any life lived according to the will of God. (Malherbe 2000: 330, giving insufficient weight to ἐν Χριστῷ, wrongly constricts εἰς ὑμᾶς.) If prophecy, as Paul later insists to the Corinthians, is more valuable than tongues and other gifts, it is because it explicitly encourages such things in a timely, practical fashion; in short, it edifies. The function of false prophecy, on the other hand—of which Paul may already have got wind in Thessaloniki, though it is only in his second letter that he addresses it directly—is to deflect us from such things. That is why prophecy, too, must be orderly and why it must be weighed and tested, not merely for its doctrinal but for its moral content (1 Cor. 12:10; 14:26–40; cf. Malherbe 2000: 333).

God's design for us, the very ground of our humanity, is that we should be eucharistic creatures who know how to give thanks and gladly do so, who are thus able to participate in an exchange of gift and gratitude and joy. Therefore the apostles urge prayer, thanksgiving, and rejoicing at all times, even and especially when things look bleak. "About midnight," in the Philippi jail, "Paul and Silas were praying and singing hymns to God, and the prisoners were listening to them" (Acts 16:25). So was God, who shook the ground and set them free, converting their jailer and his family. Such drama is not guaranteed, such rewards do not always immediately follow. But praying and singing ought in any case to come first, for in doing this we do what the holy angels do and what we will ever do in the presence of God, not to the exclusion of all else but as the foundation of all else. Thus the *Phos hilaron*, perhaps the oldest known Christian prayer outside the scriptures: "We sing thy praises, O God: Father, Son, and Holy Spirit. Thou art worthy at all times to be praised by happy voices, O Son of God, O Giver of life, and to be glorified through all the worlds" (1979 *American Book of Common Prayer*). Thus also Irenaeus: "It behoves us to make an oblation to God, and in all things to be found grateful to God our Maker, in a pure mind, and in faith without hypocrisy, in well-grounded hope, in fervent love, offering the first-fruits of his own created things." That is just what the Church is for. That is what it does, in its Eucharist, "throughout all the world" (*Haer.* 4.18, in *ANF* 1:484–85). Frequent participation in the Eucharist keeps us on the path of rejoicing, both because it reminds us that we have nothing that we did not receive and because it enables us to receive what we otherwise cannot have (cf. 1 Cor. 4:7; 10:16).

Joy is a fruit of the Spirit, the second named, after love (Gal. 5:22). The Spirit, who is both Love and Joy, plants and cultivates joy in us when we pray gratefully. This is the fire we must not quench, says Thomas (*S.1Th.* 5.2.133), whether in ourselves or another. Nor should we let circumstances quench it, as they all too easily may. Of course, rejoicing is natural and spontaneous when wonderful things happen, as they did in Philippi. Rejoicing before they happen, when it is not evident that they will happen, is another matter. The capacity to rejoice in all things is granted us *through* praying and giving thanks, which we ought always to do without losing heart (Luke 18:1). Is it necessary to observe that "in all things" is not quite the same as "for all things"? Some things are evil, and one does not rejoice or give thanks for evil. But in the midst of evil we can and should rejoice and render thanks to him who in everything and at all times "works for good with those who love him" (Rom. 8:28). For God brings good even out of evil, though he does no evil and authorizes no evil.

It belongs also to the divine design for man that he should discern good and evil, that he might ever choose the good. Desiring, choosing, and doing the good are forms of prayer, as Thomas points out here. Eucharistic man aims at being discerning man, at seeing and thinking and acting in the Spirit. In this fallen world, where he has not always chosen the good and lives with the consequences of his failure, he aims at learning to distinguish the true from the false, the real from the counterfeit, at overcoming the evil by which he has been overtaken. God does not create evil. Evil is an attack on the design of God, not a part of that design. Death, likewise, is a consequence of evil, having no place in man's first creation (Wis. 1:12–16). Yet, when God permits this attack and this consequence, he permits it in such a fashion as to force it to serve his goodness. Hence we may rejoice and give thanks in all things. In that sense, and only in that sense, even in and of our fall we can say, with gratitude to and for our Savior, *felix culpa*, "O happy fault!" But we are to cling to the good and to refuse to touch what is evil. We are to pull back from (ἀπέχω), to steer clear of, every form of evil. We cannot give thanks to God, or hope to live before God, without discerning good and evil, without hating evil and loving good (Amos 5:14–15).

God's word is good. The tree from which Adam and Eve ate was good. Desiring to be like God is good (*DCD* 13). What was evil was the serpent's aspersion of the divine goodness and man's decision to emulate the serpent and follow its advice, thus eating in untimely and disorderly fashion (cf. 1 Cor. 11:17–34). When we cling to the good—to God's word—and despise the evil of disobedience, we will discover that everything God says and makes and does is good and only good. Then we will know how to rejoice always. And how shall we cling to God's word unless we pray constantly and give thanks? What our first parents ought to have done, in their confusion, was wait for God and petition him for understanding. This, Paul implies, we may now learn to do. We may learn to test all things, to examine them carefully even when they are said to be of God and from God, lest we be misled again and again.

While it is unclear how this passage ought to be punctuated, or just what force to give to δὲ in 5:21, it is not wrong to qualify respect for the Spirit and for prophecy as fundamental to the life of the Church (cf. Acts 2:3–4; 10:30–48; and 19:1–7, not overlooking the symbolic number, twelve, that appears there) and to demonstrate that respect by testing the latter to see whether it really comes from the former. Is that not what Paul advises also in 1 Cor. 14:29? Just because "God is not a God of confusion but of peace" (1 Cor. 14:33), the fire of the Spirit is a controlled burn, so to say. It purges what does not lead men to Christ and so glorify God, while rendering newly fertile the ecclesial ground on which they may come to Christ and, through him, to the Father.

Clinging to the good means in the first place clinging to Christ, and to God as he actually is, not to some other "Christ" or supposed divine wisdom or revelation. All prophecy has that as its ultimate purpose, and by this purpose it must be weighed or tested (see Col. 1:3–3:17; cf. 2 Pet. 1–2; 1 John 2:22–23; 4:1–3; and *Demo.* 3). The same goes for teaching, naturally, by which standard very much teaching and preaching fails miserably, whatever may be said of purported prophecy. It means in the second place holding to tradition as inherited from the apostles (→2 Thess. 2:15–17; cf. Gal. 1:8). Where moral questions are concerned—not only there, but especially there—the life and example of the saints may be decisive (Matt. 7:15–20; cf. Vitoria, *Law of War* 1.1).

The call to test everything presumes that the fire of the Spirit has not been doused, of course, and that genuine prophecy has not disappeared (cf. Amos 2:12; 3:8). And where it has? There the glow of love also grows dim and the danger of dead orthodoxy looms. One can cling to the good coldly, ineffectively, fruitlessly; so can entire churches, which may despise prophecy simply by not expecting or even allowing for it. There are further consequences for that (Rev. 2:1–5; cf. Amos 7:16–17).

The eucharistic man who is also the discerning man, the man who knows good and evil in the manner God intends him to, clings to the good at all times and abstains from every form of evil. He does not presumptuously do evil that good may come, as false prophets so often advise. The notion that it is sometimes licit to do evil that good may come, so long as that foreseen good seems somehow to outweigh the evil, is the serpent's own notion, the very same demonic doctrine by which our first parents were led astray. It is the anthropological corollary of dualistic theology, of the doctrine that there is evil in God and that God creates evil along with the good. If we really mean "evil," rather than "woe" or the devastation of divine judgment on sinful man (Isa. 45:7; Lam. 3:37–39), there is no more fundamental error than that. There is nothing more basically idolatrous than that, for God is thus conceived in the image of fallen man. That is what Irenaeus attacks in *Adversus haereses*, Anselm in *De casu diaboli*, John Paul II in *Veritatis splendor*. We must not be surprised that this most perennial of heresies is being propagated again today. To test purported prophecy and ministries of teaching it is necessary to test them also by the principle that it is never licit to do evil even that good may come (*VS* 79ff.; cf. Rom. 3:8; Augustine, *Contra mendacium* 1.1).

5:23–24 May the God of peace himself sanctify you in your entirety, and your whole spirit, soul, and body be preserved blameless at the parousia of our Lord Jesus Christ. Faithful is the one calling you, who shall also effect [that for which he calls].

The letter's final task has been performed. The *peroratio* at 3:11–13 is now repeated in a slightly different form, taking account of what has been said in the intervening chapters. The God of peace, in whom alone it is possible to say "there is peace and security" without the least fear of sudden destruction (cf. 1:1; 5:3), is again petitioned to make the Christians of Thessaloniki, who were chosen and called by God for this purpose, "blameless in holiness before our God and Father at the parousia of our Lord Jesus with all his holy ones" (cf. 1:4; 2:12; 4:7). Here it is not merely their hearts that are in view, however, but their persons ὁλοτελής, completely and entirely: body, soul, and spirit. We have learned that the whole man is for the parousia and the parousia for the whole man, whether he be living or dead. Hence, though we may again translate ἐν τῇ παρουσίᾳ "at the parousia," we should allow the preposition multiple meanings, including "for the parousia" and even "by the parousia." For the parousia is the focal point of our salvation, as the cross and resurrection are its fulcrum, and it is by way of the parousia that we shall ever be with the Lord. Jesus himself warns: "But take heed to yourselves lest your hearts be weighed down with dissipation and drunkenness and cares of this life, and that day come upon you suddenly like a snare; for it will come upon all who dwell upon the face of the whole earth. But watch at all times, praying that you may have strength to escape all these things that will take place, and to stand before the Son of man" (Luke 21:34–36).

It is imperative, therefore, as Irenaeus says, that we keep to the path and make our way "by faith, without deviation, with courage and determination," toward the unity with God that will be vouchsafed to us at the parousia of Jesus Christ. "And since man is an animal made up of soul and body," that perseverance "must come about through the instrumentality of both. . . . For what is the use of knowing the truth in word, while defiling the body and accomplishing the works of evil? Or what real good at all can bodily holiness do, if truth be not in the soul? For these two rejoice in each other's company, and agree together and fight side by side to set man in the presence of God" (*Demo.* 1f., in ACW 16:48). The two agree together when the Spirit possesses both, rendering us whole, such that we too become spirit and are fit to receive from the Father incorruptibility (→4:1–8; cf. *Demo.* 5–7; *Haer.* 5.9).

Who will keep us on this path if not the one who called us to it? Has he not been doing this all along? Does he not do it when we stray? "When Adam had hid himself because of his disobedience, the Lord came to him at eventide, called him forth, and said, 'Where art thou?' And . . . just as at that time God spake to Adam at eventide, searching him out; so in the last times, by means of the same voice, searching out his posterity, He has visited them" (*Haer.* 5.15.4, in *ANF* 1:544). The Father calls, the Son communicates the call even in the deepest depths and furthest reaches, while the Spirit quickens us to answer it. That is the very assurance with which Paul prays, an assurance he elaborates most famously in the masterful eighth chapter of Romans. "I am sure," says Paul, "that neither death, nor life, nor angels, nor principalities, nor things present, nor things to come, nor powers, nor height, nor depth, nor anything else in all creation, will be able to separate us from the love of God in Christ Jesus our Lord" (Rom. 8:38–39).

God calls, and God will effect that for which he calls. God will bring us to glory, for his word runs swiftly and his call does not go forth in vain (Isa. 55:11). Yet God has called *us*. It is we ourselves whom he wishes to present blameless before his throne on the day of glory. We are those whom he wishes to make "more than conquerors." God, who made us without any help from us, neither saves nor perfects us without our contribution. *Qui ergo fecit te sine te, non te iustificat sine te* (Augustine, Sermon 169, *De verbis Apostoli Pauli* 11n13, in *PL* 38:923). Through cooperative grace he enables us to play our part in that. That we should have a part, and know ourselves to have a part, belongs to our final happiness, and this is ever God's concern, since God intends to make us like himself. It is not wrong, then, nor is it any attack on the sovereignty of grace, to say both that he will do it and that we shall do it with his help (Anselm, *DC* 3.9).

The fathers are unanimous in their testimony to the moral thrust of this entire chapter, which teaches us to expect what only God can do and, with God's help, to do what we ourselves ought to do in making ourselves ready. As Chrysostom succinctly remarks: "We are not masters of our end. Let us be masters of virtue. Our Master Christ is loving" (*Second Homily Concerning the Power of Demons* 5, in *NPNF¹* 9:190). Or, as Augustine puts it in another context, with an eye on the present darkness, the faithful must train themselves in virtue "so that the new man may be prepared through the new covenant for the new age amid the evils of this age" (*Trin.* 13.19).

5:25–28 Brethren, pray also for us. Greet all the brothers with a holy kiss. I adjure you before the Lord that this letter be read to all the brethren. The grace of our Lord Jesus Christ be with you.

Paul and his apostolic colleagues, like the Thessalonian Christians, must keep their torches lit in the night. None of them are exempt from the dangers the night presents, or from the discipline it demands. Hence, "pray also for us" (καί is textually uncertain but perfectly sensible). Here again, as at 5:12–15, we seem to have a general request to the church, followed by requests directed to those charged with oversight ("Greet all the brothers" and "I adjure you"), capped this time by a blessing used in the universal Church from that day to this, giving grace the last as well as the first word in the epistle.

Without any offense to grace we may add a brief postscript containing three observations. First, Paul's use of "greet all the brothers," rather than the general "greet one another," suggests that the letter is bound first of all for the presbyters (or presbyters in training), who will afterward bring it to the rest. His later custom is to mention some of the brethren by name, and we can only speculate as to why he does not do so here. Perhaps he is concerned about the appearance of favoritism, since there are some who must be admonished for their disorderliness. Or perhaps there were distinct house churches in Thessaloniki, whether by reason of numbers or of location and culture. (Location and culture might differ between Jewish and Gentile converts, but also among the Gentiles themselves.) That would also explain the command that the letter be read to all. Since we know neither the size nor the distribution of the church in Thessaloniki, however, it is difficult to say. What is certain is that, if there were significant divisions among them, Paul would have addressed that, as he did in Corinth. (*Pace* Harnack, it is inconceivable that the letter itself is not addressed to the whole church; cf. Malherbe 2000: 352f.)

Second, a holy kiss bespeaks a holy mission, a holy society, a holy kingdom. It is not merely casual or profane, like so much of what happens at "the peace" in many churches today. We know well enough, unfortunately, what an *un*holy kiss of greeting is, quite apart from that which is secretly sensual; for we learned it from Judas in the other garden, the garden of Gethsemane. His was an impatient kiss, a kiss of doubt tinged with despair, a kiss finally of betrayal. Such kisses come from those who no longer anticipate the parousia or any final assembling to Christ, who are working now, like Judas, to their own agenda.

Third, by invoking the Lord (ὁρκίζω ὑμᾶς τὸν κύριον) in his adjuration that the letter be read to all, Paul wields his own special apostolic authority, implicitly referencing his call to apostleship on the road to Damascus. Very likely at this point he also wields the pen, writing with his own hand (→ 2 Thess. 3:17). This should draw our attention back to 2:13, where he praises the Thessalonians for receiving what had been delivered to them, not merely as the word of men but rather for what it truly is, the word of God. Perhaps it may also draw our attention back to the fact that this letter is not as often, or as thoroughly, read in the Church as it ought to be, for it is full of the passionate tenderness and glorious severity of "Saint Paul, great Paul" (Anselm, *Oratio ad Sanctum Paulum* 10), that "winged messenger of day" through whom the notes of the gospel first sounded in literary form.

> The winged messenger of day
> sings loud, foretelling dawn's approach,

and Christ in stirring accents calls
our slumbering soul to life with him.
"Away," he cries, "with dull repose,
the sleep of death and sinful sloth;
with hearts now sober, just and pure,
keep watch, for I am very near."

Prudentius, *Hymns* 1.1–8 (ACCS 9:94)

Sermon and Deeds of Antichrist, from *Last Judgment* fresco cycle (1499–1504) by Luca Signorelli

Be strong, and let your heart take courage,
all you who wait for the LORD!

Psalm 31:24

De Agostini Picture Library / S. Vannini / Bridgeman Images

2 THESSALONIANS

Commentary on the Second Letter

1:1–2 Paul and Silvanus and Timothy, to the church of the Thessalonians in God our Father and the Lord Jesus Christ: Grace to you and peace from God the Father and the Lord Jesus Christ.

The second letter begins as the first, with the addition of "our" before "Father" and of the ἀπό phrase at the end containing a second time the divine name and the name above every name, the name at which every knee shall bow. The divine name? Only in brief, as in the *Pater Noster*, rather than in the fullness of the baptismal formula, where it (and with it the mystery of Yʜwʜ) is unfolded as an inheritance for each new member of the family of faith. As for the name above every name, the name of Jesus the Lord, that is the only name that can justly be situated alongside the divine name; for the one whose name it is, is himself situated within the Holy Trinity, being of one substance with the Father. "For us," then, "there is one God, the Father, from whom are all things and for whom we exist, and one Lord, Jesus Christ, through whom are all things and through whom we exist" (1 Cor. 8:6; cf. Phil. 2:9–11).

The church of the Thessalonians is said to be "in God our Father and the Lord Jesus Christ." In the sense just given, there is nothing unusual about that. It is by participating in the being and goodness of God that all creatures live and move and have their being, as Epimenides said. But to participate in the high and holy and unfathomable sense that the ecclesial body, the mystical body, of Jesus participates in God's being and goodness, *that* is unusual; for it is a share in the participation proper to the incarnate Son, a participation anchored not only in the goodwill of God but in the self-investment of God.

Now, the church of the Thessalonians is that mystical body insofar as it is located in Thessaloniki. Therefore a word of grace and peace from the God of grace and peace is spoken to it. A word of grace and peace from its Lord is spoken to it. In the mystical body men do not simply "feel after" God but rather hear from God and reply to God. God calls on them and they in turn call upon God, and while they are yet speaking they are heard (Isa. 65:24). That is not the case with everyone. All live and move and have their being in God. All are made to feel after God, and the word of God goes out wordlessly to the entire creation, inviting every creature to return God's call in the manner appropriate to it (Ps. 19:1–4; cf. Acts 17:27–28). But not all do, not even when the wordless word becomes the spoken word of the gospel. "When I called, no one answered, when I spoke they did not listen" (Isa. 66:4; cf. Rom. 10:11–18). Words of grace and peace require a response. When they do not get one, or the response is hostile, the word returns to him who sent it (Matt. 10:11–15), leaving no mark of protection on the lintel of the house or town to which it came.

The Thessalonians have responded, and responded enthusiastically. They have received and believed the testimony that was brought to them. Therefore the second letter begins as the first: with a word of peace followed by a thanksgiving. But the situation has changed somewhat, and the conveyors of that word have new concerns about those to whom they are writing. Their letter, therefore, has a distinct style and tone, as we will see already in the thanksgiving.

Modern commentators refer to the second letter's rhetoric as deliberative rather than epideictic, but Malherbe (2000: 361) rightly points out that this letter cannot be confined to a single epistolary type. In any case, all Paul's letters are deliberative. It suffices to say that the present letter, whatever else it is, is "a problem-solving letter" (Witherington 2006: 107n3), one that deals directly with a misunderstanding in Thessaloniki that seems to have arisen through false prophets, backed by false or falsified correspondence, who interpreted what had been said in 1 Thess. 4:13–5:11 in a false manner. Paul is about to set things straight, and that without delay, lest the Thessalonians depart somehow from the peace of God the Father and the Lord Jesus Christ.

▓ "There are indications that Paul's letters sometimes needed to be explained," remarks Malherbe (2000: 354) wryly, and the explaining was not always done by those authorized to do it. Glossed or even emended copies of his letters likely posed an additional problem.

Readers of the present commentary, itself an extended and unauthorized gloss, will no doubt be thankful, however, if we do not waste time by adverting again at any length to the second-letter-as-forgery thesis, treated briefly in the preamble. According to that thesis, the pseudonymous author sets things straight the way a good double agent would: Not-Paul pretends to be Paul by complaining about those who say they are Paul but aren't. Not-Paul then manages to imitate not only features of 1 Thessalonians but also, as Gordon Fee (2009: 237ff.) observes, many features that show up in authentic letters from Paul that have not yet been written. Perhaps Paul himself was taken in by Not-Paul? Or have those who think Not-Paul wrote long after Paul got the best of those who (taking 1 Thess. 2:14–16 as looking back at persecutions now over) think Paul must have written the second letter before he wrote the first? Who really knows? This is scholarship in the school of John le Carré, not in the service of Jesus Christ or in the school of Paul himself, and these "let's imagine" tales can be written just as the scholar in question pleases. Let my own readers be content with what was promised in the preamble—namely, to discover in 2 Thessalonians a little more of the structure of Paul's eschatology and understanding of history—and let us pursue that promise together in the company of those who share the Church's faith and its canonical judgment. The Church being "built upon the foundation of the apostles and prophets" (Eph. 2:20), that will provide some kind of authorization, at least. So we shall treat 2 Thessalonians as Paul's own gloss on 1 Thessalonians, required by the aforementioned misunderstanding—not, in the tradition of Schmidt and Wrede, as the work of a forger.

For our purposes, we can also set aside the much more legitimate question as to why the persecution in Thessaloniki was intensifying. Clearly it was not subsiding, or Paul would not have written to them thus. It is not necessary, either, to decide whether this second letter was written from Corinth just a few short months after the first, in response to a report that came back quickly regarding reception of the first, or whether some further time had elapsed—probably not much time, to judge by the way Paul picks up more or less where he left off, with comments about the parousia and misunderstandings of it, and about their mission and the problem of idleness among those who were not following the example carefully set for them. It is sufficient to say that the political situation in Thessaloniki has worsened, such that its recipients are even more closely linked to the apostles by sharing in their suffering for the sake of the gospel. Readers with no experience of that may need to remind themselves of it from time to time, lest this letter seem still more foreign to them than the first.

1:3–10 We ought always to render thanks to God for you, brethren, as is fitting in view of the fact that your faith is greatly increasing and the love of each and every one of you for one another is abounding; just as [it is fitting that] we ourselves boast of you in the churches of God, about your endurance and faith in all your persecutions and in the tribulations that you are bearing. [This is] proof of the righteous judgment of God, so that you may be counted worthy of the kingdom of God, for the sake of which you also are suffering—if indeed it is right in God's eyes to return affliction to those afflicting you and [to provide] relief with us to you who are being afflicted, at the disclosure of the Lord Jesus from heaven with his mighty angels in flaming fire, meting out vengeance on those refusing to recognize God and to obey the gospel of our Lord Jesus, who will suffer the penalty [due them]: eternal destruction, far from the face of the Lord and from the splendor of his might, when he comes on that day to be magnified among his holy ones and to be marveled at among all who have believed. For our testimony to you was believed.

This appears in Greek as a single sentence, so we will treat it as such, though it is not translated as such. The first sentence and the last, as here rendered—"on that day" having been moved with some reluctance from the very end of Paul's sentence into immediate proximity to "comes," both for ease of reading and to highlight the final clause—create an *inclusio* testifying anew to the Thessalonians' faith and love and hope and reiterating the apostles' pride in them. Packed inside the *inclusio* is a preliminary argument about the exercise of divine justice that will bring secular history to its appointed end. That is what requires our attention, after a quick look at the envelope of affirmation in which it is found.

The liturgical resonances (remarked by Aus 1973) of the opening words, "we ought always to render thanks," are still to be heard in the Church's eucharistic prayer, *Vere dignum et iustum est, aequum et salutare, nos tibi semper et ubique gratias agere.* "It is truly fitting and right, propitious and salutary, everywhere and always to give you thanks." (With 1:3, where Paul has ἄξιόν, cf. Phil. 1:7, where he has δίκαιον; these two words are rendered in Latin by *dignum et iustum*, commonly translated "right and just.") What Paul is again giving thanks for here is the faith and perseverance of the Thessalonians, a faith of which everyone has heard (→1 Thess. 1:8) and a perseverance of which the apostles can now proudly boast, a habit the Church took up in its litanies of saints and martyrs. The Thessalonians are backing the apostolic testimony with the testimony of their own suffering. This is proof of their faith and, as we will see in a moment, proof also of divine justice. And what is it they are persevering toward in these sufferings? Toward the kingdom, the kingdom that will appear with their Lord, whose marvels they will be granted to behold on the day their persecutors are punished (Wis. 11). They are persevering toward the parousia of Jesus, of which much has already been said in the first letter. Paul wants now to say more. The reason he wants to say more and the substance of what he has to say will be found in chapter 2, but what is found there will be better understood if we first grasp what is found here.

When we open up this little envelope, 1:3–10, we discover that Paul's prelimi-nary argument about divine justice has two layers, the first of which concerns their own persons. The very fact of their perseverance is already a witness to divine justice, because it demonstrates their fitness for the kingdom that is coming. The kingdom is for the just, and only the just will enter it. God is permitting the persecution they are experiencing, not because he does not care about justice but rather because he does care. Through it they are being made fit for the kingdom and their fitness is being displayed for all to see.

First Peter 1:3–9 makes the same point. Note that neither author regards God as the cause of the persecution, nor is there a theory of atoning suffering in play, though the Shepherd of Hermas develops that angle at Similitude 9.28.5 in language redolent of our text (cf. Aus 1973: 435f.; Weima 2014: 461).

At the same time it demonstrates the unfitness of their persecutors, whose judg-ment God is in fact preparing. The latter themselves have some inkling of this, or so Paul suggests in his letter to their brethren in Philippi. It is "a clear omen to them of their destruction, but of your salvation, and that from God," he tells them, when they see you "striving side by side for the faith of the gospel," not frightened in any way (Phil. 1:27–30).

That is the one layer. The second, marked in my translation by the dash, is prospective and concerns the fittingness of God's own response to the situa-tion and the eventual demonstration of his justice and righteousness. "Far be it from you to do such a thing," says Abraham (Gen. 18:25) while negotiating with God over Sodom: "to slay the righteous with the wicked, so that the righteous fare as the wicked! Far be that from you! Shall not the Judge of all the earth do right?" He shall indeed. He slays the wicked and saves the righteous; the people of Sodom perish but Lot survives. That is what he will do again, says Paul, when he acts globally through the man who has fulfilled all righteousness and upon whom he has devolved all judgment. He will destroy the wicked with fire and rescue the righteous through that fire. The Just One will act justly. He will do right by his suffering people.

The Thessalonian Christians have believed the testimony delivered to them. They have turned from idols to serve the living God and to wait for his Son from heaven. They have learned to endure in their waiting—an ill omen for their persecutors, who are confronted by a supernatural confidence of the same kind described so dramatically in the story of the Maccabean martyrs (2 Macc. 7) who already knew and served the living God. Their persecutors have nonetheless refused to believe. Like Antiochus, they have not turned toward God but turned instead, still more viciously, against the people of God. Precisely so, it is just that God should intervene to rescue the former and to punish the latter. It is right that the former should receive the kingdom, for the sake of which they are suffering and persevering, and that the latter should be shut out of it.

▨ Witherington (2006: 191f.) and Weima (2014: 458ff.) are among those who want to read this passage differently, such that the ἔνδειγμα, the proof or evidence of the justice of God, lies only in this future delivering and punishing. At 1:5, they supply "Here is" rather than "This is," so that the proof follows only at 1:6. Their reading is awkward, however, both grammatically and semantically, and it too quickly passes by the proof to be found in manifest fitness for deliverance or for punishment, the evidence of faith and unbelief to which Paul returns in the ὅτι clause of 1:10 as justification for his thanksgiving. In other words, it deprives the argument of its first layer and so of the full strength it ought to have. ▨

We should not, however, confine Paul's argument to those who actively persecute. That is its center, not its circumference. The gospel is an invitation, but not an invitation only. Being an announcement of the kingdom, it is also a word of command. "Those refusing to recognize God and to obey the gospel of our Lord Jesus" are one and the same. (The language is traditional. Τὸ τοῖς μὴ εἰδόσιν θεὸν is added, in synonymous parallelism, τοῖς μὴ ὑπακούουσιν τῷ εὐαγγελίῳ.) Their resistance to the gospel is a refusal to recognize God even before they take up the instruments of persecution. Having heard the gospel, they are not ignorant of God; nor indeed were they ever entirely ignorant of God, not even the Gentiles. They were accountable then, and they are doubly accountable now, those who refuse to recognize God by obeying his gospel, whether or not they compound their guilt by persecuting his people (cf. Rom. 1:20–21; 2:1–18; 3:21–31; Malherbe 2000: 401). God is just to exclude them.

Paul is not merely comforting his readers with this talk of divine justice; he is also counseling them. He knows that "through many tribulations we must enter the kingdom of God" (Acts 14:22; cf. 9:16). He wants to be sure their expectation of salvation, of divine relief from their troubles, does not waver. Neither is he engaging in that dubious enterprise known as theodicy. He argues from divine justice, not to it. He displays it rather than defends it, and just so applies it to the problem at hand. The question he raises with the conjunction εἴπερ—"if indeed it is right in God's eyes to return affliction to those afflicting you, and to provide relief with us to you who are being afflicted, at the disclosure [ἀποκάλυψις] of the Lord Jesus from heaven with his mighty angels in flaming fire"—is really a question about their confidence in the divine right, and the divine will, to dispense justice through a decisive intervention that delivers some and punishes others (Wis. 18:7–8). The intervention is that of Jesus, as foretold by Jesus: "And there will be signs in sun and moon and stars, and upon the earth distress of nations in perplexity at the roaring of the sea and the waves, men fainting with fear and with foreboding of what is coming on the world; for the powers of the heavens will be shaken. And then they will see the Son of man coming in a cloud with power and great glory. Now when these things begin to take place, look up and raise your heads, because your redemption is drawing near" (Luke 21:25–28; cf. Wis. 18:14–25). To build up confidence in their redemption is Paul's goal.

In asking the question, then, Paul answers it. As commentators are quick to point out, εἴπερ "introduces the protasis of a first-class condition" (Weima 2014: 204) and can just as well be translated "since indeed." For God does deem it right to repay affliction with affliction. A day of judgment is coming, a day that will arrive with the finality of the great flood but burn with a great fire, a day that will purge creation of the ungodly and bring to an end the very possibility of ungodliness. The flood destroyed the wicked in Noah's day, but did not wash away all ungodliness. How could it, when the wood of our humanity that washed up on Ararat was still the old, twisted wood? That wood has been a long time drying, but when it is dry it will burn. "Blow the trumpet in Zion; sound the alarm on my holy mountain! Let all the inhabitants of the land tremble, for the day of the LORD is coming. . . . I will give signs in the heavens and on the earth, blood and fire and columns of smoke. . . . And it shall come to pass that all who call upon the name of the LORD shall be delivered" (Joel 2:1–32, a text applied to the nations in Acts 2:19–21 and Rom. 10:11–13; cf. Luke 23:31).

Now, today some are abandoning the very idea of retributive justice and do not answer the question as Paul answers it. But no one who believes in the God of the Bible can answer it otherwise. It may be open to Marcionites to say that the true God is a God without retributive justice, but they will have to dispense with Paul in order to do so, leaving them no canon at all. The biblical God is a refining fire; for those who will not be refined, he is a consuming fire. Does he teach us to love our enemies? Yes, for he has loved his enemies. Yet he also promises to destroy them if they persist in being the enemies of those who love him. Their actions bring back into play the *lex talionis* (Eubank 2019: 146).

> Hear the word of the LORD,
>   you who tremble at his word:
> "Your brethren who hate you
>   and cast you out for my name's sake
> have said, 'Let the LORD be glorified,
>   that we may see your joy';
>   but it is they who shall be put to shame.
>
> . . . .
>
> You shall see, and your heart shall rejoice;
>   your bones shall flourish like the grass;
> and it shall be known that the hand of the LORD is with his servants,
>   and his indignation is against his enemies.
> For behold, the LORD will come in fire,
>   and his chariots like the stormwind,
> to render his anger in fury,
>   and his rebuke with flames of fire.
> For by fire will the LORD execute judgment,
>   and by his sword, upon all flesh,
>   and those slain by the LORD shall be many." (Isa. 66:5, 14–16)

It is no different, of course, where Jesus is concerned. While we were yet sinners, he loved us and gave himself for us. Yet he is also the ἔκδικος (1 Thess. 4:6), the avenger of wrongs done, among God's own people and among all people. He will come from heaven with his mighty angels in flaming fire, meting out vengeance (διδόντος ἐκδίκησιν), for it belongs to him to gain the victory over God's enemies and to exercise justice on God's behalf, in defense of the friends of God.

It should not be forgotten that Jesus himself is the one who introduces the concept of Gehenna, the fire that burns forever in "the outer darkness" (cf. Matt. 8:12; 13:36–43; 22:13; 25:30). Who else would dare to speak of such a thing? Then again, who dares deny it, now that he has spoken of it? Paul is only following Jesus when he proclaims that there will be a settling of accounts, from which no one will be exempt. Some "will go away into eternal punishment, but the righteous into eternal life" (Matt. 25:46). What happened provisionally in Eden—the banishing of Adam and Eve from the garden of God's presence, with a view to their eventual salvation—will happen again, this time irreversibly, to those who refuse that salvation. They will be driven out from before his face, not to till the ground by the sweat of their brow but rather to weep and gnash their teeth. And they will be barred from any hope of return by the flaming sword that turns in every direction.

Paul's own use of the "apocalyptic element of fire" is quite restrained, as Malherbe says (2000: 400), or at least more restrained than his Lord's; but Paul does not reduce that element to "a mere mention," nor should we. Fire is only apocalyptic because it is elemental. It wards off wild beasts and razes enemy towns and fortifications. It is a common instrument of retribution. God used it on Sodom and Gomorrah, and will use it universally when the time comes. Then "the earth and the works that are upon it will be burned up," even the heavens themselves "will be kindled and dissolved" (2 Pet. 3:10–13). The line between the literal and the metaphorical is hard to draw here, but we do not have to draw it. What we have to do is face squarely the fact of retribution. The kingdom of God would not *be* just were there no retribution for the wicked, no exclusion of the unjust. Likewise, the kingdom would not be eternal if the question of who belongs to it were to remain an open one, if its doors were never closed (Matt. 25:10; cf. Gen. 7:16). In that case, the kingdom would be no more than another phase of history. It would be another millennial kingdom at best. The eternal kingdom is possible only as a "most orderly and harmonious society to be enjoyed with God and mutually in God." It is exclusively for those who love and fear God, obediently and thankfully. The presence of any other would not be right and just but an attack on what is right and just, a perpetual assault on the kingdom, which would not then have come at all. "Thy kingdom come, thy will be done, on earth as it is in heaven," would remain an unanswered prayer.

▨ This means that the subject of hell must also be faced, and faced squarely—that appalling subject for which the burning dumps of the cursed Hinnom valley, where apostate Jews (not content to defile the temple with idolatrous abominations) had sacrificed their children to the flames, supplied the imagery employed by Jesus. His harshest language about the temple regime, about the fate that awaited Jerusalem and its inhabitants, about the individual fate that awaits all the ungrateful and impenitent, is drawn from Jer. 7, the original Gehenna text. Paul's language is indeed more restrained than that of Jesus or Jeremiah—he is talking after all to a very different audience—but he says what must be said about banishment to eternal destruction: namely, that there will certainly be such a thing. Scripture and tradition both insist that punishment for unforgiven sin is right and just in God's sight, that the punishment of the wicked is certain, and that it is, when the time for repentance and forgiveness is up, not remedial but devastating and final (Rom. 2:1–16; 9:22; cf. Wis. 12

and 17; 4 Macc. 10:15; 12:12). It is a faux Christianity that has nothing serious to say about this and no real warning to give, just as it is faux scholarship to suggest that Paul would not himself have written the sentence we are treating (cf. Malherbe 2000: 406f., in critique of Marxsen 1982: 44–52). Worse yet is dismissal of all talk of hell as theological violence, as if the very idea of hell makes God out to be a sacrificer of his own children. The same approach is used, as it must be, to dismiss traditional talk of the cross. By pitting God's mercy against his justice, these dismissals only renew man's futile attempt to divide God from God. In the end they serve no purpose other than to justify to ourselves wickedness of every kind, including the mass holocaust now taking place in our abortion mills, in our own cursed valley of Hinnom.

There are, however, more subtle ways to undermine frank talk of hell. Andrew Louth (2008: 244–46) notes with sympathy the universalist strand in Eastern theology, which has of course its Western analogues, from Origen to the present. Louth cites Isaac the Syrian, for example, who with Diodore of Tarsus claimed that "no part belonging to any single one of (all) rational beings will be lost, as far as God is concerned, in the preparation of that supernal Kingdom." Hell, like sin, once did not exist and some day will not exist, since it is an insubstantial effect produced by free will rather than a part of creation (2008: 247; cf., e.g., MacDonald 2011; Hart 2019). Yet universalism is a grave departure from tradition, and the notion that hell, like sin, is merely an effect of free will is wrong. Hell is the "eternal fire prepared for the devil and his angels" (Matt. 25:41), not a temporary fire prepared *by* the devil and his angels, of which they will later repent. It is quite true that God does not make hell when he makes the world. It is quite untrue that God does not make hell at all. Hell is the last destination of those who prefer love of self to love of God and love of neighbor, despite having been taught by God that true love of self is only possible by way of a greater love for God and a love of neighbor as oneself. Hell is the place of banishment from the presence of God who is love, and from the creaturely face of love which is the face of Jesus Christ. All who go to this place go willingly in one sense, and unwillingly in another. They go there because they have determined themselves thus; they go there because God has sent them where they belong, but where they do not, and cannot, desire to go or find satisfaction in going.

What is meant here by "place," or how to locate it vis-à-vis the good places of the new creation, need not trouble us too much. Suffice it to say that creatures belong in a place and that hell, too, is a place. Obviously neither its place nor its time is any part of the new creation, which is prepared for the righteous, not for the wicked. It is "eternal" in the sense that it has permanency, but not in the sense that it enjoys a share in the eternality of God himself, who together with the Lamb is the temple of the new creation (cf. in context Rev. 21:8 and 21:22, recalling that the Church, as the firstfruits of the new creation, already exists "in God our Father and the Lord Jesus Christ"). Hell, if you like, is the abyss, the stasis, into which the time or motion of fallen creatures runs, and with them the old creation. It is all that is left of the old creation when the heavens and earth that God originally made are dissolved and reformed into a habitation fit for those who shall always go on advancing in the delights of the divine life. It is the outer darkness in which rational souls, whether angelic or human, in their respective ways burn in the lava of an irrevocable, but unfulfilled and now unfulfillable, vocation, and in which bodies know neither pleasure nor rest (*Civ.* 13.2, 21.9). Irenaeus has it right when he says: "And to as many as continue in their love towards God, does He grant communion with Him. But communion with God is life and light, and the enjoyment of all the benefits which He has in store. But on as many as, according to their own choice, depart from God, He inflicts that separation from Himself which they have chosen of their own accord. But separation from God is death, and separation from light is darkness; and separation from God consists in the loss of all the benefits which He has in store. Those, therefore, who cast away by apostasy these forementioned things, being in fact destitute of all good, do experience every kind of punishment. God, however, does not punish them immediately of Himself, but that punishment falls upon them because they are destitute of all that is good. Now, good things are eternal and without end with God, and therefore the loss of these is also eternal and never-ending" (*Haer.* 5.27.2, in *ANF* 1:556; cf. 5.28.1, 5.36.1).

The *Catechism of the Catholic Church* is admirably clear on the fact of hell, though wisely it does not concern itself with the cosmology or, as Dante does, with the topography of hell. Its approach is christological: "Christ is Lord of eternal life. Full right to pass definitive judgement on the works and hearts of men belongs to him as redeemer of the world. He 'acquired' this right by his cross. The Father has given 'all judgement to the Son.' Yet the Son did not come to judge, but to save and to give the life he has in himself. By rejecting grace in this life, one already judges oneself, receives according to one's works, and can even condemn oneself for all eternity by rejecting the Spirit of love" (*CCC* §679). "We cannot be united with God unless we freely choose to love him. But we cannot love God if we sin gravely against him, against our neighbor or against ourselves. . . . To die in mortal sin without repenting and accepting God's merciful love means remaining separated from him for ever by our own free choice. This state of definitive self-exclusion from communion with God and the blessed is called 'hell'" (*CCC* §1033). "Jesus often speaks of 'Gehenna,' of 'the unquenchable fire' reserved for those who to the end of their lives refuse to believe and be converted, where both soul and body can be lost. Jesus solemnly proclaims that he 'will send his angels, and they will gather . . . all evil doers, and throw them into the furnace of fire,' and that he will pronounce the condemnation: 'Depart from me, you cursed, into the eternal fire!'" (*CCC* §1034).

We might leave the matter there but for the remarkable revival the universalist heresy, subtle or otherwise, is presently enjoying. To regard hell as anyone's final destination, the universalist protests, is to make belief in the goodness of God impossible. Purgative suffering there may be, but in the end there must be, as Origen thought, an *apokatastasis*, a recovery of all rational souls. Thomas Talbott (2014: 90ff.) proposes that the eternal destruction mentioned in 2 Thess. 1:9 is only destruction of the dark side of the self, which the presence of the Lord begins to drive out so that the good side may eventually emerge into the kingdom after all. All punishment being remedial, never purely retributive, we may think of hell as a prolonged and more severe sort of purgatory, as a fire at once avenging and cleansing; in short, as a salvific fire (→1 Thess. 4:13–18). Michael McClymond (2018: 953), in his comprehensive history of universalism, criticizes those of Talbott's persuasion for implying that some are saved by grace through faith in Jesus while others are saved by works; that is, by paying for their own sins in hell. A more immediate criticism in the context of 2 Thessalonians is that a divided-self dialectic is entirely foreign to the scenario Paul is setting up. Equally foreign, however, is this notion that the kingdom can be accessed after the fact, not by means of union and communion with God in Christ but rather by enduring a long and dreadful punishment. Or can one commune with Christ in hell?

The stubborn universalist, however, is not arrested even by that question. Quite the contrary. David Hart, for example, launches a counteroffensive, arraigning those who dare speak of a permanent hell for telling "sordid lies" about God (2019: 61). The πῦρ αἰώνιον, of which Jesus speaks in Matt. 25, he takes to be a fire of uncertain duration or a fire through which one may pass in an indeterminate amount of time. Likewise, then, the ὄλεθρον αἰώνιον to which Paul refers here at 1:9. Let us concede straightaway to Hart (2019: 120ff.) that the matter does not hinge on the meaning of αἰώνιος or any other isolated word. Context must be decisive. Let us also concede, or rather affirm, that God desires all men to be saved and that in Christ he provides for all men to be saved. That, however, is not to concede what Hart further believes; namely, that God intends to save all and will save all through the inexorable attraction of his own goodness. For this further belief does not arise from scripture. It arises from a certain kind of theodicy, a theodicy that proceeds by way of determinations about what goodness is and how it is known (we may start from ourselves), about the capacities and incapacities of the rational soul (we are incapable of any sin worthy of eternal punishment), and about the responsibility of the Creator if he creates freely (which includes responsibility for sin and the overcoming of sin). It arises more primordially, as Hart happily allows, from the instinctive revulsion that all feel toward suffering that has no terminus and knows no end. This revulsion, as the universalist experiences it, demands not so much that hell be avoided as that it be given a remedial purpose and effect, lest it be regarded as the most unconscionable torture. It demands the concession that rebellion is never final, that the last judgment is not literally the last judgment, that the age to come is still transitional, belonging to a much grander scheme of things the beginning and end of which scripture hides from our view.

Hart blames Augustine, most of all, for the refusal to see that what in scripture looks to be final is really transitional, arguing that remedialism was the norm among serious theologians until that Latin father worked his infernalist magic. This is nonsense, as McClymond's monumental history (*pace* Ramelli 2013) shows. It was not Augustine, but Jesus himself, who taught the Church to speak of that "baleful fire" that does not cleanse but avenge (Gregory Nazianzen, *Oration* 40.36). Of course that fire still has something of mercy in it, since it is God's fire. For it is merciful, as well as just, to set a proper limit to all things, and especially to sin. Only the love between God and those who are happy in God is without limit. But the universalist seems to think that the existence of hell somehow limits God himself. He supposes that neither God, who is happiness, nor the righteous, who are to become happy, can actually be happy if there is even a single rational creature who remains unhappy. He may even claim, as Hart does, that the permanent loss to hell of any rational creature leaves a sort of hole in creation that shows God to be subject to evil, lacking either in power or in goodness; that for God to be God, even the devil must be redeemed. To posit the devil's redemption, however, is to posit either that Jesus Christ redeems the devil or that the devil redeems himself or that someone else redeems the devil, unless perchance there is no devil but the devil within each of us, from which we redeem ourselves. None of these options can be squared with scripture; all are repudiated by tradition. And to posit that God's happiness rests on the devil's or on anyone else's is something worse than that error "based on human sentiment" (*Civ.* 21.17) that pits God's mercy against his justice. It is the kind of error that dethrones God altogether by a denial of his aseity.

Against the universalist it must be maintained that God remains good, though some of his creatures become and remain bad; that God remains holy, though some of his creatures will abide in unholiness, separated from him forever; that God remains the Almighty in consigning to hell what refuses heaven. It would be absurd, as Athanasius (*Inc.* 6ff.) points out, to posit that God our creator, in the face of evil, might not become redeemer at all, but instead let his handiwork come to naught. But it is equally absurd to posit that none of his handiwork must ever come to hell, to the avenging fire from which there is no escape, to what is not naught but rather their just end. The price universalists pay for that absurdity is that the theodicy they venture is self-defeating. They want to exonerate the Creator from any fault in his handiwork, from any responsibility for the evil that has appeared in it, by insisting on an *apokatastasis*? They want to be certain that evil, which is nothing, will be shown to be nothing by its utter eradication? But on their scheme it is not eradicated. It remains intrinsic to the entire process of creation, conceived with Origen as an eternal emanation and return. The Creator remains responsible for it and indeed becomes its first and final cause. He overcomes it only by generating and then sublating or assimilating it. Which is not the gospel of the Crucified but the crucifixion of the gospel. The universalist does not at all escape the cyclical worldview of the Greeks so devastatingly criticized by Augustine as making happiness impossible (*Civ.* 12.21; cf. Farrow 2019b).

All that can be salvaged from the universalist, whose preference for theodicy over theology betrays him, is a warning against the blasphemy he rightly decries; for God does not delight in the torment of the damned and his sovereignty in no way requires the testimony of the damned. One does not avoid this blasphemy, however, by making that torment or testimony of indeterminate duration in time. One does not even avoid the professed revulsion. For what does universalism come to in the end, if not to a God who determines, if necessary, to teach the devil (or the devilish) a damn good lesson by a very long stretch in hell? By this kind of generosity the gentle-minded universalist only digs himself a deeper pit. Time is not the issue here. We should not be concerned with setting a limit to hell but with understanding hell *as* a limit, something of which we will say more shortly.

If there is anything else to be salvaged it is a warning against setting ourselves up as knowing better than the Church how to read its scriptures, thus falling headlong into whatever pit we happen to have dug. What Paul believes, he believes on the grounds of dominical texts such as Matt. 25, on which his own text rests. On attempts to get round those texts, St. Basil rightly passes harsh judgment. "Since these and many such sayings are found everywhere in the God-inspired Scripture," he says, "this is surely one of the devil's stratagems: that many human beings, by disregarding such weighty and solemn words and declarations of the Lord, award to themselves an end of punishment in order that they may sin with greater bravado" (*Asketikon*, Shorter Responses 267, in Silvas 2005: 419). And he adds, showing his grasp both of the dominical words and of the deeper issue, "if ever there were an end of eternal punishment, then surely eternal life would also have an end," since the same adjective (αἰώνιος) is attached to both terms. Hence Basil urges on us not bravado but godly fear.

That fear, we may add, if it is godly, is not fear of hell. For it is not proper to man to fear hell but rather to fear God, just as Jesus fears God (cf. Aquinas, *ST* 3.7.6; *CCC* §1041). Yet the sinner, qua sinner, must learn to fear God in an apposite fashion if he hopes to be saved. "I will warn you whom to fear," says Jesus (Luke 12:5). "Fear him who, after he has killed, has power to cast into hell; yes, I tell you, fear him!" Thus we may say, without at all misrepresenting either the nature of man or his present situation, that "the prospect of hell ought to cause terror, just as the prospect of entering the divine rest ought to cause great joy" (Farrow 2018g: 260). We should not, however, take too seriously the advice proffered by Chrysostom, "Let us not remember the kingdom so much as hell; for fear has more power than the promise" (*Hom.* 2). It is quite the reverse, though we do well to remember both. ■

Vere dignum et iustum est, aequum et salutare, nos tibi semper et ubique gratias agere? From the side of the creature there is no justice and can be no salvation without freely offered thanksgiving. It is astonishing how readily modern Christians manage to detach the question of justice from the question of loving, fearing, and thanking God, as if that were not the essence of justice. Justice begins and ends with fearing the Lord and honoring his will; injustice by refusing to do so, by being unwilling to defer what seems delightful or desirable for happiness, precisely when and where it is contrary to the will of God. For those who repent, satisfaction for sin has been made by Christ; the justice of God, and of man before

God, has been fully upheld in Jesus's unsurpassed and unsurpassable offering of love and obedience. For those who will not repent and serve Christ, spurning the rewards of that justice, nothing remains but the justice of punishment. The sinner's own proper desert, commensurate with his own proper choice, is to be shut out from the kingdom of God and of his Christ. His refusal to be just will exclude him from happiness, for there is no such thing as happiness without justice. In God, and so also (analogically) in man, happiness and justice are one. That is why even the righteous need to be chastened, while they await the time when the judge of all the earth will rise up and "render to the proud their deserts" (Ps. 94:2; cf. 94:12). They require tempering, that they may bear the heavy weight of glory (2 Cor. 4:17). Nor will they themselves remain unexposed to the purging effects of divine justice when Christ appears. "Each man's work will become manifest," says Paul, "for the Day will disclose it, because it will be revealed with fire, and the fire will test what sort of work each one has done. If the work which any man has built on the foundation survives, he will receive a reward. If any man's work is burned up, he will suffer loss, though he himself will be saved, but only as through fire" (1 Cor. 3:13–15; cf. 1 Pet. 4:17–19).

Both deliverance and destruction are finally eternal, each in its way, because they are accomplished by the eternal God. The one delivered gains happiness in God without possibility of loss; the one consigned to destruction, banished from the presence of God and his Christ, loses happiness without possibility of gain. There is no way to measure his loss, except by contrast to the gain—to the glory and the wonder of being with the Lord on that day when he comes "to be magnified among his holy ones and to be marveled at among all who have believed."

The parallelism in ἐνδοξασθῆναι ἐν τοῖς ἁγίοις αὐτοῦ καὶ θαυμασθῆναι ἐν πᾶσιν τοῖς πιστεύσασιν may be analogous, glorified among angels/marveled at among men, or it may be synonymous, ἁγίοις already referring to the people of God. Either translation will do and both are true. In Ps. 88:5–7 LXX, however, which (along with Ps. 67:35 LXX) seems to provide the inspiration for these lines, the ἐκκλησία of holy ones in question is that of the angels around the throne. Paul, who is expecting a joint assembly of men and angels, is probably referring to both. Wis. 11:11–14 hints that the unrighteous will also marvel but to no profit.

Who as yet can speak of his glory? Paul, let us recall, was taken (whether in the body or out of the body) into his very presence, where he saw and heard things inexpressible and unutterable, where he was given hints of things no eye has seen and no ear has heard and no mind of man has ever conceived. What the Eleven experienced in the upper room, on the day the risen Lord showed himself to them, was already occasion for a delighted marveling and a joyful magnification. Still more so, when from heaven he poured out the Spirit upon them and attracted to them a marveling crowd of new converts to share their delight. But all that was only a hint of things to come.

It is human to wonder. The angels also wonder at the works of God, being filled with curiosity about his plans and purposes. There is no wonder, however, like the wonder the redeemed will experience on the day Jesus Christ is revealed from heaven personally; the day that the light of his divinity, which already shines darkly through his cross and brightly through his resurrection, will shine in its unoccluded splendor; the day when the magnificence of his and our image-bearing humanity shall also appear; the day when all shall know that justice has acceded to power and true authority as steward of creation has been given to man (cf. *Trin.* 13.17 and *Civ.* 22.9; →2:11–14). Moses coming down from Sinai, his face aglow, Simon son of Onias coming out of the inner sanctuary "like the morning star among the clouds" (Sir. 50:6), Peter emerging from the upper room on Pentecost to explain the "drunkenness" of the Twelve to wondering pilgrims and to raise up the sick and lame, even the dead: palest anticipations, barest types, meanest harbingers of the glory that is to be revealed to those who, tried by fire on earth and saved by fire from heaven, will "rejoice with unutterable and exalted joy" at the appearance of their Great King and High Priest, and of their own glorious liberty (cf. 1 Pet. 1:6–9; Rom. 8:18–21).

If all this seems somewhat foreign to believers today—those, that is, who are not suffering as the Thessalonians were suffering—it is partly *because* they are not yet suffering and partly because the societies and regimes in which they live have been crafted in such a way as to make both kingship and priesthood all but unthinkable. Modern democracies assume that real authority arises from below rather than from above (→1 Thess. 5:12–15). They have no theory of and no feeling for kingship or priesthood, unless the theory is deprecatory and the feeling antipathetic. We live now in the era of individual autonomy, in which each is his own king and high priest. In this era we strive for recognition of the brotherhood of man but not of the fatherhood of God. We stumble over nationhood and even over the natural family, which we are seeking to erase, because it is from the Father that every family is named (Eph. 3:14–21). How then are we who idolize democracy and a certain kind of democracy at that, a democracy dedicated to autonomy, to think with Paul about the fact that authority is indeed patrilineal, that it belongs to the Father and has been assigned to the Son? This was possible in the culture of the Jews and, differently, in Greco-Roman culture, but it seems impossible today. If authority arises from below, not from above, it is always disputable and can never be permitted to become a settled inheritance. The Son, then, cannot be glorified by assuming all authority, and those who do glorify him as such are the enemies of modern democracy.

"The kingdom of God, for the sake of which you also are suffering," or will suffer, is the kingdom for which the Lord bids us pray in the *Pater Noster*, the kingdom he will at his appearance claim and deliver up to the Father, that God may be all in all, after destroying every contrary rule and every false authority and every unjust power, including the rule of death itself, the last enemy (1 Cor. 15:24–28). It is the kingdom in which the will of God will be done on earth as it is done in heaven. When Jesus Christ is disclosed from heaven, his authority will be as indisputable as it is beautiful. Authority itself on that day, precisely because of him, will be indisputably beautiful and beautifully indisputable. It will not only precede argument, as in the Church it already does (*Mor. eccl.* 47); it will, on this point, preclude argument as something quite unnecessary and indeed impossible. There will be no doubt as to who in fact has the authority to judge, to vindicate or condemn, to dispose of man and of creation as such. There will be no doubt as to what the judgment is or whether it is just. What the psalmist says of God, "The heavens declare his righteousness, for God himself is judge!" (50:6), and what Jeremiah says of him who shall "reign as king and deal wisely, and shall execute justice and righteousness in the land," whose name shall be "The LORD is our righteousness" (23:5–6), will be fulfilled in this ἀποκάλυψις of Jesus Christ.

Paul, as we know, is not bashful about using of Jesus the Septuagint's κύριος, "Lord," where it plainly indicates YHWH (Fee 2009: 252ff.). The splendor of Jesus on that day will be YHWH's own. It will be a fearful and awesome display, in human form, of divine justice and power—the same that were displayed in his crucifixion and resurrection. At his crucifixion he declined the service of his Father's legions of angels. At his empty tomb, and forty days later on the mount of his ascension, only two angels were visibly posted. Now legion upon legion of angels (literally, "the ministers of his might" or "the angels of his power") will be deployed to effect judgment on the world and its inhabitants, to purge creation of all that is contrary to the divine purpose and of everyone opposed to that purpose. The kingdom of God will be a kingdom of peace, not of toleration. There will be exclusions as well as inclusions. Some will be delivered, others will be damned.

The toleration that belongs to it now (Matt. 13:24–30) is for the sake of the full harvest of faith that will belong to it then.

▓ With one important difference, the vision of 2 Thess. 1 is very like the vision of Psalm 97:

> The Lord reigns, let the earth be glad;
>   let the distant shores rejoice.
> Clouds and thick darkness surround him;
>   righteousness and justice are the foundation of his throne.
> Fire goes before him
>   and consumes his foes on every side.
> His lightning lights up the world;
>   the earth sees and trembles.
> The mountains melt like wax before the Lord,
>   before the Lord of all the earth.
> The heavens proclaim his righteousness,
>   and all peoples see his glory.
>
> All who worship images are put to shame,
>   those who boast in idols—
>   worship him, all you gods!
>
> Zion hears and rejoices
>   and the villages of Judah are glad
>   because of your judgments, Lord.
> For you, Lord, are the Most High over all the earth;
>   you are exalted far above all gods.
> Let those who love the Lord hate evil,
>   for he guards the lives of his faithful ones
>   and delivers them from the hand of the wicked.
> Light shines on the righteous
>   and joy on the upright in heart.
> Rejoice in the Lord, you who are righteous,
>   and praise his holy name. (NIV)

The difference is that what the psalmist puts in the present tense Paul, with Jesus and the prophets, puts in the future tense. The vision is for a time that is coming. It concerns a messianic event that will complete the victory of God that history has only foreshadowed. That, of course, turns history itself into a grand arena of conflict, as Augustine recognized when he wrote *The City of God* "against the pagans." It makes history to *be* history by pointing it toward an actual dénouement. It requires, as nothing else does, a proper philosophy of history, not a mythology. It requires the reinvention of political philosophy also, as treating a competition not between gods, or gods and men, or classes of men, or cities of men, but between the city of God and the city of man, between the people of God and the people of the one whom Jesus referred to as the prince or ruler of this world—the one Paul called "the god of this world [who] has blinded the minds of the unbelievers, to keep them from seeing the light of the gospel of the glory of Christ" (2 Cor. 4:4; cf. John 12:31). It requires as well, then, a practical theology of apostolic suffering, to strengthen those who look for this dénouement and for the kingdom that people of worldly power and influence neither expect nor desire.

All of this requires in turn the form outlined for it by Jesus in the Olivet Discourse, which Paul is the first to elaborate. It requires reflection on the ascension of Jesus to God's right hand, on the breach between his history and ours, and on the eucharistically anticipated spanning of that breach at the parousia, as the men of patristic and medieval times knew. Modernity, however, was characterized from the beginning by its determination to deny any such breach, to treat the Eucharist as hocus-pocus, to render the parousia of Christ nothing more than the parousia of man as such—the natural end of our own history and no real judgment at all (Farrow 1999a: 165ff.). Hence any Christianity that wishes to be modern cannot be Pauline. It is forced to be sentimental rather than biblical, progressive rather than critical, and to seek a kingdom of human design—a kingdom of peace that is no peace, of toleration that is not toleration of fellow sinners but celebration of each other's sins, of inclusion that posits all exclusion as evil.

This kingdom of toleration and inclusion, in which "they call such great evils peace" (Wis. 14:22), is not the kingdom of God but a kingdom opposed to God. It is a kingdom opposed to moral judgments under God, hence a kingdom opposed also to man qua man, to whom God gave that privilege and responsibility. It is a kingdom where power precedes justice and indeed prevents it, where authority is not earned but merely asserted. It is a kingdom whose liturgy is found in chanted slogans and shouting matches, a kingdom in which there is no true authority, only force and coercion. It is a kingdom that makes law after law that cannot bind the conscience or liberate the enslaved, because its law "has the nature, not of law, but of violence" (*ST* 1-2.93.3, ad 2). It is a kingdom that will come, as Paul has already said, to a sudden and sorry end (→1 Thess. 5:1–3). It can be confronted today by an authentic Christian witness only on the Pauline principle captured in the second article of the Barmen Declaration, the principle that underlies Christian appropriation of the vision of Ps. 97 and its political application: "Just as Jesus Christ is the pledge of the forgiveness of all our sins, just so—and with the same earnestness—is he also God's mighty claim on our whole life; in him we encounter a joyous liberation from the godless claims of this world to free and thankful service to his creatures. We repudiate the false teaching that there are areas of our life in which we belong not to Jesus Christ but to another lord, areas in which we do not need justification and sanctification through him."

Authority has been earned, has been assumed, has begun to liberate and to overthrow. At the ἀποκάλυψις of the Christ its application will be immediate and universal. Christians are not awaiting his appearance as a fresh disclosure within history of the divine mind or purpose already revealed through Moses (cf. 1 Enoch 48:5 and 2 Baruch 39:7), for they believe that to have happened already. Disclosure in history of something or someone preexisting in the mind of God is not the kind of disclosure we are talking about. Rather, he who dwelt among us as one of us, revealing the mind and will of the Father to us before returning to the Father (cf. John 1:9–18; 14:1–31; 17:1–5; 20:17), will now be revealed by the Father as Lord of history. He came from heaven then, yes, and his coming was marked by an angelic chorus, his baptism by the sound of the Father's own voice, his consultation with Moses and Elijah by a transfiguring light. But that was a crack in the darkness, a rumbling in the night. When the dawn arrives, and our ascended Lord comes with the angels of his might, we will behold, as he has desired us to, his "power over all flesh, to give eternal life to all whom [the Father has] given him" and to deprive the evil one of every remaining vestige of power (cf. John 17:2, 24). We will behold the true meaning of the cross and resurrection, and of human suffering under the sign of the cross, but not as a hermeneutic or as mystical insight only, which is open to us even now. We will behold what it is all for, what it all leads to, what it has led to. We will ourselves pass into the glory, which has its own history, of being ever with the Lord (→1 Thess. 4:13–18).

Before that happens, the books will be opened. The hearts and minds and deeds of all who have ever lived in history will in turn be disclosed by God to Christ. If he comes out "into public view from a place of concealment" (Bruce 1982: 154)—that is, from the heavenly time and place where he himself is the nucleus of the new creation—even so will everything else be forced from its place of concealment in the old creation. "For nothing is covered that will not be revealed, or hidden that will not be known" (Matt. 10:26).

As the King already exists and not only in the mind of God—for he is seated, in the flesh, at God's "right hand"—so also does the kingdom. We pray for the kingdom, suffer for the kingdom, hasten the day when the kingdom shall come on earth, but we are not *building* that kingdom, a popular Christian meme with no biblical or dogmatic warrant. We are seeking the kingdom (Matt. 6:33), receiving the kingdom (Heb. 12:28), proclaiming the kingdom (Matt. 24:14), being made worthy of the kingdom (1 Thess. 2:12), and, if worthy, entering the kingdom (Matt. 7:21), but not ourselves making or extending it. The kingdom of Jesus Christ is a kingdom made without hands, apart from those that were stretched upon the cross. It is a kingdom that descends from heaven rather than rising up from the earth. That God and his Christ are still building it may be admitted. That the Church in its ambassadorial role serves in its reception among men may be admitted. That in the Church militant the living stones of the new Jerusalem are being dressed and prepared by spiritual gifts and ecclesial ministries may be admitted (Eph. 2:19ff.; cf. *GS* 21). That through the Church the riches of the kingdom are already shared with the nations may be admitted (*GS* 11, 55, 83, etc.). That the Church is, in its way, the kingdom, and that its martyrs and saints reign with Christ now, albeit "in another and far lesser sense" than in the new creation they shall (*Civ.* 20.9), may be admitted. But that the Church is *building* the kingdom may not be admitted, except in the sense articulated in *Lumen Gentium*: Through its witness and by means of its sacraments, the Church is adding citizens of the kingdom and teaching them the virtues necessary for the kingdom (cf. *LG* 3, 5, 9, 13, 31, 36, 44, 50). For the kingdom of God is the work of God himself, a kingdom "beyond the calculations and bonds of flesh and blood" (*LG* 58; cf. John 18:36). It is a kingdom, while Christ is absent, present in sign and mystery only. In the Eucharist, to be sure, it is truly present, because Christ the King is truly present, both spiritually and bodily. Yet just as Christ remains absent even in his presence until he comes again, his humanity "being hidden in the glory of God" and presented to us only in sacramental form (Aquinas, *S.2Th.* 1.2.14; cf. Farrow 2018g: chap. 6), so too does the kingdom remain absent. While progress in earthly kingdoms, the kingdoms in which we now dwell, is "of vital concern" to the Church insofar as it "can contribute to the better ordering of human society" and hence to provisional peace on earth, such progress, where and when it occurs, "must be carefully distinguished from the growth of Christ's kingdom" (*GS* 39; cf. 1, 45), which is neither of this world nor exactly in it—not as yet! ▪

When the kingdom comes, when the distinction between heaven and earth no longer holds, the world itself, with its whens and wheres, will be transformed by the presence of Christ. It will be quite other than it has been or presently is. The nature of this otherness escapes our ken at present. Only in the regeneration of all things will we ourselves discover it. What begins to happen with the parousia, and culminates in the appearance of the new heavens and earth, will happen in such a manner that "neither the substance nor the essence [*materia conditionis*] of the creation is annihilated," since he who established it is faithful to his own design and purpose; but "the fashion [*figura*] of the world" will pass away, the fashion of things in which transgression was permitted, by reason of which both man and creation have been diminished and "grown old" (*Haer.* 5.36.1, in *ANF* 1:566). Only then will the wisdom of God, the wisdom that none of "the rulers of this age, who are doomed to pass away," have ever understood, be fully manifested to us. Only then will friendship and obedience, freedom and authority, be known to be perfectly consistent (John 15:15). Only then will we experience that manner of life which "no eye has seen, nor ear heard, nor the heart of man conceived," but which "God has prepared for those who love him" (1 Cor. 2:6–9). In that life man will join the holy angels in blessedness. Indeed, he will transcend his present limits and pass beyond the angels in excellence, by virtue of the Son's incarnate solidarity with him (*Haer.* 5.36.3; cf. Anselm 1872: 2).

This kingdom, delivered up to the Father with our world included in it, will remain the kingdom of Jesus Christ, which, as the creed says, will have no end. For the humanity assumed by the Son of God and invested with the Spirit of God and placed at the right hand of the Father is both distinguishable and indivisible from the Son's divinity. It cannot and will not pass away. Neither, then, will Jesus's mediation of all authority that is exercised in or over the kingdom, which is why authority itself will be a grateful "delivering up" to the Father rather than a seizing of power by violent and ungrateful men. The violent—this is the heart of Paul's encouragement to the Thessalonians in their exercise of endurance—will be excluded from this kingdom. It will be a kingdom without end but not a kingdom without limits or definition. Its inhabitants will have the distinctions proper to them. There will still be kinds (angels and men, for example) and ends appropriate to kinds. Moreover, there will be an inside and an outside. Neither all men nor all angels will belong to it; from it some will be banished.

What is outside is not another kingdom, but hell, where no one will marvel at anything and where no further rule will be necessary, because there nothing will be happening. In the kingdom of heaven there will be a liturgy of joy, of *Yes!* and *Amen!* "For all the promises of God find their Yes in him. That is why we utter the Amen through him, to the glory of God" (2 Cor. 1:20). In the caverns of hell, however, where man has hidden himself from God and God has turned away from man (cf. Isa. 2:9–22), there will be no liturgy at all save the liturgy of tears. There will not even be, as presently among men, a Yes and No, but only a No in place of a Yes: *No!* as a terrible and terrifying final word.

▪ The fires of Gehenna never cease burning, because that final word does not erase the creature but fixes it in itself, just as it is without God. After their fashion, then, as the judgment of God, those fires are eternal. Yet we must bear in mind that "eternal" means something different when it modifies not life but destruction. Destruction is eternal in that it is final, and final in that it is pure stasis, devoid both of movement and of rest. Life, on the other hand, is eternal in the sense that it is forever lively. To enjoy eternal life is to be at rest, to share in the Great Sabbath of the divine delight in all that has been made (Moltmann

1996: 257ff.). But God is the living God, and this rest is no mere stasis. The kingdom of heaven is the world fully ordered by man to and for God, and by God to and for man. It is the world full of resurrection life in Jesus Christ, life without death or decay. We should not think of heaven, then, as timeless, but as having a kind of time that is not entropic, a time that never runs out and never grows old. All its ends are sustained, and all its movements renewed, by the End of ends. Hell, however, may be thought of as timeless time, because in hell nothing happens. No end is reached or even reached for, save in a frozen gesture. Hell is static. Its fuel lasts and its fire perpetually burns (we are speaking metaphorically, as we must) just because it is static. It helps to bear in mind that hell is first prepared for the devil and his angels, not for man. Being active spirits, they would rather be driving swine than rotting in hell, where there is no activity. But actions require ends, and from those in hell the End of ends has decisively withdrawn. Meaningful movement is therefore impossible. (Think of Satan, encased in ice at the bottom of Dante's hell.) Humans will suffer this also in their own way, each to his own degree. The will to happiness will still be there, but all hope of happiness will be gone. *Lasciate ogni speranza, voi ch'entrate.* Happiness will be as inaccessible as the justice they did not retain for themselves and would not receive again from Christ. Their only motions, then, and their only measures of motion, will be, in the metaphor of Jesus, the weeping of their eyes and the gnashing of their teeth.

Here we may note that the universalist view rejected earlier suffers from what we might call the "durationist" fallacy, for which some blame can be placed on more conventional views insofar as they regard hell as an endless succession of moments. The universalist takes up that naïve notion, then argues that shortening the succession to something finite, something measurable, makes a great difference. In fact it makes no difference at all; or rather the difference it makes, as we have already seen, is that the universalist problem with the doctrine of hell becomes even more intractable. This problem, at bottom, has nothing to do with time or amounts of time (*pace* Hart 2019: 82ff., 203f.; cf. *Civ.* 12.13ff.). Nor is it the theodical puzzle it is made out to be. What is really at stake is not the goodness or power of God but the putative rights of unrepentant sinners. The universalist refuses to allow that these sinners should be deprived of the happiness that belongs to the righteous, conceding only (to put it as delicately as possible) such deferrals in obtaining it as correspond to their deferrals in rightly pursuing it. The annihilationist, for his part, is not quite so ambitious; for the unrepentant sinner he demands only a right to nonexistence, reducing the duration of hell to a vanishing point. These spurious rights-claims manage to gain a bit of traction from Church tradition wherever its exponents make the mistake of thinking of hell as involving, like heaven, a further history of some kind, albeit one of pains rather than of pleasures. Hell is an absolute and unyielding limit. It has no history, though that is not to say that those who enter it cease to exist. We do not have any language for this but the metaphorical language Jesus gave us, and we have no very satisfactory conceptual framework either. We may say that the second death is indeed a dying, not a living. Yet it is a special kind of dying, a dying with no outcome, a dying without ceasing to die. Aquinas (*S.2Th.* 1.2.18) observes that "the punishments of this life are not like those punishments: in this life the harsher the punishments the shorter they are, because they end; but those punishments are the heaviest, because they are the punishment of death and yet they never cease. Hence it is said that they will always be as though in the throes of death." That is almost right but not quite (cf. O'Callaghan 2011: 207). It can be made right by removing from it the remaining traces of durationism and by approaching it more christologically.

Jesus, who is the Prince of life and the way to life, suffered death and was buried. He descended to the realm of the dead, but he did not suffer the second death or enter the lake of fire. He was not, is not, and will not be present there. For that reason alone we must say that hell lacks a proper there and then. (That much can be conceded to the annihilationists, even if nothing can be conceded to the remedialists.) There is another reason as well. We must say that hell lacks a proper there and then because no form of death, much less this total death, is "inflicted on us by any law of nature, for God did not create any death for man" when he created the world. Rather, every form of death, whether partial or total, is "justly inflicted on us for sin" and by sin (*Civ.* 13.15; cf. 13.12). *A fortiori,* when the new heavens and earth appear, with God and the Lamb as their sanctuary, they appear without any form of death as even a possibility. So we should be absolutely clear that hell does not sit opposite or alongside heaven, cosmologically or ontologically. Hell is not heaven's nether region. It does not share heaven's history, its eternal glory. Yet hell is real in its own peculiar way, for it has been prepared by God for the devil and his angels, in response to sin and sinners. Just so, it is also good in its own peculiar way, for God produces nothing that lacks reality or goodness. And how is it good? It is good as the limit proper to sin and the sinner. It is good by effecting and witnessing to the justice of God, and to the freedom of rational creatures. Thus, and only thus, will it contribute to the blessedness of the world to come (cf. *ST* Suppl.94.3, ad 2), though of that world it will be no part or counterpart.

"I heard the altar cry, 'Yes, Lord God the Almighty, true and just are your judgments!'" (Rev. 16:7). Heaven and hell both attest to that most fundamental fact, though they attest very differently. In heaven, the true and just judgments of God shall bring about the fulfillment of every promise of God to his creatures, especially those at the heart of the covenant by which man is called to walk with God (Rev. 21:1–8). The substance, though not the form, of the old creation will be carried over into the new. In hell, on the other hand, there will be nothing new, and no further participation in the goodness and promise of what is old. In hell there will be only vocation without mediation, call without answer, being without communion, a hunger and thirst for happiness that cannot be assuaged. All this will be differently felt by different creatures, according to their kind and to their guilt, but we cannot say how it will be felt or experienced. And we should not make the mistake (a mistake even careful thinkers like Augustine and Aquinas sometimes make) of using existing models of time to try to give an account of it. As Thietland of Einsiedeln puts it, there will be "death without death, destruction without weakening, fire without light" (Cartwright and Hughes 2001: 47). Just so, there will be time without time and space without space. There will remain something and not nothing of the old creation, though the history of that creation will already be complete. What remains will be what sinners have prepared for themselves through injustice and what God has prepared for them as the terminus of that injustice. Injustice, by having a terminus, will be forced after all to serve justice.

Neither remedialists nor annihilationists reckon fully with the relation between freedom and justice, or factor this relation into their understanding of hell. Since our creaturely freedom, as Anselm explains in *De libertate arbitrii*, did not consist in being "able to sin or not sin" but rather in the power to preserve a God-like and God-given capacity for justice, a capacity given us in and with our creation, it follows that sin was not necessary. Neither then was death necessary, nor hell. But hell is necessary now. Without it there can be no justice, or even the concept of justice. For without it even the limited freedom we presently have evaporates. Without it our decisions do not really count. But they do count and will count. In the well-known words of the *Dies irae*,

Iudex ergo cum sedebit,	When the Judge his seat attaineth,
quidquid latet, apparebit:	and each hidden deed arraigneth,
nil inultum remanebit.	nothing unavenged remaineth.

If all unjustified sinners meet the same fate, annihilation, their individual deeds do not count. If all unjustified sinners must be beaten with rods, so to say, over a shorter or longer period of time until they wise up and have paid up, it may be supposed that their deeds count. But what is the link between paying up and wising up, between punishment and reformation of soul? (The same question that bedevils certain accounts of purgatory reappears, and becomes even more pressing, with the remedialist account of hell.) And are we not left, either way, with something much cruder than what we have found in 2 Thess. 1? What is promised there suddenly presents itself in a very flat light. Deliverance reduces to a reward, destruction to a reprisal, largely lacking in moral features. Both are reduced to something more Qur'anic than Christian, or at least more Old Testament than New. The enemies of God and of his people are utterly eliminated, while the friends of God flourish and enjoy the spoil; or if not utterly eliminated, then at least reduced to penal servitude.

Now, there is nothing wrong with deliverance and judgment in the Old Testament sense, which is corporeal and political. That very earthy, practical sense is maintained throughout the New Testament. It is filled out, however, in the light of Christ, in such a way that the individual and cosmic and spiritual dimensions are also brought to the fore, as begins to happen already in Paul's letters to Thessaloniki. At the other end of the New Testament, chronologically, the Apocalypse maintains the same delicate balance as it unites and recapitulates the Testaments. But neither the annihilationist nor the remedialist rises to the occasion. On the former's account, God's enemies are judged then promptly executed, whether one by one or all together. On the latter's account, they are judged then slowly tortured until full payment for their crimes is made *and* they have come to love their torturer. How exactly this is meant to be an improvement on those medieval accounts to which the former and the latter object (sometimes rightly) remains less than clear. The relation between freedom and justice remains less than clear. The annihilationist thinks the unjust person simply disposable. The remedialist thinks him inevitably just and loving, given sufficient time. That is not how Jesus sees it, or how Paul sees it; nor is it how we should see it.

The Thessalonian Christians, for their part, have heard the divine Yes and are saying their Amen in and through their suffering. They have believed the witness made to them, the testimony "laid upon" them (the Vulgate translates ἐφ' ὑμᾶς as *super vos*; on which see Aquinas, *S.2Th.* 1.2.22). They must not waver. When the day of the Lord arrives, it will be made manifest to all that it was right and just to have said their Amen, and that their neighbors ought also to have done so; that the latter were wrong and unjust to refuse to do so, and especially to persecute the faithful. Those worldly "brethren" who have hated them and cast them out, if they do not repent, shall be put to shame, everlasting shame, while the objects of their wrath will be comforted by their Lord and enter into his joy. (See Isa. 66:5, though here in 2 Thessalonians we must think of both Jewish and Gentile persecutors, who collaborate against the followers of Jesus as against Jesus himself.) He will be glorified in them and they in him.

1:11–12 To this very end we pray always for you, that our God may deem you worthy of the call and powerfully fulfill every aspiration to goodness and work of faith, so that the name of our Lord Jesus might be glorified in you, and you in him, according to the grace of our God and the Lord Jesus Christ.

Paul, who always keeps the beginning and the middle and the end of salvation in view, wraps up the introduction to his second letter with a benediction very like those of 1 Thess. 3:12 and 5:23. He prays that the Thessalonians may be found worthy in God's eyes through a faith that, despite persecution, aspires to good works and to goodness itself; and that God in his elevating grace, the grace that enables man to cooperate with God in the things of God, may see to it that these aspirations are carried to fruition through an anointing with power. Jesus himself, after all, was a man anointed with the Holy Spirit and with power (Acts 10:38). Paul desires that they be like him, so that the name of Jesus may be glorified through them; that there may be a communion of glory, he in them and they also in him, each having suffered for the other. It is thus that they will attain to their salvation, a salvation (in the equally eloquent language of 1 Pet. 1) "ready to be revealed in the last time" and guarded meanwhile by a faith that, proven genuine through suffering, will "redound to praise and glory and honor at the revelation of Jesus Christ."

To be found worthy in the end they must be deemed worthy in the beginning ("deemed," not "made," *pace* Malherbe 2000: 410, who jumps the gun) and continue in that worthiness. They must desire to be "doers of the word, and not hearers only" (Jas. 1:22). But they become doers, and their doing becomes fruitful, only by divine grace and power, just as they believe the word, if they do really believe, only by divine grace and power (→1 Thess. 1:2–5; cf. Jas. 2:14–26). This grace and power are both operative and cooperative. There is something that only God does or can do, and there is something that God enables them to do themselves by working in and with God (cf. Phil. 2:12–13). Paul is praying for both, and he is praying that what the Thessalonians do in and with God will be made fruitful by that fecund power that is God's, for the sake of their witness now and for the sake, ultimately, of their coming communion in glory.

Disputes about this are unfruitful, unless we count schism as their fruit. Paul knows very well that faith is necessary for faithfulness, and can use the single word πίστις for both. In the language of a later era, he knows that love is formed by faith (*caritas fidei formata*) but also that faith is formed by love (*fides caritate formata*); that is, that faith begets faithfulness and faithfulness faith. *Pace* Luther, who got only as far as admitting the *caritas fidei formata*, Paul and James are following the same script here (→1 Thess. 1:2–5). So is Aquinas when he says, "Now there are five effects of grace in us: of these, the first is, to heal the soul; the second, to desire good; the third, to carry into effect the good proposed; the fourth, to persevere in good; the fifth, to reach glory" (*ST* 1-2.111.3). Paul wishes the Thessalonian Christians to reach glory, and he prays that they will, which is what we also should do for one another, encouraging one another in faith for the sake of faithfulness and in faithfulness for the sake of faith, lest anyone, having made shipwreck of their faith, be found unworthy of the calling and fail to reach glory. *Sancte Paule, ora quoque pro nobis.*

In glory there will be nothing lacking of any good thing we desire or any good effect toward which we aspire. To reach glory is to be happy. To be glorified is to become happy, which all men want, though not all pursue it justly or worthily or in such a way as to find it. Augustine, expounding in *De Trinitate* 13 the faith necessary for that pursuit, tells us that happiness is having everything we want, while wanting nothing wrongly. The task in this life is to learn to want or aspire rightly, so that in the world to come, by divine power, we may have what we want. And so we shall, if we want rightly by wanting God first and last, and all things only in God.

■ "Why then, O little man," enquires Anselm, "do you wander many paths, seeking the goods of your soul and your body? Love the one Good in which are all goods, and it suffices. Desire the simple Good that is every good, and it is enough. What indeed do you love, my flesh? What do you desire, my soul? There it is, there it is—whatever you love, whatever you desire! If beauty delights you, 'the righteous shall shine as the sun.' If speed or strength, or liberty of movement that nothing can resist, 'they shall be like the angels of God.' . . . If a long and wholesome life, there is a wholesome eternity and an eternal wholeness. . . . If satisfaction, they shall be satisfied 'when the glory of God appears.' If inebriation, 'they shall be intoxicated from the abundance of God's house.' If melody, there the choirs of angels sing unceasingly to God. If any pleasure—pure not impure—God 'will give them drink from the river of his delight.' If wisdom, God's own wisdom shall manifest itself to them. If friendship, they will love God more than themselves and each other as themselves, and God will love them more than they love themselves. . . . If concord, there shall be one will in them all, for none shall will anything but the will of God. If power, they shall be omnipotent in the will of each, as God is in his own; for just as God is able through himself to do what he wills, so they will be able through him to do what they will. . . . If honor and riches, God will set his good and faithful servants over many things. . . . If true security, undoubtedly they will be sure that these goods, or rather that Good, will not fail them in any manner or by any means" (*Proslogion* 25, in *PL* 158:240–41, AT; cf. Matt. 19:29).   ■

2:1–5 But we beg you, brethren, with respect to the parousia of our Lord Jesus Christ and our assembling before him, that you not quickly be shaken from your senses or disturbed, whether by spirit or by word or by letter, supposedly from us, purporting that the day of the Lord has come. Let no one by any means deceive you, for [it shall not come] unless the apostasy comes first and the man of lawlessness, the son of destruction, is disclosed—the one taking an adversarial stance and exalting himself over everything said to be deity or an object of reverence, even to seating himself in the temple of God as if he were God. Do you not remember that while I was with you I was telling you these things?

Having set the stage for his main argument, Paul proceeds with some urgency to identify the problem he means to address. He wants to set the record straight about the process leading to the parousia, which is the proper focus of believing hope (*CD* IV/3, 909), and about its preconditions, lest their misunderstanding deflect them from their mission and from their aspiration to good works. In order to do that he must clarify and expand things he has already taught them regarding the "night" and its progress. Listening in, we get a better understanding of Paul's philosophy of history; that is, of the present age and of its climax in the confrontation of Christ and antichrist (though that is a Johannine term he does not employ). Just so, we get a better understanding of the situation and work of the Church.

What Paul now reveals to us about all that, he reveals in response to an error that has arisen in Thessaloniki, or at all events has made its way there. Whether that error was being encouraged by the idle—later he will have more to say about them as well, and their disruptive influence—is difficult to know, though it might have served their self-justification. That, however, is mere speculation, made doubtful by the fact that Paul himself does not make the connection. We are on much safer ground to suppose that this church was susceptible to the error in question because of an overly enthusiastic response to his assurances about the parousia, combined with an overly dramatic reading of their own sufferings as the "messianic woes" of the last days described by Daniel (Aus 1973: 438; cf. Jubilees 23), as well as an overly literal reading of Paul's first letter, with its warning about the suddenness of the Master's return. Such a reading is impossible for anyone with the whole Olivet Discourse firmly in mind, but to have it firmly in mind could hardly be expected of them, since they had neither the text of that discourse nor any sustained instruction in it. As Aquinas remarks at 1 Thess. 4:14, it might well "seem to those who do not fully understand what the Apostle is saying here that all this shall come about while the Apostle is still alive; it seemed this way to the Thessalonians. Because of this misunderstanding he wrote them a second letter in which he says: 'Now concerning the coming of our Lord Jesus Christ . . . we beg you, brethren, not to be quickly shaken in mind or excited, either by spirit or by word, or by letter purporting to be from us, to the effect that the day of the Lord has come'" (*S. 1 Th.* 4.2.96).

About the error itself, or its central claim at least, we have no need to speculate. The notion was now circulating among them that the day of the Lord had already arrived. How that notion had begun to circulate does not seem clear to Paul, who covers all the bases: Did someone put it forward in the form of a prophetic utterance? Was it passed on to the church as a report from "reliable sources" elsewhere? Were Paul and his team said to be those sources? Was someone claiming to have received a private letter from them, or had someone actually forged such a letter? It is not inconceivable that this notion was backed, or that Paul feared it would be backed, in more than one of these ways. Deceptive doctrines and enthusiasms of various kinds were and are put forward in every possible way. In our own age the means of social communication are such that they spread more quickly and more widely, but technology aside, and with it the intensification of hubris, there is nothing new under the sun.

Of more interest are the corollaries of the error. Was this claim made in support of what today we would call an over-realized eschatology? If so, that eschatology would presumably be a kind of protognosticism that approached even the resurrection of the dead as a purely psychological reality, an opening of the graves of the mind rather than of the graves in the ground. Chrysostom, perhaps, has something of the sort in view when, in his first homily on 2 Thessalonians, he says of their hope that "the devil, wishing to cut it off, as being a kind of anchor, when he was not able to persuade them that the things to come were false, went to work another way, and having suborned certain pestilential men, endeavored to deceive those who believed into a persuasion that those great and splendid things had [already] received their fulfillment." Even in Paul's lifetime, things of that nature were being mooted. Hymaenaeus and Philetus are accused in 2 Tim. 2:18 of having "swerved from the truth by holding that the resurrection is past already," which the RSVCE glosses as a collapse of the baptismal *res* into its sacramental *signum*. Already in 1 Cor. 15 he is found attacking skepticism about the resurrection of the dead, which may have existed also in Thessaloniki, particularly among Gentile converts, and perhaps continued to exist despite his assurances in the first letter. Yet Paul does not revisit that topic, so we must assume that the claim that the day of the Lord has come (ἐνέστηκεν ἡ ἡμέρα τοῦ κυρίου) is not dependent on or openly allied with such skepticism. Whether we take ἐνέστηκεν to mean that the day "has arrived and is about to break upon us" or to mean that it "is present and has already broken upon us," we need not and should not, in the absence of evidence, take it to mean that the day does not include those features Paul has already said it will include, such as bodily resurrection and a public gathering to Jesus Christ. It would seem, then, not to be an over-realized or heavily psychologized eschatology but rather a potent form of end-times enthusiasm with which Paul is contending, a doctrine not of imminency only ("be ready, for you know neither the day nor the hour") but indeed of immediacy ("*this* is the day and the hour").

That is by no means a distinction without a difference. In the language of the Apocalypse, to say "the time is now" is to assume that "there will be no more delay," that the seventh trumpet has sounded, that everything still to happen is already in the process of happening (Rev. 10:5–7). When the seventh trumpet sounds, let those who hear it act accordingly. But Paul does not think it has sounded. For Paul, as for John, imminency does not mean immediacy, and he does not want the Thessalonians to think that it does. That will not only unsettle them and throw them off course. It will disappoint them and inevitably disillusion them, leaving them prey to outright skepticism, to abandonment of their faith and perseverance, to the failure of his and their mission in the city.

A doctrine of imminency means or ought to mean that Jesus is already seated in the place of all power and authority, and is therefore ready to be revealed as Lord and to carry out divine judgment. Nothing is lacking on his side that would prevent this, other than the Father's signal. A doctrine of immediacy, on the other hand, presumes to know that the Father has given that signal. It is not really a doctrine at all, but a false start encouraged from time to time by false prophets. The solution, as we already know, is not to abandon the gift of prophecy but instead to test it. As Chrysostom says at 1 Thess. 5:20–21, making reference to the present passage, "Do not, because there are false prophets among you, on their account prohibit also" prophecy that is true (*Hom.* 11). Testing requires a certain maturity, however. "Spiritual goods," says Aquinas in his treatment of 2 Thess. 1:3, "are not safely guarded unless a man progresses in them. Now among these gifts of God the first is faith, through which God dwells in us, and our progress in faith is in connection with the understanding" (*S.2Th.* 1.1.9). Understanding of the ways of God is required for testing prophecy, and that is what Paul wishes his readers to gain. The requisite key to this understanding is found in the present chapter, which makes it all the more remarkable that our modern lectionaries suppress its main argument by omitting its middle section. This omission, lamented earlier, actually plays into the hands of false prophets or teachers, for it passes over the crucial distinction between imminency and immediacy, hence also over the true situation of the people of God in the present age.

In the twentieth century, as some will recall, Albert Schweitzer went so far as to suggest that this process of expectation and disappointment is just what happened to Jesus himself, who then betook himself in despair to the cross in one last vain attempt to push history prematurely to its conclusion. Presumably Jesus was more honest, if not more realistic, than the successors of the apostles, who in their own disillusionment, after the failure of Paul's modestly revised apocalyptic enthusiasm, invented the institutional Church and settled for something less exciting but more durable. This drab institutionalism they interpolated into dominical teaching as an antidote to general despair over the failure of the promised parousia. Or so went the story line of the generations of Protestant scholars preceding Schweitzer, as far as Harnack. Having exposed that little game, these same scholars helped (particularly in Germany) to excite their contemporaries with a new kind of kingdom-on-earth enthusiasm, the failure of which through two World Wars has drawn our whole civilization into despair, with consequences that are still unfolding.

Now, in speaking of these things, we are not getting off track but we are getting ahead of ourselves; for the Thessalonians, whatever they had heard, had heard no such blasphemous nonsense as that promulgated by modern "critical" scholars. They had, however, been fed a false teaching capable of leading them (rather like Schweitzer's Jesus and Harnack's Germany) to embrace a fundamental misunderstanding about their own place in history. And the proper antidote, thought Paul, was a better understanding of the nature of divine justice. It is in the spirit of the Song of Moses that he writes to them: "The Rock, his work is perfect; for all his ways are justice. A God of faithfulness and without iniquity, just and right is he" (Deut. 32:4).

Before we proceed with exposition of the present chapter, however, we should note that a good many commentators, even those who mean to be faithful to Paul, do get off on the wrong track by introducing speculation about the timing of the parousia already into their treatment of 1 Thess. 5—as if Paul, even there, were already fussing the way they themselves do about dates and date-setters, while managing only to encourage in his readers that very vice by banging away on the "thief in the night" motif. These same commentators often try to read 2 Thessalonians as an attempt to get the real job, the pastoral job of comfort or consolation, done properly in spite of that vice. They want to save Paul from himself, as it were, to salvage his own "obscure" efforts at some kind of timeline by insisting that whatever he says here about the parousia, or the process leading up to it, he says primarily to make his readers as comfortable in their faith as possible. This is at best a half-truth. In point of fact, Paul's first letter betrays no great concern, positively or negatively, with timelines or the setting of timelines; nor indeed does his second, except in the sense that he is very much concerned to reject immediacy, and must therefore review and expand what he himself has already told them about the process in question. And why is he concerned? Not simply because the Thessalonians are being disturbed by apocalypse-now prophecies, but because it is evident from their perturbation that they have not properly grasped what the whole process is about, which bears on their mission as much as on their mindset. For Paul it becomes a teaching moment, an opportunity to make up a deficiency in their faith—and so in ours also, if we will let him.

▨ Reading 2 Thessalonians as a "There, there, it's not so bad as all that!" letter is not a new phenomenon. Haimo, for example, thinks that Paul wrote the second letter to correct the Thessalonians' misimpression from the first letter that the parousia was expected immediately—a thought, he says, that, far from consoling them, would have terrified them because of their sins (Cartwright and Hughes 2001: 21). It is to console them properly now, by denying its temporal nearness, that he writes the second letter. Even Weima (2014: 445), in hastening to connect the doctrinal to the pastoral in 2 Thessalonians, misconstrues the pastoral, and the doctrinal with it, as primarily concerned with comfort or consolation, though he does not follow Haimo in the particulars. False enthusiasm, to be sure, is a disruptive force and a bane to pastoral leadership, as Paul is the first to say. But Paul's answer to false enthusiasm is proper education, not the subordination of doctrine to some preconceived pastoral objective, a point pastors and prelates, as well as commentators, do well to ponder.   ▨

Paul's advertised topic in this teaching moment is "the parousia of our Lord Jesus Christ and our assembling before him." The thesis to be defended is that it is not to happen today or even tomorrow, but only when the time is right. The first objective is to explain why, showing that the justice of God will not permit it and that other things must happen first. The ultimate goal is to prepare his charges for what is coming and to establish them "in every good work and word" (2:17), so that they may carry on effectively with their mission. Required background reading includes Dan. 7–12, with Ps. 110 (109 LXX), Wis. 10–19, Sir. 50, Joel, Zech. 8–14, Mal. 3–4, 2 Macc. 5–9, as well as (for readers with access) Matt. 24–25 and parallels, among other texts extending as far as the Apocalypse. Let us begin, as he does, with the topic itself.

The Christian's own ultimate goal, like Paul's, is to be with the Lord. Whatever else the parousia accomplishes, it accomplishes that. Hence Paul speaks of these as one single event: "the parousia of our Lord Jesus Christ and our assembling before him." Translation, however, does not quite do justice to the "assembling" part. As we saw in 1 Thessalonians, this assembling is no ordinary rendezvous, such as David's fighting men used to make with him; though there is something to that analogy, for David prefigures his greater Son, who is anointed both with oil and with a superabundance of the Spirit and power, who gathers round himself first the Twelve and eventually "a great multitude" that no one can number (Rev. 7:9). Even Ps. 110, the early Church's favorite messianic psalm, with its bold statements and elaborate glosses that conjure with Davidic imagery—"Yours is dominion on the day you lead your host in holy splendor"—does not quite capture the essence of this assembling to the Great King, the King of the Ages who is begotten before the morning star (110:3). If one is to speak adequately about his parousia and our assembling to him, one requires, at the very least, the imagery of Dan. 7:9–14 and of course the teaching of Jesus himself. One requires also the situation and posture so effectively portrayed by John in the opening chapter of the Apocalypse, the eucharistic situation.

◼ In the foreground, when Paul speaks ὑπὲρ τῆς παρουσίας τοῦ κυρίου ἡμῶν Ἰησοῦ Χριστοῦ καὶ ἡμῶν ἐπισυναγωγῆς ἐπ᾽ αὐτὸν, is the dominical saying at Matt. 24:31, "he will send out his angels with a loud trumpet call, and they will gather [ἐπισυνάξουσιν] his elect from the four winds, from one end of heaven to the other." Behind this is the saying found at Matt. 23:37, which brings it into focus by the sharpest possible contrast: "O Jerusalem, Jerusalem, killing the prophets and stoning those who are sent to you! How often would I have gathered your children together as a hen gathers her brood under her wings, and you would not!" Looking beyond that, we see Luke using the same word (ἐπισυνάγω) to refer to that rather chaotic rehearsal that took place while opposition to Jesus was still growing among Jewish leaders and his popularity with the people was still approaching its peak: "In the meantime, when so many thousands of the multitude had gathered together that they trod upon one another, he began to say . . ." (12:1). The word is also used at Heb. 10:25 to refer to the assembling of the Church, at once local and universal, which is so memorably compared in Heb. 12 to Israel's assembly before God at Sinai, itself a precursor to the final assembling at the parousia of the whole people of God.

We might come closer to doing justice to the present text, then, if we employed a more literal but awkward-sounding expression, "our congregating upon him." For the rehearsals— generally somewhat less chaotic than that mentioned in Luke 12—which now take place are eucharistic rehearsals, an ἐπισυναγωγή that is not only a coming together in one place but a coming together to and upon one foundation. At the birth of the Church, Mary and the disciples were all gathered together in one place (ἦσαν πάντες ὁμοῦ ἐπὶ τὸ αὐτό, Acts 2:1) and in one accord (for ὁμοῦ the *TR* has ὁμοθυμαδὸν and the Vulgate *pariter*) to receive from Christ the gift of the Spirit, who in turn would enable them to gather in many other such places to receive the gift of Christ from the Spirit. The being of the Church on earth is realized and expressed in such gatherings, gatherings both to and upon Jesus Christ, who is its one foundation. This is what the Orthodox refer to as the eucharistic synaxis, which is indeed a rehearsal for, and already a participation in, the assembling of that great *congregatio* to come, the "flocking together" of the faithful of every generation that will take place at the parousia.   ◼

This, then, is the topic or rubric with which we are concerned: the parousia, considered as the final assembling of the people of God before God and his Christ at the end of the age. But Paul's thesis under this rubric is not an ecclesiological thesis or even a christological thesis. It is an eschatological thesis about the circumstances in which it will occur, about its conditions of possibility. The final and universal gathering that every local eucharistic gathering anticipates is not yet, and it is not yet because two crucial conditions for it have not been met: the apostasy has not taken place and the man of lawlessness has not stepped forth. Therefore the time for judgment has not arrived. And if the time for judgment has not arrived, the Judge will not be arriving now either. The Church's final gathering to him must wait, for when he comes as Savior he will come also as Judge; when he comes to rescue, he will come also to carry out the divine wrath.

Those who purport that the day of the Lord has arrived are quite mistaken, because they have left out of account the fact that it cannot arrive "unless the apostasy comes first and the man of lawlessness, the son of destruction, is disclosed." How does Paul know this? Where does he get such an idea? From the prophet Daniel and from Jesus himself, who in the Olivet Discourse enlightens his disciples on the appointed time, much as Gabriel enlightened Daniel. "Behold," says Gabriel, "I will make known to you what shall be at the latter end of the indignation [τῆς ὀργῆς, 8:19 LXX]; for it pertains to the appointed time of the end." "Tell us," beg the Twelve (Matt. 24:3), "when will this be, and what will be the sign of your coming and of the close of the age?" Paul is listening carefully both to Gabriel and to Jesus as they explain, and passing on to the Thessalonians what he has learned.

> Paul is not propounding some peculiar theory of his own. What form of access he had to the discourses of Jesus we do not know, but it is clear that he did have access; in the present case, apparently, access to something like the Matthean version, in which Jesus references Daniel. As for Daniel, he is indeed "the prophet Daniel" (Matt. 24:15). Anyone who would dismiss him as a mere "scribe" or apocalyptic speculator must dismiss Jesus also. That is not to say, however, that the prophet and the legendary figure need be one person, or that the materials in Daniel have but one date. There is a difference between pseudonymity and forgery.

So what is the apostasy (ἡ ἀποστασία) of which Paul speaks? And who is this one whom he calls, using synonymous parallelism, "the man of lawlessness, the son of destruction" or "the man of sin, the son of perdition"? (Some manuscripts have ὁ ἄνθρωπος τῆς ἀνομίας, ὁ υἱὸς τῆς ἀπωλείας, while others put ἁμαρτίας for ἀνομίας, despite the precedent in Ps. 88:22–23 LXX, υἱὸς ἀνομίας; no entirely firm conclusion can be reached on the basis of manuscript evidence alone, but the use of ἀνομίας in 2:7–9 also favors it here.) Jesus mentions neither the apostasy nor the man of lawlessness directly. He does, however, warn his disciples against false messiahs who will lead the people astray by promising what they cannot deliver, and warns further that many shall take offense at him and "fall away, and betray one another, and hate one another" (Matt. 24:10; cf. Dan. 10–11). What Jesus says about taking offense, about being tripped up or enticed into sin, about falling away—σκανδαλισθήσονται can have any or all of these meanings (cf. Matt. 26:31–35; Mark 4:17; 6:3; 14:27; Luke 7:23; John 6:61; 16:1)—Paul captures with the word ἀποστασία. There will be a general forsaking of the truth, a defection from Jesus as the truth, a rebellion against the God of truth that will characterize the time of the end and precipitate the final wrath or indignation of God.

▨ The same word is later used to attack Paul himself with the allegation that he teaches Jews to forsake Moses (Acts 21:21). The verb on which it is based, ἀφίστημι, in its intransitive form means "to withdraw or desert"; transitively, "to bring about a revolt." Both the verb and the noun are associated with treachery and rebellion, as for example, in Josh. 22:22 LXX. The attempt by Ambrosiaster, Jerome, and Haimo of Auxerre et al. to read it as a cryptic reference to a *discessio* from the Roman Empire (see Hughes 2005: 76f.) is not credible and at best a serious distraction, however reasonable may be attempts to factor into the antichrist narrative the eventual failure of a revived form of that empire.   ▨

Paul elaborates on this defection by way of reference to the man of lawlessness, Daniel's "king of bold countenance" who "shall cause fearful destruction" (Dan. 8:23–24); who shall also "seduce with flattery those who violate the covenant"; who shall "magnify himself above every god, and shall speak astonishing things against the God of gods," prospering "till the indignation is accomplished" (11:32–36). Paul has already spoken in passing of Satan's opposition to the gospel and of the complicity of Jewish leaders in that opposition (→1 Thess. 2:13–16). Now he speaks of one who in satanic fashion will deceive men from all nations and oppose God himself, before the divine wrath falls at last upon him and upon them. This is ὁ ἀντικείμενος, the one who adopts Satan's adversarial stance and becomes not only a false christ but the antichrist. Jesus has pointed to him by mentioning τὸ βδέλυγμα τῆς ἐρημώσεως, the "desolating sacrilege" or "abomination that makes desolate" (Matt. 24:15; cf. Dan. 9:27; 11:31; 12:11 LXX) for which he is responsible. It is because he is responsible, because he brings destruction and goes to destruction, that he is called "the son of destruction," the one doomed to utter and everlasting ruin. (The same description, ὁ υἱὸς τῆς ἀπωλείας, is used of

Judas at John 17:12, of whom Jesus said that it would have been better for him had he not been born.)

In short, Paul makes use of Daniel to interpret Jesus and of Jesus to interpret Daniel. As the very model of the man of lawlessness, there had already appeared Antiochus IV Epiphanes, the Syrian tyrant who in the second century BC viciously attacked the people of God and violated the temple of God, until he was struck down by the hand of God and came to his end "with none to help him" (cf. Dan. 8:25; 11:45; 2 Macc. 9). Of the apostasy or defection, those "lawless men" who forsook the covenant to conform to the new Syrian regime and abandoned the temple for the gymnasium, who even sought in some cases surgically to undo their circumcision, were the model (1 Macc. 1:10–15). And in that reign of terror there were many martyrs, who became a model of the faithful who endure to the end so as to be saved (cf. 2 Macc. 7; Matt. 24:13). But all of this was viewed, whether by Daniel, Jesus, or Paul, as a mere foreshadowing of things still to happen at the end of the age, "many days hence," in which "shall be a time of trouble, such as never has been" (Dan. 12:1). Even the time of Jesus, the time spoken of by all the prophets, was not that time. It marked the beginning of that time, yes, but according to Jesus the end was not yet—"If they do this when the wood is green, what will happen when it is dry?" (Luke 23:31)—and one ought not, even in seeing signs of the end piling up one on another, become too quickly disturbed or alarmed (Matt. 24:6). Only when the gospel of the kingdom is carried to the ends of the earth "as a testimony to all nations," only when there appears that final analogue to the desolating sacrilege, only when there arises "great tribulation, such as has not been from the beginning of the world until now, no, and never will be," only then will the end come (24:14–21).

The time of Antiochus IV (175–164 BC) was certainly not the end. Nor was the destruction of Jerusalem after the revolt of AD 66–70, though the wood of that city was then dry. We know it was not the end because it was followed by no redemption or resurrection of Israel (Dan. 12:1–4) but only by a subsequent, equally futile revolt, led by a false messianic claimant dubbed Bar Kokhba. After that, Jews were banned from Jerusalem altogether and Jerusalem was rebuilt as a pagan city dedicated to Hadrian and to Jupiter. In the Olivet Discourse Jesus has these future events in view, but that is not all he has in view. He looks beyond them, as Daniel does, to a seventieth week, an ultimate not a penultimate week, that will follow unspecified wars and desolations decreed by God (Dan. 9:26–27). Likewise Paul, who understood "the times of the Gentiles" already to have begun even while the temple still stood; with Jesus, he expects those times to continue until the gospel has reached the ends of the earth and circled back to the holy city (cf. Matt. 23:37–39; Luke 21:24; Rom. 11:25–32). He then expects "one who makes desolate" to come "upon the wing of abominations," and there to meet his decreed end. Had the prophets not testified that Jerusalem must yet become "a cup of reeling to all the peoples round about" (Zech. 12:2)? Was it not to be the scene of history's final dénouement, the stage for the conclusion of Israel's struggle with God and for the contest between God and the nations?

Let the reader understand: what happens in Jerusalem is paradigmatic and must be closely studied—"from the fig tree learn its lesson" (Matt. 24:32)—since it is precisely there that the shape of history and the fate of the world are ultimately decided. Paul knew that the appointed time of the end had commenced in Jerusalem with the crucifixion, resurrection, and ascension of Jesus and would complete itself in that same city with his return in glory to destroy the enemies of God and to judge the living and the dead. He did not, however, know how long it might be in coming, and he did not want the Thessalonians to suppose that they knew, much less to suppose that it was now taking place.

▨ Reminding ourselves of these things already suffices to repudiate the falsehood on which so much modern biblical scholarship and political theology or philosophy of history rests— namely, that the "failure" of the final end to come during the generation of Jesus and the apostles precipitated a crisis of faith in the Church, leading to the Church's reinvention as a creature in and of secular history, governed entirely by its laws. Such readers are by no means readers who understand, and they do not understand because they do not want to understand. Those readers who do want to understand must not lose sight of the fact that both Jesus and Paul proclaimed that the final end would indeed come, but not yet. They must also understand why. If they do, they will not make the mistake of supposing that, since God apparently will not, they themselves can and must bring in the kingdom. They will not be among those who say, in effect, "I am he!" or "We are he!" Neither will they prematurely announce that its moment has arrived, that "the time is at hand" (Luke 21:8). They will not be too easily alarmed, but they will expect "days of vengeance, to fulfil all that is written" (Luke 21:22), and strive to "keep sane and sober" for prayer meanwhile (1 Pet. 4:7–19). They will have some grasp of the conditions requisite to the end, and when the time does come, they will lift up their heads in expectation of their salvation.   ▨

Now, in clarifying the conditions controlling the timing of the parousia, Paul wants the Thessalonians to see both that the end is not yet and why it is not yet. The reason is simple. Precisely because God is just when he punishes (→1:3–10), he punishes only at the proper time. And when is that time? It is the time when man's rebellion against God has gone as far as it can go; the time when mere discipline or chastisement will no longer do, because repentance is no longer possible; the time "when the transgressors have reached their full measure" (Dan. 8:23; cf. Gen. 15:16; Lev. 18:24–30). Like the disciples, who were corrected on the matter by Jesus, Paul has learned that the end is not yet, that it cannot come and will not come before man's response to the gospel—the negative as well as the positive response—is settled and clear. This the Thessalonians must also learn if they are to hope in divine justice and to be engaged profitably in the evangelical economy through a sustained witness to Jesus, a long-term investment in his gospel. Recall Luke 19:11–14:

> As they heard these things, he proceeded to tell a parable, because he was near to Jerusalem, and because they supposed that the kingdom of God was to appear immediately. He said therefore, "A nobleman went into a far country to receive kingly power and then return. Calling ten of his servants, he gave them ten pounds, and said to them, 'Trade with these till I come.' But his citizens hated him and sent an embassy after him, saying, 'We do not want this man to reign over us.'"

We will not have this man to reign over us? Only when the rebels are sure of that, only when they have heard and repudiated the gospel decisively, will it be time for the king of bold countenance to reign over them instead, giving form and focus to their rebellion. Which will indeed bring about the end, at its proper time, and the just judgment of both the faithful and the unfaithful. "I tell you, that to every one who has will more be given; but from him who has not, even what he has will be taken away. But as for these enemies of mine, who did not want me to reign over them, bring them here and slay them before me" (19:26–27).

If we are following here, we must conclude with Paul that the hour of the man of lawlessness, the hour of antichrist, is still unfolding. We have been in that hour ever since Antiochus. Or perhaps we should say that we have been in it ever since the heirs of Hasmonean success against Antiochus seized the vineyard and with their lies attacked Jesus and sought his death (see John 8; Luke 20; cf. Wright 1992: 158f., 217). Certainly we have been in it since Jesus began to be attacked even in the churches through denials of his deity or his humanity, hence of his atoning work and his claim on the whole man whom he has redeemed (cf. 1 John 2:18–25; 2 John 7). The top of the hour chimed long ago, and its minutes tick away with every choice about whom or what we will have to reign over us. Antichrists abound. They are an immanent feature of our age, building haphazardly one upon the other, deceiving the people and preparing them for apostasy from their true Lord and King. But the fullness of the hour has yet to arrive. When *the* antichrist comes, when the definitive man of lawlessness appears, he will come both as a product of our age and as the final sign of its end. He will come as one man and as the champion of all men insofar as they are rebels against God's Anointed. He will come corporately and individually. He will come to settle the issue and to confirm the choices that have been made.

In *Antichrist: Two Thousand Years of the Human Fascination with Evil*, Bernard McGinn attempts to trace the evolution of the antichrist idea. Fearing the readiness with which it is used to tarnish one's enemies, however, he sets out from the entirely foreign premise—foreign, at least, to Paul—that it is useful only where it warns us against ourselves (2000: xvi, 16). Certainly it ought to warn us against ourselves, in the sense just described; but unless it is merely an idea it ought to warn us also against antichrist himself, the antichrist still to come. Oddly, McGinn does not treat John Henry Newman, who might have taught him the both/and required here. While those interested in deployments of the antichrist idea can benefit from McGinn's account, more benefit will be had, for present purposes, from Newman's analysis of patristic teaching or from Kevin Hughes's *Constructing Antichrist*, which focuses on readings of 2 Thessalonians as far as the early Middle Ages. There is in McGinn too much of the modernist mistake, which by separating "the antichrist concept from the notion of an individual figure" and focusing almost exclusively on power structures concludes that "nothing can be labeled 'antichrist' once and for all; only 'antichristly' phenomena, which under Christian guise and name deny Jesus Christ, can and sometimes must be so labeled" (Klauck et al. 2011). This error, one suspects, derives from first denying individuality to the risen Christ—from refusing to allow that he has gone from here into the far country of the Father to receive his kingly power in person—before going on to deny the individuality of the man of lawlessness as well, who in Christ's absence will arise as an alternative king, the king of bold countenance.

What can we say about this man, as an individual, beyond the fact that we are on the way to his appearance and that in his time he will appear not from heaven but from earth?

First, that he is like and unlike Christ in just that respect. Though divine, Christ approached us from below, in humility; when he approaches us again, with power and great glory, his parousia will be from above. The man of lawlessness is to have his own parousia, with its own power and glory, but that parousia will not be the divine reward for having made himself a servant. It will not be from above, but only from below. It will be brought about by powers earthly and infernal, working immanently in human history. Yet it will be in hubris, not in humility. The dark powers behind it like to present themselves as angels of light. They bring word of man's own deity: "You shall be as gods." They reject the very idea of a transcendent God who stands above history and insist that "it is impossible to make a clear distinction between secular history and salvation history" (thus Kasper 1972, cited critically in Stark 2015, though Kasper merely displays the habit of religious Hegelians and of all who believe in the ascent of man or adhere to the cult of progress; cf. Kasper 1967: 148ff.). Jesus, they propose, we may regard as a fine instantiation of the unity, even the identity, of the sacred and the secular, though not as the only such instantiation. There is another and even better one coming, for whom we should wait. He will break down every idolatrous objectification of the divine and free us to recognize that Man himself is divine.

Second, that the man of lawlessness makes himself, surreptitiously at first, the adversary of Christ and the opponent of God's purposes in Christ. For, unlike Jesus, he is not trying to bring man back from the far country of sin into the Father's embrace. He is trying to convince him that the far country of sin is his proper home. He is not looking "to put an end to sin, and to atone for iniquity, to bring in everlasting righteousness . . . and to anoint a most holy place" (Dan. 9:24). For he is himself the man of sin, intent on defiling the holy place.

Third, that at every turn he casts truth to the ground and by his cunning makes deceit prosper (Dan. 8:12, 25). He knows how human regimes work and how to take full advantage of them and of those who live under them. He is able to do this, since, like Solomon and Daniel, he understands "turns of speech and the solutions of riddles" and "has foreknowledge of signs and wonders and of the outcome of seasons and times" (Wis. 8:8; cf. Dan. 8:23).

Fourth, that though he feign the form of a servant, perhaps through some philanthropy or *pro bono* labor, his humility is false rather than true, intended only to manipulate. Because he is not *homo gratus* but *homo ingratus*, he does not at all understand that "it is humility that builds a safe and true way to the heavens, lifting up the heart to God, not against God" (*Civ.* 16.4; cf. 14.13, 21.16). Instead he exalts himself at every opportunity. He does not grasp that the one who glorifies himself is nothing and by God's hand will come to nothing. He does not see that, for the rational creature, free service to God is always advantageous (*Civ.* 14.15; cf. John 8:54).

> The beginning of man's pride is to depart from the Lord;
> his heart has forsaken his Maker.

> For [even] the beginning of pride is sin,
>> and the man who clings to it pours out abominations. (Sir. 10:12–13)

Fifth, that he resents the fact that God will not glorify or exalt him. Like Satan, therefore, he seeks to be exalted above God. He exalts himself "over everything said to be deity or an object of reverence, even to seating himself in the temple of God as if he were God" (ἐπὶ πάντα λεγόμενον θεὸν ἢ σέβασμα, ὥστε αὐτὸν εἰς τὸν ναὸν τοῦ θεοῦ καθίσαι ἀποδεικνύντα ἑαυτὸν ὅτι ἐστὶν θεός). This contest with God begins through the idolization of his own autonomous will. It ends with an all-out assault on the revealed will of God. "And the king shall do according to his will; he shall exalt himself and magnify himself above every god," even the God of gods (Dan. 11:36; cf. Ezek. 28:1–19).

Sixth, that he attacks the things of God, substituting his own things for God's. He is therefore most intimately concerned not with religion in general but with the Church in particular, which he is set upon subverting, just as Antiochus was set upon subverting the people and practices of the old covenant. "He shall speak words against the Most High, and shall wear out the saints of the Most High, and shall think to change the times and the law" (Dan. 7:25); that is, to establish new regimes under which people must live (cf. 2:21, where a similar expression is used of God, who "changes times and seasons" by removing kings and setting up kings). He shall even violate the sanctuary, "take away the continual burnt offering," and "set up the abomination that makes desolate" (11:31). For it is in the temple of God that he must have his way if he wishes to overcome God.

Seventh, that he first encourages defection from God, then openly demands it, though not all will meet that demand. "He shall seduce with flattery those who violate the covenant; but the people who know their God shall stand firm and take action" (Dan. 11:32; →2:11–14). Yet even "some of those who are wise shall fall, to refine and to cleanse them" (11:35; cf. Matt. 24:24; 1 Cor. 10:12).

Eighth, that he tries at last to sit on God's throne, as Satan himself would if he could. What begins in narcissism, perhaps homosexual narcissism—

> to the god of his fathers he'll pay no heed,
>> to the desire of women likewise;
> by every god he shall be unmoved,
>> himself he'll revere above all

—progresses to speaking astonishing things against the God of gods and ends in a megalomaniac attempt, doomed from the start, to supplant God by force in the affairs of man (Dan. 11:37 AT, versification added; cf. Isa. 14:3–23). What will that attempt look like? Daniel does not say, nor does Paul, apart from the claim that he shall seat himself in the temple.

"It is uncertain," remarks Augustine, "in what temple he shall sit, whether in that ruin of the temple which was built by Solomon, or in the Church" (*Civ.* 20.19.2, in *NPNF¹* 2:437). Either way, the example of Antiochus, who profaned the altar with the blood of pigs sacrificed to Jupiter and the sanctuary with his own image, is suggestive but only suggestive. For that altar and sanctuary are no more; and even if rebuilt, as some of the fathers supposed they would be, the world in which they existed is no more. The avarice and vainglory, the ambition and infighting, the betrayal and murder, that both preceded and followed Antiochus's actions are still with us, of course. Jason and Menelaus remain familiar figures: "in those days lawless men came forth from Israel, and misled many" (1 Macc. 1:11), and in these days they still do, whether in Israel or in the Church. Antiochus himself is all too familiar. Have we not endured our Hitlers, our Stalins, our Mao Zedongs, whose crimes against God and man exceed his in scale if not in ambition? What we have yet to endure remains to be seen, however. The defiance that God will briefly—very briefly—choose to tolerate from the man of lawlessness will be something both old and new. For that man will act as if he himself were enthroned on the cherubim and ruling over the covenant.

Ninth, we can say that "without warning he shall destroy many" when he rises up against the holy people and "the prince of princes" (traditionally Michael, commander of the army of the Lord, guardian of the holy people and of the sanctuary that makes them holy; cf. Dan. 8:25 MT; 12:1). None shall have power to prevent him or be granted authority to overthrow him. When the two witnesses have departed, none shall be able in any way to withstand him. As we are about to hear, however, the Messiah himself, the ascended Lord and King, will take command of God's princely host and arrive in person, announced by that fearsome archangel, to strike him down (an eventuality hinted at, perhaps, in Josh. 5:13–15). And not only to strike him down, which he shall do with a mere word, but also to cast him down, with Satan, into the pits of hell. That is where he belongs, for he is man in the very image of Satan. He is the man Satan sought and did not find in Jesus when he tempted him in the wilderness (Luke 4:1–13): the man who will use the power lent by Satan, not by God, to turn stones into bread, that the people might flock to him for security; the man who will receive gladly the offer to unite the kingdoms of the world and to rule gloriously over them, while paying tribute to the one who offers them though they are not in fact his to give; the man who will test God, not by throwing himself down from the pinnacle of the temple but by seating himself in the temple as if he were God.

Before pursuing the question about the temple in which the man of lawlessness shall sit—no small matter, surely, if Paul thought it worth mentioning to the Thessalonians while he was still with them, even before getting round to what we might well think the more urgent task of telling them how to regard their dead (→1 Thess. 4:13–18)—we may allow John and Irenaeus to add a layer or two to our description of that man, to help us penetrate deeper into the prophetic schema of Daniel and Jesus that Paul is interpreting for the Thessalonians.

In the Apocalypse, the Danielic figure whom Paul dubs the man of lawlessness appears in chapter 13 and at 16:13 as the middle member of an unholy trinity, flanked by the dragon (Satan) and the false prophet, who plays for him the role of John the Baptist. He is portrayed there as the beast incarnate, the beast being the empire of man in league with Satan against God. This beast chafes and writhes under the bonds by which the gospel eventually chains it, but in the end is given its liberty again, marching "over the broad earth and surround[ing] the camp of the saints and the beloved city," until it falls at last to the army of the Rider on the white horse, and its three manipulators are cast into the lake of fire and brimstone, where they will be tormented day and night εἰς τοὺς αἰῶνας τῶν αἰώνων (chapters 17–19 and, in summary, 20:1–10; cf. Exod. 15:1–22).

As we know from the Old Testament, the beast appears already at Babel. Out of the post-Babel chaos emerge various pretenders to world domination, of which the Roman Empire is the last and greatest. But that empire stumbles and is broken, partly because of its own inherited flaws, as Augustine points out, and partly because it is brought down—pagan critics are not mistaken about this—by the preaching of Jesus Christ and the emergence within it of the city of God. Its eventual revival, however, is foreseen and foretold. It was and is not, but is to be again. Like the dragon or serpent, it will ascend from the abyss before it goes to perdition. In that revival, which will be neither simple nor clean, infighting will lead not only to devastation of the city of Rome itself but also to the requisite conditions for the emergence of antichrist: an Antiochus-like incarnation both of pagan power and of demonic hatred for God and the people of God, who will reign briefly during the final rebellion as if Christ himself, giving to the beast its most potent and vicious leadership ever witnessed and becoming for it "a mouth uttering haughty and blasphemous words" (Rev. 13:5). In the latter part of his reign, the city of God will flow with rivers of martyrial blood and its "continual burnt offerings" will all but cease, being driven back into underground haunts as their place is usurped by the glorification of antichrist. And then will come the vengeance from on high, inflicted on antichrist, on the false prophet who assists him, and on all who refuse "to recognize God and to obey the gospel of our Lord Jesus" (→1:3–10).

Thus far with John. St. Irenaeus, that master of biblical synthesis and theological exegesis who opens the patristic era, having expounded Jesus as the summary or recapitulation of the whole work and way of God with man (*Haer.* 5.20–22), contrasts him with Satan and the man of lawlessness. At this point he turns to our epistle, which he sets between Daniel and the Apocalypse, alongside the Olivet Discourse. He refers to the man of lawlessness as the one who "concentrates in himself every satanic error" (5.25.5). From him the beast gains its final form. Ever since Babel it has remained divided against itself and has never achieved anything more than "minglings without cohesion" (5.26.1; cf. 3.17.2f.). But the man of lawlessness, who like his predecessors is trying to press the dry chaff of our fallen humanity into a kneadable lump of dough absent the bonding effect of baptism and the Holy Spirit, achieves an illusory unity by exciting "his dupes [to] adore him as the Christ" (5.28.1). Thus "the whole of that apostasy that has taken place" since the fall of man achieves its own summing up, while the wheat of the saints is ground to flour in the maw of the beast and, wet with a baptism of blood, is baked by the fires of martyrdom into a true eucharistic offering. "For this is the last contest of the righteous, in which, when they overcome, they are crowned with incorruption," while there is "in this beast, when he comes, a recapitulation made of all sorts of iniquity and of every deceit, in order that all apostate power, flowing into and being shut up in him, may be sent into the furnace of fire" (5.29).

It is because he sums up every age of sinful man, from the judgment in the garden to the last judgment, that his name is fittingly represented by the number 666. But we are not now to speculate about that. Rather we are to "await, in the first place, the division of the kingdom into ten; then, in the next place, when these kings are reigning, and beginning to set their affairs in order and advance their kingdom," we should expect one "who shall come claiming the kingdom for himself, and shall terrify those men of whom we have been speaking, having a name containing the aforesaid number" (5.30.2; cf. Rev. 13:18). Out of chaos order will once again be imposed in draconian fashion. Antichrist will resuscitate the kingdom of the Romans, and in such a manner as to recapitulate all the evils of previous kingdoms and empires.

Something like this synthesis remains the patristic consensus about the antichrist and his times, as Newman shows in his Advent sermons of 1838. At the end of the first, he summarizes his findings thus: "that the coming of Christ will be immediately preceded by a very awful and unparalleled outbreak of evil, called by St. Paul an Apostasy, a falling away, in the midst of which a certain terrible Man of sin and Child of perdition, the special and singular enemy of Christ, or Antichrist, will appear; that this will be when revolutions prevail, and the present framework of society breaks to pieces; and that at present the spirit which he will embody and represent is kept under by 'the powers that be,' but that on their dissolution, he will rise out of their bosom and knit them together again in his own evil way, under his own rule, to the exclusion of the Church" (*DA* 56f.).

Now, there is little or nothing in Newman's summary that does not already appear in 2 Thess. 2, but a new element does very quickly appear, one that bears directly on our understanding of Paul's reference to the man of lawlessness seating himself in the temple of God. According to Hippolytus, who was a student of Irenaeus and the first to write a treatise on antichrist, antichrist will not only resuscitate the kingdom of the Romans, he will also "resuscitate the kingdom of the Jews" (Hughes 2005: 31; cf. McGinn 2000: 58–63). Hippolytus introduces this idea in order to make sense of a literal reading of 2:4—that is, of the man of lawlessness taking his seat in the temple of God. Moreover, he understands him actually to be Jewish, as does Irenaeus, and this view takes hold in the Christian tradition. "Considering that Antichrist would pretend to be the Messiah," remarks Newman, "it was of old the received notion that he was to be of Jewish race and to observe the Jewish rites" (*DA* 66).

"It is proper," writes Hippolytus (*TCA* 5, in *ANF* 5:205), "that we take the Holy Scriptures themselves in hand, and find out from them what, and of what manner, the coming of Antichrist is; on what occasion and at what time that impious one shall be revealed; and whence and from what tribe [he shall come]; and what his name is, which is indicated by the number in the Scripture; and how he shall work error among the people, gathering them from the ends of the earth; and [how] he shall stir up tribulation and persecution against the saints; and how he shall glorify himself as God; and what his end shall be; and how the sudden appearing of the Lord shall be revealed from heaven; and what the conflagration of the whole world shall be; and what the glorious and heavenly kingdom of the saints is to be, when they reign together with Christ; and what the punishment of the wicked by fire." Though he thinks he knows how to explain matters in detail (§8), these promises remain largely unfulfilled; and, where they are fulfilled, they tend to the same fault that he warns against—namely, attempting to say more than what the scriptures permit us to say (§29;

cf. 49). But Hippolytus is confident in the antichrist's Jewish origin. "The Saviour came into the world in the circumcision, and [antichrist] will come in the same manner." He is likewise confident, though the logic is far less obvious, that "he will raise a temple of stone in Jerusalem," just as "the Saviour raised up and showed His holy flesh like a temple" (§6).

Irenaeus had already identified the antichrist as a member of the tribe of Dan, who will "sit in the temple at Jerusalem" (*Haer.* 5.30). Belief in the latter part of that claim, if we are to understand it literally, requires the supposition that the temple will be rebuilt, though Irenaeus himself does not say so. Belief in the former part he derives from Jer. 8, the "peace, peace" chapter which is easily read as a last-times lament and which alludes to the "abomination" committed by the tribe of Dan, recorded in Judg. 18. That tribe did not fulfill the command of the Lord to take possession of the land of promise, whose original inhabitants had been condemned for reaching the full measure of their wickedness, but instead suddenly and viciously attacked the inhabitants of a peaceful city of Sidon and stole their land. Moreover, they did so while depending on the ministrations of a wayward Levite and a stolen graven image; that is, by relying on corrupt and forbidden forms of worship. Irenaeus notes the absence of Dan from the twelve tribes of Israel out of whom the 144,000 are sealed for redemption (Rev. 7; cf. 21:12). Since Dan typifies the kind of lawlessness with which Daniel and Jesus and Paul and John are all concerned, it seems to him fitting that the antichrist should arise from that tribe. He is followed by Hippolytus, but the latter, being a far less able bowman, first overshoots the mark by assigning antichrist credit for rebuilding the kingdom of the Jews, then undershoots it by paying too little attention to the Dan typology.

It may be noted in passing that, at Dan. 11:37, the LXX—unlike the Peshitta, which employs the singular—settles the ambiguity of אֱלֹהֵי אֲבֹתָיו by opting for the plural, rendering it πάντας θεούς τῶν πατέρων αὐτοῦ, "all the gods of his fathers." This certainly suggests a Gentile. But the Hebrew and the Syriac leave room for a Jew (as does my translation above), even if the Greek does not. Among Jews, the Greek prevailed, naturally. The legend of Armilus that arose in reaction to Christianity, taking sundry forms in the Middle Ages, posits a Gentile antimessiah who contends with the true Messiah; or rather, with the first of the two true messiahs, Messiah ben-Joseph, who rebuilds the temple but suffers death and defeat, until all is set right by Messiah ben-David. Among Christians, it was otherwise. The antichrist was widely thought to be Jewish.

That this way of thinking came to have its anti-Semitic perversion, as if the Jew qua Jew were a kind of antichrist, cannot be denied. The rise of anti-Semitism, first in the Church and then, without any gospel restraint, in the world at large—not in the Islamic world only but also in the world of the *philosophes* and in the Aryan and Russian worlds, which ignored the urgent criticisms of Berdyaev (1924) and others and pressed on toward the Holocaust—is itself a grave sign of antichrist; thus far, arguably, the gravest. Daniel allows that his godless narcissist does honor one god, "the god of fortresses" (11:38), and this god has proven himself the god of gulags and gas ovens also. It does not follow, however, that we should reject the received notion out of hand, for it is not itself inherently or intrinsically anti-Semitic. On my view, the question as to the antichrist's ethnic origin must remain open, since we have no secure basis on which to decide it. Perhaps, like Herod or Hitler, he will be of both Jewish and Gentile stock. Or perhaps, like Stalin, he will be a Gentile— Gentiles, even baptized ones, also know how to behave like the tribe of Dan!—while the false prophet, like Marx, will be an apostate Jew. Or perhaps it will be the other way round, as Solovyov has it (→3:17–18). Would it not be fitting, in any case, if the one were a Gentile and the other a Jew, in an *imitatio ecclesiae*? That is the most we can say, if we are not inclined to accept the received notion, except to add that ethnic origin is of no great importance to our reading of 2:4 except as it bears on the question of religious practice, a question to which we are still coming.　　　　　　　　　　　　　　　　　　▨

Against the received notion it can be objected that the scriptures do not actually say "that Antichrist would pretend to be the Messiah" or that he "would observe Jewish rites," an objection to which we will return. Against it can also be put the fact that Antiochus, the biblical type or protoantichrist, was not a Jew, nor was Nero or Caligula or Domitian or any other imperial forerunner. That the antichrist belongs to the beast that arises from the tumult of the sea—that is, from the chaos of the pagan nations—is worth mentioning as well (cf. Rev. 13:1–6, 18). It is the second beast, the man of propaganda who serves the man of power, who is from the earth (13:11–17). Still, it is not without all reason that antichrist should be thought a Jew, for the Jewish people remain at the heart of history even when they are scattered among the nations. "Of their race, according to the flesh, is the Christ" (Rom. 9:5). Why not also, then, the antichrist? Such is the glory and such also the burden, perhaps, of Israel's election.

Yet when we think of the man of lawlessness as an individual who sums up the godlessness of the human race, who makes himself the representative of those who, especially in the last days, "will be lovers of self, lovers of money, proud, arrogant, abusive, disobedient to their parents, ungrateful, unholy, inhuman, implacable, slanderers, profligates, fierce, haters of good, treacherous, reckless, swollen with conceit, lovers of pleasure rather than lovers of God, holding the form of religion but denying the power of it" (2 Tim. 3:2–5), have we any reason to suppose that the form of religion in question will be Jewish rather than Christian? The arena in which all this is to be played out is, after all, the global arena, even if the city in which it will be played out, come the final scene, is Jerusalem. Or if we recall with Irenaeus the appalling behavior of the tribe of Dan, and the renegade priest who blessed their perversity with a perversity, finding in this a foreshadowing of the days of antichrist, is that sufficient reason to suppose that the antitype will actually be a Danite (something no longer ascertainable anyway)? We may posit that the man of lawlessness will make himself the shepherd of such men by being still more perverse and treacherous and swollen with conceit than they, and by deploying their false and syncretistic form of religion to his own advantage. But the men in question are and will be largely Gentile, and such religion as they have may well be the dregs of a disappearing Christianity.

Nor will the man of lawlessness be content only to seize what belongs to man, as the Danites did. He will seize also what belongs to God. He will outdo even Antiochus, who seized what belonged to God chiefly to secure what he had seized that belonged to man. He will seize what belongs to God *because* it belongs to God. So if we want to wrestle further with the question of his kingdom and where he will seat himself, we must ask ourselves what it is that belongs to God. Everything, of course, belongs to God, but especially his elect people, his chosen dwelling, his word or *torah*, and the other instruments of his grace. These are the things that must be seized, perverted, suppressed, and, finally, destroyed if the man of lawlessness is to succeed. We will look briefly at each in turn.

Caution is in order here, however—much more caution than is displayed by Hippolytus. When Paul talks about the son of destruction "exalting himself over everything said to be deity or an object of reverence, even to seating himself in the temple of God as if he were God," he is simply paraphrasing what Daniel had said with Antiochus in view. Very likely Paul has Caligula in view as well, for before he was assassinated in AD 41 Caligula had hoped to repeat the outrage of Antiochus by converting the temple "into a great shrine focused on a giant statue of himself" (Wright 2018: 225). Had Paul lived long enough to see Hadrian level what was left of the temple, build the Aelia Capitolina, and construct new temples on the site to Bacchus, Venus, and Serapis, he would have had a further type with which to work. It does not necessarily follow, however, that Paul is content to move from type to antitype in a strictly literal or univocal fashion. Nor should we suppose that Jesus himself was content to do so, when he took up Daniel's warning about widespread corruption and his language about a desolating sacrilege. The outcome of the Jewish Wars fulfilled the prophecy of Jesus, but only on the near horizon. The destruction of the temple, designed as it was to be "a small working model of the entire cosmos" (Wright 2018: 48), punctuated the end of the old salvific order and the beginning of the new, an end and a beginning that Jesus himself had already brought about. It punctuated Jewish rebellion and unbelief (Matt. 21:33–46). But on the far horizon, at the close of the new age—the age

provided by God for announcing to the entire world that a new order has come
into existence with Jesus—still looms a great refusal and apostasy: that of the
Gentiles, not that of the Jews. Events on the far horizon will be analogous with,
but not identical to, events on the near horizon. A sudden and treacherous attack
on the chosen people and dwelling, on the law and other instruments of grace,
can be expected before the end comes, but in a manner befitting the form they
now have, the form given them by Jesus.

In other words, we should be thinking about a rebellion and a desolating
sacrilege suited to the last days, the exact shape of which is not immediately obvious, though it will entail sufficient knowledge of the truth to allow for a decisive
turning from it (→2:11–14). Daniel says of his vision that he was so appalled
by it as to be overcome with weakness and confined to his bed for several days,
but that he did not understand it. Paul also may not have understood very much,
beyond the fact that what had been before would be again, in its own time and
on a universal scale, after a fashion yet to be seen. In any case, not wishing his
readers to be confined to their beds but rather to be about the King's business
(→2:15–17), he does not attempt any elaboration. Only John attempts that, something more akin to Daniel's visionary experience being replicated in his case; and
even John offers us an account still wrapped in mystery, an "apocalypse" in which
much remains hidden and undisclosed. With a little help from John, however,
and from subsequent history and tradition, we may still try to say something, at
least, about the final attack on the things that belong to God—something, that
is, beyond the basic observation that the attack is Satan's, that it lasts throughout
the *saeculum* but will reach its frenzied finale in the work of the antichrist, and
that when its fury is spent judgment will fall and justice prevail; for Paul has
already made this plain.

We begin, then, with *God's people*. The elect people comprises both Jews
and Christians, the former of which have been called to join the eschatological company—the united company—of the latter and are expected by Paul
eventually to do so. Hosea foresees their present situation: "For the children of
Israel shall dwell many days without king or prince, without sacrifice or pillar,
without ephod or teraphim. Afterward the children of Israel shall return and
seek the LORD their God, and David their king; and they shall come in fear to
the LORD and to his goodness in the latter days" (3:4–5; cf. Rom. 9–11; *Civ.*
18.28). Both the former and the latter are meanwhile under attack by the enemies of God. After Christ's departure, the dragon, spoiled of his prey, pursues
"the woman who had borne the male child." The woman, however, escapes by

dispersion into the wilderness of the nations and the dragon turns "to make war on the rest of her offspring, on those who keep the commandments of God and bear testimony to Jesus" (Rev. 12:13–17; cf. Ezek. 20:33–44, which suggests that the woman's escape is for the sake of her further discipline by God, as well as her eventual salvation).

This war, which was already fierce in Paul's day and John's, grew fiercer yet in the waning days of the Roman Empire. New fronts emerged with the waxing of Islam—AD 687 saw Islamic shrines placed on the temple mount, on what Jews call the Foundation Stone, where the Roman shrines had been—and the eventual decline of Christendom. The conflict greatly intensified in our own time. In communist realms, where a bastard millennialism shaped by Marx took hold, unprecedented slaughter of Christians followed. It was in the Fascist sphere, however, with its Aryan chiliasm shaped by Hitler and his false prophet, Göbbels, that a plan was hatched to destroy completely both Jews and Christians, in that order. With Jews the plan all but succeeded. But after the Holocaust the earth opened up again, almost miraculously, to swallow the torrent from the dragon's mouth and to provide a place for those who sought refuge. This new place turned out to be the old place, which the dragon stalks round in rage and frustration, while still finding time to pursue the followers of Jesus to all points of the compass, attacking churches from Chile to Chengdu.

When antichrist comes, no doubt he will follow Hitler's example. Only this time he will try to seduce Jews, too, with false promises, as Hitler seduced Christians, before turning treacherously against both. For that he will have to come to Jerusalem. In the meantime, there is still much damage to be done by the dragon to and among the people of the new covenant, the eschatological people, the Church in which Jew and Gentile are already one new man.

▨ Hitler was not the only antichristic figure of his day. Stalin matched him stride for bloody stride, though not where the Jews were concerned. But Hitler, who did not survive long enough to carry out his plan against Christians, was perhaps more conscious of the role. He saw himself as the one who would forge unity out of chaos by the imposition of his will: "From millions of men one man must step forward, who with apodictic force will form granite principles from the wavering idea-world of the broad masses and take up the struggle for their sole correctness, until from the shifting waves of a free thought-world there will arise a brazen cliff of solid unity in faith and will" (1992: 346; Farrow 2011: 111f.). Why, we may ask, was this quest for unity in faith and will turned so systematically and so viciously against the Jews, if it is not at bottom a question of one project for "man" against another? The truth is that both Jews and Christians stand in the way of the New

Man envisioned by Satan, who therefore tries to convince Jews and Christians that they
stand in each other's way (cf. Farrow 2018g: chap. 8).

Next, *God's place*. Every people needs a place, the place God has determined for
them, a place in which "they might feel after him and find him" (Acts 17:26–27).
In the case of the people of God, to whom God revealed himself directly rather
than indirectly, the place allotted to them—the promised land—was privileged
to have within it a sanctuary where God himself dwelt. That was in Jerusalem,
on Mount Zion, where the sacrifice of his Son was also made. Jerusalem has for
a time been left desolate, however, as Jesus said it would be. During this time
God's dwelling place on earth is the Church; more specifically, the Church in its
eucharistic sacrifice, which it is mandated to make anywhere and everywhere it
finds itself. For the new and eternal temple of God is the incarnate Son himself
and, by extension, his ecclesial body (1 Cor. 3:16–17; Eph. 2:21). To violate God's
place, then, and to occupy his temple, it is necessary to violate and occupy in some
fashion his Church, which must be suborned and brought to heel, defiled and
then destroyed, like Jerusalem itself.

A new temple means a renewed city, a grander city. This David and Solomon
knew; this Ezekiel and Ezra and Nehemiah knew; this Herod the Great knew
when he did for Jerusalem something like what Augustus was doing for Rome
(Kohn et al. 1929). None of them could do what actually needed to be done, of
course, especially not Herod, that troubled forerunner of antichrist who transformed the second temple into a monument of his own glory and whom the
dragon employed in a failed attempt to snuff out the Messiah before the latter's
building project could even get off the ground (cf. Matt. 2 and John 2 with Rev.
12:4–6). Only the Messiah could do what needed to be done. Having made himself the temple of God and the headwaters of the Spirit, of the great River of Life
which gladdens the city of God (Ps. 46:4; cf. John 7:37–39), he is busy renewing
that city according to the peerless plan of God. Hence the new Jerusalem is said
to come down out of heaven from God and to have God and the Lamb for its
temple (Rev. 3:12; 21:2, 22). It is said to be expansive in a fashion Herod's city
and temple, though a miracle of human engineering, could never be (John 14:2;
cf. Ezek. 40–48). Moreover, it is impregnable. Its citizens have eternal life. The
gates of Hades shall not prevail against it, for it is built according to a blueprint
"for the fulness of time" (Eph. 1:3–23).

Yet, insofar as it is present in the world only by way of the eucharistic mystery
and not as a fully accomplished fact, it is still open to assault, from within as

well as without. It is the Church militant, not the Church glorified. It therefore cannot be ruled out as the object of antichrist's ambition. Anyone who doubts that its mortal occupants can be suborned and corrupted, even those who oversee its works, need only review the letters to the seven churches in Rev. 2–3. They would do well, however, to review as well the last few centuries, and especially the last few decades, in which an apostasy of eschatological proportions has been in progress. The apostasy Paul has in view begins in the Church, though it does not end there, and the man of lawlessness does whatever he can to encourage it. That, no doubt, is why Paul thought the subject important enough to raise with the Thessalonians in the short time he was with them.

⬛ This certainly complicates matters. To attack and destroy any people, their place must be conquered and occupied. Their gods and holy places must be defeated and replaced. But to attack and destroy the people of God now requires possession both of the holy city, Jerusalem, which is possible, and of the heavenly city of which Jerusalem is but a sign, which is impossible—or would be but for the fact that the heavenly city has, in provisional secular form, its visible expression in the world. The holy city has fallen more than once, and portions of the Church have fallen too. Full possession of both has never been achieved, however. We must anticipate that an attempt will be made to achieve it, aided by a fifth column within each (cf. *Civ.* 20.19). That attempt will be very successful, yet God will preserve for the truth a foothold in each. In the Church, there will be those who follow the Lamb wherever he goes and sing the song that only he can teach them, in whose mouths there is no lie and who are tainted by no idolatry, nor any beastly mark that obscures their baptismal birthright (Rev. 14:1–5). As for the holy city, the old Jerusalem, it will once again be the scene of a powerful, if controversial, witness to the gospel, as it was in the days of Peter and Paul and John. "Rise and measure the temple of God and the altar and those who worship there," John is told, "but do not measure the court outside the temple; leave that out, for it is given over to the nations, and they will trample over the holy city for forty-two months. And I will grant my two witnesses power to prophesy for one thousand two hundred and sixty days, clothed in sackcloth" (Rev. 11:1–3; →1 Thess. 5:1–3 and see further below). A final effort to eradicate this witness will follow: "And when they have finished their testimony, the beast that ascends from the bottomless pit will make war upon them and conquer them and kill them, and their dead bodies will lie in the street of the great city which is allegorically called Sodom and Egypt, where their Lord was crucified" (11:7–8). As Jesus rose and ascended, however, so in some manner will they, confounding their opponents. The war against God's people and God's place will not so easily be concluded. ⬛

Third, *God's word.* By "word" is meant both law and gospel, and by "law" both natural and revealed law. To seize means to take charge of and to substitute for; that is, to forbid the announcement of the kingdom of God and his Christ and to announce instead the kingdom of autonomous man and of antichrist. It means to take the deep things of God and replace them with the hollow things of Satan, "teaching and beguiling my servants to practice immorality and to eat food sacrificed to idols" (Rev. 2:20–25), just as Antiochus did. The forbidding began when the Sanhedrin tried to silence the apostles (→1 Thess. 2:14–16). The substitutions began with the false gospels of the Judaizers and of the gnostics. This continues today under the guise of a biblical scholarship that serves only to distort and suppress the genealogy of our salvation, "the genealogy of Jesus Christ, the son of David, the son of Abraham" (Matt. 1:1; →preamble), and through a theological experimentation that sets aside his designation by the Spirit as "Son of God" in power (Rom. 1:1–4; cf. Farrow 2009: 294ff.). It continues in the pandering of self-appointed pastors and preachers to men's baser instincts. It continues also in the "safe spaces" and naked public squares of secularism, in the blasphemy laws of Islamic fundamentalism, in the ideological censorship of Communism. Everywhere the word of God and the testimony of Jesus go forth, and not without their proper effect, but everywhere they are met by a perverse resistance. Mere men make great boasts under grand titles, demanding that the gospel itself do obeisance.

In Paramount Leader Xi Jinping's China, for example, it is now proclaimed that "only Sinicized churches can obtain God's love"—not because God or the love of God is thought to be real but because only Party-run churches will be allowed to pretend that it is real. In Western democracies, high courts insist that God must be left altogether out of account in determining the common good. Reality is redefined at will, and morality with it. Officials high and low insist that abortion is a right and supporting it a duty, that sexual difference is a social construct that must be deconstructed, that identity claims must be allowed to float free of any objective reference point, that bringing human beings into the world is bad and hastening their departure good. Men of every station, not least in the Church, presume to teach with an authority greater than that of Jesus, and in their attacks on natural and divine law speak astonishing words against the God of gods, whether in his name or without so much as mentioning him. Of human civilization they are making a desert, and a road in that desert for antichrist. Corrupt clerics and even princes of the Church aid and abet them, at first secretly and then more openly adopting the doctrines and practices of the Nicolaitans, reveling in those soul-destroying and society-immolating practices that are always the goal of the so-called deep things of Satan. Homosexuality is their favorite vice, though hardly their only vice, and they do not heed the warning of Christ: "All the churches shall know that I am he who searches mind and heart, and I will give to each of you as your works deserve" (Rev. 2:23; cf. 1 Thess. 4:6). They are worthless shepherds, themselves sons of destruction, after whom will come one like them, that shepherd "who does not care for the perishing, or seek the wandering, or heal the maimed, or nourish the sound, but devours the flesh of the fat ones, tearing off even their hoofs" (Zech. 11:16).

Finally, *God's sacraments*. The instruments of grace, how are they seized? By parody and by interference in their sacred use. The sacrament of orders has often been manipulated through lay investiture or state control of ordinations. Marriage has become a new battleground, by virtue of the fact that it is an instrument both of natural law and of grace, hence something always shared by church and state. In the West it has been made into a mockery of itself, by depriving it of any reference to the fact that God made man male and female and committed to their union joint responsibility with him for the gift of life and the welfare of children. Mockery is now made of the sacrament of healing also, with the introduction of assisted suicide and euthanasia into homes, hospices, and hospitals, even and especially Christian ones. States are trying to break the seal of the confessional, demanding reports of anything deemed criminal. The real prize, however, is baptism and confirmation, on the one hand, and the Eucharist on the other. Attempts are now being made on the former by forbidding the taking of children to church and/or by demanding that they be educated only in state institutions. On the latter, attempts have been made for some centuries within the sphere of the Church itself, whether by removing the requirements of unity in the apostolic faith or by denying the Real Presence and substituting an offering of man's own making. These attempts will be intensified as the day of the desolating sacrilege draws nearer. Since a people must have a place, and the Church's place is the Eucharist, that is where the attacks have been focused and will be focused. There are already symbols of sacrilege on some altars.

▪ We may mark the French Revolution as a point of departure. In it was effected briefly the sort of thing we can expect from antichrist, including the profaning of Notre Dame cathedral and other churches during the *Fête de la Raison* and the combination under Robespierre of the Terror and the *Culte de l'Être suprême*. Colonization and parody have been with us ever since. Images of tyrants replacing icons of Jesus, the elevation of notorious heretics or abusers to high office in the Church, prosperity gospels and Pachamama worship, pornography in cathedral apses, decadent liturgies and liturgies for the decadent—many are the foreshadowings of the final apostasy in an age of apostasy that is already better than half a millennium old, an age with spiritual roots that run deep into the nominalist era.

At its dawn, St. Vincent Ferrer (d. 1419) recognized the signs and warned of such things. In the first year or two of the next century, Luca Signorelli undertook his spectacular (and often spectacularly misread) *Disputation of Antichrist*, among a cycle of Apocalypse scenes begun by Fra Angelico at Orvieto. The enormous temple that appears in that painting (see page 170), with a tower leaning ever so slightly and sinister figures trampling its outer courts, provides the backdrop before which appears the unholy trinity: The antichrist appears in Christlike pose, as if resurrected but without nail marks in his hands, exalted on a pedestal embossed with a white horse and rider, gifts or spoils at his feet, presiding over the people of the Great Whore like the golden bull presided over Israel. Satan also appears, stripped of his heavenly glory by St. Michael, who is depicted far above, casting him down with disastrous effects on the objects of wrath who dwell below. Satan is now eager for revenge and whispers in antichrist's ear his diabolical plot, as that impostor rests upon him like a throne. The false prophet completes the trio, persuading whom he can to go along with it all, encouraging the learned and the simple, the pompous and the powerless, prelates as well as princes (some with recognizable faces) to recognize the greatness of what is being done. An axis of blood and violence slashes diagonally across the painting, from the somber observers at the left (one with Signorelli's face) to the beheadings of dissenters at the right, who die before the entrance to the temple court. At its heart is an empty, hollow space, for this is an empty and hollow kingdom whose fate—utter annihilation!—is already decreed. It "was and is not and is to come," before it goes to perdition (Rev. 17:8).

Signorelli's contract specified that he should consult with theological advisers in designing his frescoes. If, as some think, Ferrer's sermons also served to advise him, then (*pace* Reiss 1995) we ought not to see the crowd of religious scholars, huddled behind the antichrist with their books, as being warned off by a perceptive Dominican monk but rather as being persuaded by the false prophet, who—back turned, so that he may point up to the pinnacle of the temple—forms a tight triangle with Satan and the antichrist, while also completing an arc that comes to rest in the tower that leans darkly into heaven. As Ferrer says in his sermon on the last judgment, the light of the sun (that is, of Christ) shall be obscured. The moon (that is, the Church) shall wane, its horns reversed. Stars shall fall from heaven; that is, the learned "from the truth of the Catholic Faith." "Prelates for fear of losing their dignities, and religious and priests to gain honors and riches, will forsake the Faith of Christ and adhere to Antichrist." Taking the view that the new covenant shall seem to have failed completely, he adds that "the disputations of Antichrist with the learned will be based entirely on the text of the Old Testament, and these doctors, so far from being able to answer him, will not even be able to speak." "You may ask," he continues, "why Christ allows this, that those who defend the Faith should fail so utterly? I answer that Christ allows this for two reasons: first, according to the rule of theology: 'By what things a man sinneth, by the same is he tormented' [Wis. 11:16; cf. 11:5]; and this follows from the fact that masters and teachers no longer care for study of the Bible, but prefer the study of the poets and other profane works. The second reason why Christ permits this, is because of the scandalous and wicked lives and the many sins of learned men; for in the case of many of them, the greater their knowledge the greater also is their sin and the worse their consciences; for they are proud, puffed-up, wine-bibbers and the rest" (1954). By which observations we ourselves, if we are wise, will be advised. To Signorelli's painting we will return in a moment, but sight of his temple returns us to the question raised by Augustine as to which temple we are or should be talking about.

Now, it will be evident from this discussion of antichristic attacks on what belongs to God that we are not pursuing a Hippolytean course. The ecclesial temple rather than the Herodian is coming into focus. The line taken by Hippolytus cannot be dismissed lightly, however, given its prominent place in patristic and medieval thought. Neither should it be denied that it has its own inner coherence. Antichrist, himself a Jew, will seek to deceive Jews first of all, staking a messianic claim by seeing to the revival of a Judaism based on temple rituals and sacrifices, while at the same time seducing and beginning to suppress Christianity. He will then insert himself into those rituals in a blasphemous manner, before turning against his fellow Jews and, with unparalleled violence, against Christians. His attempt to reestablish the Levitical sacrifices already amounts to rejection of the New Testament witness to Jesus as the full and perfect sacrifice who brings to its proper end the old sacrificial system. It is already a repudiation of the Father and the Son, and antichristic in essence. Antichrist would, on these terms, become the man of lawlessness precisely by denying the effectiveness of Christ's sacrifice and by reversing the judgment of God pronounced by Christ against the temple and its keepers, the judgment later carried out by the Romans. That he might also commit the sin of King Uzziah seems likely enough. Uzziah "was marvelously helped, till he was strong," and his fame spread far, "but when he was strong he grew proud, to his destruction," becoming "false to the LORD," even entering the temple to burn incense on the altar as if he himself were a priest of the Lord (2 Chron. 26:15–21; cf. Isa. 6). That he might go so far as to commit some Antiochus- or Caligula-like act, at the point of his final breach with Judaism and with all religion other than that of his self-worship, also makes a certain sense on this scheme of things, after which he would be judged for it all, and for his slaughter of "those who keep the commandments of God and the faith of Jesus."

This being said, the Christian tradition is hardly unanimous in its support of Hippolytus's literal reading of 2 Thess. 2:4. (Jews, without consideration of antichrist, are also divided over the future of the temple. Will it be built by Messiah, as Maimonides thought, or even descend from heaven during the messianic era? Should it be built now, to usher in that era? Prayers are again being recited hopefully on the temple mount.) Reviewing Christian positions as far as the thirteenth century, Aquinas records three options, one literal and two metaphorical: Some say "the Jews will accept him at first, and will rebuild the temple in Jerusalem, and thus Daniel will be fulfilled." Others say "that neither Jerusalem nor the temple will ever be rebuilt, but that their desolation will last until the final consummation. And even some Jews believe this. So this text is explained to mean . . . 'in the Church,' since many from the Church will accept him." Still others say that "he rules and governs as though he himself with his messengers were the temple of God, as Christ is the temple with his adherents" (*S.2Th.* 2.1.40).

▨ Cyril of Jerusalem opts with Hippolytus for the first: "What temple then? He means, the Temple of the Jews which has been destroyed. For God forbid that it should be the one in which we are!" (*CL* 15.15, in *NPNF*² 7:108). Chrysostom combines the first two, remarking that antichrist "will abolish all the gods, and will order men to worship him instead of God, and he will be seated in the temple of God, not that in Jerusalem only, but also in every Church" (οὐ τὴν ἐν Ἱεροσολύμοις μόνον, ἀλλὰ καὶ εἰς τὰς πανταχοῦ Ἐκκλησίας, *PG* 62:482). Haimo's ninth-century commentary takes note of those who posit both a rebuilt temple and an antichristic session in the Church, but still makes no effort to wrestle with the relation between the two. Thietland of Einsiedeln, on the other hand, seems inclined with Augustine to the third view, presumably because he finds that relation rather obscure (cf. Cartwright and Hughes 2001: 26, 52). In his famous itinerary of antichrist, Adso, the tenth-century abbot of Montier-en-Der who was Thietland's contemporary, follows Chrysostom's path, taking a both/and approach to the first two. While mentioning the rebuilding of the temple in Jerusalem, he does not hesitate to add that "Antichrist also 'will be enthroned in God's Temple,' that is in Holy Church" (McGinn 1979: 94). Arnulf of Orléans presses the latter prospect into service in his attack on Pope John XV at the Synod of Reims, opining that John is a kind of antichrist, "sitting in God's temple and showing himself as God" (McGinn 2000: 100).

Later, some opt more decisively for the second view, as indeed Theodoret of Cyrus had done earlier (2001: 128, but cf. 130). Joachim of Fiore, writes McGinn, "always identified God's temple not with a rebuilt Jerusalem structure, but with the temple of the Church" (2000: 142), and even ventured the opinion that the antichrist might be a pope, as a pope might be an antichrist (cf. Thiselton 2011: 217; Bruce 1982: 186f.). Wycliffe and Luther did the same, and with a still more pronounced antipapalism. "For Luther, the Antichrist will betray the Church from within, undermine the Roman Empire, take God's rightful place in the Church, and mislead through false doctrines and signs. As Luther looked about him in 1520, he believed only one figure in history fulfilled all these requirements: the pope" (Whitford 2008: 34; cf. Klauck et al. 2011). Calvin followed suit, seeing in popery and also in Islam a "reign of abomination," albeit under "a succession of individuals" that Paul presents "under the name of a single individual." The day of Christ "will not come until the world has fallen into apostasy, and the rule of Antichrist has held sway in the Church." St. Paul "is predicting a general defection on the part of the visible Church, as if he were saying, 'The Church must be reduced to a ghastly and horrifying state of ruin, before its full restoration is achieved.'" Such confusion will there be that "the vicar of Satan [will] hold power in the Church and preside there in the place of God." For antichrist "is not an enemy from the outside but from the household of faith, and opposes Christ under the very name of Christ" (1961: 398–402).

Does this seem a very long way from Cyril? Perhaps it is. Yet, despite his basically Hippolytean view, Cyril himself writes: "I fear the schisms of the Churches; I fear the mutual hatred of the brethren. But enough on this subject; only God forbid that it should be fulfilled in our days; nevertheless, let us be on our guard" (*CL* 15.18). Against schism, alas, few were on guard in Calvin's day, and that century must be judged a precursor to the day of apostasy.

To try to resolve the matter is risky; to leave it unresolved, as Aquinas does, is to leave the reader at loose ends. We have seen that there are difficulties with the literal approach, not the least of which is that Paul supplies no hint of the Hippolytean scheme. He does not say that the man of lawlessness "shall falsely call himself Christ" (*CL* 4.15; cf. Lactantius, *Inst.* 7.19), but rather that he shall make himself out to be God (ἀποδεικνύντα ἑαυτὸν ὅτι ἐστὶν θεός). Neither does Jesus supply any hint of it. To be sure, he warns against false messiahs. "Take heed that no one leads you astray. For many will come in my name, saying, 'I am the Christ,' and they will lead many astray" (Matt. 24:4–5). Yet this warning is not delivered publicly to the Jewish people but privately to the apostles as a warning for the Church. And he does not speak of pretenders in the temple but of plots in inner rooms or in desert caves. Were Jesus to have identified the party responsible for the abomination "standing in the holy place" with one who would rebuild the very temple whose destruction he was announcing, surely he and the Evangelists would have made that more clear. "Let the reader understand"? Let him understand that the vision is of something near and something far, which are not the same thing. And that the holy place is one sort of place in the first instance—the temple that Pompey violated and Titus tore down and Julian the Apostate sought in vain to rebuild, being thwarted by fire and earthquake—and another sort of place in the second: the temple Jesus and the Spirit are building. The warning that follows applies equally in both cases. When you see the violation, expect the desolation. Fly!

The first or literal approach lacks the biblical warrant claimed for it, then, there being no hint of a revived Levitical worship here or anywhere else in the New Testament to support that reading of εἰς τὸν ναὸν. Moreover, it does not deal satisfactorily with the new theology of the temple of God that Jesus and Paul and John all develop, in which Jesus assumes to himself, and to his ecclesial body, the temple function. Even when combined with the second approach—which deprives the first of its internal consistency: how does a false messianic claimant who invests in old covenant rituals so that he may deceive the Jews simultaneously hold sway in the Church?—the first concentrates too narrowly and too negatively on Jews. In effect, it posits an antichrist who is just an outsized Herod or Simeon bar Kokhba, differing from the latter only in that he does not really intend to establish the kingdom of God in Jerusalem but rather to establish his own kingdom and so to play Hadrian's role in the end. Can this really be what Paul has in mind? Paul expects his fellow Jews to convert to Christ in great numbers before the age is out. Is he nevertheless expecting a Jew to arise, perhaps in opposition to that, who precisely as an observant Jew will begin exalting himself against God by presuming to rebuild the temple, not stopping short afterward of some Uzziah-like action? Or might he be expecting rather someone, Jew or Gentile, who will try by deceitful means to occupy the temple that now exists, the ecclesial temple, there to insert himself directly into the glory of God that shines from the face of Christ (cf. 2 Cor. 4:1–12)?

The literal approach seems content with one who hates Jesus but inserts himself in the place of Moses and Aaron and David only. In that respect it shares the weakness of the third proposal, which has the antichrist effecting his rule largely outside the people of God altogether. The wickedness of the latter antichrist does not seem to rise even to the level of Antiochus; the wickedness of the former does not rise as high as it might. It is therefore the middle proposal, or at least some combination of the three that features the middle proposal and does not merely include it as an afterthought, which commends itself most strongly. Whatever happens in Jerusalem, we should anticipate that there will be a lawless, antichristic attack on the ecclesial temple and on its supreme instrument of grace, the Holy Eucharist, the Great Thanksgiving.

▦ Signorelli, who with his advisers doubtless read *in templo Dei sedeat ostendens se quia sit Deus*, as the Vulgate has it, in the literal way, manages to bring into view the problem with which we are wrestling. The temple he depicts in his *Disputation of Antichrist* is a new Jewish temple, its stylized or syncretistic features notwithstanding. Presumably it is one of the wonderful works of antichrist, whose devilish scheme involves a short-lived flourishing of Jewish religion. Being the reverse image of Christ, antichrist must be accepted where Christ was rejected—in Jerusalem and among fellow Jews, particularly the temple authorities. He will therefore make a Herod-like gesture, partnering with Jews against Christians before betraying both. In the foreground, the wealthy Jew paying the whore while looking to antichrist is a sign of something more than anti-Semitic stereotyping. It belongs to the theological frame of reference, like the Jewishness of the antichrist himself.

"Something more" does not necessarily mean anything less. In Signorelli's day, a sincere desire to convert Jews—Ferrer himself had put much effort into converting Jews, with considerable success—did not preclude the old habit of putting unconverted Jews in an antichristic light, as Ambrosiaster and Jerome and others of the patristic era had done. Yet the painting transcends all stereotyping and arguably transcends the Hippolytean tradition itself. Signorelli has not overlooked Ferrer's frank talk about the corruption of the Church, a theme on which Ferrer was scarcely outdone by his fellow Dominican, Savonarola. Savonarola, to be sure, confused his draconian reforms in Florence with the establishment of a newly reformed global Christianity and was put to death during the decadent pontificate of Alexander VI, in the same year Signorelli signed his contract. *Pace* some recent interpreters of the painting, however, this does not suggest that Signorelli must have steered clear of all that. It suggests only that following Ferrer's critical line (could the man on his left possibly be Ferrer rather than Fra Angelico?) was quite compatible with portraying his false prophet (not his antichrist!) as a man in a white habit. For if the Church is also to be betrayed, it must be betrayed from within as well as from without, and there is more than one way to effect that betrayal. In fact, it is the betrayal from within that makes possible the betrayal from without.

If we keep our focus just there, we can see at least one line of convergence between the literal rendering and the metaphorical one. We need only see Signorelli's temple as a vision of the antichrist's anti-*Church*. This spares us many practical difficulties which Signorelli may have overlooked. Are we really to imagine the accomplishment of such enormously controversial matters as the removal of the Dome of the Rock, the building of a new temple, and the restoration of a functioning priesthood and regular temple sacrifice—all or most of it under the auspices of antichrist during the first part of his brief reign—followed immediately by the perpetration of some outrage in the temple? Perhaps, in a time of satanic signs and wonders, all these things are possible. But might we not think instead of a Herod-like revision of the temple already present? That is, of the modification of the visible Church by incorporation of pseudo-Christian elements, generously proposed and supported? For this there is a long history of preparation in that slowly percolating apostasy already recognized by Ferrer, replete with lesser and greater outrages in liturgy, doctrine, and morals. Here, surely, some final sacrilege is more than possible and, indeed, all but certain. That paradigm of apostasy, the golden bull that Aaron built, together with the lesser paradigms of Judg. 18 and 2 Chron. 26 and the like, has its Christian analogue in doxological expressions of solidarity with antichrist that profane the Eucharist itself, through which is received the body of the true Christ, given for the life of the world (John 6).

It is worth recalling, just here, that Urban IV commissioned the cathedral in Orvieto in the same spirit that he made Corpus Christi a universal feast; both were devoted to celebration of eucharistic orthodoxy and of the developing doctrine of transubstantiation. The cathedral's Cappella Corporale boasted a relic from Bolsena; the frescoes of Fra Angelico and Signorelli in its Capello Nuova display the same devotion to eucharistic realism, set there in its wider apocalyptic context. If indeed it is a stretch to contemplate a new Jewish temple, it is no stretch to suppose that the war made on the Lamb (Rev. 17:14) has and must have a prominent eucharistic front, as all these men would agree. Signorelli himself may safely be deemed to share Adso's both/and approach.

It may also be worth recalling that, just a decade after Signorelli painted his *Disputation of Antichrist*, Matthias Grünewald painted the Isenheim altarpiece, in which (in its partially open position) is a nativity scene that sets the Christ-child in Mary's lap, in full view of an angelic choir and a demonic chorus, with the light of the Father in heaven reflecting from his Son's brow into Mary's eyes. It is in the midst of the war between good and evil, truth and lies, beauty and ugliness, that the heavenly light breaks upon us. Grünewald thus sharpens the question for us, if perhaps unintentionally. Will the antichrist seek to insert himself even there, in the lap of the Church? Will he seek to insert himself into the very glory of the Lord?

That glory is depicted still more wonderfully in the opening chapter of Ezekiel: "And above the firmament over their heads there was the likeness of a throne, in appearance like sapphire; and seated above the likeness of a throne was a likeness as it were of a human form. And upward from what had the appearance of his loins I saw as it were gleaming bronze, like the appearance of fire enclosed round about; and downward from what had the appearance of his loins I saw as it were the appearance of fire, and there was brightness round about him. Like the appearance of the bow that is in the cloud on the day of rain, so was the appearance of the brightness round about. Such was the appearance of the likeness of the glory of the LORD" (Ezek. 1:26–28; cf. Rev. 1). Rendering a speculative account of Paul's conversion, N. T. Wright (2018: 47–54) offers a powerful meditation on this text *in persona Sauli*, so to say. He imagines him meditating on Ezekiel's words as his donkey plods on toward Damascus. As the young Saul ascends spiritually, climbing step by step up the rungs of Ezekiel's vision, he is startled to discover the face of Jesus in that "likeness as it were of a human form" that sits on the very throne of God. I wonder: Will the man of lawlessness, quite unbidden, himself try to make that ascent? Perhaps that is what Paul is intimating in 2 Thess. 2:4. But how will he make it? And where will he make it? Not on a donkey to Damascus, nor yet in a temple of stone specially built for the purpose, but in Jesus's own house, his eucharistic house, over which the Lord of Glory presides—the house Saul entered when he took the name Paul. And when his own ascent fails, this man of lawlessness will proceed with all haste to "Damascus" for the purpose of persecuting the Church, putting a halt to its sacrifice, and taking unbridled vengeance upon it.

A further codicil to these musings: The Scottish poet Edwin Muir, while recounting the path of his own conversion, mentions a dream in which he found himself approaching Golgotha. As he drew near, he was shocked to discover, hanging on the middle cross in the place of Jesus of Nazareth, a defiant and even triumphant Friedrich Nietzsche, with whom for a time Muir had been enamored. "I was bewildered by this dream," he writes, "which seemed at such odds with Nietzsche's philosophy; yet it had the profound naturalness of a dream, the cross seemed to fit the man and the man the cross; and I slowly began to realize that Nietzsche's life had been a curious kind of self-crucifixion, out of pride, not out of love" (1987: 288). At *CD* III/2, 231ff., Barth develops a similar insight into Nietzsche, which taken together with Muir's is highly suggestive of certain features of the man of lawlessness, who like Nietzsche will feel a need not only to attack Christ but in every possible way to supplant him. (In other respects, no doubt, he will be very unlike Nietzsche, who was not psychologically or socially fit, despite the virulent hatred on display in *Der Antichrist*, actually to be an antichrist.) And how can one supplant him without being seated in the Church? For if Christ once used to sit in the temple, teaching the people of Jerusalem, does he not sit now in his holy Church, teaching the peoples of the entire world?

But can the three proposals really be employed in combination? Taken on its own, the third is inadequate because it does not justify—even the alternative reading ὡς θεὸν καθίσαι does not justify—Paul's reference to the temple of God. The third may nonetheless add to either of the others a complementary dimension. The real question is whether the first, which is also inadequate on its own, might with some effort be made to cohere with the second, such that each augments the other. Some of the fathers seem to think so, and Signorelli too. For the sake of the fathers we might attempt that ourselves. Since they do not speak with one voice, however, it seems simpler and cleaner to dispense with the literal view and work only with the two metaphorical ones: The antichrist rules as if he were God, making of his followers around the world a kind of unholy temple, a tower of Babel that assaults heaven and requires those who wish its protection to put their household gods in its service or to dispose of them altogether. Not content with that, he also attempts to rule in and over the Church, as his greatest prize. As for the Jews, they get similar treatment—being alternately seduced and bullied—but no third temple.

Is that not more congenial to what we know of Paul? It is true that in the Thessalonian correspondence there is no exposition of the Church as the new temple of God. But Paul does say plainly to the Corinthians and the Ephesians that its members are growing "into a holy temple in the Lord . . . a dwelling place of God in the Spirit" (Eph. 2:19–22). If the man of lawlessness is to seat himself in the temple of God, must he not seat himself in the Church? And if he does seat himself in the Church, why would he find it necessary to rebuild the Jewish temple that he might seat himself there also? One can think of reasons to rebuild it—those of Emperor Julian, for example, who was pursuing a wider program to diminish Christianity—but attempts to draw the literal reading into the metaphorical reading lack literary cogency and fall, perhaps, to a legitimate use of Ockham's razor.

F. F. Bruce (1982: 168f.) objects that reading "in the temple" metaphorically is anachronistic, since there was at the time "no united church organization which could provide such a power base." What a curious view of prophecy! It is only one step further to Wanamaker (1990: 248), who offers his concurring judgment that the temple of stone is in view, but declares the whole passage "invalid" since the temple was later destroyed. Witherington (2006: 220) thinks that Paul would not have applied temple language to the Church because the Thessalonians would not have understood; but of course they would have understood if he had, as he says in the next verse, already told them these things. Weima (2014: 520) suggests that "the strongest evidence that Paul has in view the Jerusalem temple is that the desecration of this sanctuary" belongs to Jewish tradition. Well, yes, but this leads back again to AD 70—and then to what exactly, if not to Wanamaker's conclusion? It leads to a literal interpretation that is not really a literal interpretation, in the last analysis, but a metaphorical one, as Bruce and Weima both admit. The man of lawlessness will try to take the place of God, but not in any particular place, at least not in the Church. This, in other words, is the third proposal, not the first, and it suffers from the inadequacy already mentioned. It does not justify Paul's reference to the temple of God or any appeal to the Danielic tradition regarding its desecration.

A few disclaimers regarding my own view: First, abandoning the literal for the metaphorical, referring "the temple of God" to a structure of living stones rather than to inanimate ones (1 Pet. 2:5) does not require us to abandon Jerusalem as the geographical center of salvation history. The dominion of antichrist will entail a theopolitical claim, as every attempt to supplant God as lawgiver does, whether in the deceptively modest form of secularist democracies or in the blatant tyranny of an Antiochus. And Jerusalem is the magnet to which all such claims are ultimately drawn. Second, to retain Jerusalem as a necessary point of reference is no endorsement of the chiliasm, whether premillennial or postmillennial, that in the days of Lord Shaftesbury played such a prominent role in the rise and success of Zionism (D. Lewis 2010). That divine providence permitted both these eschatologies to play a role in the regathering of Jews to Jerusalem, making that city once again the focal point of international attention, can hardly be regarded as evidence that either of them is right. Third, to take the metaphorical option that understands "temple" as Church does not lend itself by any necessity to the antipapal sectarianism of Joachim or of Wycliffe and Luther and Calvin, which far from driving the smoke of Satan from the Church opened up hundreds of new fissures through which that smoke could billow, providing yet more cover for the eventual coming of antichrist. On the other hand, to allow that a pope or even a series of popes could themselves help provide that cover should certainly not be confused with antipapalism. To the same Peter whom Jesus blessed and to whom he committed the keys of the kingdom, he also gave the rebuke, "Get behind me, Satan!" (Matt. 16:16–23). And there is no divine promise, nor any historical or theological reason to believe, that only godly men assume the Petrine office or that the office itself has not and cannot suffer an idolatrous inflation that lends itself to a false occupation (Farrow 2018b; 2019a). Fourth, the case of Julian the Apostate—who in less than two years moved quickly on a number of fronts, including his attempt to rebuild the Jewish temple along with various pagan ones—remains thought-provoking. It is one thing to find here no reference to a new temple of stone and another to rule out altogether the possibility that Julian's abortive effort might be renewed as part of a larger program.

What then can we safely say, in light of the foregoing, about that final sacrilege or abomination? Just because the Christ was revealed to be more than a deliverer—to be both the salvation of God and the God who saves, hence the object of genuine worship as well as "ruler of kings on earth" (Rev. 1:5)—the antichrist must, to supplant him, revive in some fashion the cult of emperor worship. He must lay claim to glory and dominion on a divine scale. And he must do so in the Church, not merely in Jerusalem. He can only do that by requiring that the gospel of the kingdom become the gospel of *his* kingdom and the sacraments of the gospel instruments of his own glorification. It will not be enough that, like any other narcissist, he reveres himself above all. He will have to be revered above all *by* all. Satanic signs and wonders will help. But in the final analysis it is not ordinary human cynicism or petty jealousies or regional conflicts or the sheer unmanageability of global politics that stand in his way. Rather it is the Church's acknowledgment that "glory and dominion for ever and ever" (Rev. 1:6) belong to Jesus and only to Jesus; that is, to Jesus and his God and Father, for whom the Church has been made a royal priesthood. The sacrilege designed by the man of lawlessness must either pervert that priesthood altogether or bring about its utter destruction. In place of baptism, to use John's language, will be the mark of the beast. In place of the Eucharist will be worship of the image of the beast (Rev. 13:11–18; cf. Dan. 3).

And what are these? The mark, in the first instance, is an economic cipher, without which commerce will be impossible. Hippolytus suggests that it will also be a spiritual cipher, for it will be so arranged that censers will be universally available to test the religious loyalty of partners to commercial transactions. ("Signature here, please. Oh, yes, and a pinch of incense for the Emperor!") This conflation, in which the economic becomes the doxological and the doxological the economic, is not so bizarre as first appears, for one cannot serve both God and Mammon. In other words, the economic mark is already a spiritual mark. It does not imprint on the soul an indelible spiritual character, as do baptism and confirmation and ordination, but it witnesses to a character already there in the one who receives it: the character of readiness to submit to the beast and unreadiness to submit to God. The Apocalypse does not offer hope that one who receives this mark (visible, no doubt, only to the scanner that registers it) can still be converted inwardly. For he is possessed by what he possesses. He now belongs to the man determined to be like God on his own terms, or rather on the terms taught by the serpent, to whom he has determined to listen and to whom he will, whether deliberately or by default, render respect and obedience: "If any one worships the beast and its image, and receives a mark on his forehead or on his hand, he also shall drink the wine of God's wrath, poured unmixed into the cup of his anger, and he shall be tormented with fire and brimstone in the presence of the holy angels and in the presence of the Lamb" (Rev. 14:9–10). The Apocalypse does offer assurance that the one who entrusts himself to God and endures to the end, despite not being able to buy and sell or come and go as he pleases, will be saved, and that right soon, whether through martyrdom or through the determination of Providence that he should "live and remain until the parousia of the Lord" (1 Thess. 4:15). "For the sake of the elect," says Jesus, "those days will be shortened" (Matt. 24:22; cf. 10:17–22).

▨ We should not pass lightly over this sobering business, for fear of being alarmist or of being overly literal. It is now evident, in our age of electronic transactions, that there is no need of censers or anything of that sort. What could be simpler than to employ some tiny electronic device, hidden away like an indelible character, as the condition and mark of citizenship in the empire of the beast? (In Sweden, for example, several thousand people already sport such a device voluntarily.) The difficult thing will be to decline to receive it, since declining will bring an end, in the vast majority of cases, to gainful employment and the ability to buy and sell, or even to move "freely"—an adverb most ironic, for the device tracks every movement. Declining will mark one out, unmistakably, as a noncitizen, as disloyal, as a threat to the general well-being, as a backward and more or less dangerous fanatic. Only those who have prepared themselves will have the courage to decline or to offer any explanation, even to themselves, as to why they should decline. In the last days of our age, the match between God and Mammon will be played out on the field of each man's heart, as ever it has been, but Mammon will have its own way to measure the result. On whom or what do I rely? To whom or what shall I entrust myself? Common sense will be for Mammon. Spiritual discernment, if there is any, will be for God. "He who has ears to hear, let him hear," and let him also commit Rev. 18–19 to memory, lest he mistake what he hears.

If the mark is at once an economic and a spiritual cipher, capable of sustaining for a moment the body while witnessing to the soul's eternal destruction, it nonetheless is not the desolating sacrilege, the abomination that causes desolation. That is something launched, with a more deadly aim, directly at the heart of the Church, converting the Eucharist in some fashion from a thank offering to God in Christ to a testament of submission to antichrist. Just how is hard to say in advance, but we already know how these things go. Profaning holy things was sometimes demanded of Christians in the persecutions of the third century, for example, as was sacrifice to the imperial gods. (Eusebius, writing of the virgins Valentina and Hatha in his *Martyrs of Palestine*, highlights the appropriate response: "They dragged her to the altar, and tried to force her to sacrifice, but she kicked the altar and overturned the fire." That had its own consequence naturally. "The judge, infuriated, ordered the two young women to be bound together and hurled into the sea.") In recent centuries there have been many analogues, some even imposed by Christians on Christians. Think of the oath of supremacy required of Henry's subjects when he installed himself, with parliament's approval, as supreme head of the Church in England. (It was to highlight the fact that this was at once an absurdity and a blasphemy that St. Thomas More asked the solicitor general, Sir Richard Rich, whether parliament also had authority to declare that God was not God. That too had its consequence, as we know.) In the days of the man of lawlessness a much more profound sacrilege will be designed, one that will deliberately profane the Real Presence; and from it the final desolation will follow (cf. Matt. 11:20–24). Those of genuine faith will know it when they see it.

But "when the Son of Man comes, will he find faith on earth?" Yes, he will, though it will not be common. "Many shall purify themselves, and make themselves white, and be refined; but the wicked shall do wickedly; and none of the wicked shall understand; but those who are wise shall understand" (Dan. 12:10; cf. Luke 18:8). Paul wants the Thessalonians to be among the wise, to be among the faithful. So he reminds them of the apostasy and of the man of lawlessness, of the one who, before the Son of Man appears, must himself appear. That one will act to suborn the worship of both Jews and Christians, and to insert into each some idolatrous acknowledgment of his own person and of his lawless agenda. He will seek to gather Jew and Gentile alike into his own fold, as fodder for his self-idolization. He will do so as one man and as the lord of all men. He will do so as the last great wonder of the world, capable, were it possible, of deceiving even the elect.

If they are not to be deceived, they must be warned. And Paul means to warn, though not to frighten. Those pastors who will not warn for fear of frightening fail utterly in their duty. "Guard thyself then, O man; thou hast the signs of Antichrist; and remember them not only thyself, but impart them also freely to all. If thou hast a child according to the flesh, admonish him of this now; if thou hast begotten one through catechizing, put him also on his guard, lest he receive the false one as the True" (*CL* 15.18, in *NPNF²* 7:110).

■ St. John Henry Newman did not fail in his duty. "Surely," says he (*DA* 60), "there is at this day a confederacy of evil, marshalling its hosts from all parts of the world, organizing itself, taking its measures, enclosing the Church of Christ as in a net, and preparing the way for a general Apostasy from it. Whether this very Apostasy is to give birth to Antichrist, or whether he is still to be delayed, as he has already been delayed so long, we cannot know; but at any rate this Apostasy, and all its tokens and instruments, are of the Evil One, and savor of death. Far be it from any of us to be of those simple ones who are taken in that snare which is circling around us!"

Nor did St. Fulton Sheen fail. His famous 1947 sermon on the antichrist is worth quoting at length, despite its misleading conflation of the dragon and the two beasts into a single figure: "He will come disguised as the Great Humanitarian; he will talk peace, prosperity, and plenty, not as means to lead us to God, but as ends in themselves. He will write books on the new idea of God to suit the way people live. . . . He will explain guilt away psychologically as repressed sex, make men shrink in shame if their fellowmen say they are not broadminded and liberal. He will identify tolerance with indifference to right and wrong. He will foster more divorces under the disguise that another partner is 'vital.' He will increase love for love and decrease love for persons. He will invoke religion to destroy religion. He will even speak of Christ and say that he was the greatest man who ever lived. His mission, he will say, will be to liberate men from the servitudes of superstition and Fascism, which he will never define. In the midst of all his seeming love for humanity and his glib talk of freedom and equality, he will have one great secret which he will tell to no one; he will not believe in God. And because his religion will be [the] brotherhood [of man] without the fatherhood of God, he will deceive even the elect. He will set up a counter-Church, which will be the ape of the Church because, he the devil, is the ape of God. It will be the mystical body of the anti-Christ that will in all externals resemble the Church as the mystical body of Christ. In desperate need for God, he will induce modern man, in his loneliness and frustration, to hunger more and more for membership in his community that will give man enlargement of purpose, without any need of personal amendment and without the admission of personal guilt. These are days in which the devil has been given a particularly long rope." Every restraint against evil will be cast off, warns Sheen (1948; 1958), and is even now being cast off, which is why Christians must become disciplined in putting on the armor of God.

These predictions are proving all too accurate. Evidence is mounting that the man of lawlessness is taking his place, and will take his place, in the Church. There is great irony in the fact that Kant, as Josef Pieper (1999: 92ff.) reminds us, saw the Church itself paving the way for antichrist through its insistence on the truth of salvation history and on the observance of its laws and sacraments. This betrayal of the religion of reason and of progress by a sclerotic ecclesiastical religion, argued Kant, was causing the Church to lose its "lovableness" and turning the rest of society against it. And what now? Will the Church, like a spurned lover, try to regain the world's affections by insisting no more? Will it say that what it said before was only an ideal, to which ordinary people cannot be expected to conform? This is what in many places, even in Rome, it seems to be saying, as if it did not know the truth, as if having forgotten that it is not by being false to its own inner character, but rather by being true to it, that it ceases to be loved in a society that is whoring after antichrist (John 15:18). And in this forgetfulness, or in this unwillingness to be unloved, it is indeed paving the way for that satanic simulacrum.

We may after all agree with McGinn, then, that the chief use of the doctrine of antichrist is to warn us against ourselves, meaning this the way Gregory the Great meant it—that we should fight the antichrist within lest we find ourselves allied with the antichrist without (cf. McGinn 2000: 81). For it is from the little-by-little apostasy of Christians, who give way to the antichrist within, that the sudden and thorough rebellion of the antichrist without is made possible. Helping us to think about that is the work, not only of sermons and lectures on scripture, but of fiction as well: from Dostoevsky (1880) and Solovyov (1900) through Benson (1915) to Lewis (1943; 1945) and Williams (1945) and lately O'Brien (1996), to mention several writers who have tackled the subject. (With the exception of O'Brien, brief introductions can be found in McGinn, along with a description of Adso's antihagiography, *De ortu et tempore Antichristi*, the tenth-century mother of all informed fiction on the figure of antichrist.)

Paul does not say when the son of perdition will appear, or where. That when he appears he will come, as Jesus did, to Jerusalem, is plain enough, for the scriptures make it plain. Whether or not he will rebuild the temple of stone (our reservations about that need not rule it out), he will certainly make Jerusalem also a kind of prize. He must do so because God has already done so. Jerusalem is the city of the Great King. It is the place God chose for his sacred name and for his holy dwelling. It is the place Jesus, our Immanuel, was crucified and resurrected. It is the place where God through Jesus will complete his unfinished business with Israel, whose gifts and calling are irrevocable, and indeed with every race and nation of man, for all by then will have reached a decision about the gospel that long ago went forth from Jerusalem. Jerusalem is the place where God will manifest Jesus as "King of kings and Lord of lords" (Rev. 19:11–16). Not the Jews only, but all nations, will therefore be gathered to Jerusalem, where God's salvation and God's judgment will be made known to all—not, as already they were, in darkness from the sixth to the ninth hour, but rather in the lightning that will flash at midnight, when chimes the end of the age and of the city of man. The narrative of history will not come to its end with the end of Rome, any more than it came to its end with the end of Babylon. It is Jerusalem itself, she that is figuratively called Babylon, that must play host to the final contest and witness the last end.

In this contest the remaining Jews will, for the most part, be numbered on the side of Christ, not of antichrist. Even as the Gentiles cease believing, Jews will begin believing. When the full number of Gentiles has come in, so will the full number of Jews. The latter, suggests Aquinas in his commentary on Romans, will come to the aid of the Church and rekindle its faith. "For Gentiles are the believers who will grow lukewarm, or will fall away entirely, being deceived by Antichrist. These will be restored to their primitive fervor after the conversion of the Jews" (*S.Rom.* 11.2.890). According to the Apocalypse, those from every tribe of Israel "who sigh and groan over all the abominations" committed in the holy city will be sealed on their foreheads by the sign of the cross and the name of the Father and the Son, singing the song of the Lamb before the throne of

God (7:2–8; cf. Ezek. 9:4). They will be joined by a multitude from every nation who, having received and obeyed the gospel, will likewise stand singing "before the throne of God, and serve him day and night within his temple," sheltered by his presence (cf. 7:9–17, where "temple" is used metaphorically, and 14:1–5).

The parousia will not come before the whole number of the redeemed is complete, before all those who have been appointed to the perfection of the city of God have entered into it, spiritually speaking (cf. *Civ.* 22.1 and *CDH* 1.16), a point that will coincide with the antichrist's summing up of every abomination and his recapitulation of every offense against the Father and the Son. Which is to say, the abomination that brings desolation, accompanied by the forbidding of all true worship (cf. Dan. 9:27; 12:11–12), will not succeed in diminishing the company of the elect, for those who belong to that company will remain faithful even in the face of the antichrist's attempt at a final solution. He and all who have followed him will then discover what they ought all along to have known—namely, that there is nothing final but what God says is final. "Then I saw another angel flying in midheaven, with an eternal gospel to proclaim to those who dwell on earth, to every nation and tribe and tongue and people; and he said with a loud voice, 'Fear God and give him glory, for the hour of his judgment has come'" (Rev. 14:6–7).

Before leaving at last the opening paragraph of 2 Thess. 2, which through many departures into earlier and later tradition we have sought, perhaps over-boldly, to elaborate, we can also complete a schema begun earlier but left unfinished (→1 Thess. 5:1–3). Salvation history, like the history of the world's creation, is symbolically divided into seven days, with an eighth or eternal day to follow, prefigured in the Eucharist. This week of days, as we noted, is divided in two by the cross of Christ, the act of atonement by which man is redeemed and the old covenant passes into the new. In the run-up to that act, Daniel is told that "seventy weeks of years are decreed concerning your people and your holy city, to finish the transgression, to put an end to sin, and to atone for iniquity, to bring in everlasting righteousness . . . and to anoint a most holy place" (9:24–27). Of these the final week is reserved for "the prince who is to come," who "shall make a strong covenant with many," a deceptive counter-covenant, but after half that week will "cause sacrifice and offering to cease." This final week of years, the week for antichrist which begins, as we are about to see, when the restrainer ceases restraining (→2:6–10), is also divided in two, then, for it is a week of negative recapitulation. In the middle of it, after three and a half years, when the two witnesses have completed their task, there is a Judas-like betrayal of the strong covenant and a repetition of the repudiation of Jesus that took place on Calvary, signaled by erection of the desolating sacrilege, the cutting off of all remaining worship of God, and an attempt to "crucify" en masse those who persist in following Christ. In the following diagram, that is marked by the upside-down cross:

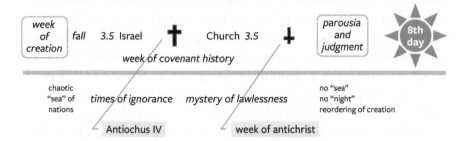

But here an anomaly appears that puzzled some of the fathers. Daniel 12:11 indicates that "from the time that the continual burnt offering is taken away, and the abomination that makes desolate is set up, there shall be a thousand two hundred and ninety days." What is the purpose of the extra month or so (cf. 8:13–14)? And why does 12:12 add, "Blessed is he who waits and comes to the thousand three hundred and thirty-five days"? Certain fathers, followed by later commentators on our epistles, took 12:12 to imply a last period of penance and conversion, some forty-five days falling between the slaying of antichrist by St. Michael and the actual appearance of Jesus—a final moment of grace, in other words, before the resurrection of the dead and the last judgment and the life of the world to come, during which men might still repent rather than calling for the mountains to fall on them in dreadful expectation of the *adventus terribilis*. That is possible, perhaps, but it seems forced; there is no hint of any such period of grace in the Olivet Discourse or here in Paul or in the Apocalypse. Nor does Daniel present it that way. Daniel 8:14 says simply that after two thousand three hundred days "the sanctuary shall be restored to its rightful state." If we are thinking of the Church as that temple and sanctuary, might we answer both questions by imagining a sudden collapse of the regime of antichrist brought about by divine intervention, followed by a brief pause for the surviving followers of Jesus to emerge from hiding, resume their public worship, and prepare themselves for the parousia of their Lord and their assembling to him? Whether this can be made to fit with what follows in 2 Thess. 2 the reader must judge, however; though Paul is working with Daniel, he is not working to quite this level of detail and it is his own argument that now reclaims our attention. ▪

2:6–10 And now you see what is delaying [the day of the Lord, namely] that he [the man of lawlessness] should be revealed in his own proper time. For the mystery of lawlessness is already at work; only [there is] one presently restraining [it] until he shall emerge from the midst [of those in whom it works].* And then [at last] the

---

* Alternatively: "until that one is ordered to stand down."

lawless one will be unveiled, whom the Lord Jesus will destroy with the breath of his mouth and bring down by the display of his [own] parousia—[the one] whose parousia is according to the working of Satan, with all [demonic] power and with false signs and wonders and with every wicked deceit, [a parousia] unto those who are perishing for want of love of the truth, which they did not receive that it might save them.

And now you see? If we are to see, a quick review is in order. In the opening chapter Paul assured the Thessalonians that divine justice would be dispensed in a timely way and their salvation effected as promised. In the present chapter he is urging patience and explaining why those who are trafficking in rumors about the day of judgment and salvation having already arrived cannot be right. They cannot be right because they have overlooked something fundamental to justice itself: that it must be timely. They cannot be right, because what Augustine called (in Edmund Hill's loose but apt translation of a phrase from *Trin.* 13.17) "the justice game" is still being played out. In that game the devil must show his entire hand before God will show his. The devil has already played his ace—he has organized the forces that, by divine permission, put Jesus to death. That was trumped by the resurrection, with which the devil had not reckoned. Now he must play his joker, whom God will overcome with his king. Only thus will the justice game be completed, which of course is no game but rather a contest in deadly earnest. The day of the Lord, then, the day of disaster for the wicked and of vindication for the righteous, is being held back until Satan's great pretender appears. Or to use a more biblical analogy: until his champion, his Goliath, his outsize man of sin, steps forward and makes himself known.

The devil sought power without justice—an absurdity, since justice and power, like justice and happiness, are one in God (→1 Thess. 2:17–20; 4:9–12). But God, whose power is infinite, made no effort to defeat the devil "at the power game," through the cross defeating him rather at the justice game. And having done that, he added power to justice through the resurrection, causing justice to accede to power. Thus, argues Augustine, did he create genuine authority among men, an authority fully invested in Jesus Christ and rightly imitated by those who, in their own station and fashion, seek justice before power. "Let mortals hold on to justice; power will be given them when they are immortal. Compared with this, the power of those men who are called powerful on earth is shown to be ridiculous weakness, and 'a pit is dug for the sinner' in the very place where the wicked seem to be able to do most" (*Trin.* 13.17, citing Ps. 94:13).

Well said! But ridiculous weakness, as Paul now indicates, must magnify itself and make of itself a false marvel. It must claim an authority that does not actually belong to it. Man will become his own judge, he will take charge of himself, he will order his own world, he will be master of all things. The ambition itself is not ridiculous. What is ridiculous is the denial of man's impotency to achieve it apart from God and without God's help. Through this denial man makes himself the son of Satan rather than the son of God, and enlists himself on the losing side. If "power added to justice, or justice acceding to power, makes judicial authority," nothing is more certain than that this authority will be exercised in its time, and that no unjust man, however inflated or exalted by satanic machinations, can prevent it. For God "has fixed a day on which he will judge the world in righteousness by a man whom he has appointed," a fact of which "he has given assurance to all men by raising him from the dead" (Acts 17:31). On that day lawless man will fall into the pit he has dug for himself, and justice shall reign.

Somewhat ironically—or does it mirror rhetorically the speed of the final dénouement Paul is describing?—the crucial paragraph now before us, explaining the delay, has itself the appearance of haste. It is, in any event, a memo to those already informed, as Paul has just said, underscoring what should by now be obvious to them. Hence it is written in elliptical fashion and cannot be translated without some effort to fill in the ellipses. The key to doing that, and to reading it without going astray, is to keep in mind the principal point—the necessity for delay if justice is to be done—and to remember that the man of lawlessness is the main subject throughout, the common referent of the paragraph's third-person singular pronouns. It further helps to keep in mind the rhetorical device of *synkrisis*, which by using the same language of two different parties enables an effective contrast between them (Witherington 2006: 21); in this case, the language of disclosure, appearance, parousia. For if we are to follow Paul's train of thought here, we must ponder further the man of lawlessness in terms of the mystery of lawlessness he incarnates, the maturation of evil that takes place in the period leading up to his appearance, and the time and manner of his appearance, including the objectives he will pursue.

This may seem a daunting task, but it is not so daunting as Augustine supposed when, near the conclusion of *The City of God*, he took refuge in the fact that no one knows quite what Paul said to the Thessalonians when he was with them. "And thus we who have not their knowledge," he says, "wish and are not able even with pains to understand what the apostle referred to, especially as his meaning is made still more obscure by what he adds.

For what does he mean by 'For the mystery of iniquity doth already work: only he who now holdeth, let him hold until he be taken out of the way: and then shall the wicked be revealed?' I frankly confess I do not know what he means" (*Civ.* 20.19, in *NPNF¹* 2:437). Augustine adds that he "will nevertheless mention such conjectures" as he has heard or read. Occasionally I will do the same, but only occasionally, for the commentators have often tied themselves knots that are not worth unpicking. And we will not retreat before this text as he retreats, or suppose it puzzling in the extreme. It is not a taxonomy of conjectures we are looking for, but actual comprehension of Paul's argument, which is quite possible. Here is the Greek text in full, which those who are able will want to consult: καὶ νῦν τὸ κατέχον οἴδατε εἰς τὸ ἀποκαλυφθῆναι αὐτὸν ἐν τῷ ἑαυτοῦ καιρῷ. τὸ γὰρ μυστήριον ἤδη ἐνεργεῖται τῆς ἀνομίας· μόνον ὁ κατέχων ἄρτι ἕως ἐκ μέσου γένηται. καὶ τότε ἀποκαλυφθήσεται ὁ ἄνομος, ὃν ὁ κύριος ['Ιησοῦς] ἀνελεῖ τῷ πνεύματι τοῦ στόματος αὐτοῦ καὶ καταργήσει τῇ ἐπιφανείᾳ τῆς παρουσίας αὐτοῦ, οὗ ἐστιν ἡ παρουσία κατ' ἐνέργειαν τοῦ Σατανᾶ ἐν πάσῃ δυνάμει καὶ σημείοις καὶ τέρασιν ψεύδους καὶ ἐν πάσῃ ἀπάτῃ ἀδικίας τοῖς ἀπολλυμένοις, ἀνθ' ὧν τὴν ἀγάπην τῆς ἀληθείας οὐκ ἐδέξαντο εἰς τὸ σωθῆναι αὐτούς.

When something we anticipated has not yet happened, we often ask the party responsible what the holdup is. ("Why is my car not ready?" "We're waiting for the new clutch to come in.") What is anticipated here is the promised day of the Lord, and the holdup, τὸ κατέχον, the thing preventing it, is that the καιρός or proper moment for the disclosure of the man of lawlessness has not yet arrived. Nor is that surprising; for this disclosure must take place in its own time, when the mystery of lawlessness is reaching its climax, since he it is who will bring it to its climax. "He is the head of all the wicked by reason of the perfection of his wickedness," says Aquinas at *ST* 3.8.8, for "the devil by suggestion infuses his wickedness more copiously into him than into all others. And in this way all the wicked who have gone before are signs of Antichrist." Only when that to which the signs point has arrived will divine judgment fall. Only then will God make good on his threats and deliver on his promises. Only then will the Lord himself, the just Judge, appear.

What is the mystery of lawlessness and how will it reach its climax? In the New Testament, μυστήριον is used to refer to the gospel as something unknowable apart from revelation (cf. *TDNT* 4:820f.; *CD* IV/4, 108f.); to the saving act of God in Jesus Christ that could not be anticipated by man; to the gracious opening made for man by the Holy Spirit in the Father's secret knowledge of the Son and the Son's exclusive knowledge of the Father; to the presence among men of the kingdom even before the kingdom comes; to the inclusion of Gentiles in that kingdom through the creation of the Church; and to the Church itself, as the

bride of Christ. It is a dominical word, but it is Paul who takes it up and develops
a theology that incorporates all these things in declaring and announcing openly
"the mystery of God" (τὸ μυστήριον τοῦ θεοῦ, 1 Cor. 2:1, which refers both to God
himself and to the formerly hidden plan of God; cf. Matt. 11:25–27; 13:11; Rom.
8; 16:25–27; 1 Cor. 2:6–10; 4:1; 13:2; 15:51; Eph. 1:9–10; 3:1–12; 5:32; 6:19;
Col. 1:24–2:3; 1 Tim. 3:9, 15–16). Paul also uses it to speak of the present alienation of fellow Jews, or rather of the secret work of God to harden them in their
unbelief and eventually to soften them again, that they may enter the promised
kingdom (Rom. 11:25; cf. Rev. 10:5–7). And he uses it here in 2 Thessalonians
to speak of a satanic alternative—of a counter-program, a counter-kingdom, a
counter-unity, and, at the right moment, a counter-revelation—just as John uses
it in Rev. 17 to speak of Babylon with its own blasphemous mystery, which can
be seen for what it is only by those who are "carried away in the Spirit" and given
the necessary insight.

   The mystery of lawlessness, like the mystery of salvation, is a mystery because
it works in secret until the time is right for it to be openly declared and for the
sins it entails to become "public and common" (Aquinas, *S.2Th.* 2.2.45). It is a
mystery because it has its own quiet *oeconomia*, which unfolds in history in ways
often unobserved. (Those ways are observed by God, naturally, who "knows what
is in the darkness" and reveals to the wise "deep and mysterious things," including
future things; see Dan. 2:17–23.) It is a mystery because it works in the Church
and depends on the Church, which provides the very soil in which it can grow
and supplies it with more than a few "falsehoods and phoneys," for, as Thietland
says, "the Antichrist comes to deceive the dead in soul" wherever he finds them
(Cartwright and Hughes 2001: 54; cf. Matt. 13:24–30, 36–43). It is a mystery also
because it effects in its own fashion a kind of union between the human and the
divine, or what claims to be divine—a union finally with one who exalts himself
above everything previously thought to be divine and who forbids the Christian
mysteries, the *sacramenta* by which men confess Christ and are united to Christ.
And it is a mystery, we may add, because it works at all and actually comes to
maturity, which it ought not to be capable of. It grows and ripens; it advances
and reaches a climax. That is counterintuitive, since lawlessness is a *defectio*, a
declension, a tendency to nothing—not something in its own right but only a
quasi-something, just as evil generally "is only non-good or the absence of good
where good ought to be found" (*DCD* 11). Hence it requires an explanation.

   As Anselm argues in the opening chapter of *De casu diaboli*, everything,
as it comes from the hand of God, has being and goodness. It belongs to that

goodness to be rightly ordered, as is the will itself in the first creation of rational beings. Sin or lawlessness, in the first instance, is a defection of the will from its rightly ordered condition, with respect to some creaturely objective that is not subjected to God's own will and purpose. It is acting autonomously in defiance of God rather than in cooperation with God, and just so it deprives the lawless agent, and with him the world in some way, of his own proper being and goodness. After Adam and Eve, Cain, who murders Abel, provides the foremost paradigm. Yet Cain builds a city, founding civilization as we know it (Gen. 4:17). How can civilization be built when it has disorder and death underlying it? How can it advance, even to the achievement of something like the universal dominion granted in principle before the fall—a dominion attempted and frustrated at Babel, as in many subsequent empires, but coming to pass in a latter-day Babylon? Is Irenaeus not right that "those things among which transgression has occurred" simply grow old rather than growing up (*Haer.* 5.36.1)? Does natural law not teach us that pursuing evil rather than good destroys even the good we are seeking? Do not our souls and bodies, and our body politic too, begin to disintegrate when corrupted by sin and lawlessness? When the human will is at odds with the divine will, or man's law with God's law, does the former not require tyrannical force, just because it aims at something other than the true good of man? And does not that force sooner or later cause societies and empires to implode? Does it not tend to anarchy, trapping us in endless cycles of order, tyranny, and collapse into disorder? Such is the "nature" of lawlessness, which is in fact contrary to nature. How then can lawlessness continue to advance? How can it develop or mature? How can it follow a line that leads to fruition in a real man of lawlessness? The answer is: only with the aid of the Church and its gospel; but this too is counterintuitive and in need of explanation.

God is only good and does only good. He makes nothing evil. Evil is strictly privative, hence parasitic on good. Rational agents, by depriving themselves of their original righteousness, produce negative effects in themselves and others (Wis. 1:12–16; cf. 11:21–26). The greater the good they eschew, the greater the evil they do. Evil can be sustained only as perversion of the good. Which is where the gospel comes in. Until the eternal gospel was announced, and the Church created as the bearer of that gospel, there was nothing in the form or fashion of this world that was more than provisional. All the privation worked by man or demon, therefore, could be worked only with things that in consequence crumbled and ran to dust, like man himself. But the incarnation of the

Word of God, and the gospel he announced, changed all that. Now the harvest of eternal life was possible. And so, by perverse derivation, was the mystery of evil or of lawlessness. The existence in the world of eternal life and truth is what accounts for the otherwise inexplicable capacity of lawlessness to come to something rather than to nothing.

To put it still more plainly: The mystery of lawlessness is the form that lawlessness takes when it seeks to occupy the gospel, the law of liberty, drawing life from it so as to produce a kind of living death. It is the form that sin takes when its self-destructive tendencies are restrained and tempered by the influence of righteousness. It is the form that evil takes when its chaotic forces converge in opposition to the unifying mysteries of the Church—and so, *mirabile dictu*, achieve a harmony and a potency not their own. The mystery of lawlessness exists and can exist only as a counter-mystery to the mystery of the gospel. It grows with the gospel and the sacraments of the gospel. It advances alongside them and in dependence upon them, borrowing what it can from them, drawing its power in perversion of them (Farrow 2011: 104ff.; 2014). Which is also why it advances in the Church itself, in the temple of God.

Now, the man of lawlessness embodies the mystery of lawlessness as the man who takes charge of peoples and of history without regard for the constraints of his own creatureliness; as the man who, Babel-like, but this time successfully, "opposes and exalts himself against every so-called god or object of worship," who "takes his seat in the temple of God, proclaiming himself to be God" (RSVCE); as the man who sits, so to say, in heavenly session while still on earth, exercising a judgment that does not belong to him, shadowing (not eucharistically, but rebelliously) the lordship and dominion that God has granted to Jesus. This man cannot emerge, full grown, all at once. Indeed it is not clear how he can emerge at all, since he has no definitive nature or form of his own. He can emerge only by aping the Christ and by despoiling the Church of its heavenly gifts through satanic arts. He therefore grows slowly, like Sauron in Tolkien's great tale. But he does grow and he will emerge eventually from the midst (ἐκ μέσου) of those in whom the mystery is at work, at just the right point in this demonic project to pervert man and to pervert him by perverting the Church, by creating a simulacrum thereof. "They believe for a while and in time of temptation fall away" (Luke 8:13). Fall away into what? Into this simulacrum; into the sphere of the Un-man, to use C. S. Lewis's label in *Perelandra*; into the universal assembly of the son of destruction. And this son of destruction—the one in whom the mystery of lawlessness will at last show itself in definitive form, the one who will bring about the abomination that causes complete desolation—will also appear in his own time. He will have his own apocalypse or parousia.

▓ Obviously we are not following the usual translation of ὁ κατέχων ἄρτι ἕως ἐκ μέσου γένηται, which the RSVCE renders "he who now restrains it will do so until he is out of the way," but preferring rather "there is one presently restraining it until he [the man of lawlessness] shall emerge from the midst." F. F. Bruce, touching on a similar sounding but actually quite different proposal—namely, "the mystery of lawlessness 'coming to pass out of the midst'"—argues that this "would require εἰς μέσον, not ἐκ μέσου" (1982: 171). That is debatable. What is not debatable is that one can draw, as he does, on extrabiblical texts to show that ἐκ μέσου γενέσθαι refers to being removed, or removing oneself, from public view or public office, for example. Weima (2014: 531), after noting that Paul's expression is unique in the New Testament, points to "close parallels" in 1 Cor. 5:2 and Col. 2:14, the first of which speaks of removing a sinner from the assembly, while the second refers to nullifying the notice of conviction contained in the law by posting it on the cross of Christ. In both cases, however, the verb is αἴρω—there is a *taking* out of the midst or out of the way. Were that the verb here, our translation would not be viable. But the verb here is γίνομαι, which has among its meanings "to arise," or "to appear in history or on the stage of history."

It may be asked whether there is anything to be gained by appeal to Jerome. At verse 6 the Vulgate reads *et nunc quid detineat scitis ut revelatur in suo tempore*, which we may render, "and now you know what must detain [him] that he may be revealed in his time," though the KJV renders it, "And now ye know what withholdeth that he might be revealed in his time." At verse 7, the Vulgate has *nam mysterium iam operatur iniquitatis tantum ut qui tenet nunc teneat donec de medio fiat*, which the KJV translates, "For the mystery of iniquity doth already work: only he who now letteth will let, until he be taken out of the way." While this translation commits to the restrainer rather than the man of lawlessness as the referent of the final clause, Jerome's *de medio fiat* is as ambiguous as Paul's ἐκ μέσου γένηται. The sense might be, "the mystery is already working, only the one who hinders it will hinder until he (the one hindering) is taken from the midst." Or it might be, "the mystery is already working, only the one who hinders it will hinder until he (the man of lawlessness) is drawn out from the midst." While the Latin text might have read *de medio tollatur* (cf. *Civ.* 20.19.3), committing itself to the first option, it does not. So we are no further ahead.

The expression ἕως ἐκ μέσου γένηται is indeed a biblical *hapax legomenon*, but there is a good contextual reason for choosing the second option. For in the background stands Dan. 7, the Greek text of which points us in the right direction. In verse 8 Daniel says, "While I was pondering its horns, suddenly another little one sprang up in their midst [ἀνέβη ἐν μέσῳ αὐτῶν] and three of the existing horns were torn away before it; and, lo, in this horn there were eyes, eyes like a man's, and a mouth making great boasts" (AT). Paul is referencing that arrogant horn. Hence we may understand the antecedent subject of γένηται to be, not the restrainer, ὁ κατέχων, or the mystery of lawlessness, but rather—as elsewhere in this paragraph—the man of lawlessness himself (Farrow 1989). Read thus, our text falls in line also with Rev. 13, which is likewise dependent on Daniel. The man of lawlessness rises up from among the nations. He appears in their midst, yes, but ἐις μέσον could not convey, as ἐκ μέσου does, the Danielic sense that Paul wishes to convey. For the man of lawlessness comes *from* them as well as *to* them. He emerges from their midst, jostling them aside. He steps forth from the throng of actors already on the stage, as the boastful mouth that loudly articulates their rejection of God and gives sharp definition to the mystery that is already at work among them. The sense is captured nicely in Benson's *Lord of the World* (1915: 318): "Peace, it was pointed out, had for the first time in the world's history become an universal fact.... [This] had been consummated by a single Person, Who, it appeared, had emerged from humanity at the very instant when such a Character was demanded." Meanwhile, that mystery is prevented from arriving at some premature climax by the one who restrains it, who retards its development so that the man of lawlessness can emerge fully formed.

What is holding up the day of the Lord and the justice to be executed on that day? The necessity that the mystery of lawlessness should run its course and that the man of lawlessness should emerge as the proper object of divine wrath. But who or what is restraining the mystery of lawlessness so that it doesn't deliver prematurely or produce an immature result? Who or what is ὁ κατέχων? Much ink has been spilt on this question, the answer to which is not of paramount importance, however great our curiosity about it. In the patristic period, what Tertullian proposed became more popular after the Christianization of the Roman Empire began; many thought the delaying factor (τὸ κατέχον) and the personal or personified "restrainer" to *be* that empire as the obvious force of law and order in the world, a force that could and would disappear eventually. The supposition that ὁ κατέχων provides the antecedent of γένηται lends itself to that proposal or to some similar proposal. Perhaps it is not the empire per se but God working through the empire? Or the Church (thus Cardinal Manning 1861) working within the empire? Or not the Church per se, but heavenly agents intervening on her behalf? Or perhaps some as yet unidentified person or force?

To say that God is restraining lawlessness is to say the obvious and the undeniable. If that is all Paul meant, however, it would have been simpler and more natural to have said, "God is restraining it," than to have employed the periphrastic expression, "there is one restraining it" or "the one restraining it will continue to do so." From the very beginning, then, speculation about the restrainer has put up other candidates, working under God. Besides the empire and the Church and the gospel and Michael or the heavenly host, even the persistent unbelief of Israel has been proposed (cf. Pieper 1999: 138), which would fit in Rom. 11 but hardly commends itself here. Various combinations of these have also been tried. Theodoret (2001: 129) creatively proposes that the *decree* of God restrains, in view of the imperative that the truth of the gospel be presented to all the world before a proper adversary of truth should appear—which makes pretty good sense, though not of the language of being "taken out of the way," unless we understand that to refer to the *enforcer* of God's decree being told to withdraw or stand down. If however, as I am arguing, the man of lawlessness is the antecedent subject of γένηται, that difficulty disappears.

Quite predictably, there are those who find that only skepticism commends itself in the face of this obscure reference to a restrainer. Hersch-Reich (1929: 60), for example, suggests that Paul combines the Jewish idea of Gentile tyrants like Antiochus and Gaius Caligula with the pagan notion of Rome as a force for law and order into a twisted doctrine about a Roman tyrant with a Jewish following who persecutes Christians. And with this, she says, apocalyptic expectation of an antichrist event "at last separates itself from any connection with historical fact and becomes purely ideal." As if to put the lie to that conclusion, Wright (2002: 148) speculates that the restrainer might be someone like Herod, for example, who tried to restrain Caligula when the latter very nearly played again the role of Antiochus. But Caligula's murderers might fit the bill rather better; which is to say, this line of thought does not seem promising either. Far the most promising line is the one Weima wisely pursues (2014: 574ff.), following Nicholl (2004: 230ff.), despite the fact that both start from a false or uncertain premise (viz., that the delaying factor and the restrainer are one and the same). That promising line is the one we also are following, for it is the line that runs between Daniel and Paul and on into the Apocalypse.

When we keep Daniel in view, as we must, and particularly if we translate Paul's text as we have, the most obvious candidate for the restrainer (ὁ κατέχων, not τὸ κατέχον, the reason for the delay) is St. Michael, the prince of the host. He it is who, under God, restrains the mystery of lawlessness by defending the people of God. The man of lawlessness cannot appear until his defense is withdrawn; conversely, Michael himself will not withdraw until the man of lawlessness is at hand. Then that man will be revealed. He will magnify himself against the powers of heaven, "even against the prince of the heavenly host," who will concede the sanctuary and the sacrifice (Dan. 8:11–12 AT). He will corrupt the sacrifice with sin (LXX: "make sin the sacrifice") and cast faithfulness to the ground. He will dominate the land and people of the old covenant and of the new also. He will wear down the saints, as Antiochus did in his day, and presume to take authority over the things of God. He will be followed by those prepared to violate the covenant but be actively resisted by those who know the God of the covenant, those who in the resurrection "shall shine like the brightness of the firmament, . . . like the stars for ever and ever" (Dan. 12:3; →1 Thess. 4:16–17).

All this we have already seen from Dan. 7–12, which Paul must have expounded to the Thessalonians, however briefly, while he was conducting his mission among them. Certainly we may acknowledge that μόνον ὁ κατέχων ἄρτι ἕως ἐκ μέσου γένηται is a sentence difficult to interpret with complete confidence, and that there is little risk in seeing here primarily a reference to God restraining lawlessness— saying to the sea, as it were, "thus far and no further" (cf. Job 38:11)—so that he may restrain at the same time his own hand of judgment. Yet we ought to take account of the fact that Paul, like Jesus, is interpreting Daniel for us, and that Daniel himself references "the prince of the host." And we must not neglect, either, that the restraint in question serves the double purpose of allowing the gospel to reach the ends of the earth *and* of enabling the little horn with the big mouth, the man of lawlessness who puffs himself up even against the powers of heaven, to emerge in his own time. In the last analysis, that is a more important thing to know than the identity of the restrainer, whom Paul does not trouble to name for them again.

▨ Were it not for the combination of these purposes, we might even suppose the restrainer to be Satan himself, who perhaps is learning that a house divided against itself (witness the rift between Hitler and Stalin, Fascism and Communism) cannot stand. But it is difficult to give any credence to that proposal, which runs against the grain of the text and what we know about Satan. The truth is that the kingdom of Satan is always roiled and violent. It is God himself, working through his heavenly host and the prince of that host, through his Church and his gospel, and through the very laws of creation, who effects the restraint necessary for things to unfold as they should.

As for Michael, Colin Nicholl supplies copious evidence for his prominence in Jewish literature of the period, including a later reference to him, with the serpent or dragon in view, as κατέχων (2004: 234ff.; cf. Rev. 20:1–3). He quite rightly observes that in Dan. 10–12 "Michael has been cast as restrainer," and that he was so regarded elsewhere. Nicholl is right again in claiming that the reference in Dan. 12:1 to "a time of trouble, such as never has been," a time which follows immediately upon a movement of Michael, "the great prince who has charge of your people," makes little sense unless that movement is a standing down, so to say, rather than a rising up. He argues that both the Hebrew word יעמד and the word used in the LXX (though not in Theodotion), παρελεύσεται, can and sometimes do refer to a cessation of action rather than to a new action—to standing aside, to withdrawal from the fray. This fits both Dan. 12:1 and 2 Thess. 2:7 very well.

Given the translation of 2 Thess. 2:7b defended above, it is unnecessary (*pace* Nicholl 2004: 245) to press that argument. We can make sense of Paul without it. To make sense of Daniel, however, it may be necessary. And if we favor this less traditional translation of Daniel, should we not also favor the more traditional translation of Paul? After all, if Paul is following Daniel closely, why wouldn't he say, "there is one now restraining it until he steps aside / stands down / is removed from the midst of God's people"? But the question now arises as to whether at 2:7b Paul has in view only Dan. 12:1 or also Dan. 7:8. If 12:1 only, then what is argued above still elucidates the pericope as a whole but cannot justify the translation, "there is one presently restraining it until the man of lawlessness shall emerge from the midst of those in whom it works." Yet why not posit—since Paul is not merely repeating what Daniel has to say but thinking it through in connection with the teaching of Jesus—that he has both these texts in view and that 7:8, with its reference to the little horn that suddenly emerges, is still guiding his thought? In that case, the proposed translation may stand.

The reader who declines to decide this point has my sympathy. The reader who decides in favor of the traditional translation will have gained something by way of understanding, and lost nothing, in considering the alternative I have offered. It may be agreed, in any case, that Michael restrains until he no longer restrains and that, when he no longer restrains, the mystery of lawlessness comes to its climax in the man of lawlessness, before whom the people of God will appear to be defenseless.

How does evil or lawlessness grow to maturity? Not by any principle inherent in itself but rather by mimicking the effects of the gospel, like a virus mimicking a healthy cell. Lawlessness by nature is self-defeating and self-destructive, as its children have ever proved it. But lawlessness that is restrained by God through the gospel of the covenant and the kingdom, and by the prince of the host charged with defending that kingdom—lawlessness, therefore, that through that very restraint is allowed to go on feeding off the gospel—can and does mature. So, too, does its power to generate that "deluding influence" of which we must shortly speak, by which it draws its own into judgment. For God can be imitated, and the gospel of God likewise, but neither can be mocked without deadly consequence (Matt. 12:31–32).

By way of illustration we may point once again to notions of autonomy and dignity; or, perhaps we should say, to the notion of dignity *as* autonomy, for in much of Western law and culture these terms now appear as a hendiadys, in which is contained an antigospel belonging to that man who knows no law but the law of his own will and choosing. God, the doctrine of creation informs us and the gospel assures us, made rational creatures as those under their own power. He made them like God, as those who must judge good and evil. But the man of lawlessness is that man who is not content to take up his task of discerning good and evil, of distinguishing the one from the other by reference to the goodness of God. He wishes to decide for himself what the good shall be. Inevitably, then, he is the man who ends up calling evil good and good evil. He is also the man who is not content to receive his own identity as a gift from God, a gift in which he and God cooperate at the deepest level of personhood (Rev. 2:17), but must determine who he is for himself and by himself. Inevitably, then, he is the man who must detach himself from reality, even from the reality of his own body, which was given him and not made by him (Farrow 2018g: 188ff.).

One telltale sign that this man is preparing his own definitive appearance in history, an appearance that cannot but be brief since it lacks all substance, is his hatred of the people of the covenant, the people who know that everything they have is a gift. Of course, in saying this we are doing more than complaining about contemporary anti-Semitic and anti-Christian movements. We are standing athwart modern philosophy of history as such, which wants to insist that history *is* progress without ever acknowledging the progress of evil or the mystery of lawlessness. One reason that so many Western "liberals" hate both Israel and the Church is that the latter stubbornly represent what all such thinking cannot abide: the knowledge that God, just because he is the great Giver, acts both in history and, where necessary, against history.

Another such sign is the state of the Church itself, quite apart from its own residual anti-Semitism. In the past half-millennium or more, and especially in the past century, and still more especially in the past few decades, there has been rebellion in it and defection from it on a massive scale. If we understand ἐκ μέσου γένηται to mean "emerge from the midst of those in whom the mystery of lawlessness is working," we certainly cannot exclude those who call themselves the people of God. The Danielic prototype does not permit that, any more than observable reality permits it. Our basic thesis, that the mystery of lawlessness depends on the evangelical mysteries, does not permit it. We introduce no novelty if we point this out. Antichrists go out from us, says John, because they are not of us. Augustine records the view that the mystery of iniquity is a mystery because it is hidden in the Church, with many members of the Church, until at last it proceeds forth from it, supplying antichrist with a great people; and that the faithful must be careful to remain faithful while this happens (*donec exeat de medio ecclesiae mysterium iniquitatis*, *Civ.* 20.19.3; cf. 1 John 2:18–19).

Theodoret suggests something similar when he identifies the mystery as taking the form of heresies and the advance of heretics, who keep "the snares of iniquity hidden" (2001: 129). For this view there is much to be said, though it must also be said that there is no basis for preferring a dynamic development of the mystery of lawlessness entirely inside the Church to a development that takes place both in the Church and in society at large through corresponding perversions of the gospel within and without. The latter option seems indeed much the more reasonable of the two, and better coheres with Paul's letter, which, despite its warning about the man of lawlessness seating himself in God's temple, does not attempt to fix its readers' attention on Church schisms. Schisms there must be, however, as Paul hints and Cyril explicitly warns, if the Antiochus scenario is to play itself out on the stage of the whole world. Of this the sixteenth century supplied a foretaste, and the present century seems set to follow suit. For the Church in our day is itself a house divided.

▨ That is not only by reason of the Protestant schisms. It is also by reason of those within the Catholic Church who have made quite clear that they intend to effect a reform from within rather than from without, meaning by "reform" the introduction of that very element of Protestantism that has, quite inevitably, divided Protestants: disdain for the binding nature of tradition, on which Paul is about to speak briefly (→2:15–17). Ironically, not a few Catholics today, being quite unwilling to face this problem now that it has penetrated to the heart of the Church, show signs of that very papolatry of which they were, in times past, falsely accused.   ▨

When this man does appear, he will be backed by false signs and wonders and by every wicked deceit (cf. Deut. 26:8; Matt. 24:24). One deceit that bears mention today, a deceit that is merely preparatory and requires no signs and wonders, is the secularist lie that there are spheres—particularly political spheres—in which the existence of God and the will of God need not be taken into account by man, indeed, *must* not be taken into account. No deceit could be more transparent, since this claim is really an assertion that if God exists at all, he is not such a God as could or would lay claim to the public sphere or to the political arena, which is manifestly a theological assertion and one entirely at odds with the biblical tradition (*CCC* §676; cf. Farrow 2015: 87ff.). It beggars belief that so many Jews and Christians have failed to see through this lie or to recognize its source in the father of lies, who wishes them to think that there is some "neutral ground on which to stand and wait" (Schwarz 2000: 386). Over this ground flies the tricolor flag of democracy and pluralism and solicitous care for human dignity, but alongside it waves the rainbow flag of sexual perversion and other symbols of his hatred of the truth and of the people of the covenant. Which do they suppose are his true colors? If they fall so easily for what is transparently false, what will they do when confronted with still more innovative claims that are backed by signs and wonders?

■ According to Rev. 13:1–4, a scene Signorelli does not fail to include and a text to which tradition has paid much attention (Hughes 2005: 43ff., 57ff.), the beast from the sea suffers a seemingly fatal blow from which, in a display of corporate *fortuna imperatoris* (Pieper 1999: 135f.), it makes an astonishing recovery that causes the inhabitants of all the earth to follow it with wonder. This has generally been taken to refer to the fate of the Roman Empire in the Christian era. Newman observes in his third lecture that the judgment that began in Jerusalem in AD 70 "steadily tracked its way for centuries round and round the world, till at length, with unerring aim, it smote the haughty mistress of the nations herself, the guilty woman seated upon the fourth monster which Daniel saw" (*DA* 83). The empire failed, through a great *defectio*, yet it did not quite die but was kept alive in its Christian hospice—always a very hopeful sort of place, as Pieper observes (1999: 85f.)—from which it must emerge to rise up one more time against Rome, the whore that used to rule it or try to rule it. And then comes antichrist, who will pick up the pieces for the sake of global order. "Antichrist is to head it; yet in another sense it dies to make way for Antichrist, and this latter form of death is surely hastening on, whether it comes sooner or later. It may outlast our time, and the time of our children; for we are creatures of a day, and a generation is like the striking of a clock; but it tends to dissolution, and its hours are numbered" (*DA* 103).

We recall this, just here, that we may note with Newman a prescient peculiarity in Hippolytus (*TCA* 27), who in treating the Danielic background "expressly says that the ten states which will at length appear, though kingdoms, shall also be democracies" (*DA* 72). Such are the ten toes of the image in Nebuchadnezzar's dream, among which we ourselves now live. But do we realize where and when we live? Is our situation sufficiently clear to us? Or has the advent of democracy lulled us to sleep and extinguished any sense that great matters are still afoot? Here among the "toes," are we even conscious of the great image looming above us? While Satan, says Newman, may soon "adopt the more alarming weapons of deceit," he may also hide himself for a time in things that seem to us quite ordinary and hardly worthy of close attention. "He may attempt to seduce us in little things, and so to move Christians, not all at once, but by little and little from their true position. We know he has done much in this way in the course of the last centuries. It is his policy to split us up and divide us, to dislodge us gradually from off our rock of strength." Too true. And is secularist democracy not a fit instrument for the pursuit of that policy? Does it not invite minglings without cohesion? Is it not being used to relativize and suppress the gospel? Is it not becoming increasingly bold in that suppression, even to the point of persecution?

"And if there is to be a persecution, perhaps it will be then; then, perhaps, when we are all of us in all parts of Christendom so divided, and so reduced, so full of schism, so close upon heresy. When we have cast ourselves upon the world, and depend for protection upon it, and have given up our independence and our strength, then he may burst upon us in fury, as far as God allows him" (*DA* 105f.).

Newman later appeals to Bishop Horsley's account of Christian apostasy, which is also prescient: "This desertion will begin in a professed indifference to any particular form of Christianity, under the pretence of universal toleration; which toleration will proceed from no true spirit of charity and forbearance, but from a design to undermine Christianity, by multiplying and encouraging sectaries. The pretended toleration will go far beyond a just toleration, even as it regards the different sects of Christians. For governments will pretend an indifference to all, and will give a protection in preference to none. All establishments will be laid aside. From the toleration of the most pestilent heresies, they will proceed to the toleration of Mahometanism, Atheism, and at last to a positive persecution of the truth of Christianity. In these times the Temple of God will be reduced almost to the Holy Place, that is, to the small number of real Christians who worship the Father in spirit and in truth, and regulate their doctrine and their worship, and their whole conduct, strictly by the word of God. The merely nominal Christians will all desert the profession of the truth, when the powers of the world desert it" (quoted in *DA* 107f.).

To suffer a great *defectio*, in other words, is also the fate of the Church. And here we may observe that Exod. 32 remains the paradigm of apostasy or defection where the people of God are concerned. It is as easy now, as it was then, to grow weary of waiting for the Master to descend from the mountain, to begin ignoring the words spoken "out of the midst of the fire on the day of the assembly" (ἡμέρᾳ ἐκκλησίας, Deut. 9:10 LXX; cf. Isa. 65:11–12), to become impatient, to seek some other way forward than the way God has pointed out to us. Or rather it is much easier yet. Christians "are not very good at such waiting" (Pelikan 2005: 43), and they have had a very long while to collect their trinkets and produce their rationalizations for ignoring what they were told. The Master who ascended, ascended long ago. Perhaps the whole idea of a Messiah, not to speak of a returning Messiah, is a myth—a myth that is best set aside now? The messianic imagination has been useful, to be sure, making possible conceptually a golden age of peace, a peace to be constructed in the future rather than consigned to some irretrievable past. But let us be honest about the fact that it represents a development of the human spirit rather than a divine promise, or a divine promise in the form of a development of the human spirit; more precisely, that it is a mythological product of the Axial Age, rather than a prophetic inspiration with a real fulfillment that we may now anticipate through some special intervention of God. And let us not forget that if messianism is dangerous in its utopian fervor, it is equally dangerous in the possibility of its collapse into nihilism (cf. Salvatore 2011). Messianism must be tamed, domesticated, democratized if it is still to be useful at all. After that? Well, we shall see.

So they speak among themselves, those of the *defectio*. But what the prophets foresee is a sudden collapse of democracy and an equally sudden revival of messianism, a tyrannical messianism.

As the final day of assembly approaches, they will indeed be confronted with signs and wonders, false signs and wonders produced for a satanic Sinai. And what will they do? They will assemble to antichrist rather than to Christ. When at last that lawless one is being unveiled, these signs and wonders will be given in abundance. What they will be like or how they will be offered is difficult to say. As when Moses and Aaron confronted Pharaoh and the magicians of Pharaoh, there will be signs appropriate to the times yet defying simple explanation; they will cause men to marvel. There will be devilry in them, as there was in Egypt, not merely technological prowess. Satan does not require human technology, though he certainly makes good use of it, to work his perverse wonders. ("Miracles," says Thomas in *S.2Th.* 2.2.50, "are called *lying* either because they fall short of the true nature of the supposed deed, or because they fall short of the true nature of a miracle, or because they fall short of the due end of a miracle," which is to glorify God. It is the third reason that matters here.) Then men will forget the warning of Jesus that no truly decisive sign is given to an apostate generation except the sign of the prophet Jonah—in this case, his suffering and decimated, yet still faithful, Church, which for three days and three nights, as it were, will lie still in the belly of Leviathan. This Church they will despise, despite the power of its testimony and the severe grace of preliminary judgments from God—the fire from heaven that destroyed Sodom and Gomorrah when God's patience ran out, the fire "the sons of thunder" called for before they had even begun to learn what patience is (cf. Mark 3:17; Luke 9:51–62; Rev. 16:8). Unmoved for long by these warnings or by their own sufferings, and still more impressed by the power of the man of lawlessness and his false signs and wonders, they will be like the subjects of Antiochus: "Then the king wrote to his whole kingdom that all should be one people, and that each should give up his customs. All the Gentiles accepted the command of the king. Many even from Israel gladly adopted his religion" (1 Macc. 1:41–43; cf. Rev. 11).

Here a further word must be said about Israel. Now, as then, some in Israel will make their peace with the man of lawlessness and his lawless ways, as will many in the Church. But now, as then, some will not. According to Paul, a great many will not. For long centuries, seed was cast to little effect on Israel's stony soil, and to much effect on the better soil of the nations. But now the situation will be reversed. The Gentiles who have not believed will hate the Gentiles who have believed, just as the Jews who did not believe once hated and hindered those who had. And the Jews who do believe will again help the Gentiles who believe. They will at the last repudiate their claim against Jesus, "We do not want this man to reign over us," and they will do so at the very point where the nations are saying, "We do not wish to be what God has called 'Man'" (Pieper 1999: 135, quoting Philipp Dessauer). For God, we are told, "will pour out on the house of David and the inhabitants of Jerusalem a spirit of compassion and supplication, so that, when they look on him whom they have pierced, they shall mourn for him, as one mourns for an only child." They shall wash in the font "opened for the house of David and the inhabitants of Jerusalem to cleanse them from sin and uncleanness" (Zech. 12:10; 13:1). On that day, the one-third that have been left alive, preserved like Daniel's friends through the refining fires of persecution, will call on the name of the Lord and he will answer them. He will say, "You are my people!" and they will say, "The LORD is our God!" (cf. 13:7–9; Farrow 2018a: 497f.). The ministry of his two witnesses, who, backed by genuine signs and wonders, will complete his prophetic task in Israel (Rev. 11:1–14; cf. Zech. 4:11–14), will see to it that when Jesus descends from heaven there will be those who have been brought out from the camp to greet him at the base of the holy mountain. The faithful dead of every generation will rise to join them. The question, "Who is on the LORD's side?" (Exod. 32:26), will receive a definitive answer from the living and the dead, among Jews as among Gentiles.

As for those Gentile Christians who congregate to antichrist rather than to Christ, they can expect nothing but the divine wrath as the reward for their apostasy. He who "did not spare the natural branches" when they declined to receive the Messiah will not spare them either (Rom. 11:21). And the man of lawlessness himself? He will be destroyed by the breath of Messiah's mouth (Isa. 11:4; cf. Fee 2009: 291). To borrow Luther's phrase, "a single word shall fell him." Antiochus III the Great, who established a divine ruler cult based on himself and his consort, met a gruesome fate in a temple of Baal near Susa, whose treasures he coveted. Antiochus IV Epiphanes, like Herod Agrippa who also fancied himself a god, was struck down suddenly by devastating disease (cf. 2 Macc. 9:5–6; Acts 12:22–23). Antiochus the Last, if we may assign that moniker to the man of lawlessness—or should we call him Tarquin the Proud (cf. Rev. 17:9–10)?—will be brought down far more dramatically by the display of our Lord's parousia. The angels shall bind him and the false prophet and cast both into hell (Rev. 19:17–21; cf. 20:7–10). Or, as Thomas puts it (*S.2Th.* 2.2.46), at our Lord's command

"Michael will kill him on Mount Olivet whence Christ ascended," settling his temporal fate, his eternal fate following in the bright light of the last judgment. Then shall be fulfilled, on a cosmic scale, what is foreshadowed of Jesus in Luke 13:17: "All his adversaries were put to shame; and all the people rejoiced at all the glorious things that were done by him."

We should not be so rash as to try to say what any of this will look like. Just as we do not know the day or the hour, and do not know exactly what will transpire beforehand during the ministry of the two witnesses and the antichrist's reign of terror, we do not know—it is quite impossible to know—what the disclosure of the Messiah from heaven will entail, except that it will entail the end of the whole order of things as we perceive it. Paul makes no further effort, beyond that of his first letter, to speak of this. Instead he directs our attention to the fact that those who will perish with the man of lawlessness will do so because they have been deceived by him, mistaking the false parousia for the true. How or why will they do that? Because they have not loved the truth, which would have saved them. And that is the case also with those who perish even before he has come, insofar as they prefer lies to truth and so help prepare the way for him. "Many will come in my name," says Jesus, meaning not only those who profess to *be* the anointed one, like Judas the Galilean before him or Simeon bar Kokhba after him, but false prophets of all kinds, including those who profess to further his own work and mission. Of these there are many today, even many in holy orders, twisting truth into lies and liberty into lawlessness.

Echoing Jesus's warning about "false Christs and false prophets" who sometimes "show great signs and wonders" (Matt. 24:24), the *Didache* counsels us to take care lest our love of the truth wane:

> But often shall you come together, seeking the things which are befitting to your souls: for the whole time of your faith will not profit you, if you be not made perfect in the last time. For in the last days false prophets and corrupters shall be multiplied, and the sheep shall be turned into wolves, and love shall be turned into hate; for when lawlessness increases, they shall hate and persecute and betray one another, and then shall appear the world-deceiver as the Son of God, and shall do signs and wonders, and the earth shall be delivered into his hands, and he shall do iniquitous things which have never yet come to pass since the beginning. Then shall the creation of men come into the fire of trial, and many shall be made to stumble and shall perish; but they that endure in their faith shall be saved from under the curse itself. And then shall appear the signs of the truth; first, the sign of an outspreading in heaven; then the sign of the sound of the trumpet; and the

third, the resurrection of the dead; yet not of all, but as it is said: The Lord shall come and all His saints with Him. Then shall the world see the Lord coming upon the clouds of heaven. (§16, in *ANF* 7:382)

The *Catechism of the Catholic Church* speaks in the same sobering vein: "Before Christ's second coming the Church must pass through a final trial that will shake the faith of many believers. The persecution that accompanies her pilgrimage on earth will unveil the 'mystery of iniquity' in the form of a religious deception offering men an apparent solution to their problems at the price of apostasy from the truth. The supreme religious deception is that of the Antichrist, a pseudomessianism by which man glorifies himself in place of God and of his Messiah come in the flesh" (§675). Otherwise put: by which man takes to himself "the pretension to rule history in place of the one who rules only as the crucified," forgetting that all such pretenders have already been disempowered by Christ's resurrection and ascension (Gunton 2002: 169).

2:11–14 **For this very reason God sends upon them a deluding influence, that they might credit the lie, so that they should be judged—all those who have not believed in the truth but taken pleasure in unrighteousness. But for you we ought always to render thanks to God, brethren beloved by the Lord, because he selected you as firstfruits for salvation in consecration of spirit and conviction of the truth, unto which he called you through our gospel for possession of glory, [the glory] of our Lord Jesus Christ.**

"Let no one by any means deceive you," writes Paul at 2:3, and now he closes the envelope there opened, the envelope in which he has deposited his explanation of the necessity for delay, by remarking that God will send upon the apostate an ἐνέργειαν πλάνης, a deluding influence, an energetic error, a misleading zeitgeist, a wind of wandering that will blow them ever further off course, carrying them to the very edge of the abyss. Under this influence they will be persuaded to embrace the lie and to believe what is manifestly false, to enter ever more deeply into the mystery of lawlessness and even to swallow the preposterous self-deification of the man of lawlessness. Thus will they be ripened for judgment, a judgment they will deserve because they have repudiated the truth and preferred the lie, reveling in their own unrighteousness. Because they have not loved the truth, because they have willingly "exchanged the truth about God for a lie" (Rom. 1:25), he will allow the lie to have free rein among them. He will not himself deceive them, for he is

Truth and cannot lie. He will not even withdraw from them his witnesses to the truth, but send them Elijah as he once sent John the Baptist (cf. Chrysostom, in *Hom.* 4 on 2 Thessalonians, who emphasizes the restored confidence Elijah will bring to the faithful). Yet he will permit the father of lies to have his way with them, to blind their minds and lead them to destruction (2 Cor. 4:3–4). What they want, he will grant them.

▨ As Aquinas says, "their sin and punishment is their deception," while "the punishment only is eternal damnation" (*S.2Th.* 2.3.54). He points us to Isa. 19:14, "The LORD has mingled within her [Egypt] a spirit of confusion," and to 1 Kings 22:19–23, where God permits a spirit to entice Ahab into battle by becoming "a lying spirit in the mouth of all his prophets." Note that God reveals this to Ahab through Micaiah, for God does not lie. Yet Ahab does not believe God, for he has been given over to a base and reprobate mind; he disguises himself and enters the fray, where he is slain. Note, further, that the confusion God permits in Egypt, he permits also in Israel. He permits it likewise in the Church, though never without sending Micaiah or, at the last, Elijah. And he does not permit it for those who abide in his love: "The beloved of the LORD, he dwells in safety by him" (Deut. 33:12; cf. Fee 2009: 299). ▨

The lie at bottom is that God need not be thanked or served, that his word need not be obeyed, because his motives are false and he wishes to suppress rather than perfect man. That is the lie that was told in the garden, and it is the lie that is still being told. "Establish your own identity! Worship and serve yourselves! You shall be as gods!" Since they credit this lie, and obey the liar who told it, God gives them up to its effects and consequences. It is not just that they trip all over themselves in this false service. It is not just that they become "foolish, faithless, heartless, ruthless," pushing each other to new lows, heaping up their sins, spelunking in caves of depravity. It is not just that they want wrongly and receive "in their own persons the due penalty for their error," spoiling their own souls and dishonoring their own bodies, even to the denial of souls and resentment of bodies. It is also that they prepare themselves through all this, through their greed "which is idolatry" (Col. 3:5), to do Satan's bidding: to side with antichrist, to assemble to antichrist, to choose antichrist rather than Christ to reign over them. They make themselves dupes of Satan and of the man of lawlessness, party to the latter's persecutions and to his blasphemous crimes. This happens slowly at first, through experimental prototypes, but all too rapidly at the end. And when it has happened, judgment, richly deserved judgment, shall fall on them, as on him.

They will come with dread when their sins are reckoned up,
    and their lawless deeds will convict them to their face.
Then the righteous man will stand with great confidence
    in the presence of those who have afflicted him,
    and those who make light of his labors.
When they see him, they will be shaken with dreadful fear,
    and they will be amazed at his unexpected salvation.
They will speak to one another in repentance,
    and in anguish of spirit they will groan, and say,
"This is the man whom we once held in derision
    and made a byword of reproach—we fools!
We thought that his life was madness
    and that his end was without honor.
Why has he been numbered among the sons of God?
    And why is his lot among the saints?
So it was we who strayed from the way of truth,
    and the light of righteousness did not shine on us,
    and the sun did not rise upon us.
We took our fill of the paths of lawlessness and destruction,
    and we journeyed through trackless deserts,
    but the way of the Lord we have not known . . ."

The hope of the ungodly man is like chaff carried by the wind,
    and like a light hoarfrost driven away by a storm;
it is dispersed like smoke before the wind,
    and it passes like the remembrance of a guest who stays but a day.
But the righteous live for ever,
    and their reward is with the Lord;
    the Most High takes care of them.
Therefore they will receive a glorious crown
    and a beautiful diadem from the hand of the Lord,
because with his right hand he will cover them,
    and with his arm he will shield them.
The Lord will take his zeal as his whole armor,
    and will arm all creation to repel his enemies;
he will put on righteousness as a breastplate,
    and wear impartial justice as a helmet;
he will take holiness as an invincible shield,
    and sharpen stern wrath for a sword,
    and creation will join with him to fight against the madmen.

> Shafts of lightning will fly with true aim,
>> and will leap to the target as from a well-drawn bow of clouds,
>> and hailstones full of wrath will be hurled as from a catapult;
> the water of the sea will rage against them,
>> and rivers will relentlessly overwhelm them;
> a mighty wind will rise against them,
>> and like a tempest it will winnow them away.
> Lawlessness will lay waste the whole earth,
> and evil-doing will overturn the thrones of rulers.
>> (Wis. 4:20–5:7; 5:14–23)

Men of lawlessness, rebels against God, shall find that even the lower nature, over which they thought they had dominion and should have had dominion, will rebel against them. This is described in the Apocalypse. But so will higher nature, as the same book testifies and as Paul has already testified. The heavenly host will rise up against them. When the lie has reigned and the righteous have suffered, the Lord himself will appear with that host, meting out his righteous judgment, "meting out vengeance on those refusing to recognize God and to obey the gospel of our Lord Jesus" (2 Thess. 1:8), while bringing salvation to those who do.

> Vengeance is mine, and recompense,
>> for the time when their foot shall slip;
> for the day of their calamity is at hand,
>> and their doom comes swiftly.
> For the LORD will vindicate his people
>> and have compassion on his servants,
> when he sees that their power is gone,
>> and there is none remaining, bond or free. (Deut. 32:35–36)

At this point Paul strikes again his opening note, this time with a new emphasis: "For *you* we ought always to render thanks to God" (2:13, which leads with Ἡμεῖς; cf. 1:3). He thus invites them to recall that earlier assurance, "To this very end we pray always for you, that our God may deem you worthy of the call and powerfully fulfill every aspiration to goodness and work of faith, so that the name of our Lord Jesus might be glorified in you, and you in him, according to the grace of our God and the Lord Jesus Christ" (1:11–12). The Thessalonians were selected by God personally as firstfruits of the harvest of salvation from among both Jews and Gentiles, like the believers in Antioch who were first to be called Christians. (In 2:13, some texts have ἀπ' ἀρχῆς, "from the beginning," for ἀπαρχήν, "firstfruits," but the idea is the same; cf. 1 Cor. 15:20; Jas. 1:18.) They were chosen "for salvation in consecration of spirit and conviction of the truth." (Most translations render ἐν ἁγιασμῷ πνεύματος "through sanctification by the Spirit" rather than "in consecration of spirit," but again the idea is the same, since the human act rests on the divine act; cf. 1 Thess. 3:13; 4:3–8; 5:23. What Fee 2009: 300 calls "the first of nearly forty proto-Trinitarian soteriological moments in Paul's letters" is somewhat muted, however, by maintaining here the synonymous parallelism between ἁγιασμῷ πνεύματος and πίστει ἀληθείας.) This consecration or conviction is a work of the Holy Spirit, a work of God who sanctifies them in their entirety, preserving them blameless in their "whole spirit, soul, and body." The spirit of error that energizes the mystery of lawlessness and the man of lawlessness leads to destruction, but sanctification in the truth leads to salvation, to a share in the kingdom and glory of Jesus Christ (→1 Thess. 2:12).

2:15–17 So then, brethren, stand fast and cling to the traditions you were taught, whether in person or through our letter. And may our Lord Jesus Christ himself, and God our Father, who loved us and in [his] grace gave [us] eternal comfort and good hope, encourage your hearts and confirm you in every good work and word.

Those who think their steadfastness already amply demonstrated may well suppose the day of the Lord to be at hand, not only in principle but in fact, not merely imminently but immediately. It has been the major burden of this second letter to make clear, however, that the negative correlates of divine justice—the maturation of evil and the appearance of the man of lawlessness who is ripe for judgment— have yet to be realized, hence that the conditions for the final exercise of justice have yet to be met. The Just One will judge justly, which means also that he will judge nothing before its time (1 Cor. 4:5), and the time has not yet come. Now that the Thessalonians have a better grasp of this, now that the inner dynamics of the times and turning points that lead to the parousia are clearer to them, Paul returns to the task of inculcating perseverance "in every good work and word," joining his second letter securely to his first. (Even the military imagery in 1 Thess. 5 reappears here with στήκετε; cf. Malherbe 2000: 439.) He knows, though he does not say, that Daniel fainted with foreboding. He knows that, according to Jesus, many will faint with fear. He understands that it is altogether necessary to inculcate courage and perseverance in the people of God. For what is already bad enough will get worse, and there still lies ahead a time to bear testimony

(Luke 21:13). Now, then, is the time to "strengthen the weak hands, and make firm the feeble knees," to "say to those who are of a fearful heart, 'Be strong, fear not! Behold, your God will come with vengeance, with the recompense of God. He will come and save you'" (Isa. 35:3–4). Now is the time to say, Stand fast!

▨ In Abram's patient waiting for God to arrive and ratify the covenant, and in his driving away of the birds of prey that descended upon the divided carcasses laid out for the purpose (Gen. 15), Augustine finds a promise that the last heirs of the covenant will indeed stand fast. For "even among these divisions of the carnal against the carnal, the truly faithful will persevere to the end." And in the smoking fire pot and flaming torch that passed between the pieces, he finds a foreshadowing of that final coming of God, in salvation and judgment, for which they stand fast. "For, just as the dark dread that came over Abraham toward sunset—that is, as the end of the world was approaching—signifies the affliction of the city of God that is expected to come under Antichrist, such affliction as there never was before, so also this fire, appearing as the sun was actually setting—that is, at the actual end of the world—signifies the day of judgment, separating those of the carnal who are to be saved by fire from those of the carnal who are to be damned in fire" (*Civ.* 16.24, trans. Babcock). Yet it is only "when nature has failed and is at an end that God's work is clear" (16.28). Therefore, when all seems lost, just then the call to stand fast must go forth again. ▨

The traditions in question, passed on orally or by letter (διὰ λόγου εἴτε δι' ἐπιστολῆς), serve as stabilizers. They are what Paul had taught them about the gospel, the sacraments, and the moral life (Wright 2002: 150). They are the biblical, dominical, and apostolic teachings vouchsafed to all properly prepared catechumens, as summarized in the *Didache*, in the Apostles' Creed, and eventually in the Nicene Creed (*CL* 5.12). They are the crucial theological affirmations developed and applied by the ecumenical councils. They are the things guarded, or that ought to be guarded, by the successors of Peter, the things that help make sense of the confession of Jesus as "the Christ, the Son of the living God" (Matt. 16:16). They are the things lauded and prayed in the divine liturgy, wherever the liturgy remains divine. They are authentic readings of holy scripture, known to be authentic by their harmony with what has been said everywhere and always in the Church. They are the spiritual disciplines that the Church has hallowed, the moral virtues it has inculcated, and that whole "divine training" the goal of which is "love that issues from a pure heart and a good conscience and sincere faith" (1 Tim. 1:3–7; *ST* 3.25.3, ad 4).

These traditions have come under attack from the beginning and are now facing a fearful assault from both inside and outside the Church. One way they are assaulted today is virtually opposite to the way that concerns Paul in the present letter, and more like that identified in Peter's second letter. For it is not so much by foolish talk about the day of the Lord having already arrived that the traditions are now undermined, as by failure to keep in mind that it *will* arrive and that it is drawing ever nearer. That failure is a failure to recognize the night and the darkness. It is to pretend that night is day and darkness light. It is the "onwards and upwards" narrative of those who have baptized the cult of progress—the deceptive narrative that offers "eternal comfort and good hope" not from above, not from the grace of God, who loves us and gave his only Son for us, but rather from below, through the myth that belongs to the mystery of lawlessness. In that cult and according to that myth, we know better than our forefathers in the faith. We stand above tradition, which in our advanced state we may modify more or less freely to keep abreast of the times. Neither by word nor by letter are we bound.

▨ This spirit emerged among the nominalists in the early years of the second millennium. It took firmer shape in the Protestant Reformation and loomed large in the new reformation of the Enlightenment. It prevails today, and characterizes what some are calling the Francis reformation. (All three, curiously, originated in Germany, though the father of nominalism was the French philosopher and theologian Roscelin, and it was Teilhard de Chardin who eventually gave eschatological shape to this cross-denying spirit that confuses the grace of God with the aspirations of fallen man; see Farrow 2018e and, for a contemporary example, Rohr 2019.) The man imbued with it is the man who will call lawlessness "law" and antichrist "Christ," extending a false hope and comfort in place of the true, that he may move others to adopt the same posture and take up the same practices.

To stand fast is to refuse this. It is not to stand motionless, however, or to be "rigid" or stuck in the past (to use a favorite expression of Pope Francis). Far from it. For standing fast means holding to all three articles of the creed and faithfully living their implications. It means affirming the goodness of creation, hence also of growth and change, and hoping in God to see his creatures through to their proper ends. "The Christian attitude to history," insists Pieper (1999: 149), "contains both affirmation of creation and readiness for the blood-testimony; only the man who combines in himself this affirmation and this readiness will retain the possibility of historical activity, arising out of a genuine inner impulse, even in the midst of the catastrophe." Chrysostom was thinking along the same lines: "This is the comfort of Christians, to do something good and pleasing to God," who quickens them with hope. "For when any one is not [shaken or] turned aside, he bears all things, whatever may happen to him, with much longsuffering; whereas if his mind be shaken, he will no longer perform any good or noble action, but like one whose hands are paralyzed, so also his soul is shaken, when it is not fully persuaded that it is advancing to some good end" (*Hom.* 4).   ▓

Those who do not cling to the apostolic traditions, whatever justification they offer for not doing so—be it biblicism or determination to bring the Church up to date, to effect some groundbreaking *aggiornamento*—do not stand fast. They either open themselves to the lie or are already crediting the lie. Whether they stand in some sectarian corner or sit on an episcopal throne concerns only the degree, not the character, of their fault. Whatever protestations are made, precisely what is wanting is love of the truth. After observing that his disciples "are not of the world," Jesus prays: "Sanctify them in the truth; your word is truth. As you sent me into the world, so I have sent them into the world. And for their sake I consecrate myself, that they also may be consecrated in truth" (John 17:16–19). The apostolic traditions, the things handed down, are the means of consecration. Those who let them go will sooner or later pass from worshiping the true God falsely to worshiping a false one truly. In the end, should they come to the end, they will find themselves caught up in the worship of antichrist, the man of lawlessness, the son of perdition who loves all things only for his own sake and not at all for God's, and so falsifies the truth of each thing. And that worship will lead them to perdition.

3:1–5 It remains to say: Pray, brethren, for us, that the word of the Lord may advance triumphantly, just as it did among you, and that we may be rescued from perverse and evil men; for the faith is not [the faith] of all. But the Lord is faithful, who will steady you and protect you from the evil one. And we are convinced in the Lord about you, that you are following our directives and will continue to do so. May the Lord guide your hearts in the love of God and the constancy of Christ.

Thus commences the conclusion of Paul's correspondence with the Thessalonians, when his itinerant and epistolary ministry was still in its fledgling stage. The ambassadors of the Lord request petitions to the Lord that their mission may prosper, that his gospel might τρέχη καὶ δοξάζηται—that it might run ahead of him and be celebrated, becoming victorious among the nations. That request would be pointless were their mission conducted in territory that did not already belong to him. But all territory, all life, all peoples, belong to him now (Matt. 28:18–20). Those who pray, then, seek what is in his power to grant (→1 Thess. 5:23–24; cf. John 14:12–14). They seek from him what concerns him before it concerns them, the glorification of God for which the world was made. "I give you thanks, O LORD, with my whole heart; before the angels I sing your praise," says the psalmist. "I bow down toward your holy temple and give thanks to your name for your mercy and your faithfulness; for you have exalted above everything your name and your word" (138:1–2).

Paul seeks nothing less and nothing else. The conclusion of his correspondence with Timothy at the end of his ministry, not long before he laid his head to rest on Nero's block, testifies that the very same desire and goal are still on his mind. "The Lord stood by me," he writes after his first defense in the imperial court, "and gave me strength to proclaim the word fully, that all the Gentiles might hear it" (2 Tim. 4:17).

> On the day I called, you answered me,
>   my strength of soul you increased.
> All the kings of the earth shall praise you, O LORD,
>   for they have heard the words of your mouth;
> and they shall sing of the ways of the LORD,
>   for great is the glory of the LORD. (Ps. 138:3–5)

As the book of Acts is designed to show, the word of the Lord had by then advanced triumphantly from Jerusalem to Rome, turning the world upside down, with Paul "preaching the kingdom of God and teaching about the Lord Jesus Christ quite openly and unhindered" in Caesar's own city for some two years before his trial (28:31; cf. 1 Thess. 2:11–13). The prayers of the Thessalonians and of all who besought the Lord on his behalf were thus gloriously answered, and even the Caesars themselves would one day be numbered among those who sing of the ways of the Lord.

How sharply this contrasts with so much contemporary "witness" to Christ in our own place and time, and with what passes these days for the prayers of the people, which too often are no more than banalities about peace and justice and feeling included. Do we no longer believe in the mission? Do we no longer consider it our business, or indeed God's business, to exalt the name of Christ? Have we lost all confidence in the power of his word? Then we ourselves have been hindered by perverse and evil men, who have taught us not to be too quickly shaken or disturbed by God himself, and have led us away into somniferous myths about peace and progress. That would explain why we, for our part, no longer follow a great many of Paul's directives and why 2 Thessalonians in particular is scarcely read in our churches, much less expounded with understanding. It would explain why our priests and pastors no longer heed Paul's closing words to his colleague in mission: "I charge you in the presence of God and of Christ Jesus who is to judge the living and the dead, and by his appearing and his kingdom: preach the word, be urgent in season and out of season, convince, rebuke, and exhort, be unfailing in patience and in teaching." For we are those who live in the time he said was coming, the time "when people will not endure sound teaching, but having itching ears . . . will accumulate for themselves teachers to suit their own likings, and will turn away from listening to the truth and wander into myths" (2 Tim. 4:1–5; cf. 1 Tim. 6:3–10).

To Timothy he adds, "As for you, always be steady, endure suffering, do the work of an evangelist, fulfil your ministry." And here already at the end of 2 Thessalonians, where Paul has one eye on the road ahead and the other on those whom he and Silvanus and Timothy have left behind, it is steadiness he desires to see in them. Steadiness is what they, like the apostles, require—steadiness of faith, steadiness of nerve, steadiness in witness—a steadiness that can only come from God. Turning the world upside down is not for the squeamish or the unsteady. Bearing witness to Christ, even to being crushed under the barrage of persecutions that are thus shaken out of the world, is not for the squeamish or unsteady. Glorifying God's name and God's word in a world that does not know or acknowledge God, a world in which the evil one is at work hindering the gospel wherever and however he can, is not for the unsteady. "Therefore lift your drooping hands and strengthen your weak knees." "Be grateful for receiving a kingdom that cannot be shaken" and offer to God "acceptable worship, with reverence and awe" (Heb. 12:12, 28).

But let us return to the text before us and attend more closely. The Thessalonians have need of deliverance from their persecutors—that will happen in due course, at the appearance of him who is to come again in glory to judge the quick and the dead—and also from those who have upset and alarmed them with false rumors of that coming. Paul has sought in this letter to rescue them from the latter. Now he covets their prayers both for the continued success of the apostolic mission and for the apostles' own deliverance from those perverse and evil men who are determined to arrest that mission. "For the faith is not common to all" (οὐ γὰρ πάντων ἡ πίστις) or "the faith," the true faith, "is not the faith of all." This is a litotes, a deliberate understatement, negatively expressed, that strikes a somewhat ironic note (cf. Weima 2014: 590). The word has a long way yet to run, in other words, and it is running a race fiercely contested by those Jews and Gentiles who, as his readers know all too well, detest it as something subversive of their way of life. It is also in turn a target for subversion, as some seek to bend it to their own purposes. It is not merely by enthusiasts with an inadequate understanding of biblical eschatology that a threat to the faith is posed.

"*The* faith," not faith or faithfulness, though πίστις can mean either. *Pace* Marshall (1983: 198), the definite article points to *fides quae* before it points to *fides qua*. In the last analysis, however, it comes to the same thing. Not all have faith, and not all who say they have faith are faithful to the faith. Where *fides qua* is lacking—the faith that the Spirit gives as a form of participation in Christ (→1 Thess. 1:2–5)—so usually is sound knowledge of what ought to be believed, of what one must cling to in order to stand fast. This correlativity between *fides qua* and *fides quae* puts the lie to universalism, just as it puts the lie to the Judaizing of the Judaizers: "I am astonished that you are so quickly deserting him who called you in the grace of Christ and turning to a different gospel—not that there is another gospel, but there are some who trouble you and want to pervert the gospel of Christ. But even if we, or an angel from heaven, should preach to you a gospel contrary to that which we preached to you, let him be accursed. As we have said before, so now I say again, If any one is preaching to you a gospel contrary to that which you received, let him be accursed" (Gal. 1:6–9; cf. 5:6–12). For strength to outrun and grace to outlast such accursed people, Paul is seeking the Thessalonians' prayers.

That men resist the grace and goodness of God, assaulting the faith that can save them, shows them to be perverse and evil, be they Jews falsifying the faith of Moses, such as those whom Satan used to prevent Paul from returning to Thessaloniki; or Christians falsifying the faith of Jesus, such as Hymenaeus and Alexander, whom Paul "delivered to Satan that they may learn not to blaspheme" (1 Tim. 1:20; cf. 2 Tim. 4:14); or pagans stirring up opposition in the name of some false god by which they are prospering, as did Demetrius the silversmith (Acts 19). To the middle category endless examples can now be added from among the gnostics and Arians and Islamists and their modern counterparts, who for all their diversity are united in a common movement of corruption and apostasy, a movement (as Manning observes in his first lecture) that "has accumulated its results from age to age, and that at this time . . . is more mature and has a loftier stature and a greater power and a more formal antagonism to the Church and the faith than ever before" (1861: 19). The man of lawlessness will give it its final form when he attempts to seat himself in "the city of God, the house of God, the temple of God" (*Civ.* 18.47), lauded no doubt by men of the cloth, even of red or purple cloth; for among them also the true faith is not the faith of all. The full measure of his perversity and theirs can only be taken by reference to the Faithful One himself, of whom the faith, if it is the faith, always speaks. He it is who embodies the divine constancy and who remains faithful even when men are faithless, "for he cannot deny himself" or the Father from whom he came (2 Tim. 2:13). "The testimony of Jesus is the spirit of prophecy" (Rev. 19:10).

Paul adroitly moves from requesting prayer for protection from men of perverse faith to promising protection to those of genuine faith, the protection of Jesus. Jesus is capable of keeping us calm and vigilant at our posts. He is capable of delivering us from the evil one, for which deliverance he taught us to pray (→1 Thess 2:17–20; cf. Marshall 1983: 200). Those who can see heaven opened, as eventually for better or worse all will, can already see what John saw: "Behold, a white horse! He who sat upon it is called Faithful and True, and in righteousness he judges and makes war" (Rev. 19:11). Those who cannot can still plead, "Lead us not into temptation." They can still ask that their hearts be guided in the love of God and in the constancy of Christ. As they ought to do, since many things there are "that turn us aside from love, and many paths that draw us away from thence. . . . For this is to love God: to endure, and not to be troubled" (Chrysostom, *Hom.* 5).

▨ Aquinas is equally succinct: "Now there are two things through which we advance on the way of salvation, namely the good things we do and the bad things we endure. But works are not good unless they are directed to the goal of love" (*S.2Th.* 3.1.68). Both these commentators take the genitival phrase "love of God" as objective rather than subjective, understanding the guidance or direction in question as enabling our proper response *to* God in Christ, through loving him and loving him consistently, even under pressure. The second genitival phrase, "constancy of Christ" (καὶ εἰς τὴν ὑπομονὴν τοῦ Χριστοῦ), would then seem to be subjective, for it is a share in Christ's own strength and an *imitatio Christi* that is in view. The alternative, which makes both genitives subjective, such that Jesus guides us in allowing *God's* love, as well as his own constancy, to work in and through us, fits the context equally well. But if Paul is alluding here to David's prayer in 1 Chron. 29 (cf. Fee 2009: 322), if he too is thinking of God's people "offering freely and joyously" to God what is God's own, trusting God to instill in them his own "purposes and thoughts" and to "direct their hearts" to himself (29:17–18), then we should probably not confine ourselves to one or the other of these alternatives, but read the genitives both ways. Only thus will we arrive at the full sense.

However we read it, we should not overlook the relevance of this passage to the very act of prayer, which is, in the first place a beseeching of the Father that his name be hallowed, his kingdom come, his will be done on earth, as already in heaven; and, in the second place, a pleading for ourselves, that the requisite advance on the kingdom, and safe conduct to it, be granted. This is the kind of prayer Paul seeks here, and he seeks people to pray who are taught by Christ himself how to do so; who are taught also by the Holy Spirit, who "helps us in our weakness." Since so often "we do not know how to pray as we ought," the Spirit also "intercedes for us with sighs too deep for words . . . according to the will of God" (Rom. 8:26–27), which ought to make us constant in prayer despite our weakness. It is true that we have only a limited knowledge of the will of God and of the shape of his kingdom, and only an imperfect desire for God and his kingdom. But we must not throw up our hands and say, like the wicked servant in the parable of the talents, "You reap where you do not sow; you do not require my prayers." For our safe conduct to the kingdom is a process of learning the love of God and the constancy of Christ, which cannot be done without prayer. That we stumble in our lessons; that neither our words nor our intentions are properly conformed as yet; that we do not as yet see God, like the saints in glory, with God's own eyes or hear him with his own ears; that we do not know fully even what is in our own mind, never mind what is in the mind of God; that our knowledge of self and our knowledge of God are alike confused at many points; that we desperately need those sighs of the Spirit, especially when they are most inaudible and inaccessible to us—is no reason not to pray, but rather a reason to pray. For only what is in motion toward God can be directed.

3:6–12 And we command you, brethren, in the name of the Lord Jesus Christ, to withdraw yourselves from every brother living in a disorderly manner and not in accord with the traditions you received from us. For you yourselves know how it is proper to imitate us: We were not undisciplined among you, nor did we consume anyone's bread like freeloaders, but [were among you] rather as those who labored, with toil and trouble night and day, so as not to be a burden to any of you—not that we had no right [to impose on you], but [we behaved as we did] in order that we might make ourselves an example to you, that you might imitate us. For even when we were with you, we were issuing this order, that if anyone refuses to work, neither shall he eat. Yet we hear that some among you are [indeed] disorderly, doing no work but the work of interfering with others. To such as these, we command and exhort in the Lord Jesus Christ that, working with quietness, their own bread they should eat [not another's].

The present directives elaborate on 1 Thess. 2:9; 4:9–12; and 5:14, employing the same language but much more forcefully. They are, perhaps, like some of the directives with which the first letter concludes, addressed first of all to the presbyters; but, if so, very much in the hearing of all the brethren, among whom are some whose behavior is still disorderly and disruptive, despite the fact that they too have received clear instructions as to how Christians must live. (Some manuscripts have "they" or "he" for the second "you" in 3:6; see Weima 2014: 629.) Paul uses the adverb ἀτάκτως twice in this paragraph and the verb ἀτακτέω once. Though commentators make much of "the problem of the idle," and though these words certainly point to such a problem, the idea is broader than that. Disorderliness, unruliness, troublemaking—soldiers of Christ who lack the appropriate discipline and shirk their duty, who disregard authority and tradition, whose idea of comradeship is to consume the rations of others and to have a bit of fun at their expense, or to stir up dissent and grumbling—that is the spirit and manner of life Paul is rebuking here. In doing so he uses παραγγέλλω ("command" or "order") three times, accompanied in the third usage by παρακαλέω ("urge" or "exhort"), for of course the army of Christ is a brotherhood of faith, not a band of conscripts to be whipped into line.

It is not as if "the hand of the diligent will rule, while the slothful will be put to forced labor" (Prov. 12:24). Were it so in the Church, Paul would not have had to repeat himself so often. Nor his commentators, for that matter, though the present one must confess the fault as his own.

In the communal life of the churches, however, as in the liturgy at the heart of that life, good order must prevail (1 Cor. 11–14). How can a church fulfill its ambassadorial mission if the kingdom it represents appears to be a kingdom of chaos, or of slackers, freeloaders, and busybodies? That authority in the church extends as far as instructions about decent order in daily affairs will surprise no one who grasps its mission. Anyone who understands the gospel—"for you know the grace of our Lord Jesus Christ, that though he was rich, yet for your sake he became poor, so that by his poverty you might become rich" (2 Cor. 8:9)—will also understand the vehemence with which Paul later complains to Timothy about a certain kind of slacker: "If any one does not provide for his relatives, and especially for his own family, he has disowned the faith and is worse than an unbeliever" (1 Tim. 5:8). He takes, he receives, but he returns nothing. He makes promises and does not keep them. He undermines the welfare of his family and of his community. What we have called "the economy of gift" grinds to a halt with him. Moreover, he often diverts the energy that ought to have gone into his work to disrupting the work or lives of others. "He who is slack in his work is a brother to him who destroys" (Prov. 18:9).

Idleness and indiscipline, as everyone knows, tend to troublemaking. "Put him to work, that he may not be idle, for idleness teaches much evil" (Sir. 33:27). "And therfore seith seint Ierome: 'doth somme gode dedes, that the devel which is our enemy ne finde yow nat unoccupied.' For the devel ne taketh nat lightly un-to his werkinge swiche as he findeth occupied in gode werkes" (Chaucer, "The Tale of Melibeus" §51). Therefore saith Saint Paul himself that we should work with quietness and pray without ceasing. "With quietness" (μετὰ ἡσυχίας) does not mean silently or solitarily, as in hesychasm, but humbly and harmoniously; that is, responsibly, minding one's own affairs with the good of others in view (→1 Thess. 4:9–12; in that light, cf. 1 Tim. 2:11–12). The monastic movement as a whole sought to realize that ideal by way of a still more highly ordered life than parishes could provide, and on its success rested the renewal of an entire civilization (see Woods 2012). On discipline, hard work, and generosity, on following the example of the apostles, rested the future success of the mission in Thessaloniki. That their presbyters in particular should build on the foundations of that example was, in Paul's mind, not merely proper (as in any community that practices psychagogy or prizes spiritual friendship) but also necessary if the economy of gift was to take hold and flourish. Sometimes the righteous, though they give and do not hold back, must hold back from the sluggardly (cf. Prov. 21:25–26; 2 Cor. 9:6).

Paul acknowledges the principle that those who devote themselves to overseeing the mission and life of a church are worthy, not only of hospitality but of remuneration—it is not as if we had no right to your support, he says—and he defends that principle again to Timothy when the latter has oversight of overseers: "Let the elders who rule well be considered worthy of double honor, especially those who labor in preaching and teaching; for the Scripture says, 'You shall not muzzle an ox when it is treading out the grain,' and, 'The laborer deserves his wages'" (1 Tim. 5:17–18). But he points out to the Thessalonians that, in their own case, he and Silvanus and Timothy had waived its application precisely in order to kick-start their Christian economy. Now he orders that those who are undermining that economy by abusing the hospitality of the brethren should be marginalized. Orders are given to withdraw from them all support, even that of ordinary friendship. Those who abuse accompaniment, to employ that popular and much-abused term, are not to be accompanied any longer.

▨ The eucharistic economy, as we have already had occasion to note, transcends the economy of friendship, hospitality, and gift-giving expounded so admirably by Cicero, which the early Christians inherited and incorporated but also extensively revised by resituating it within the larger economy of salvation and the morality of the two great commandments (cf. Malherbe 2000: 256ff.). "Friendship itself, lived according to the Christian ideal" of charity, as a process of mutual sanctification in Christ, is integral to the Christian mission (André Marie 2006: 2). So, then, is its defense from those who would abuse it. As Paul knows, even Cicero's economy cannot function without the element of self-sufficiency, which requires a willingness to work. As for the economy of Christ, it requires a willingness to work in order to give: "Let the thief no longer steal, but rather let him labor, doing honest work with his hands, so that he may be able to give to those in need" (Eph. 4:28; cf. Ezek. 16:49). On the need to withdraw from those who refuse to work, Paul is about to remark further. Meanwhile, we may remark what he doesn't; namely, that the good, whether of oneself or of others, also requires rational limits around work.

This means, first of all, respect for the Sabbath. God's "rest" from creative activity permits creaturely freedom, so that man may also be a creator of sorts. But man, too, is to rest, turning freely from his own concerns and responsibility, in which he becomes over-absorbed, in order to fulfill his obligation of thanksgiving and to be reminded of the ground of his being and the goal of his work. "For we are his workmanship, created in Christ Jesus for good works, which God prepared beforehand, that we should walk in them" (Eph. 2:10). Work, whether of a mundane or a spiritual kind, belongs to the *imago dei*. It is not a product of the fall or of the curse, but it certainly suffers from both. Only work that is performed in the light of the Lord's day, which the Lord gives us to praise him with happy voices and to anticipate the eternal rest of that day when he shall "be glorified through all the worlds" (*Phos hilaron*), will be work that is redemptive rather than destructive. Work becomes destructive whenever it is no longer subject to the principle of charity or subservient to the goal of reaching the divine rest (Eccl. 12:13–14.; cf. Heb. 13:1–7 and 13:16), but is instead a means of evasion or an attempt to squeeze from this world what can no longer be found in it. "There is great gain in godliness with contentment; for we brought nothing into the world, and we cannot take anything out of the world; but if we have food and clothing, with these we shall be content. But those who desire to be rich fall into temptation, into a snare, into many senseless and hurtful desires that plunge men into ruin and destruction. For the love of money is the root of all evils; it is through this craving that some have wandered away from the faith and pierced their hearts with many pangs" (1 Tim. 6:6–10). And again: "No one can serve two masters; for either he will hate the one and love the other, or he will be devoted to the one and despise the other. You cannot serve God and mammon. ... But seek first his kingdom and his righteousness, and all these things shall be yours as well" (Matt. 6:24–33).

Second, it means responsibility to balance different kinds of work. The replacing of work by undisciplined play or amusement is one way to shirk our greatness under God and our duty before God. Another is to allow the less important to shoulder aside the more important, as when career work, even in support of marriage and family, displaces the work proper to marriage and family; or household work, even the work of hospitality, displaces the labor of love for the things of God (Luke 10:38–42). What Aquinas says on 1 Thess.

4:11 applies here also: "Things occur in a disorderly manner if they are not governed within the limits of reason, for example, when somebody drives himself excessively; they occur in an orderly manner if the dictates of reason are observed in regulating them. The latter is commendable" (*S. 1 Th.* 4.1.90).

But what are we to make of Paul himself in this regard, or of Aquinas for that matter? Even those who have eschewed marriage and family for the sake of the kingdom (cf. 1 Cor. 7; Mark 10:28–30) may sometimes fail to observe the proper limits of work, particularly if they are trying, like Paul, both to minister the word and, as it were, wait on tables. "I worked harder than any of them," he says, "though it was not I, but the grace of God which is with me" (1 Cor. 15:10). So hard did he work that people sometimes supposed him to be disordered himself, as they did Jesus, whose example he was following: "My food is to do the will of him who sent me, and to accomplish his work" (John 4:34; cf. Mark 3:20–21). "We must work the works of him who sent me, while it is day; night comes, when no one can work" (John 9:4; cf. 5:17; 2 Tim. 2:15). There is a time, let us allow, for extra toil and trouble, especially for the Lord's sake. Only in the eternal "rest" will the perfect balance of work and rest be struck; and there it will indeed be struck, for there we shall be fully human by rightly imaging God, who works on the creature's behalf and also rests for the creature's sake. Yet we should, even now, seek quietness of soul and body where we can, whatever our vocation, lest we give way to anxiety and forget that the yoke of the Lord is easy and his burden light (Matt. 11:30; cf. 6:25–34; Mark 6:31).

"May our Lord Jesus Christ himself . . . encourage your hearts and confirm you in every good work and word" (2:17)? This is possible on the strength of his own confirmation through his ascension to the Father's right hand, where he both rests and rules (Ps. 110). But, as Karl Barth so astutely observes, the exaltation of Jesus Christ, God's true coworker, has the effect of exposing our sloth, our inertia, our tendency to let ourselves fall rather than to rise and advance toward God, as we may now do. It reveals the sin of sloth for what it is. "It is the knowledge of the man Jesus which forces us to, or rather frees us for, a knowledge of sin" (*CD* IV/2, 383), including this sin. He who was put to shame on our behalf now shames us where we are slothful. "We are confronted by the man who is with and for God as God is with Him, at peace with God and therefore with His fellows and Himself. But this means that we are all asked by Him who and what we ought to be as His brothers" (386). We are probed in regard to our refusal to live the genuinely human life that can only be lived as he lived it, by way of the two great commandments.

If we hear these commandments but do not obey, we reveal our "practical atheism," writes Barth (415). We also carry on exploiting our fellow man, either by working only for ourselves when we ought to become coworkers with God, or alternatively by refusing to work at all. "In every one of us . . . there is a vagabond who will not accept discipline, and therefore will not exercise it in relation to himself, however gladly he may do so in relation to others." This vagabond "prefers to receive permissions rather than commands" (454). He forgets that for man in Christ it is possible to set to work "as one whom God has endowed with freedom" (595), that doing so is proper to one who wishes to attain God's rest rather than to go down to ruin by reason of the fact that he "can always merrily escape the discipline that is brought to bear on him" (455). The ruin of this man, who will not rise to every good work and word but lets the vagabond in him prevail, is just what concerns Paul. It is what he is trying to prevent.

3:13–15 And you, brothers, [we urge] not to grow weary in doing good. Should any one refuse to listen to our instruction through this letter, mark that man [and] do not associate with him, that he might be ashamed. Yet do not regard him as an enemy, but rather discipline [him] as a brother.

At 1 Thess. 5:12–14 we heard Paul entreating the whole church to honor those toiling among them, and asking those doing the toiling to discipline the disorderly and encourage the discouraged, seeking the good of all. Here we find him urging the latter to keep this up, despite any temptation to discouragement in their encounter with those whose lives are stubbornly disordered. He later sends the same message to the church in Galatia, speaking to them all: "Let him who is taught the word share all good things with him who teaches. . . . And let us not grow weary in well-doing, for in due season we shall reap, if we do not lose heart. So then, as we have opportunity, let us do good to all men, and especially to those who are of the household of faith" (6:6–10). And the Ephesians he likewise encourages, adding a further promise to the commandment, to continue "rendering service with a good will as to the Lord and not to men, knowing that whatever good any one does, he will receive the same again from the Lord, whether he is a slave or free" (6:7–8). For the Lord can never be outgiven.

Whomever Paul has in mind here by "brothers," the presbyters or the people as a whole, this passage reminds us that it is certainly possible to discourage leaders, whether by failing to follow or by failing to give back; and that leaders, like followers, sometimes give up just when they should be most careful to persevere. It is a very great good, for the one as for the other, to know the word that will sustain the weary (Isa. 50:4) or the deed that will encourage a person to press on when it seems easier to turn back, to finish the race and earn the crown of righteousness that "the Lord, the righteous judge, will award . . . to all who have loved his appearing" (2 Tim. 4:8). But Paul's focus now is on those who do the opposite, on protecting the community from people who stubbornly distract or disobey; indeed, on protecting the latter from themselves as far as possible. It is the grace of discipline he has in view, when the grace of encouragement has failed. So he issues a sterner order, the order to withdraw from their company.

This order must not be misunderstood, as if Paul were encouraging the Thessalonians to turn away from the man or woman who, spiritually speaking, has fallen amongst thieves and is lying beaten and bloody in the ditch. A church is a field hospital. It is the place where our Lord sends such people for help, "commending to the Holy Spirit his own man, who had fallen among thieves, whom he himself [through his incarnation] compassionated, and bound up his wounds, giving two royal denaria; so that we, receiving by the Spirit the image and superscription of the Father and the Son, might cause the denarium entrusted to us to be fruitful, counting out the increase to the Lord" (*Haer.* 3.17.3, in *ANF* 1:445). There can be no economy of gift if not this economy, the economy with which we ourselves have been graced lest we die, each of us, in our own ditch. Paul does not want us to turn aside from the spiritually broken in order to keep our own hands or parishes clean, metaphorically speaking. God forbid! He is not talking about such as these, any more than he is talking about those who are physically broken and unable to work, whom together with widows and orphans (cf. Acts 6; 1 Tim. 5, etc.) it has always been the practice of the churches to support. He is talking, rather, about the contrary and the disobedient; about those who wish to take advantage of the community without conforming to the faith and morals and discipline of the community. They are like the shameless "Christ-mongers" of whom the *Didache* speaks, and the church that fears to shame them risks becoming shameless itself through the corruption of its faith and manner of life (cf. Rev. 2:5; 3:3, 17). That faith and manner of life cannot be imposed on them, but discipline can be imposed. They can be deprived of the ordinary benefits of the community they are abusing.

"I wrote to you in my letter not to associate with immoral men," Paul says to the Corinthians, "not at all meaning the immoral of this world, or the greedy and robbers, or idolaters, since then you would need to go out of the world. But rather I wrote to you not to associate with any one who bears the name of brother if he is guilty of immorality or greed, or is an idolater, reviler, drunkard, or robber—not even to eat with such a one. For what have I to do with judging outsiders? Is it not those inside the Church whom you are to judge? God judges those outside" (1 Cor. 5:9–13). The basic idea is clearly the same: Discipline a brother because he is a brother, depriving him of ordinary society in hopes that he will recognize the error of his ways, repent, return, receive forgiveness, and be restored to full fellowship (cf. 2 Cor. 2:5–12; Rev. 3:19–20). This will help him in the way he most needs help, while protecting the church from his bad example. But in Corinth Paul is having to deal with something worse than that—a scandalous case of *porneia* that requires him to move from the lesser discipline of shunning to the greater discipline of excommunication: "Drive out the wicked person from among you." Nothing of that sort is said to the Thessalonians, yet the question arises as to how far Paul means them to go in imposing discipline. They are to mark out offenders and dissociate from them. Might this also entail excommunication?

▓ Positively, Paul encourages the Philippians to "mark those who so walk as you have an example in us" (3:17). The Romans, on the other hand, he instructs to "take note of those who create dissensions and difficulties" and to "avoid them. For such persons do not serve our Lord Christ, but their own appetites" (16:17–18). The verb in both those texts is σκοπέω. Here, however, it is σημειόω, which can mean "to give notice of" rather than "to take notice of"; and this has fed speculation that he has excommunication in mind. ▓

Chrysostom does not seem to think so. He points out that a natural brother who behaves badly is admonished privately, not publicly; even when deprived of familial fellowship, he remains a family member. Paul is calling here only for social discipline, then. Haimo and Aquinas take a harder line. Aquinas (*S.2Th.* 3.2.85–87) speaks of *sententia excommunicationis* and suggests that the marking out takes place in the form of a letter to the apostles identifying the offender, who pending apostolic judgment is excluded from the church's fellowship on account of his disobedience, albeit not "from hateful spite but from a loving eagerness" for his ultimate welfare. (Commentators generally are careful to underline the motive and goal of the discipline, however harsh the discipline itself; cf. Weima 2014: 627.)

One problem with Thomas's view, even if we ignore certain syntactical hurdles, is that it assumes a degree of apostolic oversight that did not exist and seldom if ever has existed. Another and more serious problem is that it turns what gives every appearance of being a simple pastoral text into a highly juridical one. A problem with Chrysostom's view, on the other hand, is that it is difficult to see how this retreat from happy congress in homes and other social settings would play out in the *agape* feast, the fellowship meal which was then the primary context for the Eucharist. Were the offenders to be excluded from that also, or only from communal or familial meals that had no liturgical function?

▓ Neither mentions the *agape* meal directly, which by the time of Chrysostom had already disappeared. Chrysostom does seem to have it in mind, however, when he takes up this lament: "For like men who inhabit one house, and are under one father, and partake of one table, so did they then dwell in every Church. How great an evil therefore was it to fall from so great love! But now it is not even thought to be a great evil, because neither is it considered any great thing when we are united with one another. What was then in the order of punishment, this, on account of the great coldness of love, now takes place even apart from punishment, and we withdraw from one another causelessly, and from coldness. For it is the cause of all evils that there is no love. This has dissolved all ties, and has disfigured all that was venerable and splendid in the Church, in which we ought to have gloried" (*Hom.* 5, in *NPNF¹* 13:396). Indeed! But if, as Malherbe thinks, "withdrawing from an individual at the very least meant that he would not be admitted to the church's fellowship meals" (2000: 460), how then would that individual have access to the Eucharist itself? To sustain Chrysostom's approach it would seem necessary either to confine the discipline to nonliturgical meals or to posit a restriction on the offender's involvement in the church's main fellowship meal.   ▓

That is a good question, but surely Chrysostom has the better of it. Means must be proportionate to ends. The offenders' combination of sloth, taking advantage of others, troublemaking, and stubborn disobedience warranted isolation within the church family, though not (or not yet) exclusion from it.

Exactly how to carry out Paul's order may have puzzled his first readers as much as it puzzles us, but military men would call it *Auftragstaktik* or "mission command": those on the ground, nearest the situation, must work it out. These were early days and Paul himself may have been procedurally uncertain. One notes that even in the scandalous situation in Corinth, which soon escalated into a fully juridical one, several attempts to clarify the appropriate sequence of actions proved necessary. One also notes that the maxim "he who does not work shall not eat" is capable of being applied even to the *agape* feast, without precluding a sharing in the sacred body and blood, if presbyters are prepared to act pastorally and shoulder the burden of supervision. In any case, the *agape* feast was a good thing, not a necessary thing. Otherwise Paul could hardly have advised the Corinthians to satisfy their hunger at home rather than at church, if satisfying it at church meant perpetuating the problems in the church (1 Cor. 11:17–34). Perhaps he expected the Thessalonians, if it came to it, to be ready to make the same adjustment. And one notes, above all, that while Paul clearly intends the discipline to have teeth—excluding a person socially, particularly at mealtime, is no minor discipline, as even ordinary family life attests—he sends none of the signals requisite to an application of the Church's ultimate sanction.

■ Here we ought to acknowledge that there are different kinds and degrees of sin, which have different effects on the sinner and on the community; hence that there are different kinds and degrees of discipline in the Church. Discipline must not be regarded lightly (Heb. 12:1–11). Just as it is a sign of sickness in a community or a soul when categorizing sins and punishments becomes an obsession, so also when all is covered by rationalizations or made over into an occasion for accompaniment, such that discipline disappears. Now, the sentence of excommunication is the highest form of discipline, though it may or may not be allied with lesser forms such as forfeiture of office, say, or shunning. There is no graver penalty the Church can impose than to say to the baptized that, through refusal to repent of mortal sin, he has forfeited his place in the fellowship of the redeemed at the altar of the Lord, that his saving relation to the One coming in judgment is no longer secure. That is what it means to deliver someone "to Satan for the destruction of the flesh, that his spirit may be saved in the day of the Lord Jesus" (1 Cor. 5:5; →1 Thess. 5:12–15), the day the Eucharist anticipates. He is stripped of every illusion that the life he is living is compatible with the prospect of salvation. He is handed over to life in the far country, where there is nothing to eat but worthless husks. He is turned out into the realm in which man is ruled by the fear of death and ought to be ruled by the fear of body and soul being cast into hell.

Let us not forget that the same Jesus who told the parable of the man picked up out of the ditch and conveyed to the innkeeper was asked, "Lord, will those who are saved be few?" His answer was sobering: "Strive to enter by the narrow door; for many, I tell you, will seek to enter and will not be able. When once the householder has risen up and shut the door, you will begin to stand outside and to knock at the door, saying, 'Lord, open to us.' He will answer you, 'I do not know where you come from'" (Luke 13:22–30). Baptism and excommunication are the two ways by which the Church acknowledges this ineradicable distinction between inside and outside. If one of these ways is not taken seriously, neither is the other; that is why in 1 Corinthians Paul moves back and forth between them. It is also why his judgment on the man to be excommunicated is so clearly a juridical act, why it is rendered from the place where the whole Church is present—where Paul himself is present (ἀπὼν τῷ σώματι παρὼν δὲ τῷ πνεύματι, 1 Cor. 5:3), where the saints and the heavenly hosts are present, where we must be sure not to "refuse him who is speaking," where the "immoral or irreligious" ought not to be present (Heb. 12:12–29).

But again, there is nothing like that here in 2 Thess. 3, which does not return us to the contrast at work in 2 Thess. 1–2. A distinction is drawn between inside and outside only as regards concourse in the ordinary affairs of daily life. It is drawn however as a warning to all, and particularly to the unruly who have refused counsel already given, that in the Church ordinary human life does not cease to matter. It matters more than ever, because in the Church it is brought, eucharistically, into the sphere of the extraordinary and divine.

3:16 Now may the Lord of Peace himself give you peace in all things and in every way. The Lord be with you all.

Against disorder and its danger to the church, Paul has warned the Thessalonians. Now at the last he directs them once more to the true source of tranquility of order; that is, to Jesus Christ, whom he calls "the Lord of Peace," since it is through him, with him, and in him that peace in all things and in every way is possible.

Augustine, without reference to our text, famously parses peace in all things and in every way, as nature intends it and as the Author of our redemption achieves it through overcoming all disorder of sin: "The peace of the body then consists in the duly proportioned arrangement of its parts. The peace of the irrational soul is the harmonious repose of the appetites, and that of the rational soul the harmony of knowledge and action. The peace of body and soul is the well-ordered and harmonious life and health of the living creature. Peace between man and God is the well-ordered obedience of faith to eternal law. Peace between man and man is well-ordered concord. Domestic peace is the well-ordered concord between those of the family who rule and those who obey. Civil peace is a similar concord among the citizens. The peace of the celestial city is the perfectly ordered and harmonious enjoyment of God, and of one another in God. The peace of all things is the tranquillity of order" (*Civ.* 19.13.1, in *NPNF¹* 2:409).

Aquinas, in treating our text (*S.2Th.* 3.2.89), parses the peace of God just as concisely: "God is said to be the God of peace in relation to two things. For peace consists of two things, namely that a man be in harmony with himself and that he be in harmony with others. And both can only be had sufficiently in God. For apart from God a man does not have harmony with himself, much less with others, because a man's emotions are in harmony with themselves when what is sought to fulfill one desire suffices to fulfill all desires, and nothing but God can do this: 'Who satisfies your desires with good things' (Ps. 103:5). For anything else but God will not be enough for all desires, but God is enough: 'In me you have peace' (John 16:33). Similarly, men are only united amongst themselves in that which is had in common among them, and this is most of all God."

Neither parsing works, of course, or is meant to work, without coming to rest in the mediation of Jesus Christ, who himself is our peace—the "at-oneing" peace between God and man, between a man and himself, between Jew and Gentile, between male and female, between man and man generally, between body and soul, and hence also between the living and the dead (→1 Thess. 4:13–18).

Peace in all things and in every way is nonetheless a relative peace at present. Paul is not expecting the Lord to give the Christians in Thessaloniki, just yet, that "perfectly ordered and harmonious enjoyment of God, and of one another in God," that belongs to the kingdom of God. He is expecting God to give them such peace as they need to complete the mission he and Silas and Timothy have begun in their city, to announce to their neighbors that this kingdom is coming and to tell them whose kingdom it is, to do so despite their appointment to tribulation (1 Thess. 1–2). Peace in all things and in every way means peace in perplexity and in persecution. It means a refusal of resignation or despair (1 Thess. 3). It does not mean tolerance of all things in every way. It does not mean making peace with sin, whether the sin of sloth or of disobedience or of sexual immorality or any other kind of sin. It does not mean accepting disorder as if it were a reasonable substitute for good order, whether in our souls or in our bodies or in our life together (1 Thess. 4). It does not mean learning how to live and thrive in "the real world"—as if the world we know were the real world, the world without end, rather than merely the provisional world in a sin-disordered and death-disordered state, the world that faces traumatic reordering through divine judgment and salvation (1 Thess. 5). It *does* mean the calmness and courage that derive from knowing the One who will effect that judgment and salvation with absolute justice and all power and authority, from knowing the Lord of Peace who can and will say to the wind and waves "Peace! Be still!" when he comes to be glorified among his holy ones (2 Thess. 1). It does mean being unshaken meanwhile by false teachings, false prophets, and false messiahs; even by antichrist, the man of lawlessness, whose dupes will say "Peace, peace!" when there is no peace. It means being unshaken by lawlessness itself, by wicked and evil men and the wicked and evil things they do and will yet do, when the wood is dry and ready for the fire (2 Thess. 2). It means clinging to the fact that the Lord is faithful and will guard his saints from evil, helping them to stand fast. "For in everything, O Lord, you have exalted and glorified your people; and you have not neglected to help them at all times and in all places" (Wis. 19:22).

Who is offering this prayer for peace? It comes from the man who used to be known as Saul of Tarsus. Saul, it must be said, was not originally a man of peace. He had witnessed the martyrdom of Stephen, who stood like an unassailable tower of peace before the people of Jerusalem and before a council of lawless men and their false witnesses. Full of the Holy Spirit, the Comforter who brings peace, Stephen "gazed into heaven and saw the glory of God, and Jesus standing at the right hand of God," ready with the verdict of the heavenly court. The protomartyr's face, as they could all see, "was like the face of an angel." But they would not hear out his testimony. In the name of the temple that Herod built, they became enraged to the point of an impromptu execution. That was their verdict, for what it was worth, coming from so low and corrupt a court. Saul, who as a rising star from Gamaliel's stable must have known the lawlessness of their actions, was himself highly agitated. "Still breathing threats and murder against the disciples of the Lord," he headed for Damascus, only to encounter, as he drew near that city, the very one whom Stephen had beheld. From out of the blinding light of heaven, from the glory of the heavenly bench itself, he heard Jesus ask him a question. Not the provocative question Stephen had asked of the Sanhedrin—"Which of the prophets did not your fathers persecute?"—but a more personal question: "Saul, Saul, why do you persecute me?"

Such answers as he thought he had no longer seemed cogent. He made his peace with Jesus (who had heeded Stephen's prayer, "Lord, do not hold this sin against them") and his commissioning as an apostle was carried out. He "increased all the more in strength," confounding his former friends and new opponents "by proving that Jesus was the Christ," until they sought to kill him as well. Escaping from Damascus by night, he embarked on a new course, with a new mission, under a harmless sun for his glorious wandering (Wis. 18:3). That wandering would bring him eventually to Philippi and Thessaloniki. Jail awaited in the former, and the necessity of flight (yet again!) in the latter. But those songs in the night that broke up the jail in Philippi testified to the fact that he had now become a man of peace. With complete credibility he could write to the brethren there, as more briefly here: "The Lord is at hand. Have no anxiety about anything, but in everything by prayer and supplication with thanksgiving let your requests be made known to God. And the peace of God, which passes all understanding, will keep your hearts and your minds in Christ Jesus" (Phil. 4:5–7).

Paul the apostle, unlike young Saul the bailiff, was a man of peace. Unless, of course, we mean by "man of peace" someone who in all things and in every way is interested chiefly in avoiding scandal and trouble. Paul was not that sort of man, for no apostle of Jesus is or can be. No, he was still the very soul of scandal and trouble, for the gospel he preached is a *skandalon*. Because of that gospel, trouble and scandal dogged his every step, even when he was doing his best to give it a wide berth, as he later did when, at James's advice, he took vows in Jerusalem (Acts 21:26). That didn't turn out quite as hoped. But Jesus stood by his bed in the night, after a day in which Paul, like Stephen, stood before the Sanhedrin threatened by a violent and untimely death. "Take courage," said the Lord, "for as you have testified about me at Jerusalem, so you must bear witness also at Rome" (23:11). Having been heard in Rome by another lawful council of lawless men, he would meet his worldly fate with peace and confidence. "I am already on the point of being sacrificed," he wrote to Timothy. "The time of my departure has come. I have fought the good fight, I have finished the race, I have kept the faith. From now on there is laid up for me the crown of righteousness, which the Lord, the righteous judge, will award to me on that Day, and not only to me but also to all who have loved his appearing" (2 Tim. 4:6–8).

Among this "all" Paul hoped and expected to find the Thessalonians, whom he here entrusts to the Lord of peace to keep in peace through all their own tribulations. "In me you may have peace," promises Jesus (John 16:33). "In the world you have tribulation; but be of good cheer, I have overcome the world."

3:17–18 [Here is] the greeting in my own hand, [the hand] of Paul, which is a sign [of authenticity] in every letter—this is how I write. The grace of our Lord Jesus Christ be with you all!

Saul's story is told in Acts 7–9. The first time we hear the name Παῦλος is in Acts 13, where Luke tells us that in Paphos "they came upon a certain magician, a Jewish false prophet, named Bar-Jesus. He was with the proconsul, Sergius Paulus, a man of intelligence, who summoned Barnabas and Saul and sought to hear the word of God. But Elymas the magician (for that is the meaning of his name) withstood them, seeking to turn away the proconsul from the faith. But Saul, who is also called Paul, filled with the Holy Spirit, looked intently at him and said, 'You son of the devil, you enemy of all righteousness, full of all deceit and villainy, will you not stop making crooked the straight paths of the Lord? And now, behold, the hand of the Lord is upon you, and you shall be blind and unable to see the sun for a time.' Immediately mist and darkness fell upon him and he went about seeking people to lead him by the hand. Then the proconsul believed, when he saw what had occurred, for he was astonished at the teaching of the Lord" (13:6–12). After this remarkable episode, for Luke it's always "Paul" not "Saul."

▒ Why is not clear. Σαῦλος means "asked for," as in: the Israelites asked for a king and were given what they asked for. They were given a man by that name, who stood head and shoulders above the rest of them; a man, however, who turned back from the teaching of the Lord and from following his word, and was handed over to a tormenting spirit; a man who made an unlawful sacrifice and was reduced in the end to consulting a medium; a man who eventually fell on his own sword. Saul of Tarsus was a different sort of man altogether—much more like David than Saul, as Luke intends us to see, for he fought the battles of the Lord and planted the flag of the Lord and proclaimed the astonishing teaching of the Lord in cities around the empire, until he was felled by Caesar's sword. It is likely that he was "also called Paul" for quite mundane family reasons, however, unless perhaps as an affectionate joke. Παῦλος was a common diminutive—Sergius Paulus being roughly the equivalent of Sergius Jr.—but Saul was diminutive in stature, standing head and shoulders below other men. Anyway, he was "Paul" to his friends and to the churches he founded, and "Paul" from this point in Acts.   ▒

It is not the introduction of Saul's other name that is important here, however. What is important is that Paul recognized in the false prophet, Bar-Jesus or Elymas, not a divine magician, for God does not have magicians, but rather just about everything critiqued in one of Paul's favorite scriptural sources, the Wisdom of Solomon. He needed to make no inquiry into the counsels of this ungodly man "to convict him of his lawless deeds" (Wis. 1:9). Here again was a Jew, acting like a Gentile and preventing a Gentile from receiving the word of God from a Jew. Paul rebuked him with the same forthrightness that Stephen had rebuked the council. His rebuke left Elymas sightless and groping, like the men of Sodom, in need of others to lead him (Wis. 19:17). This was a parable with which Paul was personally familiar, having himself tried to stymie the gospel until he was brought up short on that road to Damascus and briefly "imprisoned in darkness," before going out to bring the imperishable light of the gospel to the world (Wis. 18:1–4). A signal was again being sent, this time to Elymas, that the Lord of all the earth would not permit his gospel to be stymied, that his word would without fail go forth to the "rulers of the earth," and that those who reasoned soundly would receive it (Wis. 1:1–5), as Sergius in fact did.

In Philippi and Thessaloniki, however, the situation was otherwise than in Paphos. Here, too, Jews were preventing Jews from reaching Gentiles, but the Gentile rulers were themselves hostile to the gospel and its messengers. To know the peace of Christ in all things and in every way, at all times and in all places, meant for Paul, and might mean for his converts also, knowing it in jail or out on the road by night under cover of darkness. Moreover, there were Christians confusing Christians about the gospel, or at least about the character of the age in which the gospel must be preached. To the church of the Thessalonians, therefore, Paul had things to say that others (in the summary of 2 Pet. 3:15–18) have sometimes found "difficult to understand," things about "the forbearance of our Lord" and "the error of lawless men" and the need to "grow in the grace and knowledge of our Lord and Savior Jesus Christ" lest they lose their stability. These things included, as we have seen, the need to reckon with the dialectic of divine patience and divine justice, and so also with the coming of that lawless one who must precede the coming of the Judge—to reckon with that son of Satan, with that "enemy of all righteousness, full of all deceit and villainy," who (together with his own Bar-Jesus, as the Apocalypse tells us) will perfect the art of making crooked the straight paths of the Lord.

"Here is the greeting in my own hand," in the "large letters" of my own hand (Gal. 6:11). This is a sign of authenticity and so of authority, but also of intimacy and affection for his brethren in the privilege of suffering for the sake of the gospel. His deep affection Paul has made crystal clear in the first letter. Authenticity and authority he makes clear here, for the man of fraud is still coming, but the danger of fraud is already present. Nowhere is that danger greater than in the Church of Jesus Christ, because nowhere are the stakes as high. Today's attacks on the authenticity of 2 Thessalonians may be seen in that light, but we will not return to so calculated a distraction. It is better in conclusion to reflect instead on the relevance of this epistle to our own situation, which promises to become as difficult or even more difficult than that of the Thessalonians, and in some parts of the world already has. For from the fig tree we should learn its lesson, as our Lord said, and from the roaring of the sea also.

The fig tree is beginning to bloom again, which is a sign that the times of the Gentiles are running out. Paul's second letter warns us that they will not run out quietly. Already the wind has begun to howl and the waves to heap up. From those waves the outline of a beast is rising. The mystery of lawlessness is growing more transparent and the man of lawlessness bolder by the day. The beast we face is one with those that have come before it, yet it is behaving differently now, just as we were warned it would. For it has caught sight of *Ha-Maschiach* and his kingdom, the kingdom that shall never be destroyed. It hates the people of that kingdom, whether Jew or Gentile. And it has today new means at its disposal, both technological and psychological, for deceiving and manipulating them. To these the old means, even those of Elymas, will be joined more openly in due course; ours is the era of the "deep fake" as well as the "deep state."

The Church has a final Passover to undergo as it confronts this beast. It has already entered upon a painful Gethsemane-like struggle, a struggle that is internal before it is external. Because of the sins that have beset it during this age of apostasy, the Church's struggle, unlike its Lord's, must be purgatorial before it is martyrial. But the one will lead to the other, after a respite likely to be brief. Then the kingdom will come, "not by a historic triumph of the Church through a progressive ascendency, but only by God's victory over the final unleashing of evil, which will cause his Bride to come down from heaven" (*CCC* §677). In this final Passover, while we await the kingdom, we must watch and pray that we "may have strength to escape all these things that will take place, and to stand before the Son of man" (Luke 21:36). We must learn how to dwell in the peace of Christ in all things and in every way. We must discover, even in moments of doubt or fear, that we are not alone, because Christ is secretly present with us. For the time will come when we are scattered each to our own home or indeed driven from our homes, as our brethren in so many times and places have been. "Why do you sleep? Rise and pray that you may not enter into temptation" (Luke 22:46; cf. John 16:33)!

Before our Lord appears and we assemble to him, that we may be with him forever in the mansions of the God-filled creation he has been preparing for our occupancy, the mystery of lawlessness that is already at work must run its course and the man of lawlessness appear without disguise. We are much nearer to this than the Thessalonians were. That does not mean that we, unlike the Thessalonians, should leave our stations or abandon our ordinary duties in life, thus becoming ourselves those who are disorderly. There remains much work to be done in the service of God and neighbor. Yet neither should we overlook the fact that our situation is not quite the same as theirs, nor even as that of those who afterward suffered the writhings and the wrath of a collapsing Roman Empire (cf. Dawson 1942: 8ff.). Periods of chaos and extraordinary suffering the world has always known, and the Church both with it and from it. But our Lord said that the time of the end would be unlike any other.

Those who lack the peace of Christ will find this truly terrifying. Luminous hints of God's just judgment are flashing on the horizon. There are signs in the sun, moon, and stars (→2:1–5). Antichristic tyrannies are arising, whose subjects are under blanket surveillance, whose churches are razed, whose babies are poisoned or cut asunder, whose undesirables suffer vivisection for organ harvesting. (Was it a glimpse of such things that sickened Daniel and sent him to his bed?) The violence of thunder reverberates ominously in the heavens, as the love of many grows cold and even the embers of reason flare and die out (Wis. 19:13). The foundations of civilization are crumbling under the unbearable weight of human disbelief in God and defiance of his law. The very constitution of man is collapsing. As the late Leonard Cohen (1994) predicted, "things are going to slide in all directions," for "the blizzard of the world has crossed the threshold" and "overturned the order of the soul." Or as Étienne Gilson put it, summarizing Nietzsche's famous warning, "the entire human order totters on its base" (1949: 8), like the image in Nebuchadnezzar's dream with its toes partly of iron and partly of clay. As it falls, those who have preferred sleep to wakefulness and watching, who have noticed nothing out of the ordinary, who have allowed themselves to become "captives of darkness and prisoners of long night," who are now "paralyzed by their souls' surrender" to the ways of darkness and to secret sins, will be overwhelmed "by sudden and unexpected fear" (Wis. 17). But the wakeful, the people who know their God and look for the appearing of their Lord, shall stand firm, as Gabriel assured Daniel, and Paul the Thessalonians.

Hippolytus, whom we met earlier, had not read any of our modern authors, of course, but he had read Deuteronomy and Daniel and Paul. What he found already in Deuteronomy, where apostate Jews are in view, he recognized with Daniel and Paul as applying also to Gentiles. For all is foretold, the whole history of the world is foretold, in the Song of Moses. "They did slide, therefore, in all things, as they were found to be in harmony with the truth in nothing" (*TCA* 58; cf. Deut. 32:35). Such will be the case, he says, in the democracies of the latter days, at the extremity of lawlessness. For they belong to a kingdom that cannot and will not hold together, a majestic kingdom with the strength of iron but the weakness of miry clay (*TCA* 27; cf. Dan. 2:41–43). It and they will give way to the kingdom of antichrist, who will relieve men of their anxiety about the chaos, when the toes crumble, when their foot slips, when the center no longer holds.

Antichrist will promise peace and security. He will seem steady and sure-handed, a timely savior. His peculiarities and excesses will be overlooked. "As Christ at His coming was believed to be the carpenter," warns Manning in his second lecture, "so Antichrist may be visibly no more than a successful adventurer. Even his preternatural character, true or false, may pass either as scintillations of insanity, or as the absurdities of his partisans, or the delusions of his flatterers" (1861: 33). But his true purpose and program will out in the end, and he will sweep the peoples of the earth to their doom, as Satan's tail swept the stars of heaven to theirs. At first, says Cyril, "he will put on a show of mildness (as though he were a learned and discreet person), and of soberness and benevolence: and by the lying signs and wonders of his magical deceit having beguiled the Jews, as though he were the expected Christ, he shall afterward be characterized by all kinds of crimes of inhumanity and lawlessness, so as to outdo all unrighteous and ungodly men who have gone before him; displaying against all men, but especially against us Christians, a spirit murderous and most cruel, merciless and crafty. And after perpetrating such things for three years and six months only, he shall be destroyed by the glorious second advent from heaven of the only-begotten Son of God, our Lord and Savior Jesus, the true Christ" (*CL* 15.12, in *NPNF²* 7:107f.).

▧ The passage in Manning is, alas, tainted by traces of contemporary anti-Semitism. As for Cyril's "beguiled the Jews," I have suggested rather "beguiled apostate Christians" or, better yet, "beguiled all those who have exchanged their biblical heritage for a mess of pottage, be they Jew or Gentile." That brings it into line with Solovyov's "Short Tale of the Antichrist," where the *in templo dei* question (with a few hedged bets) is handled thus: The "coming man," in his bid to bring religious as well as political unity to the world, headquarters his regime in Jerusalem with a grand new structure on the temple mount that is more palace than temple, though it serves as a temple in his own honor. Jews are at first seduced by the hope that Jerusalem and Israel are to be at the heart of the new world empire, and by their understanding that he himself is a Jew. Christians are seduced in all the ways Ferrer said they would be, and Christians are those whom this narcissist—who regards Jesus as his own forerunner—is most intent on seducing. He even arranges for his false prophet, an Elymas-like figure who in syncretistic fashion combines sorcery with corrupt Catholicism, to become pope. In the process, a false ecumenism that gives allegiance to antichrist has the unintended effect of bringing about a true ecumenism among those who remain loyal to Jesus. Before he can fully destroy the latter, he is brought down by an act of God while facing (after discovery that he is uncircumcised) another Jewish revolt. Jews then join Christians in welcoming the true Messiah.

Now, the teller of this tale acknowledges both that the story's end is somewhat uncertain in its particulars, from our present vantage point, and that it may suffer from an overly literal reading of scripture and tradition. Quite true. But he also underlines the fact that scripture and tradition, however difficult to understand on this or that point, are clear in their basic outline and cannot be gainsaid. For the actual end, in all its particulars, is already known to God and thus capable of being revealed to the people of God. Like the beginning of the world, the end of the world (as we know it) rests on the will and power of God, a fact we seem to have forgotten, as Solovyov notices. ("Such ideas as God *creating* the universe *out of nothing* were no longer taught even in elementary schools. A certain high level of ideas concerning such subjects had been evolved, and no dogmatism could risk a descent below it.") And having forgotten it in regard to the beginning we overlook it with regard to the end. This belongs to our decadence and is a sure sign of our readiness for the coming man and for the divine judgment he will precipitate. So is the syncretism and false ecumenism that seem to unfold with the daily headlines.   ■

Here, as Cyril underscores, "is a call for the endurance of the saints, those who keep the commandments of God and the faith of Jesus" (Rev. 14:12). And not for endurance only, but also for wisdom and discernment, lest we mistake the false for the true (*CL* 15.18). We must not mistake it! Yet on most accounts, whether patristic or modern, many will. Indeed, there are many in the Church even now who argue—displaying that urbane wisdom Solovyov so sharply criticizes, a wisdom backed (in the words of his antichrist) by a "free examination of the sacred Scriptures from all points of view and in all possible directions"—that it is better not to concern ourselves with such things when we wish each other the peace of Christ. Indeed, it is better that we not read texts such as 2 Thessalonians. Paul may or may not have dictated it and signed it with his own hand, but in any case he never repeated in any other extant letter quite what we find here. Nor are these things mentioned in the creed, which may require us (with the first letter) to find something to say about a parousia, a resurrection, and a judgment, but does not require us to become apocalyptic enthusiasts invested in antichrist narratives.

It is highly revealing, however, what else this urbane wisdom overlooks in deciding to overlook the unwanted features of Paul, to ignore his "apocalyptic streak" and the texts on which he draws. It overlooks the unity of scripture and picks apart tradition. It overlooks dominical and apostolic authority. It overlooks just judgment, pining for a mercy without judgment. It objects to the distinction between inside and outside. It doubts the reality of damnation and, sooner or later, of salvation. Truth be told, it habitually refuses to receive scripture "not as the word of men but as it truly is, God's own word," and believes very little that is found in the creed, from *creatio ex nihilo* to the life of the world to come. To echo Yeats in "The Second Coming," even inside the Church the best, if these are the best, lack all conviction while the worst (leaving aside the Christ-mongers, the scoundrels, and the predators) become passionate about their own messianic and utopian projects, over which is draped a dark curtain of moral forgetfulness that precludes any participation in the peace of Christ.

Do we drink from the destabilizing spirits that Paul warned the Thessalonians against if we observe that our times are now ripe for the affairs of which he spoke? Or do we drink from the Rock from which he himself was drinking? If two millennia on, we cannot recognize around us, inside the Church as well as outside, the advance of the mystery of lawlessness and the appearance of the signs of the end, then there *is* no advancing mystery nor any approach of the end. If we cannot see, in the theoretical and practical atheism with which we have been experimenting for several centuries, and in today's sudden repudiation of the body and of any God-given moral order, preparation for the appearance of the man of lawlessness, then no doubt we can say that such a man is always with us and will never be with us. In which case, neither will the Son of Man come. For we *are* that man, as D. F. Strauss claimed (1879: §151). Which means that the long arc of justice, to employ that popular phrase, will never terminate in any actual judgment.

But what says the Rock? What says the one whose "work is perfect, for all his ways are justice"? He says:

> I lift up my hand to heaven,
>   and swear, 'As I live for ever,
> if I whet my glittering sword,
>   and my hand takes hold on judgment,
> I will take vengeance on my adversaries,
>   and will requite those who hate me.' (Deut. 32:40–41; cf. Rev. 10:5–7)

He says, or will soon say, "There will be no more delay!"

> Behold the storm of the LORD!
>   Wrath has gone forth,
>   a whirling tempest;
>   it will burst upon the head of the wicked.
> The fierce anger of the LORD will not turn back
>   until he has executed and accomplished
>   the intents of his mind.
> In the latter days you will understand this. (Jer. 30:23–24)

The kind of thinking that passes for wisdom today, in an age that (in Solovyov's sardonic commendation) may well be "so advanced as to be actually the last," wants nothing to do with such texts, just as it wants nothing to do with the letters of Paul to the Thessalonians. But we have been given these letters and these texts to teach us how to stand firm, how to be stable in our manner of life, how not to be quickly shaken in mind, how to wait for what, in the justice and mercy and faithfulness of God, we have been told to expect—in a word, how "to serve the God who is living and true, and to wait for his Son to appear from the heavens, whom he raised from the dead: Jesus, the one rescuing us from the wrath that is coming."

The long night draws to a close. The man of lawlessness approaches, but so too does the Son of Man. They will arrive together, more or less; the one first, and then the other. Only the latter and those united to the latter will remain. Of this St. Paul assures us, and signs his assurance with his own hand. Of this Jesus himself assures us, having signed already in water and blood. Wait, then, for him. Watch and pray. Do not fear those who can kill the body. Refuse to surrender your soul to the night, for we are sons of the light and of the day.

Mary! You whom Gabriel told to fear not, because you had found favor with God: you who were filled with grace, that your foot not slip before the serpent's head was crushed by your Son's heel: you who from your own conception were kept in the holy peace of the Lord of Peace, who would be conceived in you: Pray for us, that by grace upon grace we too may persevere in peace until the Great Interruption for which we long—until we behold with our own eyes the eternal Light in his glorious face, and marvel evermore. Μαρανα θα!

WORKS CITED

André Marie. 2006. "Friends Forever: St. Augustine, Friendship, and Catholic Evangelism." Paper presented at Saint Benedict Center Conference, available at http://catholicism.org/downloads /St_Augustine_Friendship.pdf.

Anscombe, G. E. M. 1993. "Contraception and Chastity." In *Why Humanae Vitae Was Right*, edited by Janet E. Smith, 119–46. San Francisco: Ignatius.

Anselm of Canterbury. 1872. "Of Christ." Meditation 13 in *St. Anselm's Book of Meditations and Prayers*. Translated by M. R. London: Burns and Gates.

———. 2006. "*Oratio ad Sanctum Paulum,*" no. 10. In *Prayers and Meditations of St. Anselm with the Proslogion*, translated by Benedicta Ward, 141–56. New York: Penguin Classics.

Asiedu, F. B. A. 2019. *Paul and His Letters: Thinking with Josephus*. Minneapolis: Fortress.

Augustine. 1610. *City of God*. Translated by John Healey. London: Griffith Farran Okeden & Welsh.

———. 1887. *City of God*. Translated by Marcus Dods. *A Select Library of Nicene and Post-Nicene Fathers of the Christian Church*. 1st series. Edited by Philip Schaff. Vol. 2. New York: Christian Literature. Reprint, Peabody, MA: Hendrickson, 1994.

———. 2018. *City of God*. Translated by William Babcock. New York: New City.

Aus, Roger D. 1973. "The Liturgical Background of the Necessity and Propriety of Giving Thanks according to 2 Thes 1:3." *Journal of Biblical Literature* 92, no. 3 (September): 432–38. https:// doi.org/10.2307/3263583.

Banner, Michael. 1999. *Christian Ethics and Contemporary Moral Problems*. Cambridge: Cambridge University Press.

Barth, Karl. 1933. *The Epistle to the Romans*. Translated by Edwin C. Hoskyns, from the 6th ed. London: Oxford University Press.

———. 1956–75. *Church Dogmatics*. 4 vols. Edited by G. W. Bromiley and T. F. Torrance. Translated by G. W. Bromiley et al. Edinburgh: T&T Clark.

Bauckham, Richard, Daniel R. Driver, Trevor A. Hart, and Nathan MacDonald, eds. 2009. *The Epistle to the Hebrews and Christian Theology*. Grand Rapids: Eerdmans.

Benedict XVI. 2007. *Spe salvi*. Rome: Libreria Editrice Vaticana.

Benson, Robert Hugh. 1915. *Lord of the World*. London: Sir Isaac Pitman & Sons.

Berdyaev, Nikolai A. 1924. "The Jewish Question, as a Christian Question." *Rul* (The Rudder, Berlin), March 18–19, no. 999–1000. Available at http://www.berdyaev.com/berdiaev/berd_lib/1924_301.html, translated by S. Janos in 2006.

Bridges, Linda McKinnish. 2008. *1 & 2 Thessalonians*. Macon, GA: Smyth & Helwys.

Bruce, F. F. 1982. *1 & 2 Thessalonians*. Word Biblical Commentary 45. Waco: Word.

Calvin, John. 1961. *Epistles of Paul the Apostle to the Romans and to the Thessalonians*. In *Calvin's Commentaries*, edited by David W. Torrance and Thomas F. Torrance, translated by Ross MacKenzie. Edinburgh: St. Andrews Press.

Campbell, Douglas A. 2009. *The Deliverance of God: An Apocalyptic Rereading of Justification in Paul*. Grand Rapids: Eerdmans.

———. 2014. *Framing Paul: An Epistolary Biography*. Grand Rapids: Eerdmans.

Cartwright, Stephen R., and Kevin L. Hughes, eds. and trans. 2001. *Second Thessalonians: Two Early Medieval Apocalyptic Commentaries*. Haimo of Auxerre, *Expositio in Epistolam II ad Thessalonicenses*, and Theitland of Einsiedeln, *In Epistolam II ad Thessalonicences*. Kalamazoo, MI: TEAMS.

Celano, Thomasso da. 1902. *Dies Irae*. Translated by William Josiah Irons. In *The Seven Great Hymns of the Mediaeval Church*, edited by Charles Cooper Nott. New York: Church Missions House.

Chaucer, Geoffrey. 1900. *The Canterbury Tales*. In *The Complete Works of Geoffrey Chaucer*, 2nd ed., edited by Walter W. Skeat, vol. 4. Oxford: Clarendon. Available at https://ebooks.adelaide.edu.au/c/chaucer/canterbury/skeat/index.html.

Cicero. 1912. *Letters to Atticus*. 3 vols. Translated by E. O. Winstedt. Loeb Classical Library. London: William Heinemann.

Cohen, Leonard. 1994. "The Future." In *Stranger Music: Selected Poems and Songs*. New York: Vintage Books.

Coleridge, S. T. 1956. *Confessions of an Inquiring Spirit*. Reprinted from the 3rd ed., 1853, edited by H. StJ. Hart. London: Adam and Charles Black.

Congregation for the Doctrine of the Faith. 2008. Instruction *Dignitas Personae* on Certain Bioethical Questions. Rome: Libreria Editrice Vaticana. Available at http://www.vatican.va/roman_curia/congregations/cfaith/documents/rc_con_cfaith_doc_20081208_dignitas-personae_en.html.

Corbon, Jean. 2005. *The Wellspring of Worship*. Translated by Matthew J. O'Connell. San Francisco: Ignatius.

Damian, Peter. 1982. *The Book of Gomorrah*. Translated by Pierre J. Payer. Waterloo, Ontario: Wilfrid Laurier University Press.

Davies, Brian, and G. R. Evans, eds. 1998. *Anselm of Canterbury: The Major Works*. Oxford: Oxford University Press.

Dawson, Christopher. 1942. *The Judgment of the Nations*. Washington, DC: Catholic University of America Press.

Donfried, Karl Paul. 2002. *Paul, Thessalonica, and Early Christianity*. Grand Rapids: Eerdmans.

Dostoevsky, Fyodor. (1880) 1981. *The Brothers Karamazov*. Translated by Andrew H. MacAndrew. Toronto: Bantam Classic.

Ehrman, Bart D. 2008. *The New Testament: A Historical Introduction*. 4th ed. New York: Oxford University Press.

Eire, Carlos M. N. 2016. *Reformations: The Early Modern World, 1450–1650*. New Haven: Yale University Press.

Emery, Gilles. 2011. "The Dignity of Being a Substance: Person, Subsistence, and Nature." *Nova et Vetera* 9, no. 4 (Fall): 991–1001.

Eubank, Nathan. 2019. *First and Second Thessalonians*. Catholic Commentary on Sacred Scripture. Grand Rapids: Baker Academic.

Farrow, Douglas. 1987. *The Word of Truth and Disputes about Words*. Winona Lake, IN: Eisenbrauns.

———. 1989. "Showdown: The Message of 2 Thessalonians 2:1–12 and the Riddle of the Restrainer." *Crux* 25 (1), 23–26.

———. 1999a. *Ascension and Ecclesia: On the Significance of the Doctrine of the Ascension for Ecclesiology and Christian Cosmology*. Edinburgh: T&T Clark.

———. 1999b. "A Response to Robert Jenson's *Systematic Theology*." *International Journal of Systematic Theology* 1, no. 1 (March): 89–95.

———. 2007a. *Nation of Bastards: Essays on the End of Marriage*. Toronto: BPS Books.

———. 2007b. "Resurrection and Immortality." In *The Oxford Handbook of Systematic Theology*, edited by John Webster, Kathryn Tanner, and Iain Torrance, 212–35. Oxford: Oxford University Press.

———. 2009. "Melchizedek and Modernity." In *The Epistle to the Hebrews and Christian Theology*, edited by R. J. Bauckham, D. R. Driver, T. A. Hart, and N. MacDonald, 281–301. Grand Rapids: Eerdmans.

———. 2011. *Ascension Theology*. London: T&T Clark.

———. 2014. "On the Maturation of Evil." In *Serving God's Community: Essays in Honor of W. Ward Gasque*, edited by Susan Phillips and Soo-Inn Tan, 41–51. Vancouver: Regent College Publishing.

———. 2015. *Desiring a Better Country: Forays in Political Theology*. Montreal: McGill-Queens University Press.

———. 2018a. "Blessed Is He Who Comes in the Name of the Lord: Jews and the Parousia of Jesus." *Communio* 45, no. 3–4 (Fall–Winter): 494–514.

———. 2018b. "The Conversion of the Papacy and the Present Church Crisis." *Catholic World Report*, November 10, https://www.catholicworldreport.com/2018/11/10/the-conversion-of-the-papacy-and-the-present-church-crisis.

———. 2018c. "Jew and Gentile in the Church Today." *Nova et Vetera* 16, no. 3 (Summer): 687–701.

———. 2018d. "'The Lady Left for Dragon's Meat': Comments on the Paris Statement." *Communio* 45, no. 1 (Spring): 1–7.

———. 2018e. "The Problem with Teilhard." *Nova et Vetera* 16, no. 2 (Spring): 377–85.

———. 2018f. "Reckoning with the Last Enemy." *Theoretical Medicine and Bioethics* 39, no. 3: 181–95.

———. 2018g. *Theological Negotiations: Proposals in Soteriology and Anthropology*. Grand Rapids: Baker Academic.

———. 2019a. "The Church's One Foundation." *Catholic World Report*, March 4, https://www.catholicworldreport.com/2019/03/04/the-churchs-one-foundation.

———. 2019b. "Harrowing Hart on Hell." *First Things* (October): 57–62, available at https://www.firstthings.com/article/2019/10/harrowing-hart-on-hell.

———. 2020a. "Anselm and the Art of Theology." *Fellowship of Catholic Scholars Quarterly* 42, no. 4 (Winter): 255–72.

———. 2020b. "The Secret of the Saeculum." *First Things* (May): 27–35.

Fee, Gordon D. 2009. *The First and Second Letters to the Thessalonians*. New International Commentary on the New Testament. Grand Rapids: Eerdmans.

Ferrer, Vincent. 1954. "On the Last Judgment." Sermon on Luke 21:25–28 (Advent II, Sermon 3). In *Angel of the Judgment: A Life of Vincent Ferrer*, edited by Sister Mary Catherine, 102–17. Notre Dame, IN: Ave Maria Press. Available online at http://www.svfsermons.org/A061_Last%20Judgment.htm.

Fletcher, Joseph F. 1966. *Situation Ethics: The New Morality*. Philadelphia: Westminister.

Furnish, Victor Paul. 2007. *1 Thessalonians, 2 Thessalonians*. Abingdon New Testament Commentaries. Nashville: Abingdon.

Gilson, Étienne. 1949. *The Terrors of the Year 2000*. Toronto: University of St. Michael's College.

Gray, Tim. 2002. "From Jewish Passover to Christian Eucharist: The Story of the Todah." *Lay Witness* (November/December).

Gunton, Colin E. 2002. *The Christian Faith: An Introduction to Christian Doctrine*. Oxford: Blackwell.

Hart, David Bentley. 2019. *That All Shall Be Saved: Heaven, Hell, and Universal Salvation*. New Haven: Yale University Press.

Hastings, Adrian. 2000. "Devil." In *The Oxford Companion to Christian Thought*, edited by Adrian Hastings, Alistair Mason, and Hugh Pyper, 164–66. Oxford: Oxford University Press.

Hendrix, H. L. 1984. "Thessalonicans Honour Romans." ThD diss., Harvard University.

Hersch-Reich, Beatrice Maria. 1929. "Antichrist." In *Encyclopedia Britannica*, 14th ed., 2:59–62. Chicago: William Benton.

Hitler, Adolf. (1925–26) 1992. *Mein Kampf.* Translated by Ralph Manheim. London: Pimlico.

Hughes, Kevin L. 2005. *Constructing Antichrist: Paul, Biblical Commentary, and the Development of Doctrine in the Early Middle Ages*. Washington, DC: Catholic University of America Press.

Jewett, Robert. 1986. *The Thessalonian Correspondence*. Minneapolis: Fortress.

John Paul II. 1981. *Laborem exercens*. Rome: Libreria Editrice Vaticana.

———. 1993. *The Splendor of Truth*. Rome: Libreria Editrice Vaticana.

———. 1997. *Theology of the Body: The Redemption of the Body and Sacramentality of Marriage, from the Weekly Audiences of His Holiness, September 5, 1979–November 28, 1984*. Rome: Libreria Editrice Vaticana.

Kasper, Walter. 1967. "Gott in der Geschichte." In *Gott heute, 15 Beiträge zur Gottesfrage*, edited by Norbert Kutschki, 138–51. Mainz: Matthias-Grünewald Verlag.

———. 1972. *Einführung in den Glauben*. Mainz: Matthias-Grünewald Verlag. English translation: *An Introduction to Christian Faith*, translated by V. Green. London: Burns and Oates, 1980.

Klauck, Hans-Josef, Volker Leppin, Martin George, and Walter Sparn. 2011. "Antichrist." In *Religion Past and Present*, edited by Hans Dieter Betz, Don S. Browning, Bernd Janowski, and Eberhard Jüngel. Leiden: Brill. http://dx.doi.org/10.1163/1877-5888_rpp_COM_00789.

Kohn, Hans, Herbert Martin, James Loewe, and Michael Avi-Yonah. 1929. "Jerusalem." In *Encyclopedia Britannica*, 14th ed., 13:6–8. Chicago: William Benton.

Lahey, Lawrence. 2007. "Evidence for Jewish Believers in Jewish-Christian Dialogues." In *Jewish Believers in Jesus*, edited by Oskar Skarsaune and Reidar Hvalvik, 581–639. Grand Rapids: Baker Academic.

Lessing, G. E. 1956. *Lessing's Theological Writings*. Edited and translated by H. Chadwick. London: A&C Black.

Levering, Matthew J. 2019. *Did Jesus Rise from the Dead? Historical and Theological Reflections*. Oxford: Oxford University Press.

Lewis, C. S. 1943. *Perelandra*. London: Bodley Head.

———. 1945. *That Hideous Strength*. London: Bodley Head.

Lewis, Donald M. 2010. *The Origins of Christian Zionism: Lord Shaftesbury and Evangelical Support for a Jewish Homeland*. Cambridge: Cambridge University Press.

Louth, Andrew. 2008. "Eastern Orthodox Eschatology." In *The Oxford Handbook of Eschatology*, edited by Jerry L. Walls, chap. 12. Oxford: Oxford University Press.

Luther, Martin. 1910. *Concerning Christian Liberty (On the Freedom of the Christian)*. Translated by R. S. Grignon. Harvard Classics Edition 36. New York: P. F. Collier & Son.

MacDonald, Gregory, ed. 2011. *"All Shall Be Well": Explorations in Universal Salvation and Christian Theology from Origen to Moltmann*. Eugene, OR: Wipf & Stock.

Malherbe, Abraham. 2000. *The Letters to the Thessalonians*. Anchor Bible 32B. New York: Doubleday.

Mangina, Joseph L. 2010. *Revelation*. Brazos Theological Commentary on the Bible. Grand Rapids: Brazos.

Manning, Henry Edward. 1861. *The Present Crisis of the Holy See*. London: Burns & Lambert.

Manson, Thomas W. 1953. "St. Paul in Greece: The Letters to the Thessalonians." *Bulletin of the John Rylands University Library of Manchester* 35 (2): 428–47.

Marshall, I. Howard. 1983. *1 and 2 Thessalonians*. New Century Bible Commentary. Grand Rapids: Eerdmans.

Marxsen, Willi. 1982. *Der zweite Thessalonicherbrief*. Zurich: Theologischer Verlag.

McCarthy, John F. 1998. "Neo-Patristic Exegesis: Its Form and Method." *Roman Theological Forum* 75 (May).

McClymond, Michael J. 2018. *The Devil's Redemption: A New History and Interpretation of Christian Universalism*. 2 vols. Grand Rapids: Baker Academic.

McGinn, Bernard. 1979. *Apocalyptic Spirituality: Treatises and Letters of Lactantius, Adso of Montier-en-Der, Joachim of Fiore, the Franciscan Spirituals, Savonarola*. Mahwah, NJ: Paulist Press.

———. 2000. *Antichrist: Two Thousand Years of the Human Fascination with Evil*. New York: Columbia University Press.

Milligan, George. 1908. *St Paul's Epistles to the Thessalonians*. London: Macmillan.

Moltmann, Jürgen. 1996. *The Coming of God: Christian Eschatology*. Translated by Margaret Kohl. Minneapolis: Fortress.

Muggeridge, Malcolm, and Alec Vidler. 1972. *Paul: Envoy Extraordinary*. London: Collins.

Muir, Edwin. 1987. *An Autobiography*. London: Hogarth.

Nicholl, Colin R. 2004. *From Hope to Despair in Thessalonica: Situating 1 & 2 Thessalonians*. Society for New Testament Studies Monograph Series 126. Cambridge: Cambridge University Press.

O'Brien, Michael D. 1996. *Father Elijah: An Apocalypse*. San Francisco: Ignatius.

O'Callaghan, Paul. 2011. *Christ Our Hope: An Introduction to Eschatology*. Washington, DC: Catholic University of America Press.

O'Donovan, Oliver. 1996. *The Desire of the Nations: Rediscovering the Roots of Political Theology*. Cambridge: Cambridge University Press.

———. 2005. *The Ways of Judgment*. Grand Rapids: Eerdmans.

Paddison, Angus. 2005. *Theological Hermeneutics and 1 Thessalonians*. Society for New Testament Studies Monograph Series 133. Cambridge: Cambridge University Press.

Paul VI. 1968. *Humanae vitae*. Rome: Libreria Editrice Vaticana.

Pelikan, Jaroslav. 2005. *Acts*. Brazos Theological Commentary on the Bible. Grand Rapids: Brazos.

Penner, Todd. 2004. "Madness in the Method? The Acts of the Apostles in Current Study." *Currents in Biblical Research* 2, no. 2 (April): 223–93.

Peterson, Erik. 2011. *Theological Tractates*. Edited and translated by Michael J. Hollerich. Stanford: Stanford University Press.

Pieper, Josef. 1999. *The End of Time: A Meditation on the Philosophy of History*. Translated by Michael Bullock. San Francisco: Ignatius.

Pitre, Brant. 2016. *Jesus and the Jewish Roots of the Eucharist: Unlocking the Secrets of the Last Supper*. New York: Image.

Pius XI. 1930. *Casti connubii*. Rome: Libreria Editrice Vaticana.

Pius XII. 1955. *Address to Midwives on the Nature of Their Profession*. Address to members of the Congress of the Italian Association of Catholic Midwives, October 29, 1951. London: Catholic Truth Society.

Plato. 1961. *The Collected Dialogues of Plato Including the Letters*. Edited by Edith Hamilton and Huntington Cairns. Bollingen Series 71. Princeton: Princeton University Press.

Pruss, Alexander. 2013. *One Body: An Essay in Christian Sexual Ethics*. Notre Dame, IN: University of Notre Dame Press.

Raith, Charles, II, ed. 2018. *The Book of Acts: Catholic, Orthodox, and Evangelical Readings*. Washington, DC: Catholic University of America Press.

Ramelli, Ilaria. 2013. *The Christian Doctrine of Apokatastasis*. Leiden: Brill.

Ratzinger, Joseph. 1988. *Eschatology: Death and Eternal Life*. Translated by Michael Waldstein. Washington, DC: Catholic University of America Press.

Reiss, Jonathan B. 1995. *The Renaissance Antichrist: Luca Signorelli's Orvieto Frescoes*. Princeton: Princeton University Press.

Richard, Earl J. 1995. *First and Second Thessalonians*. Sacra Pagina 11. Collegeville, MN: Liturgical Press.

Rohr, Richard. 2019. *The Universal Christ: How a Forgotten Reality Can Change Everything We See, Hope For, and Believe*. New York: Convergent.

Rowe, C. Kavin. 2009. *World Upside Down: Reading Acts in the Graeco-Roman Age*. New York: Oxford University Press.

Salvatore, Armando. 2011. "Politics and the Messianic Imagination." In *The Politics of Imagination*, edited by Chiara Bottici and Benoit Challand, 124–41. Abingdon, UK: Birkbeck Law.

Schleiermacher, Friedrich. 1989. *The Christian Faith*. Edinburgh: T&T Clark.

Schwarz, Hans. 2000. *Eschatology.* Grand Rapids: Eerdmans.

Sheen, Fulton J. 1948. *Communism and the Conscience of the West.* Indianapolis: Bobbs-Merrill.

———. 1958. "Signs of Our Times." Address given on January 26, 1947. In *Light Your Lamps*, 8th ed., 11–23. Huntington, IN: Our Sunday Visitor.

Silvas, Anna M. 2005. *The Asketikon of St. Basil the Great.* Oxford Early Christian Studies. Oxford: Oxford University Press.

Skarsaune, Oskar, and Reidar Hvalvik, eds. 2007. *Jewish Believers in Jesus.* Grand Rapids: Baker Academic.

Solovyov, Vladimir. 1900. "Short Tale of the Antichrist." In *War, Progress, and the End of History: Three Conversations.* Translated by Alexander Bakshy. Great Barrington, MA: Lindisfarne, 1990.

Stark, Thomas Heinrich. 2015. "German Idealism and Cardinal Kasper's Theological Project." *Catholic World Report*, June 9. https://www.catholicworldreport.com/2015/06/09/german-idealism-and-cardinal-kaspers-theological-project.

Strauss, David F. 1879. *The Life of Jesus, Critically Examined.* Translated by George Eliot. 2nd ed. 2 vols. London: Williams & Norgate.

Stump, Eleonore. 2018. *Atonement.* Oxford: Oxford University Press.

Synod of Barmen. 1962. *The Barmen Declaration.* In E. H. Robertson, *Christians against Hitler.* London: SCM.

Talbott, Thomas. 2014. *The Inescapable Love of God.* 2nd ed. Eugene, OR: Cascade.

Tanner, Norman, ed. 1990. *Decrees of the Ecumenical Councils.* 2 vols. London: Sheed and Ward.

Tellbe, Mikael. 2001. *Paul between Synagogue and State: Christians, Jews, and Civic Authorities in 1 Thessalonians, Romans, and Philippians.* Coniectanea Biblica: New Testament Series 34. Stockholm: Almqvist & Wiksell International.

Theodoret of Cyrus. 2001. *Commentary on the Letter of St. Paul.* Vol. 2. Translated by Robert Charles Hill. Brookline, MA: Holy Cross Orthodox Press.

Thiselton, Anthony. 2011. *1 and 2 Thessalonians through the Centuries.* Oxford: Wiley-Blackwell.

Tolkien, J. R. R. 1993. "Athrabeth Finrod ah Andreth." In *Morgoth's Ring*, edited by Christopher Tolkien, 303–66. Boston: Houghton Mifflin.

Torrance, Thomas F. 1992. *The Mediation of Christ.* Colorado Springs: Helmers and Howard.

Vitoria, Francesco de. 1991. "On the Law of War." In *Vitoria: Political Writings*, 295–357. Cambridge: Cambridge University Press.

Wanamaker, Charles A. 1990. *The Epistles to the Thessalonians.* New International Greek Testament Commentary. Grand Rapids: Eerdmans.

Weima, Jeffrey A. D. 2014. *1–2 Thessalonians.* Baker Exegetical Commentary on the New Testament. Grand Rapids: Baker Academic.

Weima, Jeffrey A. D., and Stanley E. Porter. 1998. *An Annotated Bibliography of 1 & 2 Thessalonians.* Leiden: Brill.

Whitford, David M. 2008. "The Papal Antichrist: Martin Luther and the Underappreciated Influence of Lorenzo Valla." *Renaissance Quarterly* 61, no. 1 (Spring): 26–52.

Williams, Charles. 1945. *All Hallows' Eve.* Grand Rapids: Eerdmans, 1981.

Witherington, Ben, III. 2006. *1 & 2 Thessalonians: A Socio-Rhetorical Commentary.* Grand Rapids: Eerdmans.

Woods, Thomas E., Jr. 2012. *How the Catholic Church Built Western Civilization*. Washington, DC: Regnery History.

Wright, N. T. 1992. *The New Testament and the People of God*. COQG 1. Minneapolis: Fortress.

———. 1996. *Jesus and the Victory of God*. COQG 2. Minneapolis: Fortress.

———. 2002. *Paul for Everyone: Galatians and Thessalonians*. London: SPCK.

———. 2003. *The Resurrection of the Son of God*. COQG 3. Minneapolis: Fortress.

———. 2013. *Paul and the Faithfulness of God*. COQG 4. Minneapolis: Fortress.

———. 2018. *Paul: A Biography*. New Haven: Yale University Press.

Yeats, William Butler. 1920. "The Second Coming." In *Michael Robartes and the Dancer*. Churchtown, Dundrum (Ireland): Chuala.

Zizioulas, John D. 1985. *Being as Communion*. Crestwood, NY: St. Vladimir's Seminary Press.

SCRIPTURE INDEX

SUBJECT AND NAME INDEX

Printed and bound by CPI Group (UK) Ltd, Croydon, CR0 4YY

13/04/2025

14656456-0003